READINGS IN WORLD DEVELOPMENT

DEVELOPMENT MANAGEMENT IN THE TWENTY-FIRST CENTURY

READINGS IN WORLD DEVELOPMENT

K. C. ROY – SERIES EDITOR

UNIVERSITY OF QUEENSLAND, AUSTRALIA

Readings in World Development: Growth and Development in the Asia Pacific
K. C. Roy and S. Chatterjee (Editors)
2006. ISBN: 1-59454-947-8

Growth, Development and Poverty Alleviation in the Asia-Pacific
Kartik C. Roy and Srikanta Chatterjee (Editors)
2007. ISBN: 1-59454-931-1

Development Problems and Prospects in Pacific Islands States
Biman Prasad and K. C. Roy (Editors)
2007. ISBN: 1-60021-793-1

Globalization and Development: Country Experiences
K. C. Roy, A. Medhekar and Hemant Chittoo (Editors)
2010. ISBN: 978-1-60876-851-6

Development Management in the Twenty-First Century
Kartik Roy and Sandip Kar (Editors)
2012. ISBN: 978-1-62100-699-2

Education, Human Capital and Development
Kartick Roy, Mike Roberts and Ershad Ali (Editors)
2012. ISBN: 978-1-62081-760-5

READINGS IN WORLD DEVELOPMENT

DEVELOPMENT MANAGEMENT IN THE TWENTY-FIRST CENTURY

KARTIK ROY
AND
SANDIP KAR
EDITORS

Nova Science Publishers, Inc.
New York

For permission to use material from this book please contact us:
Telephone 631-231-7269; Fax 631-231-8175
Web Site: http://www.novapublishers.com

Library of Congress Cataloging-in-Publication Data

Development management in the twenty-first century / editors, Kartik Roy, Sandip Kar.
p. cm.
Includes index.
ISBN 978-1-62100-699-2 (hbk.)
1. Economic development. 2. Economic development--Environmental aspects. 3. Economic development--Developing countries. I. Roy, K. C. (Kartik Chandra), 1941- II. Kar, Sandip.
HD82.D38957 2011
338.9--dc23
2011037411

Published by Nova Science Publishers, Inc. † New York

CONTENTS

PREFACE

The use of the term 'management' is no longer confined to the domain of academics in management disciplines in college and universities, of those working as management personnel in enterprises who are managing human resources or project implementation. It is now being increasingly used in Economic and Political systems to describe policy failures or policy successes in economic and political governances.

This book: Development Management in the Twenty First Century has aimed to highlight several important issues which policy makers as well as state and private sector agents are confronted with while implementation different types of programs to improve social and economic conditions of beneficiaries of these programs. However, the process of implementation of one development project may produce unfavorable effects on several other projects and on beneficiaries of some other projects. In such a situation, project implementing agents will be required to take measures to ensure that adverse externalities stemming from the implementation of each project are minimized.

Therefore, the crucial factors which enables a development projects to be successfully implemented are simply not the availability of the resources but also more importantly, the efficient management of project implementation process. This Book examines many such issues, which make the task of development management a complex one indeed. All papers, which have been included in this volume, have successfully passed through a two-stage referring process under which the Editorial Board first reviewed papers before sending those to an external referee.

The editors wish to thank Nova Science Publishing Company, which has set up the Readings in World Development Series under which this volume will be published. The editors also wish to thank all others who have been associated with the preparation of the manuscript and with all other aspects of the task involved in publication of this volume.

Finally, Kartik Roy, after serving university of Queensland in Brisbane, Australia for nearly four decades has joined the Auckland Institute of Studies (AIS) in Auckland, New Zealand, in 2011 as its Research Professor.

Kartik Roy[1] and Sandip Kar[2]
Auckland Institute of Studies St Helens, (AIS), Auckland, New Zealand.[1]
International Institute of Management Sciences, Calcutta, India.[2]

In: Development Management in the Twenty-First Century ISBN: 978-1-62100-699-2
Editors: Kartik Roy and Sandip Kar

Chapter 1

Development Management in the Current Global Order: An Overview

Kartik Roy*
Research Professor, Auckland Institute of Studies St Helens (AIS), Auckland, New Zealand

Introduction

Economic development is usually expressed in terms of improvement in economic and social indicators in a country. When an economy grows at a robust rate, the state authorities obtain larger amount of revenue via tax collection, and returns from state's own enterprises and spend that revenue to create new facilities and improve the condition of existing facilities for citizens to enjoy a better quality of life than before. However when any individual, private organisation or the state produces and supply new types of goods and services, old products or services become redundant and new resources are utilised to supplies newer types of goods and services. Hence destruction and creation go hand-in-hand. But one creation creates a continuous process of further creation and destruction of existing entities. The best example is that of a mining company starting its operation in India in a remote area inhabited by tribals. The mountain, forest and the river constitute their bio-mass which provide these tribals with foods, other necessities and sustain their livelihood for future years. So before the construction activity begins these people are driven out of their land and forest and land is cleared. Then the secondary process commences. Larger tracts of land are further cleared to make way for the construction of township to accommodate labourers, engineers, to set up markets, schools, hospitals, rail line etc. Again larger number of original inhabitants of those lands are driven out of their land and bio-mass. Even if those people uprooted from their lands are well-settled somewhere else, their link with their land and nature are lost for ever.

In this whole process of destruction and creation, forest, environment and poor people become casualties. In 1919-20, 60 per cent of undivided India's land (including Bangladesh and Pakistan) was covered with dense forest. Today that dense forest covers less than 20 per

* kartikr@ais.ac.nz; kcroy20@gmail.com.

cent of total India's land area (excluding those of Bangladesh and Pakistan). The effects of the loss of forest cover and of the growth of industries, transport networks, buildings and of manufactures of consumer goods using natural resources are clearly evident in change in monsoon pattern, enormous rise in temperature throughout the year, spread of viral infection and in occasional droughts in different parts of the country in different years. Similar situation prevails in China and other developing countries as well. So the question that may be asked is how did we get to this situation? To find an answer we comment on the historical process of the growth of consumerism.

From Hunters and Gatherers to Modern Day Consumers

Only the primordial instinct for survival forced these human and animals to kill other animals for food. These animals and nature also provided these humans with clothing and shelter. Since the size of the global population was extremely low, the demand for consumer goods was low. The loss in natural resources could be replenished quickly. But the situation began to change after the industrial revolution which greatly increased the demand for labour and consequently higher wage rates. Malthus felt that rising wages would encourage workers to get married and have children. In this way, the rising population, if remained unchecked would depress wages and workers' living standard would be brought down to the subsistence level. Meanwhile since population grows at geometric rate and food supply at arithmetic rate, the gap between the two would continue to widen. This would force the nature to impose positive checks in the form of floods, famines, pandemic disease which would destroy excess population and therefore excess demand for foods. Although the prediction of Malthus did not prove to be correct for nearly two centuries, the broader implications of the Malthusian theory are being felt today. Malthus was primarily concerned with the supply of basic foods to feed the rising population. But the industrial revolution which began in England and spread to Germany and France was destroying nature to manufacture machines to make non-food consumer goods for domestic use and for exporting to colonies where local import competing products made with simple hand made tools could not withstand the competition from European ones produced on a large scale with heavy machines. For example, the import of cheaper cotton clothes made by Lancashire cotton mills into British India virtually destroyed Indian historic cotton textile industry (Roy 1986) which consisted of millions of individual household firms. So what we see here now is that the demand for non-food consumer goods was no longer created only in Europe, it was also being created in colonies by European powers. Hence the extraction of non-renewable resources to satisfy the rising global demand for non-food consumer goods began to increase at a rapid rate.

The World War II and its Aftermath

During the second world war, a significantly larger proportion of the Earth's resources was directed to the production of machines, arms, ammunitions, other ancillary products needed to strengthen war efforts of allied and axis powers and a smaller proportion was directed to the production of essential and non-essential consumer goods. The global trade was severely disrupted. Consumers around the globe got used to living with limited supply of even essential consumer goods such as butter, bread and so on.

At the same time, it can also be said that the production of consumer goods was not largely responsible for the adverse environmental effects of the destruction of earth's resources during the Second World War.

POST WORLD WAR II PERIOD

During the 1950s, the reconstruction of the war-ravaged Europe used substantial proportion of Earth's resources to manufacture steel, copper wire, cement, bricks and mortars and aluminium products and so on.

It was also during the 1950s and 1960s Term-lending and hire-purchase financing schemes began to be made available to consumers by banks, manufacturers and retailers of different types of essential and non-essential consumer goods.

A person's or a family's consumption expenditure could no longer be defined as a function of that person's or family's disposable income during a certain period of time. Consumption expenditure can be defined as a function of disposable income and credit income of an individual or of a family in a year. However, a number of factors prevented the growth of production, supply and consumption of non-essential consumer goods.

First, the availability of credit money to consumers was limited due to the inability of domestic banks and other financial institutions to access global financial capital. This inability resulted from the lack ofcapital market liberalization in many countries.

Second, consumers were not very keen to take on additional burden of repayment of loans incurred to purchase a semi-durable consumer good such as a transistor, radio, camera etc. They were saving enough money first before they could buy such goods by making payment in cash. Third, the price of consumer durables was also quite high due to lack of adequate increase in consumers' demand for these products, and consequently to lack of competition among suppliers of those products. The following momentous events changed the whole fabric of production, supply and consumption of consumer electronics and other consumer durables around the world:

(i) The Rise of Hong Kong and Taiwan

In the 1950s when the war devastated Europe was being rebuilt, consumers had little income to spend on durable and semi-durable consumer goods. Also at the same time American producers ran out of their patent rights in Europe. Hence these producers shifted their production of all kinds of consumer durables to Hong Kong and Taiwan. In Hong Kong, the efficient civil administration and the global marketing network of the British rulers were combined with capital and technological expertise of Shanghai textile manufacturers who fled to Hong Kong to save themselves from being caught by the rapidly advancing People's Liberation Army (PLA) and cheap labour force from mainland China to create a low cost labour intensive manufacturing hub for all kinds of consumer goods (Clark and Roy 1997) which American entrepreneurs began to manufacture and supply to the rest of the world. One such simple consumer semi-durable which became a household name in developing Asia was

Eveready Torch Light. A parallel scenario also emerged in Taiwan. To evade the advancing red army, many capitalists also fled with the nationalist army to Taiwan even local islanders provided cheap labour. Thus emerged also in Taiwan a vibrant labour-intensive low cost manufacturing sector which American manufacturers of light consumer durables gleefully embraced.

(ii) The rise of Japan as the Electronics' Giant

Under General McArthur's rule since Japan had to relinquish any ambition it might have had of becoming a military super power, all efforts of Japanese entrepreneurs were directed towards making Japan an economic super power. Hence during the 1950s and 1960s, Japan was able to develop highly efficient consumer durables' brand names such as Sony, Sanyo, National Panasonic, Suzuki, Hitachi, Mitsubishi etc. and began to export durable goods of all kinds to developed countries. Consequently, the number of manufacturers increased greatly and as a result the supply of non-essential consumer goods of all varieties began to increase in the global market. To increase the demand in the export market of such goods, the government provided subsidy to exports and allowed almost tax free import of imported inputs which were to be used as inputs in the manufacture of exportable goods (Dowling &Valenzuela 2004). But domestic consumers were deprived of the availability of such consumer durables at the same low price as paid by foreign consumers as the price of the same product was higher in domestic market than in the foreign market.

(iii) Technology transfer and the rise of East Asia

Since the early 1970s, higher labour and other input costs began to raise the per unit cost of production of non-essential goods. This trend forced the Japanese manufacturers to shift their production structure to Taiwan, Hong Kong, Malaysia and Singapore initially and later to Thailand and the Philippines under the flying geese pattern of development (Akamatsu 1961).

Trade Structure, Monopolistic Competition and Consumer Sovereignty

These above noted events tend to explain how and why the global supply of consumer durables increased substantially during a 30 year period from 1960 to 1990. But the question that has to be advanced now is how did the purchasing capacity and desire of consuption of consumer goods of global consumers' rise.

Two Factors Can Provide the Answer

One factor is that the global economy experienced a period of sustained growth with low inflation and stable prices over a period of more than 20 years from 1951 to 1973. This period came to be known as the golden age in world economic history.

Such a sustained economic growth raised the purchasing capability of global consumers by increasing their disposable income and by creating demand for more full – time job opportunities in domestic manufacturing and services sectors.

Furthermore, several of former colonies of European powers, prominent among them being India gained independence from their colonial masters. The pent-up demand for simple consumer durables of consumers in India and in other countries now could be met.

INDUSTRY STRUCTURE AND MONOPOLISTIC COMPETITION

Under 'flying geese' pattern of development, the industry structure initially exhibited features of inter-industry trade. Inter industry trade which is based on the principle of comparative advantage as expounded by Ricardo and Heckhscher-Ohlin (Salvatore 2001) consists of free trade between two countries in two different types of goods which can be complimentary to each other and which are produced with abundant supply of factors. Generally in inter-industry trade, the quantum of environmental resources to manufacture a principal and a complimentary product would be considerably less than that in intra-industry trade under which both countries produce and export same products. For example, if country A is exporting a motor vehicle to country B and country B is exporting all components of that motor to country A then that trade can be characterised as being intra- industry trade.

Under the 'flying geese' pattern of development, the importance and size of inter-industry trade in total trade declined while those of intra-industry trade in total trade greatly increased. Such trade can only prosper under monopolistically competitive market structure. Under monopolistic competition, product differentiation via some superficial changes in design, colour and body structure of a product undertaken by monopolistically competitive firms led to a phenomenal increase in production and export of different varieties of the same product.

This rise in intra-industry trade increased competition among producers of different varieties of the same consumer durables in each country to supply their products in foreign markets at a highly competitive price. In the home market also retailers of imported vehicles facing steep competition were forced to lower their price and to offer other incentives to lure domestic consumers to buy their products and thereby to help consumers develop 'brand loyalty'. To aid the growth of consumers, 'brand loyalty', manufacturers and retailers joined hands to undertake advertising in television during prime-time viewing, radio and print-media which together could produce Duesenburry's demonstration effect on consumers' mind. Furthermore, both manufacturers and retailers began to make available to customers, credit money to buy consumer durables and to allow repayments of the loan in installments. The global economy witnessed a phenomenal increase in the supply of such credit money since the early to mid 1980s due to the liberalisation of rules governing the flow of capital in developed and developing countries. Also during this time, apart from banks and other financial institutions, retailers of consumer durables, supermarkets, and department stores began to issue credit card to their customers.

The ultimate objective of such efforts was to motivate a consumer to buy their products even when that consumer's disposable income was just sufficient only to pay for all essential expenses per month or per year.

Since 1995, under globalization, the flow of capital into short term money market increased greatly, the liquidity of banks in both developed and developing countries. This liquidity enabled banks to extend credit to domestic customers for investment in such speculative activities as stock market and building construction. Also a part of that credit money was lent out to clients to buy houses and apartments.

Even when couples in Western countries did not have enough guaranteed disposable income to pay for all their monthly household expenses and to make monthly repayment of house mortgage interest rate and of principal of the loan, they still purchased houses at unrealistically high prices.

Eventually when first home buyers began to default on loan payment, the panic spread among lenders who had almost exhausted their liquidity and began to repossess those houses to sell those at whatever price they could fetch to recover a part of the loan.

The collapse of the building construction industry contributed to the East Asian financial crisis in 1997 and to the global financial crisis in 2008-09. Hence it is the demand for consumer goods fuelled by credit money that governs consumption expenditure now rather than disposable income driven the demand for consumer goods which governs consumption expenditure.

CONSUMER SOVEREIGNTY

On the one hand there is unsustainable increase in expenditure on consumption of all kinds of semi-durable and durable consumer goods; on the other hand, millions of people die of starvation every year in the world.

Manufacturers of consumer durables direct their Research and Development (R&D) activities to develop improved versions of other brands with monotonous regularity so much so that the time lag between the appearance in the market of older version and improved version of a particular brand of consumer durable good has been regularly shortening. Consumers are enticed to buy improved version of the older model by offering them attractive terms of purchase by retailers of consumer durables even when the old brand is operating all right. The examples are mobile phones, digital cameras and so on.

The consequences of all these are (i) that additional consumption expenditure is incurred by consumers even when there is no need for it, (ii) that the older model of the product now is sent to the junkyard to be melted which then causes environmental hazards, (iii) that consumers are burdened with more debt as such purchases of newer models are mostly undertaken with loan money and (iv) that the money saved by refraining from the consumption of many varieties of non-essential consumer durables can be used to buy such serial goods as better education, better healthcare, better recreation and so on.

WHY HAS SUCH A SITUATION COME ABOUT?

Such a situation has come about due to the total absence of consumer's sovereignty in the product market. When pure competition prevails among producers in the product market and among labourers in labour markets, information on features of various products flow freely, to sovereign consumers to decide what kind of goods they want the market to supply. Market then sends the green signal to producers through relative changes in prices of preferred and non-preferred goods.

However as the size of population in each country continues to rise, the number of complex economic and social transactions that each human being is required to be engaged in also rises. As knowledge about anything is not a public good and information flow is asymmetric, consumers are unable to advise the market of what goods they want to purchase and what features they would like those goods to contain.

Hence monopolistically competitive and oligopolistic firms have taken over consumers' decision –making power to determine what kind of goods consumers would be required to buy and what features such goods would consist of. After that, while products are being manufactured, the manufacturers and retailers begin disseminating to consumers through all media outlets the information on main features of goods, prices and on retail outlets from where those products can be obtained.

Then finally, manufacturers and retailers, media outlets also inform consumers of the availability of credit with easy repayment facilities to customers willing to buy those goods. Naturally with so much incentive, consumers cannot resist the temptation of buying such consumer durables even when they can live comfortably without them.

But producers in private sector are primarily interested in maximising monetary returns for the company from a given level of investment on the production of a good.

UNSUSTAINABLE CONSUMPTION EXPENDITURE AND ENVIRONMENT

A country's Gross Domestic Product (GDP) which consists of four components is explained in the following ways:

$$Y = C+I+G+(X-M)$$

Where, Y = Income

C = Consumption expenditure
I = Investment expenditure
X = Export earnings
M = Import earnings

A country's economic growth rate therefore could depend on the growth rate of each of these items of expenditure.

John Maynard Keynes (1936) suggested that a country can increase its national income by increasing any one of its four components of GDP while not reducing other expenditures. Different countries may choose different courses of action to achieve economic growth. For example China substantially increased investment expenditure as a proportion of GDP. Then first it created a net trade surplus and increased it as a proportion of GDP and finally it kept consumption and government expenditure at very low level. By repressing consumption expenditure, the Chinese state was able to significantly cut down import payments on consumer durables. This in turn also helped China to maintain a healthy trade and balance of payment surplus.

The course of action that India took was diametrically opposite to that taken by China. The West Minister style of democratic government sys tem with many political parties at federal, provincial and local levels, thousands of democratic elections every year to form governing bodies for all kind of political, economic and social organisations and with high level of corruption penetrating the entire fabric of the Indian society as well as with anti-growth regulatory regime still in place – makes it virtually impossible for India to significantly raise its investment expenditure on consumer durables and to cut non-essential import payments to create and enlarge its net trade surplus. Hence India chose to increase its economic growth rate by raising private consumption and government expenditure as a proportion of GDP while its trade deficit continued to rise as a proportion of its GDP.

Since any expenditure whether for consumption of necessary or luxury goods or for investment projects uses natural resources, and since directly or indirectly such expenditure produces adverse effects on a country's environment, the country that chooses to spend more on investment and less on consumption will be able to sustain its economic growth and development outcomes for a longer period of time than that which depends on more consumption and less on investment for its economic growth.

On that basis one would say that economic development outcomes in China would have more long term sustainability than those in India. Also within investment expenditure a part consists of consumption of social goods.

Any increase in investment on social capital and increase in consumption serial goods do not imply refer to hefty increase in salaries of teachers and administrative staff without any quantifiable increase in productivity of teachers and bureaucrats in schools, colleges, universities and public sector organisations. This is exactly what has happened in India. Such a rise in salaries is unproductive as it increases the demand of the middle class for consumer durables and as it contributes on the creation of social and human capital and on the consumption of social good.

Therefore, since a country's air, water, diverse biological species, and natural resources including forest, river and mountains are its valuable natural resources and since all economic activities use the environment as a dumping ground for waste products, environmental damage apart from lowering a country's GDP growth rate can also produce substantial effects on the country's health and over all welfare of its citizens (Radelet, Snodgrass, Gillis and Roemer 2001). Heavy dependence on fossil fuels of large and growth –oriented developing countries is accompanied by substantial air-pollution and escalating greenhouse gas (GHG) emissions. China today is the largest emitter of GHG in the world and China's share in the global GHG emission is set to continue to rise further as developed countries continue to export their manufacturing industries producing consumer and producer durables to China. Asia which is also the world's biggest user of wood fuels accounts for 44 percent of global wood fuel consumption. This wood fuel consumption and open fire which burn bio-mass and coal increase the levels of such indoor pollutants as sulphur and nitric oxides and arsenic compounds.

The destruction of forest results from legal and illegal logging, as well as by growing encroachment on forested land by rapidly growing ego-centric and politically powerful villagers to meet their increasing demand for food and by overuse of forest by poverty stricken rural poor. As a result, seventy two percent of Asian's total forest cover is lost. Only

6 percent of Asian's original forest can now be considered as 'frontier forest'. Out of these six percent, about sixty percent are under threat from coastal development (Dowling and Valenzuela 2004).

DEVELOPMENT MANAGEMENT IN THE TWENTY FIRST CENTURY

While many people think that economic development and environmental management are not congruent as higher economic growth can only be achieved at a considerable cost to the environment, a sound management of economic development must include environmental management as well. If decisions on the value of investment expenditure, and types of goods to be produced and imported are left to the free market mechanism and to the private sector businesses, then such business operators would likely invest more on the production and import of luxury consumer goods and less on essential goods on the assumption that there is no compulsory requirement to include the monetary cost of project specific damage to environment only then the expected net return from an investment project would come closer to the social rate of return from that project after its completion.

Similarly, consumers' preferences particularly of those belonging to the middle and the rich class if not redirected towards the consumption of necessary and holistic goods, then much of expenditure of these classes would be directed to the consumer durables.

For redirecting expenditures on investment and consumption, away from luxury goods to necessary goods including expenditure on social infrastructure, social and human capital formation and other social and holistic goods consumption, the state has to play a very assertive role.

A sustainable development management regime would have to accept that no robust growth and development outcomes can be achieved at zero environmental cost. The more the society can cut down on the consumption of material goods, less would be the cost to the society of environmental damage.

A robust development management programme must first eliminate absolute poverty in rural sector by redeveloping agriculture by joining it with industries and by creating opportunities for service sector industries to grow while at the same time maintaining subsidies on food grains, fuel and on a few other essential items. In the urban sector, the growth of labour intensive medium sized industries and service trade can create employment and thereby eliminate absolute poverty.

One service sector industry which has backward linkages to many ancillary service industries as well as to agriculture and which can be less damaging to environment is tourism. A well developed tourism industry can be one of the biggest foreign exchange earning industries in a country. In Thailand, tourism is the largest export and foreign exchange earning industry.

Tourism is a conglomerate industry as it includes diverse industries such as hotels, agriculture, manufacturing, plumbing, electrical, dry cleaning, transport and so on. Those countries which are endowed with beautiful forests, rivers, sea beaches, mountains, agricultural, historic, cultural and religious sites can draw tourists with diverse interests to satisfy from around the world. Consequently the capacity of a well developed tourism industry to generate employment and to alleviate absolute poverty is quite considerable.

Furthermore, the tourism conglomerate can produce a multiplier effect of around two. For every one dollar of expenditure that a foreign tourist incurs, about two dollars of income can be created in the host country.

The development of such service sector industries by alleviating poverty can narrow the rich and poor divide which usually widens in a booming economy in the developing world.

Other issues such as trade relationship among regions and between countries also will have to be managed in a way that benefits both sides and continues to remain sustainable and environment friendly. A robust development management programme must also include the expansion of education, healthcare and employment for women because women are the best micro level managers and also carers of nature and environment with their proven expertise in the management of household economy. An educated and income earning woman will take care of the health of her children and thereby will help create the foundation of human capital formation.

In the end we must never forget Gandhi's teaching that human mind is a restless bird; the more it gets, the more it wants and still remain unsatisfied (Narayan 1960). What Gandhi really meant was that the only way to cut down the production of newer and newer models of consumer durables is to drastically cut down consumers demand for such newer varieties of non-essential consumer goods. This can, however be done only if consumers themselves improse limits on their demand for material goods. Since the global society has been living on coal, oil, natural gas, iron ore and other valuable minerals which are its capital and not on the income derived from the capital it is not limiting its annual draft on capital. Consequently, it will eventually run out of its capital. Hence it has to learn to subsist on income without further limitless drafts on capital (Schumacher 1960).

The principal task of development management is to find a way either by price mechanism alone or by a combination of price mechanism and government decrease social individuals satisfy their consumption needs largely by their disposable income and by income derived from assets as well marginally, if necessary, by credit money which is a draft on capital.

REFERENCES

Akamatsu, K. (1961), 'A Theory of Unbalanced Growth in the World Economy', *Welwirtschaftliches Archive,* 86 (2), pp. 196-215

Akamatsu, K. (1962), 'A Historical pattern of Economic Growth in Developing Countries', *The Developing Economies* , 1(1), pp.3-25

Clark, C. and Roy, K.C. (1997), 'Comparing Development Pattern in Asia', *Boulder, Co.: Lynne Rienner.*

Dowling, J.M. and Valenzuela, R. (2004), 'Economic Development in Asia', Signapore: *Thompson Learning.*

Keynes, J.M. (1936), 'The General Theory of Employment, Interest and Money', New York: *Harcourt Brace and Co.*

Malthus, T. (1798), 'An Essay on the Principles of Population', London: *Pickering*

Narayan, S. (1962), 'Principles of Gandhian Planning', Allahabad, *Kitab Mahal.*

Perkins, J.S. Raadelet, and Lindauer, D. (2006), 'Economics of Development', *Norton:* New York.

Roy, K.C. (1986), 'Foreign Aid and Indian Development: A study from the view point of Peace and Development', Ahmedabad: *Gujarat Vidyapith.*

Salvatore, D. (2001), 'International Economics'. New York: *John Wiley and Sons.*

Schumacher, E.F. (1960), 'Roots of Economic Growth', Varanasi: *Gandhian Institute of Studies.*

In: Development Management in the Twenty-First Century ISBN: 978-1-62100-699-2
Editors: Kartik Roy and Sandip Kar

Chapter 2

MANAGEMENT OF INTERNATIONAL TRADE PATTERN IN CHINA'S RISE AS SUPER POWER

Ershad Ali *
Director, Centre for Research in International Education,
Auckland Institute of Studies St Helens, Auckland, New Zealand

INTRODUCTION

Although China has begun its political reform since 1950, it has adopted economic reform from 1978. Since then, China adopted open door policy to welcome the foreign investors for which the success of Chinese economy has become a concern for the world. With a rapid economic growth at annual rate of around 9% for the past three decades, China has become the third largest economy in the world in 2008. Even after the world financial crisis in 2008, China has been maintaining the steady economic growth. The Emerging Markets Monitor (2009) gave the forecast that the global economy has grown by 1.7% in 2010; however, a growth of 8.1% is expected for China for 2009-2010. The evidence shows that China is emerging as a new economic superpower. Therefore, China has been following a planned trade pattern in the world backed by necessary management techniques which have been driving this trade growth.

There are plenty of literature available related to the growth of international trade of China but very few have explained the link between trade pattern and the management techniques which have been driving the country to achieve the growth pattern. This paper contributes to fill that gap.

The paper examines the pattern of international trade of China and identifies the management techniques which have contributed to achieve that pattern. Data for this paper were collected from the published documents of the government of China. We have used export and import data and trade policies reforms that were developed by the country during last three decades. As the trade pattern of China might have significant implication in the

* ershada@ais.ac.nz.

world trade communities, findings of the paper might be of interest for researchers, policy makers and educationists.

MAJOR CHARACTERISTICS OF CHINA'S INTERNATIONAL TRADE

Prior to 1978, China had very minimal trade with the outside world, exporting just enough raw materials and simple manufactured goods to cover payments for imports of strategic minerals and other necessities which were not available at home. Since opening economy in 1978, the international trade has been increasing. During the 1980s, the value of imports exceeded that of exports as capital goods were brought in to equip manufacturing industry (China's Customs Statistics, 2010). During the 1989-91 slowdown, demand for imports fell below that of exports, and China's external trade has since remained in surplus, resulting in the accumulation of a mountain of foreign exchange reserves (China's Customs Statistics, 2010).

Although China's economic policy reform started in 1978, its decisive external opening, and with it sweeping industrial and agricultural restructuring, belong more to the post-Tiananmen phase, especially since 1994. China undertook enormous trade and Foreign Direct Investment (FDI) liberalisation during the 1990s, before World Trade Organisation (WTO) accession in 2001 followed by another big dose of liberalisation in line with its WTO commitments. Its WTO commitments are very strong. They exceed those of other developing countries by a wide margin. This holds for disciplines on border and non-border restrictions in goods and services. In addition, there are detailed commitments on transparency procedures to make sure trade-related laws and regulations are implemented, backed up by management and legal environment to which individuals and firms are supposed to have recourse (Fredrik, Patrick & Razeen 2010).

While the liberalisation of its markets and the development of foreign trade relations has been delayed by the gradual reform of its trade and foreign investment policy framework, China's goal to align itself with prescribed international requirements and standards is well underway. China has continued to modify its trade related management and preferential treatment to free trade agreement signatories. In addition, continuous structural reforms since its last Trade Policy Review (TPR) have continued to introduce market-oriented measures, which have contributed to a more efficient allocation of resources and a surge in foreign direct investment (Fredrik, Patrick & Razeen 2010). For example, in 2008, total two-way trade was valued at US$2,561.6 billion, an increase of 17.8% year on year. Merchandise exports rose 17.2% to US$1,428.6 billion while imports increased more rapidly, by 18.5%, to reach US$1,133.1 billion, leaving a trade surplus of US$295.5 billion, 12.7% higher than in 2007 (China's Customs Statistics, 2010).

China has succeeded more than most developing countries because: firstly in generating very high rates of growth; secondly in translating the growth into employment, poverty reduction and human-welfare improvement for a broad section of the population; and thirdly efficient management of resource allocation and utilization. High rates of saving and investment have driven this process, but trade and FDI have also been very important, especially in ramping up labour-intensive manufactured exports. China still has high regulatory barriers that waste resources, restrict internal trade and generally stifle domestic sources of growth. Tackling these barriers is the next big challenge (Fredrik, Patrick & Razeen 2010). This indicates that China still needs attention on its efficient management and its implications.

DRIVERS OF CHINESE INTERNATIONAL TRADE

The main driver of the growth of the Chinese international trade and economic growth is the reform of trade regulatory system. During last three decades, China has adopted few dozens of economic and trade policies to meet global challenges of international trade. Some important regulatory reforms are as follows.

1979 The law of the People's Republic of China on Chinese-Foreign Equity Joint Ventures: It is the first foreign related economic law in China, with a view to expanding international economic co-operation and technical exchange, the People's Republic of China permits foreign companies, enterprises, other economic organizations or individuals to joint with Chinese companies, enterprise or other economic organizations in establishing joint ventures in the People's Republic of China in accordance with the principle of equality and mutual benefit and subject to approval by the Chinese Government (China Internet Information Center, 2010).

1986 Law of the People's Republic of China on Foreign Capital Enterprises: In order to expand economic cooperation and technical exchanges with foreign countries and promote the development of China's national economy, the People's Republic of China permits foreign enterprises, other economic organizations and individuals to establish foreign capital enterprises in the territory of the People's Republic of China and protects the lawful rights and interests of foreign capital enterprises (China Internet Information Center, 2010).

1986 Law of the People's Republic of China on Enterprises Bankruptcy: This law is formulated in order to suit the development of the planned socialist commodity economy and the needs of the reform of the economic structure, to promote the autonomous operation of enterprises owned by the whole people, to strengthen the economic responsibility system and democratic management, to improve the state of operations, to increase economic efficiency and to protect the lawful rights and interests of creditors and debtors (China Internet Information Center, 2010).

1987 Customs Law of the People's Republic of China : This Law is formulated for the purpose of safeguarding state sovereignty and interests, strengthening supervision and control by the Customs, promoting exchanges with foreign countries in economic affairs, trade, science, technology and culture, and ensuring socialist modernization (Standing Committee of the National People's Congress, 2010a).

1988 Law of the People's Republic of China on Chinese-Foreign Contractual Joint Ventures: This Law is formulated to expand economic cooperation and technological exchange with foreign countries and to promote the joint establishment, on the principle of equality and mutual benefit, by foreign enterprises and other economic organizations or individuals and Chinese enterprises or other economic organizations of Chinese-foreign contractual joint ventures within the territory of the People's Republic of China (Trade Union of Xiamen, 2010).

1993 Company Law of the People's Republic of China: The law is formulated in conformity with the Constitution in view to establishing a modern enterprise system, standardizing the organization and operation of companies, protecting the legitimate rights and interests of companies, shareholders and creditors, maintaining the socialist economic order and promoting the development of the socialist market economy (Standing Committee of the National People's Congress, 2010b).

1994 Foreign Trade law of the People's Republic of China: This Law is formulated with a view to developing foreign trade, maintaining the order of foreign trade and promoting a sound development of the socialist market economy (Standing Committee of the National People's Congress, 2010c).

2000 Customs Law of the People's Republic of China: The revised Customs Law of the People's Republic of China was also released at the same time and came into force on January 1, 2001. As a big event for China Customs at the turn of the century, an important step for China Customs to improve the legal construction and carry out the administrative policies in conformity with the law, a significant reform of promoting the fair competition and increasing the trade efficiency in face of the development of international trade, and an important measure to strictly enforce the discipline and fight against the corruption, the revision of Customs Law caused wide concerns from the governmental authorities and social public.

The revised Customs Law has strengthened the forces to fight against the smuggling and established a new anti-smuggling system. In addition to supplementing and improving the existing legal systems of the Customs Law, the revised Customs Law has set up some new Customs legal systems, such as system of the Customs administrative ruling, the system of Customs security etc, which strengthened the supervisory force on the Customs. As a cross-century Customs law, the revised Customs Law has a significant meaning to the clearance reform, the modernization of China Customs and the prosperity of our country *(Shanghai Customs District, 2010).*

2003 Regulations on Import and Export Tariffs: These Regulations are formulated in accordance with the relevant provisions of the Customs Law of the People's Republic of China (hereinafter referred to as the Customs Law) for the purposes of implementing the policy of opening to the outside world and promoting the development of foreign economic relations and foreign trade and the national economy.

2004 Foreign Trade Law of the People's Republic of China: These laws and regulations related to standards, anti-dumping, countervailing and safeguard measures, and intercultural property rights. The present Law is enacted for the purpose of broadening the opening to the outside world, developing foreign trade, maintaining the order of foreign trade, protecting the lawful rights and interests of the foreign trade business operators, and promoting the healthy development of the socialist market economy

The present Law applies to foreign trade and the protection of foreign-trade-related intellectual property. China promotes and develops foreign trade relations with other countries and regions, concludes or accedes to regional economic and trade agreements such as customs or tariff union agreements, free trade zone agreements, etc., and joins regional economic organizations according to the principle of equality and reciprocity. In international trade sector, China grants, according to the international treaties and agreements it concluded or acceded to, most-favored-nation treatment or national treatment to other contracting parties or members, or grants most-favored-nation treatment or national treatment to its counterparts according to the principle of mutual benefit and reciprocity (Standing Committee of the National People's Congress, 2010d).

2006 Company Law of the People's Republic of China: This Law is formulated for the purposes of regulating the organization and operation of companies, protecting the legitimate rights and interests of companies, shareholders and creditors, maintaining the socialist economic order, and promoting the development of the socialist market economy (China Daily, 2010).

2006 Agricultural Product Quality Safety Law of the People's Republic of China: The present Law is formulated in order to guarantee the quality safety of agricultural products, maintain the health of the general public and promote the development of agriculture and rural economy (Standing Committee of the 10th National People's Congress, 2010e).

2006 Regulations on the Administration of Foreign funded Banks 2006: These Regulations are formulated for the purpose of meeting the needs of opening up to the outside world and economic development, strengthening and improving supervision and regulation over foreign-funded banks, and promoting safe and sound operation of the banking industry (China Banking Regulatory Commission, 2010).

2006 Regulations on Customs Statistics: The present Regulation is formulated in accordance with the relevant provisions of the Customs Law of the People's Republic of China and the Statistics Law of the People's Republic of China. for the purpose of carrying out the work of customs statistics in a scientific and effective way, and ensuring the accuracy, timeliness, and completeness of the customs statistics (State Council of the People's Republic of China, 2010).

2006 Regulations on Export Products Responding to Anti-dumping Cases: Firstly, they reflect an institutional change10 in antidumping investigating authorities. The Ministry of Commerce (MoC) shall be responsible for the investigation and the determination of both dumping and injury. Secondly, they encourage the authorities to consider public interest as an important factor to accept an offer of price undertaking and to provide that the collection of anti-dumping duty shall conform to the public interests. Thirdly, they also stipulate that MoC may take necessary measures to collect retroactive anti-dumping duties after launching an investigation (Thi, Van & Tong, 2009).

2007 Property Law of the People's Republic of China: It defines the concept of ownership of property and stipulates the protection of property rights of both private and public entities. The law covers the creation, transfer, and ownership of property in the mainland of the People's Republic of China (PRC) and is part of an ongoing effort by the PRC to gradually develop a civil code (Standing Committee of the National People's Congress, 2010f).

2007 Law on Enterprise Bankruptcy: It aims in regulating enterprise bankruptcy, stipulating procedures relating to the settlement of credit and debt, and outlining the standards of rights and interests of creditors and debtors. This Law is formulated for purposes of regulating the procedures for enterprise bankruptcy, fairly resolving the settlement of debts and credits, safeguarding the legitimate rights and interests of creditors and debtors, and maintaining the market order of the socialist economy (Standing Committee of the National People's Congress, 2010g).

IMPLICATION OF REFORMS ON INTERNATIONAL TRADE POLICY

The regulatory policy reform has been contributing positively to the different sectors of the Chinese economy and hence on international trade. However, in this section, we have discussed some important sectors of the economy such as import and export; trade related further policy reform; tariff; private sector; and foreign capital.

Implication of International Trade Related Policies

The export and import data of China from 1980 to 2009 is presented in Figure 2.1.

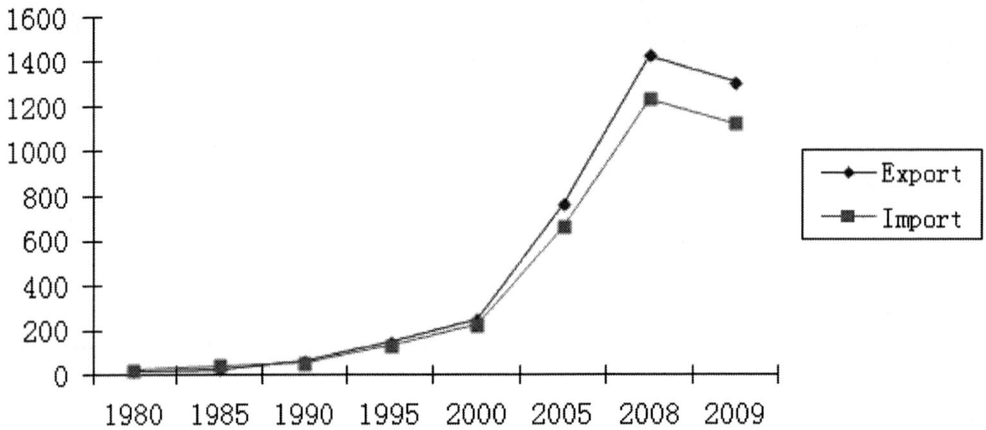

Figure 2.1. Export and Import of China from 1980 to 2009. Source: Prepared from the data National Bureau of Statistics of China, 2010.

Figure 2.1 shows that China's trade increased steady with the rest of the world since 1980. However, because China needed to bring in capital goods to equip manufacturing industry, until 1990, the value of imports exceeded that of exports.

From 1990 to 2000, China assumed the active role in the world through opening up to the outside world and building of a sound socialist market economy. It started to involve in the international cooperation and competition on larger scale. The value of exports exceeded that of imports, which led to the trade surplus and foreign exchange reserves accumulation.

After 2001, the total value of imports and exports of China increased significantly. The accession to WTO in December 2001 became a new stage for China's opening up. After China entered WTO, it shifted its regional approach opening up to multidimensional method. Also, China shifted its open sectors from traditional goods transaction to the service trade. Because of the commitments to WTO entry, Chinese market became more accessible and Chinese market environment became more transparent and well regulated, which promoted China's exports and imports significantly. In 2009, the global economic crisis caused China's trade surplus fall especially the rapid drop of exports.

Under with the reform and opening up policy decision, the reform of Chinese foreign trade system became important. In order to attract and utilize foreign capital, as well as lay the foundation for building a preferential environment for foreign investment, on July 1979, Chinese government enacted the first foreign-related economic law – the Law of the People's Republic of China on Chinese-Foreign Joint ventures. Following, Chinese government enacted other two important foreign-related economic laws, including the Law of the People's Republic of China on Foreign Capital Enterprises in 1986, and the Law of the People's Republic of China on Chinese-Foreign Contractual Joint Ventures in 1988. These three laws formed three basic laws of China in attracting foreign capital.

Implication of Tariff Related Policies

During last three decades, China has been reducing import tariff significantly compare to its major trading partner countries in the world such as EU, USA, Russia, India, etc.

Tariff is a trade barrier which increases the governments' revenue, improves the domestic producers' competitive ability, and raises the cost of imported products. Figure 2.2 shows the trend of China's tariff reduction level during last three decades.

It appears from Figure 2.2 that Chinese government has concerned to minimize and eliminate trade tariff during last three decades in order to create more trade with the rest of the world, to fit with its opening up policy.

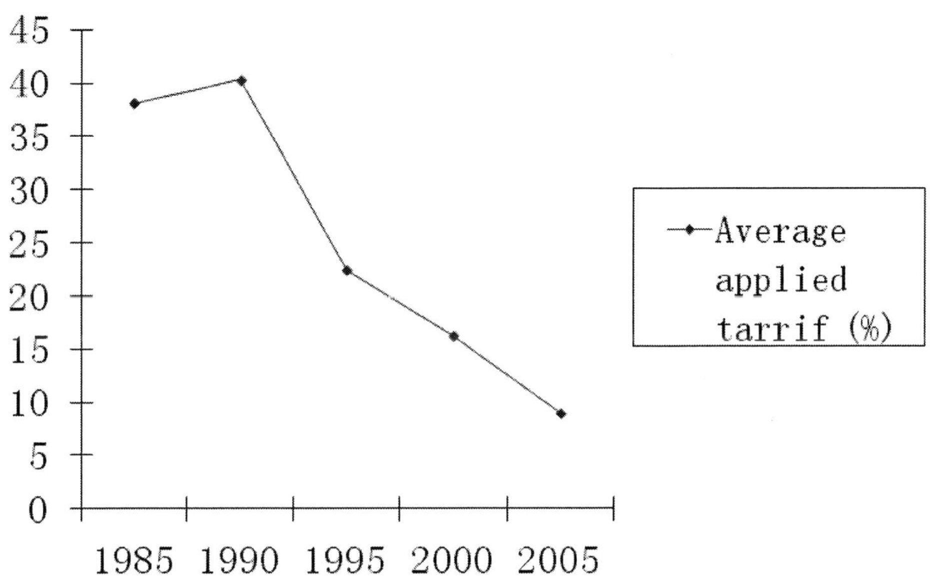

Figure 2.2. Changes of Chinese tariffs during last three decades. Source: China's Custom Statistics (2010).

Implication of Policy Reform on Private Sector

China's entrepreneurs have been successful in creating the institutions of private markets. In 1978, state owned enterprises generated about 80 percent of China's GDP, while the rural sector produced the rest 20 percent. There was no business in private sector. By 1997, there were 961,000 private owned enterprises and 28.5 million small family private firms. By 2002, the private sector's share exceeded two-thirds of GDP. By 2004, there were more than three million private companies employing more than 47 million workers. Before 1980, entrepreneurial activity in China was illegal. Presently, there are over 40 million entrepreneurs, whose businesses employ over 200 million and generate two-thirds of industrial output. The state had no choice but to accept the reality of burgeoning farmers' markets and private trade.

The improvement in product quality and the disappearance of long food lines convinced urban residents, as well as government leaders, of the power of grassroots entrepreneurial activities. The state could not curtail such activities without inflaming the entire populace, although it periodically tried. In 1988, the government made it theoretically legal to own private businesses but in practice imposed strict controls over private urban markets, including steep fees to regulate them. Private business originated in agriculture, spread to the cities, and then returned to the countryside as rural-based industry. Some examples are such as the Hoep Group in agribusiness; Wang Guoduan in rural sector business; and Huanyuan in air conditioning business (Gregory and Zhou, 2010).

The international trade involves not only the trade between countries but also between private companies across board. In China, before 1980 economic reform, there were no private businesses, especially in rural China. The implication of policy reform on private sector is presented in Figure 2.3.

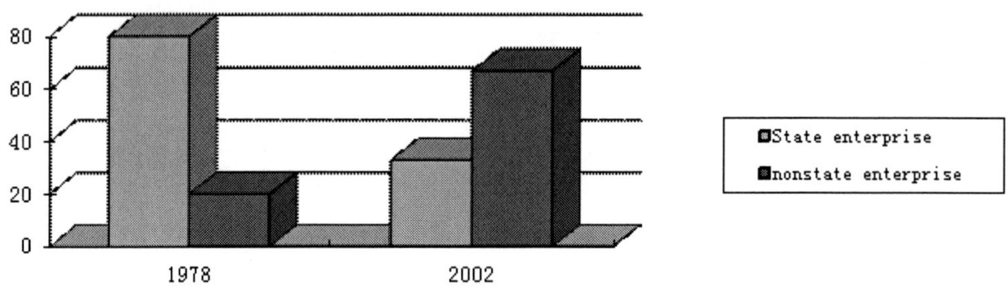

Figure 2.3. The success of private sector during last three decades. Source: Gregory & Zhou, 2010.

Private companies increased significantly, which not only produced the large share of Chinese GDP but also promoted the international trade.

Implication of Policy Reform on Foreign Capital

China's success in attracting foreign capital and know-how and selling manufactured products in foreign markets is well established. Over the 30 years since the reforms and opening-up to the outside world, Chinese foreign trade has increased from USD20.6 billion in 1978 to USD2.1738 trillion in 2007, average annual growth of 17.4%.

As a country attracting the most FDI among the developing world for 15 consecutive years, China not only expands the FDI scale but also optimizes its structure. Foreign-invested companies are playing more and more important role in China's national economic growth, industrial and technological advance, export expansion and generation of job opportunities (China Foreign Investment Administration, 2010).

Foreign capital is very important factor promoting China's foreign trade as it increased the trade volume of foreign invested companies. China has become the most attractive destination in the world for FDI during last three decades, in terms of its smooth investment promotion and investment protection agreements, which not only protects Chinese interests but also the legitimate rights of foreign investors.

Conclusion and Policy Implications

The paper analyses the management of China's international trade pattern in last three decades, in order to describe the major characteristics of the trade at different periods, and identifies the major drivers on each period.

In order to understand the trend of management of international trade of China, the paper reviews data on China's export and import for last three decades. We have identified three clear periods to describe the different characteristics of international trade of China. The first period is from 1980 to 1990, in which the international trade of China had the steady increase but the value of imports exceeded that of exports in terms of bringing in capital goods to equip manufacturing industry. The second period is from 1990 to 2000, in which the international trade of China still increased steady as well as with the value of exports exceeding that of imports in terms of its socialist market economy and involvement of international cooperation and competition on larger scale. The third period is after 2001, in which the international trade of China increased significantly, in terms of its accession to WTO and shifts from regional approach opening up to multidimensional method, and open sectors from traditional goods transaction to the service trade. The more accessible Chinese market and more transparent well regulated market environments drove China's booming of exports and imports.

In order to identify the major reasons driving Chinese international trade during each period, we have examined four major factors such as trade related policies, reduction of trade tariff, development of private sector, and inflows of foreign capital.

Various trade related polices and regulations created by China during last three decades shows that the reform of Chinese foreign trade regulations was very important factor in driving Chinese international trade during last three decades. Before 2001, the Law of the People's Republic of China on Chinese-Foreign Joint ventures, the Law of the People's Republic of China on Foreign Capital Enterprises in 1986, and the Law of the People's Republic of China on Chinese-Foreign Contractual Joint Ventures in 1988 are three laws formed three basic laws of China in attracting foreign capital. After joining WTO in 2001, China's foreign-related economic policy has been gradually perfected and the transparency of trade policies has been constantly strengthened, through accelerating the reform step of the import and export management system, and promulgating the foreign trade regulations.

Pattern of tariff level reduction in China during last three decades shows that minimizing and eliminating trade tariff during last three decade is also a factor driving Chinese international trade increasing trend. The reform of private sector during last three decades shows that the booming of private companies in China produced the large share of Chinese GDP as well as promoted the international trade, especially one of important factor in driving China's significant increase of international trade after 2001. Similarly the inflows of foreign capital during last three decades shows that foreign capital is very important factor promoting China's international trade as it increased the trade volume of foreign invested companies.

Finally, based on above analysis, the paper concludes that China's management of its trade pattern including policy formulation and implementation is fully competent to raise this country as a super power in the world.

REFERENCES

China Banking Regulatory Commission. (2010), 'Regulations on the Administration of Foreign funded Banks.' http://www.cbrc.gov.cn/english/home/jsp/doc.

China's Customs Statistics. (2010), 'China's Exports & Imports', 1952-2009. http://www.chinability.com/Trade.htm

China Daily. (2010), 'Company Law of the People's Republic of China.' http://www.chinadaily.com.cn/bizchina/

China Foreign Investment Administration. (2010), Foreign capital in China's national economic development. http://www.fdi.gov.cn/pub/FDI_EN

China Internet Information Center. (2010), Law of the People's Republic of China on Enterprise Bankruptcy. http://en.148365.com.

Emerging Markets Monitor. (2009), China: BMI Raises 2009 Growth Forecast To 8.1%. Emerging Markets Monitor. 15 (16), pp. 5-6.

Fredrik, E., Patrick, M. and Razeen, S. (2010), 'China's Trade Policy', Post-WTO Accession: Focus on China-EU Relations. http://www.ecipe.org/people/fredrik-erixon/

Gregory, P.R. and Zhou, K. (2010), 'How China Won and Russia Lost', http://www.hoover.org/publications/policyreview/

National Bureau of Statistics of China (2010), 'China's Exports & Imports, 1952-2009'. http://www.chinability.com/Trade.htm/

Shanghai Customs District. (2010), 'Customs Law of the People's Republic of China.' http://shanghai.customs.gov.cn/

Shenzhen Customs District. (2010), 'Regulations on Import and Export Tariffs', http://shenzhen.customs.gov.cn/publish/

Standing Committee of the National People's Congress. (2010a), 'Company Law of the People's Republic of China', http://www.lawinfochina.com/law/

Standing Committee of the National People's Congress. (2010b), 'Customers Law of the People's Republic of China', http://www.lawinfochina.com/law/

Standing Committee of the National People's Congress. (2010c), 'Foreign Trade law of the People's Republic of China', http://www.nti.org/db/China

Standing Committee of the National People's Congress. (2010d), 'Foreign Trade Law of the People's Republic of China', http://www.lawinfochina.com

Standing Committee of the National People's Congress. (2010e), 'Law on Enterprise bankruptcy', http://www.lehmanlaw.com/resource-centre/laws-and-regulations

Standing Committee of the National People's Congress. (2010f), 'Property Law of the People's Republic of China', http://en.wikipedia.org/wiki/Property_Law

Standing Committee of the 10th National People's Congress. (2010g), 'Agricultural Product Quality Safety Law of the People's Republic of China', http://jckspaqj.aqsiq.gov.cn/zcfg/gnflfg/

State Council of the People's Republic of China (2010), 'Regulations on Customs Statistics', http://www.asianlii.org/cn/legis/cen/laws/

Thi, L., Van, T. and Tong, S.Y. (2009), 'China and Anti-Dumping Regulations, Practices and Responses', EAI Working Paper. No. 149.

Trade Union of Xiamen. (2010), Law of the People's Republic of China on Chinese-Foreign Contractual Joint Ventures. http://xmzgh.org/frame/

In: Development Management in the Twenty-First Century ISBN: 978-1-62100-699-2
Editors: Kartik Roy and Sandip Kar

Chapter 3

MANAGING ECONOMIC AND SOCIAL DEVELOPMENT IN SOUTH EAST ASIA IN THE CHANGING GLOBAL ORDER

Katarzyna Anna Nawrot*
Department of International Economics, Poznan University of Economics, Poznan, Poland

INTRODUCTION

South East Asia constitutes an unique example of a region composed of ten countries, which could be located on different side of a letter of economic and social development. Singapore is for instance one of the most technologically developed country in the world and then Cambodia or Lao are still economies with agriculture as a main sector of production and are rank among the poorest countries in the world economy. One of the biggest countries in the region – Indonesia – is located next to the small city-state Singapore. Indonesia, next to China is also rank among the most populated countries in the world, as Brunei is one of the smallest. All the main religions – Buddhism, Christianity and Islam – are spread around the region. There are countries like Lao – without the sea access, on the contrary to Indonesia with one of the longest sea line. All this contribute to the fascinating collage for research studies in numerous dimensions.

Furthermore there is a genuine opportunity to be observed in South East Asia in terms of the changes which took place in the last decades, concerning the agrarian transition in particular countries and the rise of economic growth and social and economic development. Specific countries took the benefits from the globalisation and internationalisation processes, comparative advantage and international division of labour. Causality between the transition, economic development and ongoing process of integration in the region could also be observed. Besides the crucial issues in the changing global order are to be observed in the region including the impact of the global financial crisis on Asian economies with reference

* k.nawrot@ue.poznan.pl.

to Asian financial crisis of '98th and the lesson learned. Furthermore essential concern is the rise of China and India and its impact on the economic development of the countries in the whole region and the ongoing integration processes of China and other countries in terms of creating free trade agreements and cooperation approaches.

So, the chapter is an attempt to analyse the managing of economic and social development of Southeast Asian countries of ASEAN (*Association of Southeast Asian Nations*) in the light of the above mentioned issues of contemporary international relations in the changing global order. First of all the state of economic and social development of particular countries will be presented followed by the achievements over the last two decades. On that basis a discussion on determinants and managing of economic growth and development will be raised focusing on three dimensions: internal, regional and international. Furthermore the impact of issues like global financial crisis, ASEAN itself and the impact of the rise of China and India on economic and social development of Southeast Asian countries will be analysed resulting in the conclusions on perspectives of development of the economies in the region.

The Pattern of Grow and Economic Development in South East Asia

Although the eighties of the XX century could be perceived as the beginning of the transition in the Southeast Asian countries, the very first symptoms of all globalization and liberalization processes which marked the new pattern of grow and development started in February 1977 by the signing of the ASEAN Preferential Trading Arrangements (ASEAN PTA). In the late eighties also ASEAN itself changed the character from political arrangement to an organization in which economic co-operation became the main purpose of activity (Khoman 1992; Rajaratnam 1992)[1]. As a result intra-regional cooperation was intensified (creation of AFTA – ASEAN Free Trade Area), import-subsidized policy was replaced by export orientated policy and it all led to the rapid development of all the member countries.

Following object lessons from Japan and the Asian NIE's, ASEAN began to open its borders to international competition and, as a result, the region moved into the spotlight as world's fastest-growing economy with GDP growth rates reaching 10% (Figure 3.1).

After the Asian financial crisis of 98th "V-shape" recovery and the slowdown in the world economy at the beginning of the XXIth century registered growth rates of Southeast Asian countries were 5%-8% per annum and only China's rate of growth was significantly higher.

The changes towards the industrialization and internalization of Southeast Asian economies could be observed in the share of sector of production in GDP. The changes were especially radical for ASEAN-5 economies, with a declining share of agriculture from around 30% of GDP in the 70s till even around 10% in 2010 in case of Malaysia and Thailand. The share of agriculture in GDP for ASEAN-BCMLV hasn't changed significantly over the last 30 years with the exception of Vietnam and its impressive transformation (compare tables 3.1 and 3.2). The actual rise of agriculture share in GDP in Myanmar (from 30% till even 60% in

[1] Although in the first decades after establishment of ASEAN the stability and politics were the main issues of concern, the founders of ASEAN indicate strongly the initial economic purposes of the Association and its creation as a non-military organization based on the example of European Economic Community (EEC).

2001) over the last forty years resulted largely from the sluggish growth of the non-agricultural sectors due to socialist economic policies which tended to prevent the inflow of capital and technology (Lim Chong Yah 2004, pp. 46-47).

Those factors were in turn essential for the industrialization of particular countries in the region (namely ASEAN-5) in line with the economic potential derived from the factor endowments – mainly capital (inward capital formation) and labor (qualitative and qualitative dimension) next to the chosen technique of production (Skawińska, Grabka-Sobiech, Nawrot 2010, p. 64).

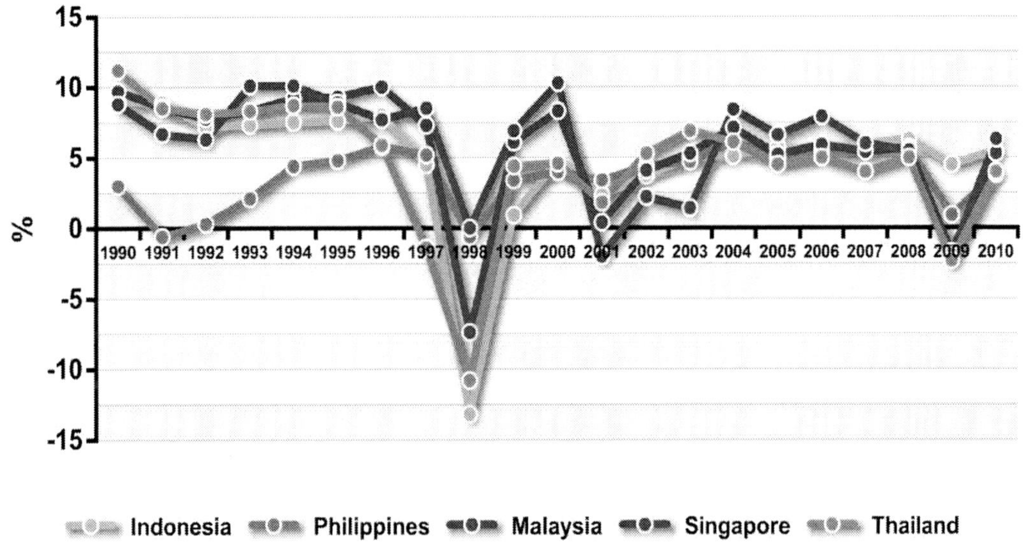

Figure 3.1. GDP rates of growth of ASEAN-5 in 1990-2010 (%). Source: based on ADO (1996), pp. 76-222; ADO (2002), pp. 19-211; ADO (2005), pp. 90-303; ADO (2010), p. 261.

The positive direction of economic development processes is reflected in dynamics of quantitative indices, showing that all countries in the region improved their standard of living measured by per capita income.

Nevertheless the ten countries differ considerably in terms of the level of economic development as they could be located on two different side of the same letter of economic development. Singapore achieved one of the highest incomes in the world with GNI in PPP reaching 50000 USD, in line with Brunei (compare figure 3.2) and then Cambodia or Lao are still economies with agriculture as a main sector of production and are rank among the poorest countries in the world economy with income per person hardly reaching 1500-2500 USD. While using the World Bank Atlas methodology GNI per capita approximate 540-580 USD accordingly, thus not reaching 2$ poverty line for an average citizen of those countries and classifying them next to Myanmar and Vietnam as low income economies (*Atlas of Global Development* 2009, pp. 128-129). All the remaining economies are rank as middle income countries, with Malaysia as upper-middle-income country and Thailand, Indonesia, Philippines and lower-middle-income countries.

Table 3.1. Share of sectors of production in GDP in ASEAN-5 in 1970-2008 (%)

	Agriculture						Industry						Services					
	1970	1980	1995	2001	2004	2008	1970	1980	1995	2001	2004	2008	1970	1980	1995	2001	2004	2008
Indonesia	35,0	24,4	15,9	16,2	17,0	14,0	28,0	41,3	42,2	36,0	46,0	48,0	37,0	34,3	41,9	47,8	38,0	37,0
Philippines	28,2	23,5	21,5	20,1	14,0	15,0	3,7	40,5	35,5	34,0	32,0	32,0	38,1	36,0	43,0	46,0	54,0	53,0
Malaysia	28,0[a]	22,9	13,9	8,2	10,0	10,0	25,0[a]	35,8	47,1	43,1	48,0	48,0	47[a]	41,3	39,0	48,7	42,0	42,0
Singapore	2,2	1,1	0,2	0,1	0,1	0,0	36,4	38,8	42,7	30,7	33,7	28,0	61,4	60,0	57,1	69,2	66,2	72,0
Thailand	30,2	20,2	10,9	8,0	10,0	12,0	25,7	30,1	42,2	44,0	44,0	46,0	44,1	49,7	46,9	48,0	46,0	43,0

Descriptions: a – data for 1965

Source: based on ADO (1996), pp. 76–222; ADO (2002), pp. 19–211; WDR (2006), pp. 292–293; WDR (2010), pp. 384-385.

Table 3.2. Share of sectors of production in GDP in ASEAN-BCMLV in 1970-2008 (%)

	Agriculture						Industry						Services					
	1970	1980	1995	2001	2004	2008	1970	1980	1995	2001	2004	2008	1970	1980	1995	2001	2004	2008
Brunei	0,6[b]	Nd	nd	1,8[a]	nd	nd	82,4[b]	nd	nd	41,6[a]	nd	nd	17,0[b]	nd	nd	56,6[a]	nd	nd
Cambodia	nd	44,7	44,6	32,0	36,0	32,0	nd	20,3	18,7	24,0	28,0	27,0	nd	35,0	36,7	44,0	37,0	41,0
Lao	d	53,9	56,5	51,3	49,0	40,0	nd	17,3	18,9	23,1	26,0	31,0	nd	28,8	24,6	25,6	25,0	29,0
Myanmar	49,5	47,9	46,1	60,0[a]	54,6[c]	nd	12,0	12,3	15,3	9,0[a]	13,0[c]	nd	38,5	39,8	38,6	31,0[a]	32,4[c]	nd
Vietnam	nd	42,7	33,9	22,7	22,0	20,0	nd	26,3	27,7	36,9	40,0	42,0	nd	31,0	38,4	40,4	38,0	38,0

Descriptions: a – data for 2000, b – data for 1965, c – data for 2002, nd – no data available.

Source: based on ADO (1996), pp. 76–222; ADO (2002), pp. 19–211; WDR (2006), pp. 292–293, WDR (2010), pp. 384-385

SOCIAL DEVELOPMENT OF SOUTHEAST ASIAN COUNTRIES

Precise diagnosis of social development requires the use of qualitative indices what enables to explore different dimensions of the situation in developing countries, then by means of quantitative measures only. The example of Southeast Asian countries proofed that economies with the same or similar GDP per capita can significantly differ when taking into account qualitative measures like HDI (*Human Development Index*), HPI (*Human Poverty Index*), SDI (*Sustainable Development Index*), or IEF (*Index of Economic Freedom*) (compare figures 3.2, 3.3).

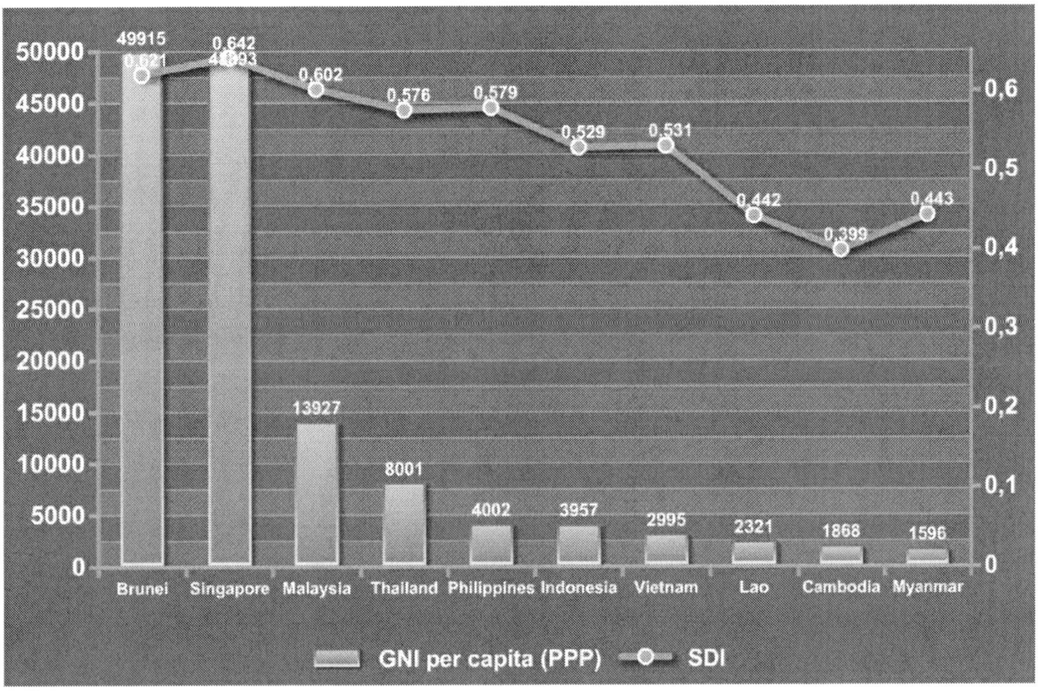

Figure 3.2. Comparison of GNI per capita (PPP) and SDI (Sustainable Development Index) of Southeast Asian countries in 2008. Source: based on UNDP (2010), pp. 143-146; Nováček P., Mederly P. (2002), pp. 67-69.

All of the countries in the region are rank as those with high or medium human development. However Singapore and Brunei, according to the latest typology by UNDP are economies with very high human development, above 0,9 (UNDP 2009, p. 171). It is worth pointing out that all of the countries in the last 10/20 years achieved significant progress shifting from low or medium level to medium, high and very high level. The evidence of poverty is significantly differential in the region. There is still very high level of people in poverty in Lao and Cambodia (around 30%) and in Myanmar (around 25%). In case of Singapore, Malaysia, Thailand and Brunei the HPI doesn't exceed 8% (UNDP 2009, p. 171).

In 1993 HDI for 37 countries was twenty position lower or higher then GDP *per capita*. Good examples are Vietnam and Pakistan – countries with similar income per person but quite different level of human development. Economic policy of Vietnam, especially after joining ASEAN, focused on qualitative grow of a society led to spectacular outcome transforming the growth of production into improvement in the quality of life. The decrease of poverty in case of Vietnam from more than 30% at the beginning of the nineties till around 12% in 2010 is exceptional illustrating the proper managing not only of economic but also social development of a country.

The research study and observation lead however to the conclusion that there is no automatic link between economic growth and human progress in many countries. Thailand, for example, achieved high level of human development with relatively low level of income per person. It underpins the thesis that human development is possible during the economic slowdown. So in the short term, countries can achieve significant improvements in human development without satisfactory economic growth.

However, in the long term no improvement in human development is possible without growth and, by analogy, no sustained growth will be achieved if accompanied by low human development (Nawrot 2008, p. 117).

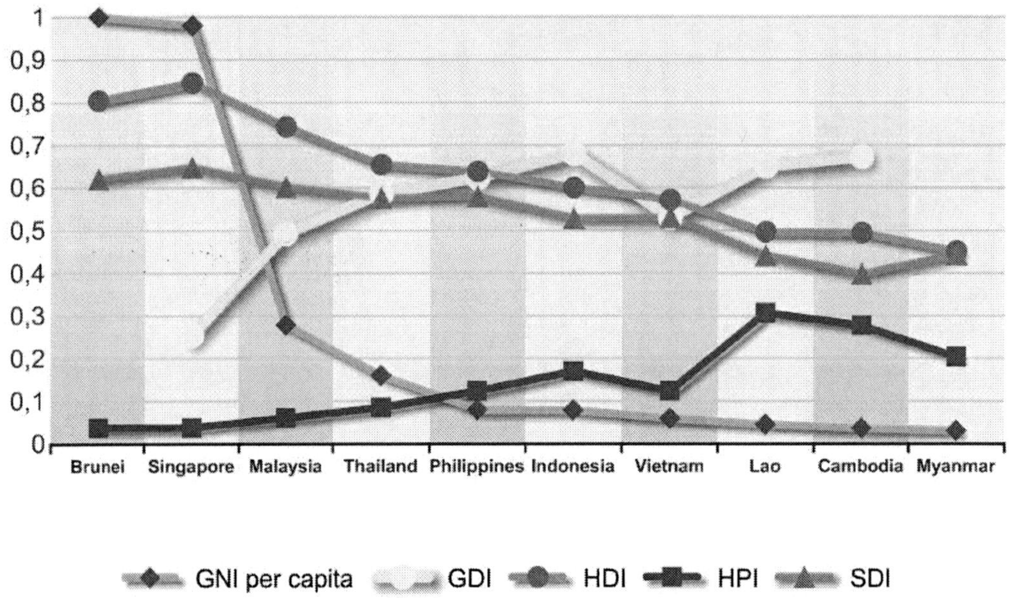

Figure 3.3. Comparison of qualitative and quantitative measures of economic development in Southeast Asian countries (2010). Source: based on UNDP (2009), pp. 171-184; UNDP (2010), pp. 143-146.

Comparing the qualitative and quantitative indicators analyzed in the study analogical results could be derived (Figure 3.3). The value of per capita income of Philippines and Indonesia were on similar level of around 4000 USD (PPP).

However the qualitative indicators show that the Philippines has higher human development in all dimensions what resulted from higher level of education, better social care and higher empowerment of women. Similar situation could be observed in case of Vietnam and Cambodia, which differ significantly in human development and poverty level. Comparing Philippines with Thailand slightly different conclusion can be derived, as those countries differ significantly in terms of GNI per capita (PPP) but on the other hand the level of human development is very much the same (compare figure 3.2 and 3.3).

DISCUSSION ON MANAGING AND DETERMINANTS OF ECONOMIC GROWTH AND DEVELOPMENT IN SOUTHEAST ASIAN COUNTRIES

Conducted research, based on literature studies and diagnosis of the level of development of Southeast Asian countries lead to the statement that the transition, the level of economic and social development of particular countries and its dynamics were determined by the combinations of factors of endogenous and exogenous character, which were influencing each other and could be systematize in three infiltrating dimensions (Nawrot 2008, pp. 72-73):

- internal dimension,
- regional dimension,
- international dimension.

The endogenous factors include: the endowment of a country in factors of production and related to this choice of technique of production and change in technique of production, economic freedoms, cultural background and disaster risk. Among exogenous determinants, resulting from the involvement of a country in the global economy are in the first place international trade and capital flow. Concerning capital flow, foreign direct investment and financial markets influenced the change in the fundamental way. The crucial influence of regional integration in stimulating agrarian transition and economic development cannot be omitted and should be examined in relation to trade, capital flow and regional initiatives in the field of production and agriculture. Development aid and assistance is also important in the analysis of exogenous determinants of economic growth and development of the region.

The analysis resulted in an attempt to state the hypothesis, that direction of specialization of Southeast Asian countries and the choice of technique of production with relation to the endowment of factors of production were the cause generating the growth of international exchange (international trade and flow of capital), what with the particular civilization and cultural background, institutional factors and pro-integration regional policy led to the growth and development of the particular countries. In all of those mentioned dimensions, starting from the domestic, through regional and international the role of the state and institutions was crucial and in many aspect primary in managing development in South East Asia.

Bearing in mind the volume of the elaboration the focus will be made on the significance of regional dimension and the impact of ASEAN as an Association on economic growth and development of the member countries what will be further discussed in this chapter. It is worth mentioning that initially, the liberalization in the region encompassed only the member countries of ASEAN, and was adjusted to the capabilities of each participant. The main aim of introduced PTA (Preferential Trading Arrangements) was to intensify intra-regional trade through the granting of trade preferences on a product by product basis (Bende-Nabende 1999, p. 33). The agreement included trade preferences through long-term contracts, open accounts on preferential lending rate, liberalization of non-tariff barriers on preferential terms, and extended tariff preferences. According to the above arrangement, member countries were supposed to grant each other a minimum 20-25% margin of preference (MOP) on products already established by ASEAN PTA (Lim Chong Yah 2004, p. 200). Year by year the margins of preference have been deepened, non-tariff barriers have been cut and the list of products to liberalize has been extended. Additional initiatives which have contributed to preferential trading included ASEAN Industrial Joint Ventures (AIJVs) and ASEAN Industrial Complementation (AIC) schemes. Although the intense trade preferences were adopted, an expected trade creation effect did not occur, but instead trade diversion effect was observed.

In the nineties the aware steps have been made in order to intensify intra-regional cooperation – creation of AFTA – ASEAN Free Trade Area and AIA (ASEAN Investment Area). Despite the criticism – as compared with other developing countries – ASEAN might be regarded as the most successful developing regional economic block.

Concerning the economic development and the agrarian change it is also important to indicate the significance of sub-regional cooperation – regional economic initiatives called growth triangles (Tongzon 2002, pp. 81-84). With reference to the analyzed region SIJORI growth triangle is worth mentioning. It was the very first triangle launched in South East Asia and consist of Singapore (SI), Malaysian province Johor Baharu (JO) and Indonesian Islands of Riau (RI). The economic rationale of SIJORI resulted mainly from the comparative and competitive advantages arising from the differences in factor endowments among the three participating ASEAN partners (Lim Chong Yah 2004, p. 212). The initiative was aimed at attracting investors because of advanced transport and communication infrastructure and high quality human capital of Singapore, relatively inexpensive industrial land and unskilled labour of Indonesia and semi-skilled labour and accessible large industrial land of Malaysia.

The formation of SIJORI growth triangle was in fact formalization of previous business connections with Malaysia. Participation of Indonesian Riau Islands was a new conception of cooperation. Effective functioning of a triangle is resulting in bilateral relations on the line Singapore-Johor and Singapore-Riau. Cooperation between Johor and Riau is very limited what is combined with similar endowment in factors of production, so the economic structure between them is rather competitive then complementary.

New possibilities for SIJORI growth triangle appeared in 2003 in line with implementing the U.S. – Singapore Free Trade Agreement – USSFTA (Ikuo Kuroiwa, Toh Mun Heng 2008, p. 114). This opportunity should be perceived as a chance for small and medium enterprises from Johor and Riau for incorporating in global production networks through a closer cooperation with Singaporean and international firms exporting to the USA. Particular countries are standing in front of a possibility to take advantage of geographical proximity and at the same time having different comparative advantage and specializing in products at different stages of a life cycle can create pan national cluster. The other sub-regional economic zones include Indonesia-Malaysia-Thailand Growth Triangle – IMTGT or Northern Growth Triangle; East ASEAN Growth Area (EAGA).

The growth triangles in Southeast Asia should be perceived as tools managing regional development through accelerating industrialisation processes, regional trade and capital liberalisation. Those initiatives are not marketed to compete but to gain from bilateral complementarities. The future of functioning of this sub-regional form of cooperation lies in private sector which should pursue the initiatives initiated by the government.

The integration processes and cooperation in the region were not inward looking path strategy of development but a part of global orientated trading policy management. So, global orientation of all member countries of ASEAN should be indicated which, however, are still subordinate compared with the global trade and trade with the industrialized countries. The members of ASEAN are world leaders in trade and a share in world's export and import approximates 6%. Export growth in all member of ASEAN-5, except Indonesia was exceeding the global average for the nineties. A significant share of exports in national income was recorded as well; which in 1995 reached 25% for Indonesia, 96% for Malaysia, 36% for the Philippines, 172% for Singapore and 42% for Thailand (ADB 2005, p. 170). Compared with the eighties this indicator rose twice. Despite the export orientation of ASEAN, the member countries still compete between themselves not only for export markets in developed countries but also for FDI and as low cost manufacturing bases for multinational corporations from North East Asia, EU, and North America (Jones and Smith 2006, p. 107; Camilleri 2003, p. 229).

Current Issues Shaping the International Relations in the Region

An Integrating Asia

In parallel with economic integration of ASEAN cooperation in the whole region of East Asia and Asia and Pacific was initiated, along with the integration into the global economy. ASEAN played a significant role in that process as a group which succeeded to avoid the ineffectiveness in cooperation, typical for many initiatives undertaken by developing countries. Nevertheless unlike economically developed integrated regions like EU the share of intra regional trade is relatively small and in 2008 the intra regional export of ASEAN approximated 28% (Jones and Smith 2006, p. 107; Nawrot 2008b, pp. 59-60). However in the mid nineties, especially after the Asian financial crisis the regional identity has strengthen and "ASEAN plus" process has began. One of the most important initiatives is so called ASEAN+3 including Japan, South Korea and China and ASEAN+3+1 together with India. ASEAN plus process could be perceived as a crucial step towards East Asian regionalism or even further Pan Asian regionalism. East Asian Summit (EAS) is another manifestation of East Asian power in international relations with ASEAN holding the balance of power between China and Japan as Eastern Asian representatives, India as Southern Asian leader and Australia representing the Western powers. It is worth indicating that EAS does not include USA or EU. The only international institution functioning in the whole Asia and the Pacific region is APEC (Asia-Pacific Economic Cooperation). Another important cooperation including ASEAN is ASEAN Regional Forum – ARF – established with Russia, India, China, Japan, EU and USA.

Until the mid nineties the cooperation and industrialization in East Asian were both combined with Japanese led flyeeing geese model of development introduced at the beginning of the thirties by K. Akamatsu. The growth of production and regional division of labour were following the life cycle of different branches of industry. The main channels of relocation of production from one country to the other through the shift in competitiveness were trade and foreign direct investment. After obtaining specialised skills and competences the producers from Japan, Hong Kong, South Korea and Taiwan started to search for locations in less developed countries in the region, creating regional production networks. In the second half of the eighties the relocation of labour intensive branches of production were additionally intensified by the currency appreciation i.e. Japanese yen and the high dynamics of foreign direct investment flows, which were also stimulated by the integration initiatives of ASEAN (Nawrot 2009a).

According to the model, less developed countries from the region benefited from the experience of more advanced economies, imitating their development and industry restructuring strategies and then while being on different level of development started to shift to more advanced economies, industrialisation and wealth (Nawrot 2009b, p. 352). An integrating Asia has been though reshaped between the late nineties and the beginning of the twenty-first century in favor of China what will be discussed in further part of the text.

The Rise of China and India

The global order, as the landscape of international relations in Asia and the Pacific has changed along with the rise of China and India. In case of ASEAN and East Asian community China is playing a crucial role directing economics and politics in the region. The turning point was signing a few agreements in 2002 at ASEAN+1 summit in Phnom Penh, namely: Joint Declaration of ASEAN and China on Cooperation in the Field of Non-traditional Security Issues, Declaration on the Conduct of Parties in the South China Sea and Framework Agreement on Comprehensive Economic Cooperation. On the basis of the latest the establishment of the ASEAN-China Free Trade Area (ACFTA) came into effect. Both sides have targeted the realisation of ACFTA in 2010 for ASEAN-6 (Brunei Darussalam, Indonesia, Malaysia, Philippines, Singapore, Thailand) and China, and 2015 for ASEAN-CMLV (Cambodia, Lao PDR, Myanmar and Viet Nam). The stabilization of bilateral relations between ASEAN and China resulted in closer economic cooperation, therefore placing China as a main trading partner of ASEAN. The analysis of the trade pattern of East Asian economies shows that China is the very first trade partner for the majority of its neighbors. Thus the rising power of China on both regional and international arena indicates that neither economic nor security issues in South East Asia cannot be raised without China. Furthermore the economic agreements with China dominate the cooperation processes in the region, challenging the meaning of U.S.-led APEC, the ADB framework preferred by Japan. The important issue in the establishment of ACFTA lies in political logic and peaceful rise and development policy of China.

The cooperation between India and ASEAN has also been accelerated strongly over the last two decades and especially after signing the Framework Agreement on Comprehensive Economic Cooperation in 2003 at the Bali Summit. The strengthening of bilateral relation between ASEAN and India was a part of Indian Look East Policy (LEP) adopted in 1991 and the indication of globalization processes in the region. Both India and ASEAN could play significant role in the Asia-Pacific international relation: ASEAN as a bridge to cooperation with the Northeast Asian economies toward wider Pan Asian integration and India for ASEAN and North East Asia as a link to Central and West Asian countries (Kumar, Sen, Asher, p. 2). Emerging broader economic cooperation between ASEAN, India, Japan, South Korea and China should also be considered.

Furthermore there is a chance for a region in broader cooperation among the partners of the emerging Asian Triangle of China, India and ASEAN+ process (Figure 3.4), as they form obvious boundaries for potential cooperation in the region although with the substantial support of Japan, USA and EU, which on the other hand structure the other strong group of countries. The interconnections and interdependence between particular actors of the two triangles will be very interesting to observe in the future and require further research. The importance of Russia in the region of East Asia should also be taken into consideration, especially with the rising power of the BRIC countries (Brazil, Russia, India, China). It should be further indicated that the decade of the Triad countries phenomenon may to be not applicable any longer while watching the fast changing global order. It seems that Asian triangle would be the core of growth in manufacturing sector in Asia and although it is a provocative phenomenon it can underpin the idea of East Asia as a (future or contemporary) centre of global economy.

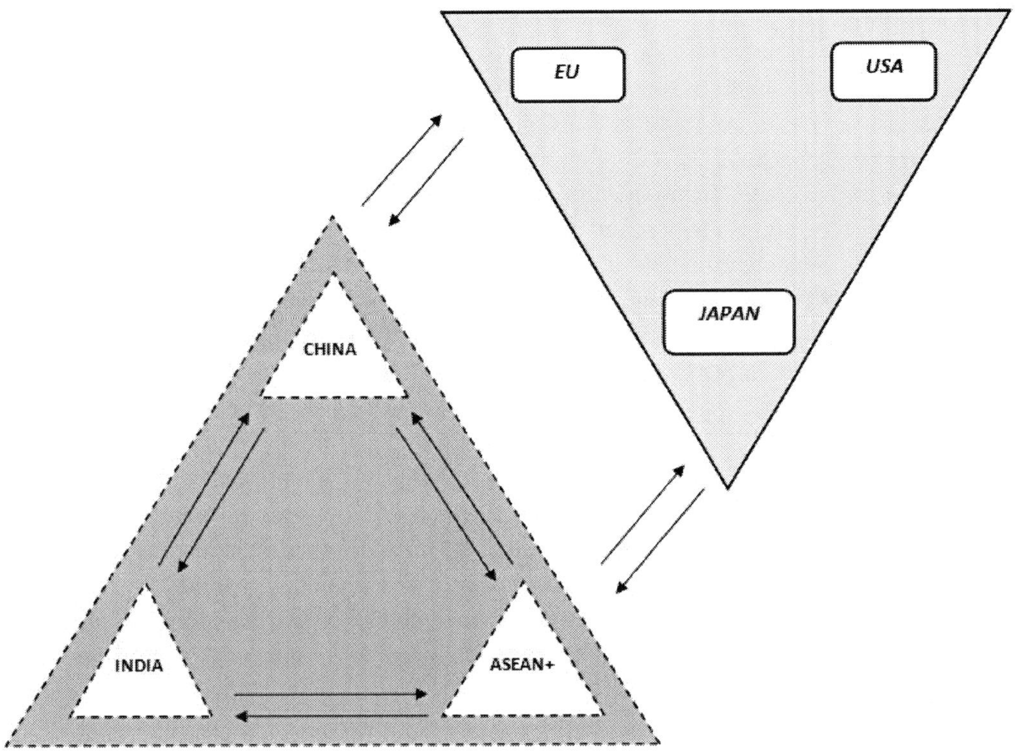

Figure 3.4. The concept of the Asian Triangle.

Financial Crisis

All of the countries in South East Asia are aware that their development was closely correlated with the expansion to the global markets and that they have to continue this strategy. The regional cooperation was the bridge leading to the higher competitiveness at the international level. The particular economies grasp the edge of globalization processes and ridged it into prosperity and development. On the other hand liberalization of international trade and furthermore liberalization of financial sectors made the Asian markets very responsive to the global fluctuation, resulting on one hand in success, but on the other in the reverse. The exemplification of the later was the Asian financial crisis of 1997/98. So the dynamism of economic growth and development processes were combined with the rise and functioning of the financial markets, which were simultaneously a source of a breakdown and destabilization what resulted in the crisis on the regional scale. The situation actually led to the realization of not only ASEAN countries but also other East Asian economies, that their markets are significantly interdependent and common efforts to avoid future breakdown are necessary and inevitable part of a joint strategy and management. Although the crisis raised doubts concerning the effectiveness of ASEAN as an organization, finally it closed up the regional bonds and strengthened the cooperation not only in South East Asia but in the whole Asia and Pacific. Because of an inability to take a joint action preventing the crisis, lack of elaborated mechanism of immediate reaction and broader cooperation of countries in the region several initiatives have been undertaken in order to work on institutional solutions of common character. One of the first attempt have been made in 1997 during the ASEAN Summit in Malaysia, while the informal meeting of leaders of ASEAN, China, Japan and South Korea took place and started the cooperation in a shape of "ASEAN plus" formation (Chien-Huei Wu 2010, p. 331).

The process have been institutionalized in 1999 at the ASEAN Summit in Manila along with launching the Joint Statement on East Asia Cooperation and further underpinned with the Second Joint Statement on East Asia Cooperation and ASEAN Plus Three Cooperation Work Plan (2007-2017). The financial crisis of 1997/98 became a crucial accelerator in the process of buil ding regional identity. Particular countries also have been encourage to cooperate more closely in the financial sector and as a result they took institutional initiatives to build regional financial structure stabilizing and protecting the economies in case of the financial meltdown.

In the aftermath of the crisis Japan proposed to establish "Asian Monetary Fund" (AMF) among the member states of Asian Development Bank (ADB). This was suppose to deepen the economic and especially monetary integration in the region with the lead taken by Japan due to its economic potential and the character of international relation with the USA (Hungdah Su 2010, pp. 28-29). At the end Japan withdraw from the idea and signed the Chiang Mai initiative which should be mention here as a network of bilateral swap agreements worth 80 bln USD signed by all ASEAN+3 economies. Thus ASEAN countries seems to have learned from the lesson of the Asian crisis and realize that liberalization should be properly manage and control by the governments concerned, so the extent to which the economies are subordinate to foreign markets is not destructive. The experienced showed that the international organisations of regional and global character played a significant role in the financial and afterwards economic crisis recovery. However the importance of those of regional character was revealed strengthening countries determination for further cooperation.

Conclusion

Over the last two decades Southeast Asian countries, gathered in ASEAN have surpassed in development and modernization other developing regions recording faster economic growth and what is more social change. As a result the poverty in the region was eradicated and higher human development was achieved. In 2011 three of the ASEAN countries Singapore, Brunei Darussalam and Malaysia reached high human development, and the rest:

Indonesia, Thailand, Vietnam, Cambodia, Laos and Myanmar are classified as countries of medium human development. The paper captured the success of particular Southeast Asian countries but on the other hand records the gaps that still exist between more affluent societies and those that have lagged in economic and social progress. The clear distinction can be observed between initial members of ASEAN and their later cosignatories. The main goal of the future is to diminish and finally suppress all those differences in development. Furthermore while managing development in the changing global order in light of all the above mentioned issues it will be necessary to work out new institutional solutions in South East Asia, including those with less formal forms of cooperation. What is more, the changing global order indicates a transformation of the existing system of leading economies. We will then have a chance to observe a conversion of Triad countries into the new system of different character which will include more players, next to USA, UE, Japan, China and India also other emerging markets with the leading share of those from East Asia. It seems that in the changing global order the importance of institutions and organizations of international and regional character will be rising in the context of managing economic and social development. So, in the coming decades we can expect new forms of global governance, where the coexistence of a state and a market will be closer to the conception of "the state capitalism" propagated as an alternative for the pure market economy in the aftermath of the crisis. Facing the rise of China and India the chance for development of South East Asia lies in one integrated market of composed economies. The region should be thus perceived as one competitive market for global producers where positive cumulative causality between a growth centre and the peripheries can be a reality leading to the more integrated region with the increasing economic and social development of each particular country.

REFERENCES

ADB (2005), 'Key Indicators of Developing Asian and Pacific Countries 2005'. *Asian Development Bank.*

ADO (1996), 'Asian Developement Outlook 1996–1997'. New York: *Oxford University Press.*

ADO (2002), 'Asian Developement Outlook 2002'. New York: *Oxford University Press.*

ADO (2005), 'Asian Developement Outlook 2005'. New York: *Oxford University Press.*

ADO (2010), 'Asian Developement Outlook 2010'. New York: *Oxford University Press.*

Atlas of Global Development (2009), second edition, Washington DC: *The World Bank.*

Bende-Nabende, A. (1999), 'FDI, Regionalism, Government Policy and Endogenous Growth'. A Comparative Study of the ASEAN-5 Economies, with Development Policy Implications for the Least Developed Countries. *Aldershot: Ashgate.*

Camilleri J, A. (2003), 'Regionalism in the New Asia-Pacific Order'. The Political Economy of the Asia-Pacific Region. II. *Cheltenham: Edward Elgar.*

Chien-Huei Wu. (2010), The ASEAN Economic Community Under the ASEAN Charter; Its External Economic Relations and disputes Settlements Mechanisms, in: Eauropean Yearbook of International Economic Law, ed. C. Herrmann, J. P. Terhechte. Berlin Heidelberg: *Springer-Verlag.*

Hungdah Su. (2010), 'The Eu's Taiwan Policy in a New Context, Issues and Studies', A Social Science Quarterly on China, Taiwan, and East Asian Affairs, 46 (1), March, Taipei, Taiwan (ROC): Institute of International Relations, National Chengchi University.

Jones D. M. and Smith M. L. R. (2006), ASEAN and East Asian International Relations. Regional Delusions, Cheltenham: *Edward Elgar.*

Khoman, T. (1992), 'ASEAN Conception and Evolution. The ASEAN Reader', Singapore: Institute of Southeast Asian Studies.

Kumar N., Sen R., Asher M. ed. (2006), 'India-ASEAN Economic Relations. Meeting the Challenges of Globalization', Singapore/New Delhi: Institute of Southeast Asian Studies /Research and Information System for Developing Countries.

Lim Chong Yah. (2004), 'Southeast Asia. The Long Road Ahead', Singapore: *World Scientific.*

Nawrot K. A. (2008a), 'Determinanty rozwoju gospodarczego państw ASEAN', Warszawa: *Wydawnictwo Naukowe Scholar.*

Nawrot K. A. (2008b). Ewolucja procesu integracji regionalnej w Azji Południowo-Wschodniej, in: Procesy integracyjne we współczesnej gospodarce światowej, ed. T. Rynarzewski, Poznań: *Wydawnictwo Akademii Ekonomicznej w Poznaniu.*

Nawrot K. A. (2009a), Production networks and industrial clusters in the process of development and integration of South East Asia – the causality between growth centre & the peripheries in development. Preliminary draft of a paper prepared for The Biennial Conference of The Canadian Council for Southeast Asian Studies „Engaging Southeast Asia: Centres and Peripheries". Vancouver: University of British Columbia.

Nawrot K. A. (2009b), Production networks and industrial clusters in the process of regional integration of South East Asia, in: Integracja Azji Wschodniej. Mit czy rzeczywistość? ed. B. Skulska, Prace Naukowe Uniwersytetu we Wrocławiu, nr 67. Wrocław: *Wydawnictwo Uniwersytetu Ekonomicznego we Wrocławiu.*

Nováček P. and Mederly P. (2002), 'AC/UNU Millennium Project Central European Note, Global Partnership for Development', Olomouc: Palacky University, United Nations University.

Production networks and industrial clusters. Integrating Economies in Southeast Asia, (2008) ed. Ikuo Kuroiwa, Toh Mun Heng, Singapore: Institute of Southeast Asian Studies.

Rajaratnam, S. (1992), 'ASEAN: The Way Ahead', The ASEAN Reader. Singapore: Institute of Southeast Asian Studies.

Skawińska, E., Grabka-Sobiech, K. G. and Nawrot, K. A. (2010), ' Makroekonomia. Teoretyczne i praktyczne aspekty gospodarki rynkowej', Warszawa: *Polskie Wydawnictwo Ekonomiczne.*

Suehiro, A. (2008), 'Catch-up Industralization. The Trajectory and Prospects of East Asian Economies', Singapore: *NUS Press.*

Tongzon, J.L. (2002), 'The Economies of Southeast Asia. Before and after the Crisis', Second edition. Cheltenham: *Edward Elgar.*

UNDP (2009), 'Human Development Report 2009: Overcoming barriers: Human Mobility and Development', Oxford University Press. New York: United Nations Development Programme.

UNDP (2010), 'Human Development Report 2010': 20th Anniversary Edition. The Real Wealth of Nations. Pathways to Human Development. Oxford University Press, New York: United Nations Development Programme.

WDR (2006), 'World Development Report 2006' : Equity and Development. New York: *The World Bank & Oxford University Press.*

WDR (2010), 'World Development Report 2010': Development and Climate Change. Washington DC: The World Bank.

In: Development Management in the Twenty-First Century ISBN: 978-1-62100-699-2
Editors: Kartik Roy and Sandip Kar

Chapter 4

MAJOR ISSUES IN HUMAN RESOURCE MANAGEMENT AND ECONOMIC DEVELOPMENT

***Maureen Fatiaki Karan Dayal*[*,1] *and Narendra Reddy*[†,2]**
[1] Assistant Lecturer, School of Management and Public Administration, Faculty of Business and Economics, University of the South Pacific, Laucala Campus, Fiji
[2] Associate Professor & Head of School, School of Management and Public Administration, Faculty of Business and Economics, University of the South Pacific, Laucala Campus, Fiji

INTRODUCTION

Public enterprise reforms have gained a global perspective over the last few decades. This has drawn the attention of both policy makers and academics. There have been wider implications of such reforms for the people working in them as well as the society. Accompanied by the inefficiency and lowered productivity of many public enterprises along with the increasing global competition and rapidly changing technologies. This has intensified the need to improve the performance and competitiveness of the public enterprises all over the world.

BACKGROUND OF PUBLIC SECTOR REFORMS IN FIJI

The private sector in Fiji is a relatively new phenomenon and it has a weak industrial base with a high proportion of public enterprises. In the period the country's independence in 1970, the last couple of decades have been marked by instability in the political environment. This has negatively affected the economy that led to the introduction of economic reforms at the persistence of the international financial institutions. To facilitate the process saw the

* dayal_m@usp.ac.fj.
† reddy_n@usp.ac.fj.

enactment of the Public Enterprise Act in 1996. This was later reviewed in 2004 (Strategic Development Plan 2003-2005:53).

Public enterprise reforms in Fiji have taken place in three phases. The first phase of reforms imposed by the World Bank was during the 1980s when the government of the day was losing popular support in the wake of the trade union led political parties gaining ground and the balance of payments misfortune (Reguri 2004). The second phase of reforms took place in 1984; the government introduced a small dose of reform in the form of wage freezes. This resulted in massive protests, hence, forcing the government to reduce the pace of reforms. Eventually, it resulted in a change of power from the ruling Alliance Party to a trade union dominated coalition pursuant to the April 1987 elections. The two military coups of that year led to the set-up of a military appointed administration, in which, the government, had no legitimacy and little alternative but to surrender totally to the agents of global monopoly capital (the International Monetary Fund, the World Bank, the Asian Development Bank, etc.). As a result, a large dose of structural adjustment program (SAP) was launched in 1989. It included 33 per cent currency devaluation; a freeze on public expenditure and investment, labour market reforms, and public sector wage cuts. The reforms were not introduced by acts of parliament but imposed by military decrees (Prasad 1995). When the SVT-led government came into power in 1992 under a controversial constitution, there was a further push in the economic reform process. During 1992 to 1998, there was a large-scale program of commercialisation and corporatisation and some preliminary attempts at privatisation of the public sector. However, when the People's Coalition government led by the Fiji Labor Party came to power in May 1999, there was a progressive shift in the state policies. The new government had suspended the Public Finance Management Act and associated public sector reforms, re-introduced price control, and exempted essential consumer items from the VAT, quota and tariff protection to local industries, and took steps to rejuvenate the labour market institutions. On the whole, these moves were aimed at reducing the ill effects of earlier liberalisation and economic reforms, particularly on the working class and poorer sections (Reguri 2004). In the third phase, after the coup of May 2000 the interim Qarase government had put an end to the previous labor party policies and introduced free market policies. The military appointed government subsequently through elections surrendered its economic policies to the dictates of the World Bank, IMF, ADB, Australian Aid, and the local business community.

The key aspects of the wholesale reform package adopted by the SDL government included: further deregulation of the economy through the reduction of tariffs and license control; labour market reforms aimed at dilution of trade union power by placing restrictions on strikes, promoting enterprise unionism and individual employment contracts; civil service reforms and further corporatisation and privatisation of public enterprises; and removal of controls on prices and re-introduction of VAT on exempted items (Prasad and Snell 2002).

LITERATURE REVIEW

Globally, there is extensive literature on the reform of State Owned Enterprises and some literature on Fiji. Graham (1997) and Osborne and Gaebler (1992) stated that the competition-based nature of the private sector meant that it would always provide services more efficiently and achieve greater customer satisfaction than public sector bureaucracies. Authors such as Ashworth (1991), Farazmand (1996), Burnes, (2000) comment that in the three decades from 1945, across the world, there was an enormous increase in the size and range of activities undertaken by the public sector. Hughes (2003) highlights that in the United Kingdom and the United States of America the reform process was led by rightwing governments. This was described as the move to roll back the state. It has been driven by ideological and economic concerns. Reguri and Venkataiah (2003) contend that the agents of the capitalist world continuously profess to the developing world to open up their economies, privatise everything, withdraw from social welfare and await the foreign investors to return and save their people. Prasad and Snell (2001) and Reguri (2003) have taken a political economic approach and have argued that the reforms of SOEs were driven by external forces such as IMF and World Bank. Appana (2003) informs that with the support of the international organisations, SOE reforms in Fiji have been based on the New Public Management (NPM) model. In addition, there are a number of unpublished Master of Arts and Master of Commerce theses written by post-graduate students at the University of the South Pacific. First, Chand (1999) highlighted about the Performance Management in the Public Sector in Fiji and Implications of Leadership, Culture and Competency on the Performance of Public Sector Organisations. Nath (2000) examined the Performance Measurement and Evaluation Techniques in the 'Fiji Housing Authority'. Singh (2002) looked at the reform process in the case studies of 'Airports Fiji Ltd' and 'Ports Authority'. Narayan (2004) focused on the reform in Government Shipyard and Public Slipway. Karan (2009) looked at the reform process in TFL. There have been a number of newspaper articles in the Fiji Times and the Fiji Sun on the reform process in TFL since 1989.

METHODOLOGY

The paper is based on first hand primary empirical research conducted by the authors between 2006 and 2010. Three main research methods were used for this empirical study. First, face-to-face interviews were conducted with major stakeholders relating to the TFL reforms. The interviews were by the use of semi-structured and structured questionnaires. The first set of stakeholders who were interviewed included different levels of staff of Telecom Fiji Limited such as senior management (CEO, General Manager, and General Manager Human Resources).

The second stakeholders interviewed were current employees of TFL at various levels and ex-workers of the company. A total of 50 employees were interviewed. Employees that participated in the survey were from supervisory staff, technical and customer service staff. It was ensured that at least 5 employees from every section were interviewed. The employees who were working for TFL for more than 10 years were outspoken and relayed a lot of information.

The ex-workers of TFL were more open and willing to reveal more in-depth information about the company than current workers because there was fear of victimisation by the company. The third stakeholders interviewed were government officials namely from Ministry of Public Enterprises.

The fourth stakeholders interviewed were trade union officials of the Fiji Public Service Association and the Fiji Post and Telecom Employees Association.

The fifth stakeholders interviewed were the customers of TFL- 200 customers along Suva- Nausori corridor. The second research method used was observation techniques since one of the authors was a former worker of TFL. The third research method used was literature review of primary company and government documents and Hansard[1] reports. Furthermore, secondary published articles on SOE reforms were reviewed.

Major Changes during the Reform Process

Battle for Recognition as Trade Unions between Fiji Public Service Association and Fiji Post and Telecom Employees Association

Prior to reforms in 1989 the majority (95 percent) of the workers in the old Department of Post and Telecom (DPT) were trade union members of the Fiji Public Service Association (FPSA).

In 1989, when the government started the reform process, the FPSA (as the main representative of the workers) initially was neither informed nor consulted about the reform program but were only told after enquiring about this from government authorities (Interview with General Secretary of FPSA, March 2010). The officials of FPSA and workers of DPT were totally against the proposed reform and were worried about job security, job losses, redundancies and loss of trade union density.

Overseas Consultants and Management Hand in Reform of TFL

The TFL management and overseas consultants played a major hand in the reform of IR environment in TFL. To further complicate this industrial relations environment the overseas consultants and the top management personnel of the company adopted a 'divide and rule' policy, and encouraged the formation of a rival 'in-house' trade union, often through intimidation of those who refused to join (Interview with FPSA official based in TFL, 2007).

For example, the New Zealand based 'Hay Management Consultant Limited' in their report recommended that the workers of the new company to be represented by an 'in-house' enterprise union and not FPSA which is a 'general union'. They wrote "trade union would have to be organised and structured to operate within a commercial environment rather than a civil service environment…it is suggested that an in-house union is needed." As a result of the recommendation of Hay consultants in 1991, a new in-house trade union called the 'Fiji Posts & Telecommunication Employees Association' (FPTEA) was formed. After six months, in August the Registrar of Trade Unions defying the court order and re-registered FPTEA and since this date FPTEA has been representing the workers at TFL and Post Fiji.

[1] Hansard Reports are records of all that is said in the House of Representatives, during Parliamentary sessions in Fiji.

INDUSTRIAL DISPUTES DURING REFORM PERIOD

First Industrial Strike: June 1992

The first strike took place, on June 27 1992, because one of the General Managers of Telecom, who opposed the reform at FPTL, was sacked by the Telecom Board. The reason given by the Board was that the GM had engaged in 'subversive action' to topple the Board of Directors. Workers had strongly supported the GM and they feared that if the GM was not re-instated then the management will have no opposition in making them redundant.

As a result of this about 1,000 FPTL workers around Fiji went on strike and it continued for two weeks and only ended after the GM was re-instated and the Board members resigned (The Fiji Times, 16 July 1992: 1). This industrial action taken by the workers showed the first major concerted effort by workers to oppose the managerial prerogative of sole decision making during the reform process. The workers and trade union had some 'teeth' in opposing management and government officials' decisions.

Second Industrial Strike: July 1992

Few weeks after the first strike, on July 15 1992, workers frustrated at not getting anywhere with their attempts to have Mr Naqova reinstated as a CEO went on strike for the second time. This time around the workers used sabotage tactics and damaged cables at the Suva Telecom exchange, affecting about 14,000 telephone lines (Interview with a Telecom technician, 2007). With the crisis escalating, the government gave in and Mr Naqova was subsequently reinstated as the CEO. As a result of the strike, FPTL suffered a $F200, 000 losses from the sabotage and four employees were charged by police. This cost the company thousands of dollars. Estimates of repairs and labour costs were put at $F150, 000 (Interview with GMHR TFL, 2007).

Research Findings

Telecom Fiji Limited has three subsidiary companies; Connect Fiji Limited, Xceed Pacifica and TransTel Fiji Limited. The researcher interviewed around 50 employees' altogether since most of the employees did not wish to participate in this survey because they were scared that their jobs might be at risk.

The employees were interviewed from the 3 subsidiaries as well. Employees that participated in the survey were from management and supervisory levels as well as technical and customer service staff.

Figure 4.1 shows that 74% of the staff interviewed had agreed that there was very little improvement in the operations of TFL after the restructure. Some 8% said that there was not much improvement and 18% said that the organisation remained the same after the restructure. This shows that restructure within TFL was not able to achieve its objectives.

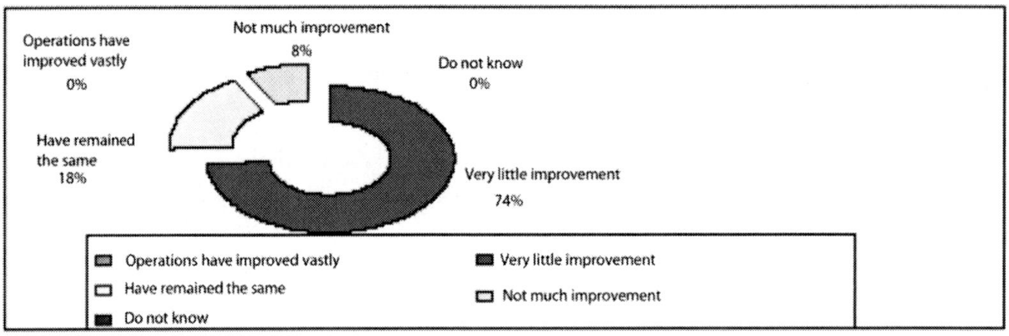

Figure 4.1. Employees Perception about the Operations of TFL after the Restructure.

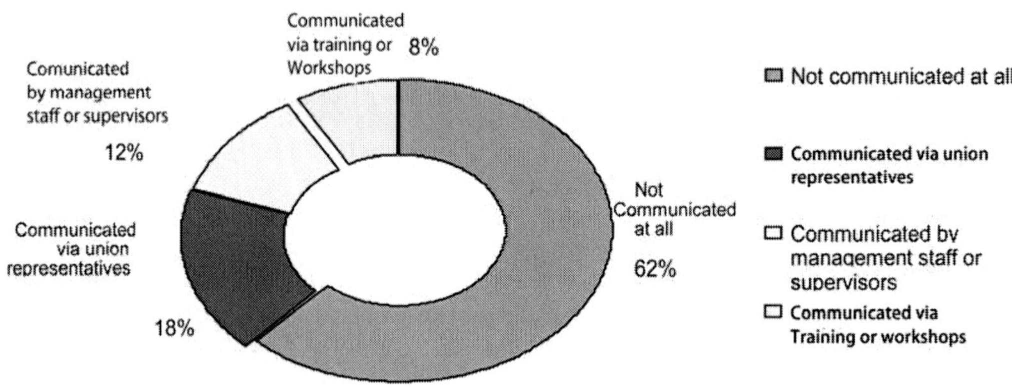

Figure 4.2. Employees views about the Reform Process at Telecom Fiji Limited.

Figure 4.2 illustrates that communication to TFL staff about the reform process was very poor. 62% of the interviewers felt that employees had not been included at all in the reform process.

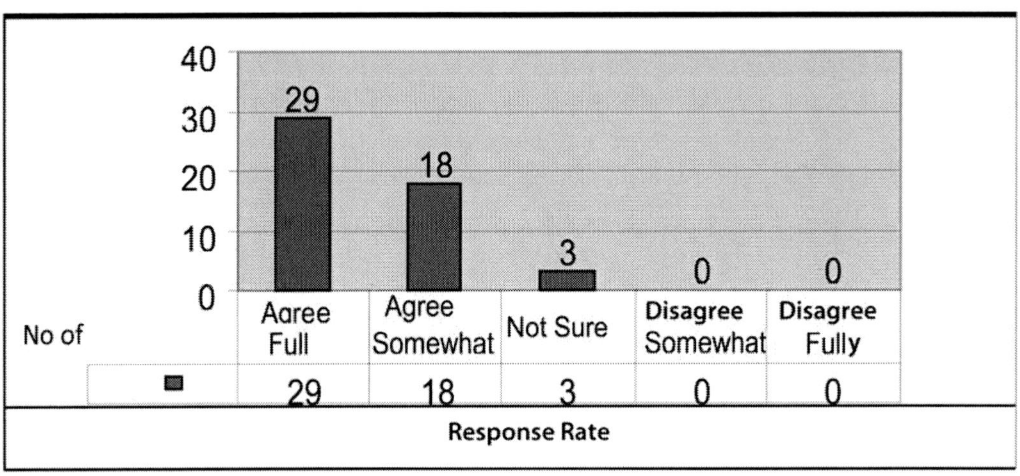

Figure 4.3. The Restructuring Process within TFL created ‘Job Insecurity’.

Figure 4.3 shows that there was a lot of job insecurity during the restructure process.

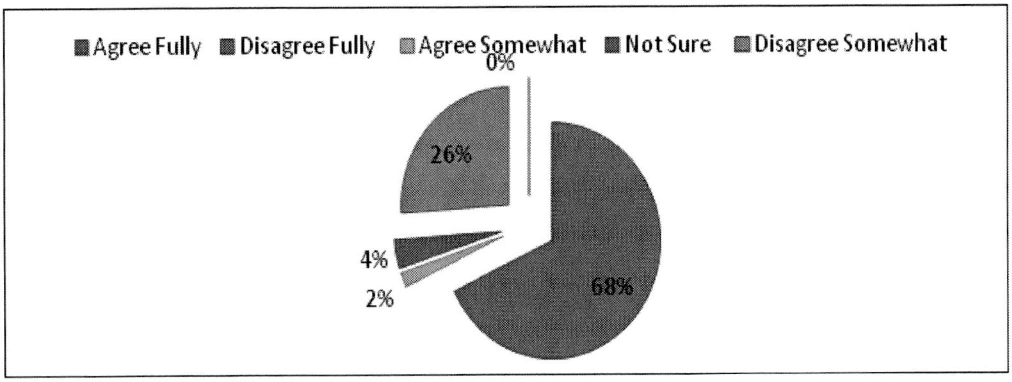

Figure 4.4. The Restructure has Improved the Working Conditions within TFL.

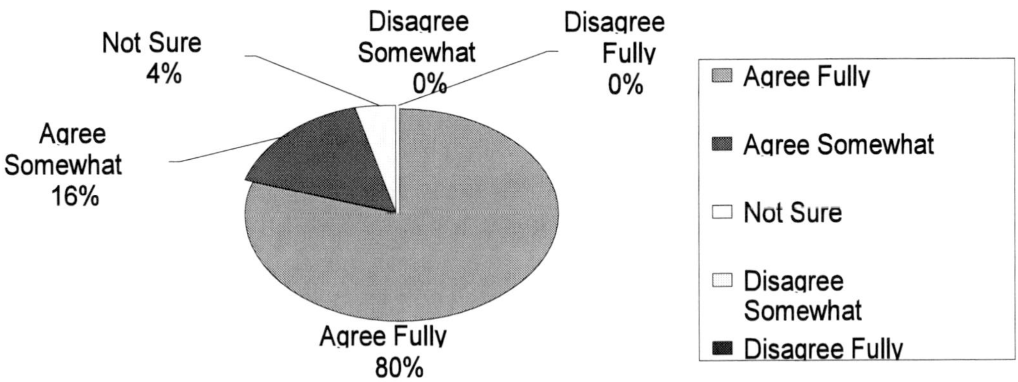

Figure 4.5. Skilled People Left for Overseas.

Figure 4.4 shows that a majority (68%) of the staff disagrees that the working conditions had improved due to the restructure of the organization.

Figure 4.5 shows that 80% of the staff interviewed agreed fully that due to the restructure process skilled staff left for greener pastures.

Figure 4.5 shows that 80% of the staff interviewed agreed fully that due to the restructure process skilled staff left for greener pastures.

RECOMMENDATIONS

The study shows that the government has not observed proper guidelines in restructuring the telecommunications industry as there were a lot of loopholes, lacked transparency, accountability and a lot of political interference for the personal gains of Ministers and Board Members.

The study found out that workers and union officials were not consulted at all and were mostly left in the dark while management unilaterally forced their decisions on to workers.

Debates About Increasing Efficiency/Reducing Costs

The public sector has always been labeled as inefficient in providing services due to bureaucracy and red tape.

Hence the move to privatise has made an attempt for private firms to provide services more efficiently. However, this is not the case in the findings of this research, as it contradicts this claim that privatisation reduces cost and increases efficiency. In the case of Telecom Fiji since the restructuring costs have started to increase and customer service become less efficient. Fiji Posts and Telecommunications used to be the most profitable government department before it became corporatised. During the difficult year of 1987, it realised a $F6m profit, which rose to $F8m in 1989. As a government department, it provided an essential social service yet remained viable and cost efficient. Hence, one can question why it was reformed in the first place.

The move towards privatisation (yet to happen) has been a disastrous experience for the company. Privatisation has resulted in substantial revenue loss to the public reserves, led to marked decline in profits for the company, lowered worker morale and resulted in the loss of some highly experienced and skilled staff, the company forced by one crisis after another; there have been scandals, abuse of privilege, mismanagement and exploitation by Board Members pursuing their own self interest. According to government published statistics FPTL profits have declined each successive year nose-diving from $F12m in the first year of privatisation in 1990, to $F10m in 1991 and dropped markedly to $F3.8m in 1992,. Such a significant decline in profit cannot simply be explained away through a claim of increased capital expenditure.

As a result of restructuring the government also loses control of activities it is financing and this will affect the end users who are in most need of this service. The private sector will only serve those sections of the market that are most profitable, ignoring the needs of the neediest in the community. In addition to this, while restructuring focuses on economic benefits it often ignores the issues concerning transparency, accountability, equity of access to services, and the quality of those services.

Debates About Selling Like the Rest (First World Countries)

The sale of a government trading enterprises is necessary because the industry is privatised in other countries. The latest 1998 survey of the Organization for Economic Cooperation and Development (OECD) of the communications sector in its industrialised member nations shows that 100% private ownership of telecommunications is far from common.

In only 6 of the 29 OECD member countries United States, United Kingdom, Canada, Denmark, Mexico and New Zealand - are the telecommunications networks that are privately owned. Partial privatisation appears the norm in most of the industrialised world; this includes Japan, countries of Eastern Europe, France and Germany.

In the case of Fiji it was an approach used to follow the first world countries without even considering the consequences and the relevant data. Public owned enterprise which was based on traditional public enterprise is now being altered into a more market based enterprise. This paper shows that the reform process has transformed (re-engineered) Telecom Fiji Limited from a public owned enterprise into a more efficient and market oriented organisation. This paper shows that both the external environment (structure) as well as individuals (agencies) had influenced in driving the reform process for example government policies led to the restructure, at the same time individuals such as top management, board members and overseas consultants had a major input in steering the restructuring process.

PROPOSED MODEL FOR SUCCESSFUL REFORM

In this paper we would like to propose a model for undergoing a successful Public Sector Reform Process. The model is shown in Figure 4.6.

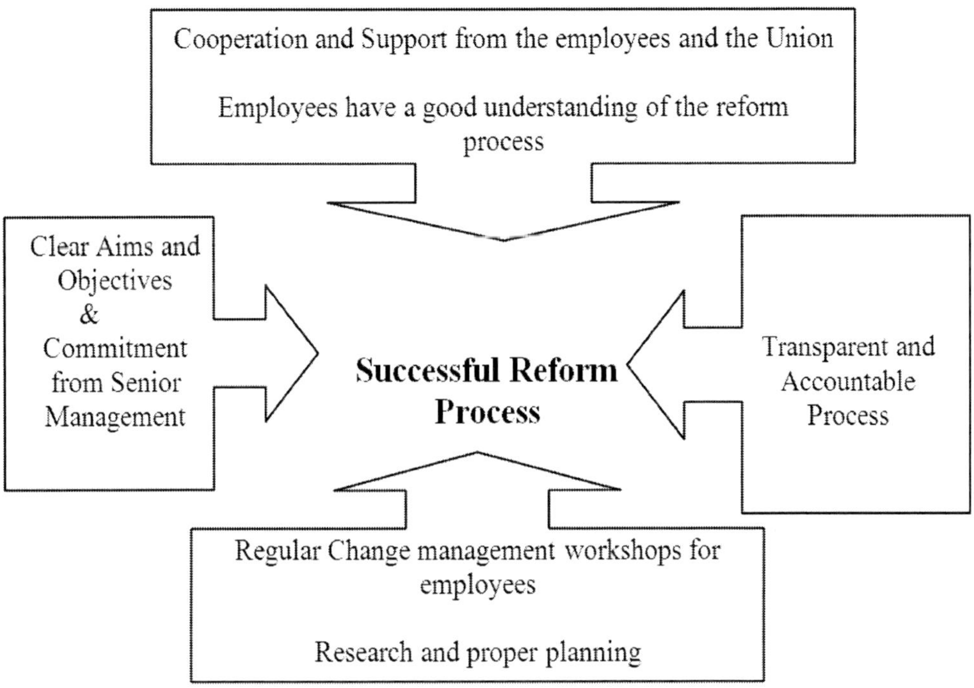

Figure 4.6. Proposed model for Successful Reform. Source: Karan, M., 2009.

Figure 4.6, which is developed by the author after conducting extensive research and surveys on the stakeholders of TFL, proposes that for a successful reform of an enterprise the following are needed:

- Cooperation and support from the employees and the union
- Employees have a good understanding of the reform process
- Transparent and accountable process
- Clear aims and objectives and commitment from senior management
- Regular change management workshops for employees
- Research and proper planning

CONCLUSION

Telecommunications is one of the most dynamic sectors of the Fiji Economy. One of the triggers for change was new technology that necessitated large-scale investment in telecommunication systems. Major technical, economic, and political challenges confront TFL in a transitional global telecommunications market. TFL lies at a cross road in a transitional telecommunication sector that is no longer isolated from global reforms and advancement. The company has to learn to compete. By putting themselves up against the best, initially, they had to learn to appreciate the network of global telecommunication giants, their resources and the activities they perform in transforming these resources. Through this process, TFL will be able to adjust their mechanisms, learning instruments, and focus. The telecommunications industry is a thriving industry especially in this information age. It is therefore very important for a small developing nation like Fiji to actively pursue and formulate national policies and strategies that will promote an environment in which restructured industries can thrive and be productive. This will eventually benefit the country and the grass root people. It should stress shared visions, both at horizontal and vertical levels, of planning and management. This entails involving and educating communities at the grass root level in dialogue and decision making at the public policy and practice levels. Future privatisations and reform processes to be handled more cautiously so that the main objectives of restructuring are achieved.

REFERENCES

Ashworth, W. (1991), 'The State in Business: 1945 to the Mid-1980s', *Palgrave,* London.

Burnes, B. Katsouros, M. and Jones, T. *'International Journal of Public Sector Management',* 17, (1), 2004.

Burnes, D. (2000), 'Perspectives on Total Rewards: Recruitment and Retention', *Tower Perrin.*

Chand, K. (1999), 'Performance Management in the Public Sector in Fiji: Implications of Leadership, Culture and Competency on the Performance of Public Sector Organisations', Unpublished Master of Arts Thesis. Department of Management and Public Administration, the University of the South Pacific, Suva.

Farazaman, A. (1996), Introduction: The Comparative State of Public Enterprise Management' in Ali Farazamand (ed.) Public Enterprise Management: International Case Studies. *(Westport: Greenwood Press).*

Graham, A. (1997), 'The UK 1979-95: Myths and Realities of Conservative Capitalism' in Crouch, C., Streeck, W. (Eds), *Political Economy of Modern Capitalism, Sage,* London, Pp.117-32.

Hughes. E.O., (2003). 'Public Management and Administration - An introduction', Third Edition, *Palgrave Macmillan,* New York.

International Telecommunications Union- World Telecommunications Indicators, ATH and TFL, (2002-2010).

Karan, M. F. (2009), 'Public Enterprise Reform in Fiji: A case Study of Telecom Fiji Limited'. Unpublished Master of Commerce Thesis. School of Management and Public Administration, The University of the South Pacific, Suva.

Mcmaster, J. (2001), 'Public Enterprise Reform in Fiji: Policy Implementation and Reversals', *Asian Journal of Public Administration,* 23 (2), pp. 229-246.

Narayan, J. (2004), 'Public Enterprise Reforms in Fiji: How 'Not' to Privatize – the Case of Government Shipyard and Public Slipways'. *E-published Master of Arts Thesis. COOPERJAL Ltd,* London.

Nath, N.D. (2000), 'Performance Measurement and Evaluation Techniques: The Housing Authority of Fiji – a Case Study'. Unpublished Master of Arts Thesis. Department of Accounting and Financial Management, the University of the South Pacific, Suva.

Osborne, D.E. and Gaebler, T. (1992), 'Reinventing Government: How the Entrepreneurial Spirit is Transforming the Public Sector'. New York: *Penguin Books.*

Prasad, S. and Chandra, R. (1995), 'Globalization and its Impact on the World of Employment'. Report prepared for ILO/Asian Network of Labor Institutions Collaborative Research Program, ILO – Bangkok.

Prasad, S. and Snell, D. (2002), 'Globalization and Workers Rights in the South Pacific' ILO.

Primary Source Interview with General Secretary of FPSA, March 2010. Interview with General Secretary of FPTEA, February 2006. Interview with Acting HR Manager- Post Fiji, March 2010. Interview with GMHR –Telecom Fiji Limited 26, March 2007. Interview with former GMHR – FPTL 28, February 2006. *Interview with current and former employees of TFL,* August 2007.

Reddy, N. (1997), 'The Implications of Public Sector Reforms on Human Resource Management in the South Pacific': The Case of Fiji, Paper Presented at the Conference on Human Resources and Future Generations in Islands and Small States, 6-8 November. University of Malta. Valletta.

Reddy, N. (2005), 'Public Sector Reforms in Fiji: Progress to date'. *Paper Presented at the fifth International Conference of the International Institute for Development Studies,* 1-4 December, 2005. Suva, Fiji.

Reguri, R.R. and Venkataiah, K. (2003), 'Public Enterprise Re-organization in India: The Content, Process and the internal labor markets', International Industrial Relations Association (IIRA) 13th World Congress.Available:http://www.fuberlin.de/iira2003 /papers/track_1/Workshop_1_4_Reguri.pdf,September 8-13, (2004,Jan.02)

Richard O. L., Joseph S. K. and Randolph J. M. (2003), 'Trends in the competitiveness of Telecommunications Markets: Implications for Deregulation of Retail Local Services, the Progress & Freedom Foundation'. *The Progress and Freedom Foundation.*

Rothschild group, Report on the Fiji Telecommunications Industry, May 1996.

Secondary Source Appana, S. (2003), 'New Public Management and Public Enterprise Restructuring in Fiji', *Fijian Studies: A Journal of Contemporary Fiji,* 1 (1), pp. 51-73.

Singh, A. (2002), 'Public Enterprise Restructuring and Industrial Relations in Fiji: With Case Studies of Ports Authority of Fiji and Airports Fiji Limited', Unpublished Master of Arts Thesis, University of the South Pacific, Suva.

Strategic Development Plan, (2003-2005), November 2002. Parliamentary Paper No. 72 of 2002. Pp: 52-53.

The Fiji Times, (1992), 16th July 1992, *Fiji Times* Pp1.

The Fiji Times, (1992), 'Political appointment of chairman of FPTL board' 15th July 1992, *Fiji Times* Pp1.

In: Development Management in the Twenty-First Century
Editors: Kartik Roy and Sandip Kar
ISBN: 978-1-62100-699-2

Chapter 5

MANAGEMENT OF MICROPROJECTS IN SPECIAL TRADE CONSTRUCTION SECTOR IN INDIA

Sandip Kar*

International Institute of Management Sciences, Kolkata, India

INTRODUCTION

India has exhibited the second fastest economic growth rates among the major economies in the world in recent time. One of the striking features of this growth has been the dynamism of the service sector which includes finance, education, health care, hospitality, IT, construction, etc. As per National Accounting Statistics, during 2008-09, the share of service sector was about 57 per cent. This growth trajectory, which has been termed "service-led" industrialization, or even a "service revolution" (Gordon and Gupta 2004, Singh 2006) seems to stand out from the traditional path from agriculture to manufacturing, with services becoming important at a later stage. Between 1951 and 2000, the share of agriculture in GDP fell from 58 to 25 per cent, while share of service sector increased from 27 to 48 per cent. The substantial share of the service sector in employability has contributed maximum increase in employment in the past few decades; the sector accounted for 73.2 per cent of additional employment generated during the early years of 21st century (Joshi 2004). The economic survey of 2006-07 (GOI 2007) states that the share of service sector in GDP has grown to 55.1 per cent and it has contributed to the tune of 68.6 percent of the average growth in GDP.

CONSTRUCTION SECTOR

Construction industry, being one of the main segments in the service sector, constitutes the second largest economic activity in India, and offers substantial employment generation opportunity for its vast population. The sector is now poised for growth on account of industrialization, urbanization, economic development and people's rising expectations for

* sandip.kar@rediffmail.com.

improved quality of living. In India, construction industry accounts for nearly 65 per cent of the total investment in infrastructure and is expected to be the biggest beneficiary of the surge in infrastructure investment over the next five years. Investment in construction accounts for nearly 11 per cent to touch 102 per cent of India's GDP. The investments made in this sector amounted to Rs. 6.6 trillion in FY 2005-06. An estimated 239.68 billion Euros is likely to be invested in the infrastructure sector over the next five to 10 years – in power, roads, bridges, city infrastructure, ports, airports, telecommunications, which would provide a huge boost to the construction industry as a whole (India-Italy Chamber Report 2010).

Investment into this sector could go up to 93 Billion Euros by FY 2010-11. With the present annual rate of asset addition of Rs. 340,000 crores, the industry employs over 31 million citizens 83 per cent of which is categorized as unskilled work force belonging to unorganized sector. Low value addition and lower productivity are some of the obvious resultants, leading to lower quality of life and no career growth prospects for the work force (CIDC Report, 2010).

The construction sector is one of the largest employers in the country. In 1999-2000, it employed 17.62 million workers, a rise of 6 million over 1993-94. The construction workers also constitute one of the largest categories of workers in the unorganized sector. According to the Sample Survey conducted by National Sample Survey Organization (NSSO) in 2004-2005, about 2.57 crore workers are employed in the construction activities.

The 61st round sample survey done by NSSO shows that there has been acceleration in growth of employment, since 1999-2000 to 2004-05. Growth of employment during this period (1999- 2000 to 2004-05) is estimated at 2.62 per cent per annum. The sector also recorded the highest growth rate in generation of jobs in the last two decades, doubling its share in total employment. The main advantage of the construction sector in employment generation lies in the fact that it absorbs rural labour and unskilled workers (in addition to semi-skilled and some skilled), it provides opportunity for seasonal employment thereby supplementing workers' income from farming; and permits large-scale participation of women workers.

The share of construction sector in gross domestic product (GDP), which was 5.4 per cent in 1970-71, came down to 4.4 per cent in 1990-91. Subsequently it picked up and stood at 5.1 per cent in 1999-2000 (Planning Commission, Govt. of India, 10th Five Year Plan). It contributed more than 5 per cent to the nation's GDP and 78 per cent to the gross capital formation.

The construction industry sets in motion the process of economical growth in the country; investment in this sector contributes 6.5 per cent of Gross Domestic Product (GDP) growth (Das, 2003). Every Re.1 investment in the construction industry causes an Rs. 0.80 increment in GDP as against Rs.0.20 and Rs.0.14 in the fields of agriculture and manufacturing industry, respectively (Laskar and Murthy 2004).

With the cost per job created in construction lower than any other sector of the economy, construction is seen as an "employment-spinning" sector (Vaid 1999). China has seen a very dramatic increase in employment in the construction industry in the past few decades. The construction workforce was just under 10 million in 1980 and grew to 30 million by 1993, more than doubling its share of the total workforce from 2.3 per cent to 5 per cent (Lu and Fox 2001).

MICROPROJECTS

Among the various categories of projects, the majority falls into the smallest category of projects known as Microprojects. The reason behind is the fact that any Mega Project gradually streamlines into Microprojects at the base level. As they have all adopted the phenomenon of subcontracting basis, every project ultimately gets fragmented into several Microprojects. ILO defined microprojects as "A project with investment size lesser than enhancement figure, having time frame about 90 days and involving lesser number of human resource with minimum technological support and system." According to Standish Group International, an USA based research group on small size projects, "a Micro Project is any project that lasts three months or less and costs $2,50,000 or less in labour" (Johnson 2001). Many researchers preferred the term "small project" to mean the similar size projects (Awad *et al.* 2004, Behrendt 2004). Sohail and Baldwin (2004) reported that the majority of public works contracts undertaken in developing countries have a total cost of less than US $15 000. They include the provision of enhanced water and sanitation, access ways and pavements, small community buildings and solid-waste related construction. These are termed 'micro-projects' and there is a general lack of information for such projects.

Most of the Microprojects in India fall under the Unorganized category and workers involved in this field belong to the "Unorganized" or "Informal" sector. World Employment Report (ILO 1998) of ILO characterises the informal sector as the "Informal units comprise small enterprises with hired workers, household enterprises using mostly family labour, and the self-employed. Production processes involve relatively high levels of working capital as against fixed capital, which in turn reflects the relatively low level of technology and skills involved."

SPECIAL TRADE CONSTRUCTION

A construction project is accomplished or coordinated by a number of contractors, who specialize in one of construction such as masonry, carpentry, painting, electrical, plumbing, air conditioning, etc. which fall under a broad term of "Special Trade Construction" (National Employment Matrix, USA 2008). General promoters often obtain orders for their works from architects or owners. They then subcontract most of the works to specialized working groups. Repair work is almost always done on direct order from owners, occupants, architects, or rental agents. In the U.S., there were about 884,300 construction establishments in 2008: 269,700 were building construction contractors; 57,600 were heavy and civil engineering construction or highway contractors; and 557,000 were specialty trade contractors.

WORKFORCE IN THE MICROPROJECTS

The small size construction projects, what are described as microprojects or more specifically, Special Trade Construction, have been run in India for years without due attention to scientific approach in managing its human resources. However, with the advent of *Globalization* and *Liberalization* that have taken place in India, companies here are taking new approach with regard to its manpower involved (Bahuguna *et al.* 2009). Workers in micro projects are characterized by their casual nature, temporary relationship between employers and employees, uncertain working hours, lack of basic amenities and inadequacy of welfare facilities. Practically the Micro projects take a reactive rather than proactive approach while managing their HR which involves active and innovative participation by the Project Managers and other support staff (Narang and Singh 2010).

The construction sector in India is one of the largest employers in the country most of which belong to unorganized sector. The sector represents about 380 to 400 Million workers, or about 91 to 92 per cent of the active population of our country. In other words the organized sector represents only 8 – 9 per cent of the active population. The first National Commission on Labour (1966-69) has defined unorganized labour as those who have not been able to organize themselves in pursuit of common objectives on account of constraints like casual nature of employment, ignorance and illiteracy, small and scattered size of establishments and position of power enjoyed by employers because of the nature of industry etc. Nearly 20 years later the National Commission on Rural Labour (NCRL 1987-91) visualized the same scenario and the same contributory factors leading to the present status of unorganized rural labour in India.

The evidence in India and many other parts of the world indicate that construction workers do not view their employment in a very favourable light. Construction is regarded almost everywhere as a low status job (ILO 2001). A recent survey of 2,600 construction workers in five towns in India found that 90 per cent were working in construction because they had no choice, but they did not want their children to work in the industry (Vaid 1999). Only 3.8 per cent of respondents in another survey in Delhi thought that construction was a suitable occupation for their sons (Anand 2000).

It provides employment for those with little education or skill, many of them from the poorer sections of society. Recent surveys of construction workers in a number of Indian cities have revealed that they are predominantly young, from the lower castes and the Muslim community and poorly educated (Vaid 1999, Anand 2000). A significant proportion is illiterate: 69 per cent of the workforce in Delhi, 56 per cent in Pune, 40 per cent in Mumbai and the entire workforce in Hyderabad and Visakhapatnam were found to have had no schooling (Vaid 1999).

The role of knowledge and upgraded skill has been found to be paramount and necessary prerequisite for improving the earnings and standard of living of the poors specially those belonging to unorganized sectors (Chadha 2004). The idea of labour productivity is gaining much attention as the labour productivity directly contributes to the national production.

While 13 per cent of the population had primary education, 16 per cent of them had middle level of education. The share of educated persons i.e. those with secondary and above education was higher at 24 per cent. Even among the 15-29 years population in 2004-05, educational attainment was still very low, with 31 per cent of them having below primary level of education and 38 per cent of them with primary or middle level education only. Only 2.5 per cent of total unorganized sector workers had formal training while 12.5 per cent had informal training. In the NSS survey in 1993-94, revealed a separate question on skill along with the questions on education and technical education. It showed that 90 per cent of the population above 15 years did not have any skill.

The World Competitiveness Year Book, 2008 made a statement giving the labour productivity measures in terms of Gross Domestic Product (Purchasing Power Parity) per

Person Employed per Hour and Overall Productivity- Real Growth i.e. Percentage Change of Real GDP per Person Employed in Asian Countries and four benchmark countries during 2007. "Percentage Change of Real GDP per Person Employed" in India during 2007 is 5.92 per cent, which is 10.55 per cent in China (World Competitiveness Yearbook 2008). One estimate indicates the need for a 20 million increase in skilled workers by 2015 (CII-McKinsey 2004) or incremental skilling of 1.5 million people every year.

KEY ISSUES IN MANAGING MICROPROJECTS IN CONSTRUCTION SECTOR

I. Lack of Latest Technology: Microprojects in India generally do not use the latest technologies available for a given work resulting in cost over run and poor quality. The manpower involved in the microprojects are unable to master and follow the modern technology which need special skill sets. The issue therefore arises about the training required and way to impart it.

II. Majority of Microprojects belongs to Unorganised Sector: Microprojects in India by and large falling in unorganized sector .A number issues are associated with a project in unorganized sector. The sector is characterized by the employment of unorganized labour. The term 'unorganized labour' has been defined as those workers who have not been able to organize themselves in pursuit of their common interests due to certain constraints, like, casual nature of employment, ignorance and illiteracy, small and scattered size of establishments, etc (NSSO, 2004-05).

III. Participation of Unskilled Labour with Low Productivity: The construction industry is characterized by the predominance of migratory and unskilled labour. The Microprojects employed mostly unskilled labours. The major sources are rural migrated labours who have very little educational background. As a result they are unaware and least interested about formal training which requires a basic educational background. Augmentation of skilled and productivity through on job training also unavailable to them largely because of unavailability of any suitable training process. Lack of training and skill cause poor quality work and low productivity which naturally affect natural growth.

National Council for Enterprises in Unorganised Sector (NCEUS, 2007) highlighted the need for developing the potential and productivity of the huge workforce, from the point of view of both the economy as well as the individual. Several studies and policy documents have highlighted the acute mismatch between the workforce needs and the availability of skilled manpower to sustain the economy's growth rates (Sengupta 2009). With a very low level of labour productivity, the need for large numbers of skilled people is felt more acutely in the context of the country's need to compete internationally in manufacturing as well as services and to emerge as a significant player in the knowledge economy.

IV. Lack of Proper Planning: Microprojects are often given a shorter duration for completion than they really need. This makes the implementing agency to take hectic offset in growing up execution plan, collecting quality materials and most impractically the human resource. Inadequate time spent in almost all the phases leave with fewer options but to go for whatever resources available leading to major compromise in quality and productivity. While planning most microprojects, mobilization time of HR and materials is not considered.

V. Absences of on-site Training: Mirocroprojects in the construction sector involves unskilled and unorganized labours, largely lacking required training; most even lack the basic education which is required for institutional training. Further more, the projects do not have the provision for on-site training. As a result, the human resource involved in the special trade constructions fail to deliver standard productivity, consequently contribute to the low quality and profitability of the projects. Should the desired productivity and quality of the products are to be met, an introduction of a need based, on-site training regime for the labours is a must in special trade construction sector in India.

VI. Lack of Social Security: Microprojects are characterized by short duration and small fund which is why this sector has little to offer to its workforce in terms of job security and social security. Some recent government initiatives are directed to address the plight of the human resources involved in unorganized sector. Productivity of worker is affected due of uncertainties which always loom large on them.

To summarized the scenario reviewed in the article a few things need to be pointed out. The construction sector, like developed nation, in India is coming up fast to foster the national growth. The construction is again classified into Mega to Micro projects. Major part of the construction activities fall under the microporject category. The microprojects are comprised of some specialty trade construction which employ majority of workforce in India. These workers are largely unorganized and lack required skills for the construction projects to be successfully completed. The poor state of skill contributes to remarkably low level of productivity. The result is evident from cost and time overrun, deterioration of quality, etc. The overall outcome is negative, eventually rendering majority of microprojects to be categorized under "Challenged" status.

References

Anand, H. S. (2000), 'Critical HRD issues pertaining to construction and other workers in the informal sector', Draft report prepared for IFP/SEED under a project entitled "Urban Informal Sector Support Programme in India" funded by the ILO and the UNDP Awad, S. Hanna, P. E., Asce, M. and Gunduz, M. (2004), 'Impact of change orders on small-intensive projects', *Journal of Construction Engineering and Management,* 130, (5), pp. 726-733.

Bahuguna, P.C., Kumari, P. and Srivastava, S.K. (2009), 'Changing face of human resource management: A strategic partner in business', *Management and Labour Studies,* 34, (4), pp 563-580.

Behrendt, V. (2004), 'Best Practices for small Project', cost engineering, 46(10) pp. 10-12.

Chadha, G. K., (2004), 'Hauman capital base of the Indian labour market: identifying worry Spots', *The Indian journal of Labour Economics,* 47 (1), pp.3-38.

CII-McKinsey, (2004), Report on 'Made in India: the next big manufacturing export story'. October, 2004.

Construction Industry Development Council, (2010),file://I:\ConstructionDevelopment Council.htm.

Das, T.K., (2003), 'Development of Highways and Airports in India,' Proceedings of the 6th National Conference on Construction, 10-11 November 2003, New Delhi, *CDROM, Technical Session 1, Paper No.7.*

Gordon, J. and Gupta, P. (2004), 'Understanding India's Services Revolution', *Paper presented at IMF-NCAER Conference.*

Government of India, (2007), 'Economic Survey 2006-07', New Delhi: Government of India.

ILO (1998), New prevention strategies for labour inspection. Labour Administration Branch, (56). Geneva.

India-Italy Chamber Report, (2010), 'Construction Industries in Indian – An Overview', pp. 1-8. www.indiaitaly.com.

Johnson, J.H. (2001), 'Micro projects cause constant change.' *A report by The Standish Group International Inc.,* USA, pp. 132-135.

Joshi, S. (2004), 'Tertiary sector driven growth in India' – Impact on employment and poverty, *Economic and Political Weekly,* Sept., 11, 2004.

Laskar and Murthy, (2004), 'Challenges before construction sector in India', *A study Report, Indian Institute Technology, Kharagpu.* pp. 1-18.

Lu, Youjie; Fox, Paul W. (2001), 'The construction industry in the 21st century: Its image, employment prospects and skill requirements': Case study from China. *Unpublished report for the ILO.*

Narang, L. and Singh, L. (2010), 'Human Resource Practices in Indian Organizations: An Empirical Study', *Management and Labour Studies,* 35 (1), pp. 25-32.

National Commission for Enterprises in the Unorganised Sector, NCEUS, (2007), *Report on Conditions of Work and Promotion of Livelihoods in the Undorganised Sector.* Govt. of India.

Sengupta, A.K. (2009), 'Skill formation and employment assurance in unorganized sector'. *National Commission for Enterprises in the Unorganised Sector,* Govt. of India.

Singh, N. (2006), Services led industrialization in India: Assessment and Lessons, UNDESA.

Sohail, M. and Baldwin, A. N. (2004), 'Performance indicators for 'micro-projects' in developing countries. *'Construction Management and Economics,* 22, pp. 11–23.

Vaid, K.N. (1999), 'Contract labour in the construction industry in India', in D.P.A. Naidu (ed.): Contract labour in South Asia. Geneva, ILO, Bureau for Workers' Activities.

World Competitiveness Yearbook, (2008), 'World Competitiveness Yearbook 2008', Institute of Management & Development, Lausanne, Switzerland (National Productivity Council is the Partner from India), www.imd.ch/research/publications/wcy/index.cfm.

In: Development Management in the Twenty-First Century ISBN: 978-1-62100-699-2
Editors: Kartik Roy and Sandip Kar

Chapter 6

MANAGEMENT OF TOURISM DEVELOPMENT AND COMPETITIVENESS OF AGRICULTURAL AREAS

Katarzyna Anna Nawrot* and Łukasz Nawrot†
Dept. of International Economics, Poznan University of Economics,
Poznan, Poland

INTRODUCTION

The development of tourism and the advantages resulted from the concentration of tourists movement may occur in locations being able to attract a potential tourist due to sufficient intensity of tourist attractions. One of them could be constituted by the agriculture and no urbanized areas. Their unique character and recreation functions may become crucial factors of a stay of touristic nature. It is critical to indicate that a tourist function may be one of the essential functioning dimensions of agriculture and non urbanized areas and those with low level of economic development by contributing to the increase of their competitiveness potential. Furthermore the rise in competitiveness of a region or a country through management of tourist development may constitute additional incentive in the process of interregional convergence, especially in case of those regions which are less developed. It is even more important as economic growth and development indicate the inflow of capital investments which in case of tourism investment could be perceived as effective from macroeconomic perspective while contributing more than proportional to the rate of economic growth. So the main aim of the chapter is to work out the conditions for tourism to constitute an essential factor for increasing the competitiveness of agriculture areas which is the complex process of management and programming. It will require an attempt to specify the importance and competitiveness of tourist function in agriculture areas, what will further result in describing the influence and spillover effects of tourist function on the other crucial economic functions in agricultural areas and revealing the bilateral and multilateral interactions of complementary and subsidiary character with reference to the competitiveness

* k.nawrot@ue.poznan.pl.
† l.nawrot@ue.poznan.pl.

of a tourist region and also showing the experience from selected regions and economies. It is the very first step for the effective stimulation of the process of tourism development and its management in order to increase competitiveness of agricultural areas.

THE ESSENCE OF COMPETITIVENESS OF A TOURIST REGION

When it comes to the influence of tourism on a competitiveness of a given region we take the real influence rather than potential one referring to the process of competition. Thus the most vital issue is being competitiveness of the region as a trade – tourism. If we talk then about a region of intense tourism the competition should be first narrowed to tourist economy and only after draw conclusions about the region itself as a whole. The key to the question about the influence of tourism on the competitiveness of economically less developed regions would be then introducing the competitiveness system of a tourist region – as a spatial market subject – where tourism attractions occur.

The debate about the matter of competitiveness of a tourist region is based on a question of what do the areas compete for on a tourist market. The concept of the system of competitiveness of a tourist region is thus the starting point for creating general development strategies and implications for the economical politics on the local level. The most important issue seems to be the approach to the space, that is in a way organized, administered and closed as such within administrative borders, has a certain internal trading ties, and within that space the tourist attractions occur even on a small scale that is on the early stages of development. The basis of the development processes in so organized space is in turn competition i.e. a process that takes place on many levels of the socio-economical life including the regional level too. What it means really is that it is not only the economic subjects that are competing for certain profits but the competition affects also the territorial units. Competition or rivalry means that one needs to find a way to dominate or diminish the gaps and that enforces certain adjustment changes. Individual subjects though do not have as elastic structures as companies so the changes are not easy to introduce or what should the character of those be. That makes the regional development difficult to plan and manage.

The notion of competitiveness is strictly connected to the process of socio-economical development and is one of the most important ones from the point of view of the aim of the chapter but initially ascribed to micro economical level in economy. It goes without saying that competitiveness is considered to be one of the most vital subjects in the economic studies and furthermore is related to the concept of competition. It arises many controversial issues and opinions. The characteristics of the notion is that it can be associated with any stage of aggregation i.e. with a separate product, company, branch, sector, general trade, region or national economy. The concept depends thus on the level of aggregation. Nevertheless, the notion of competitiveness is connected with the idea of competition. It is worth mentioning that in literature competition is mainly associated with business not so much with other socio-economical activities which gets a special meaning in regional analyses. Competition is thus primary to competitiveness.

Competitiveness in its broadest aspect means the ability to act in competitive conditions (Godlewska and Typa 2002, p. 7). It can be assumed then that it is an ability to compete which means act and survive in competitive environment (Gorynia 2002, p. 48). This definition can be developed though after defining the aim of a competition which is more complicated in the case of regions as compared to companies. The increase in competitiveness of regions is definitely a positive phenomenon and the basis for many development strategies. It has to be born in mind though that this should be the indirect aim the realization of which opens the gate to final intentions of regional development politics. Competitiveness as well as efficiency of the economical system are first of all meant to be useful for people (Winiarski 1999, pp. 9-20). The main issue thus seems to be the structure and quality of the processes so that they benefit the general development, lead to decrease in poverty and protect the natural environment (Nawrot 2008, p. 117).

It is worth noticing that the notion of competitiveness has evolved in meaning from the traditional factors of competitiveness of a country or company (the amount of resources) to so called "soft" factors connected with the social and institutional environment (cultural, ethical and religious aspects) (Dołęgowski 2002, p. 10; Dziembowska-Kowalska, Funck 1999, pp. 1381-1398). It leads to more complex approaches to the quantification of competitiveness.

There is a certain kind of regularity that can be noticed as far as the study of competitiveness on different levels of economy is concerned. The lower the level of a study the more it applies to the problem of competition and at the same time they seem to be methodologically correct. The higher the level, on the other hand, so applying to countries or companies, the study comprises not only the idea of competition but also the socio-cconomical development. One might even try to put a thesis that in the study of competitiveness on the level of individual subjects, the borderline between the socio-economical development of a country or region and competitiveness of a country or region is not clearly cut. It seems, thus, that the notion that originates from competition is slightly over evaluated. This process can be observed in various aspects of studies including the tourist economy (Ritchie, Crouch 2003). The subject of competitiveness on this level must at some stage be related to the aspect of development and differentiating these categories is very important.

The concept of the competitiveness system of a region is closely related to the micro economical theories of competitiveness (Krugman 1994; Krugman 1996) rather than the macro economical ones (Porter 1990; Ritchie, Crouch 2003; The World Competitiveness Yearbook 2000). It applies to the basics of the theory of the developing processes pointing out certain ways of operating on the tourist market but does not substitute them.

Tourist region, similar to national economies, has to keep up with the international competitiveness as it functions in an open system and what it means is that even local areas have a status of international tourist subjects functioning on the tourist market (Meethan 2001, p. 53). The analysis of competitiveness of a tourist region has thus international implications even in relation to mainly agricultural and not urbanized areas where inflow of tourists is recorded. It happens together with the processes of globalization, liberalization of the human flow progress in computer technology and transport leading to an argument that segmentation of receivers according to the division: national-international tourists is basically losing its meaning (Nawrot, Zmyślony 2009b, p. 37). According to K. Weiermair those regions that are not competitive on the international market might be actually considered nonexistent (Weiermair 2001). For example Mazury lake region in Poland is competing for tourists not only with the Baltic coast but also with Finish lake districts, Greek cicladas or The golden Shore in Australia. Poznan on the other hand competes not only with Wroclaw but also with Bilbao, Glasgow, Atlanta or Wellington. Many regions or cities similarly to international corporations have a trade mark recognized in the whole world: Paris, Roma, Barcelona, Florida, Tuscany, Hawaii are among the most famous (Nawrot and Zmyślony 2009b, p. 37).

Competitive ability of the individual subjects in the international environment that is dependent on a good functioning of territorial socio-economical systems is based on the recourses that a tourist region has. Regions have certain virtues that tourists have to have access to. Putting the virtues in space determines their uniqueness and that means they cannot be replaced and are the basis of the tourism in a given region. It is very important matter as far as the competitiveness of the region is concerned because unlike other regions competing for investors or better conditions, these regions compete for a tourist. One might even say that this is one of the most important matters of the competitiveness of a tourist region. For this reason the notion of competitiveness of regions should be broadened by one vital element that makes the tourist region exist namely a tourist. It so happens that private subjects compete for tourist but the competition takes place also on the regional level[1]. It can be thus stated that it is a direct competition for a tourist between regions since the tourist traffic is limited, defined and if there are less tourists coming to one region another region will benefit from that (Rapacz 2004, p. 57). It is of paramount importance then to constantly improve the competitive position which in this case could be measured by the participation of a region in generating tourism on the level of a country or a group of countries.

Similar to regions in general, tourist regions can compete directly and indirectly. Indirect competition means creating good environment for the tourist subjects operating within its boundaries which allows to get a competitive advantage in elements that are beyond the control of the subjects. Thus indirect competition is based on the competing abilities of the subjects. Direct competition means that territorial subjects compete among themselves for various kind of advantages like income and work places, investors, access to financial resources or organization of tourist attractions and events (Jędrzejczyk 2000, p. 27). The final aim of the competition although indirect should be socio-economical development of a given region.

The key to the idea of increasing the competitiveness of a region apart from companies and investors is a tourist. It is connected with the complexity of the tourist trade and the issue of the tourist product. According to indirect notion of competitiveness tourist region should be creating appropriate conditions for a tourist analogically to creating conditions for the economic subjects functioning within it. It is then important to properly coordinate the subjects in the region for none of them can individually offer the whole tourist product. It results from complement of a tourist supply in the region. The competitiveness of a tourist region has both direct and indirect character applying to economical subjects operating within as well as tourists – the most important part of it. All the subjects in the region are related in many different ways (resulting from the idea of the system of a tourist region (Zmyślony 2008). These relations have impact on the competitiveness of a tourist region as a whole, the competitiveness also influences the subjects functioning within the region. Moreover, the competitiveness of a tourist region remains dependant on the environment especially macro economic factors, the central government, cooperation with tour operators and transport

[1] International Tourist Fairs, marketing and advertising campaigns are some of the instruments of attracting potential tourists by particular local governments and spatial subjects.

companies (Figure 6.1) and all this results from the presence in an open market system – international environment.

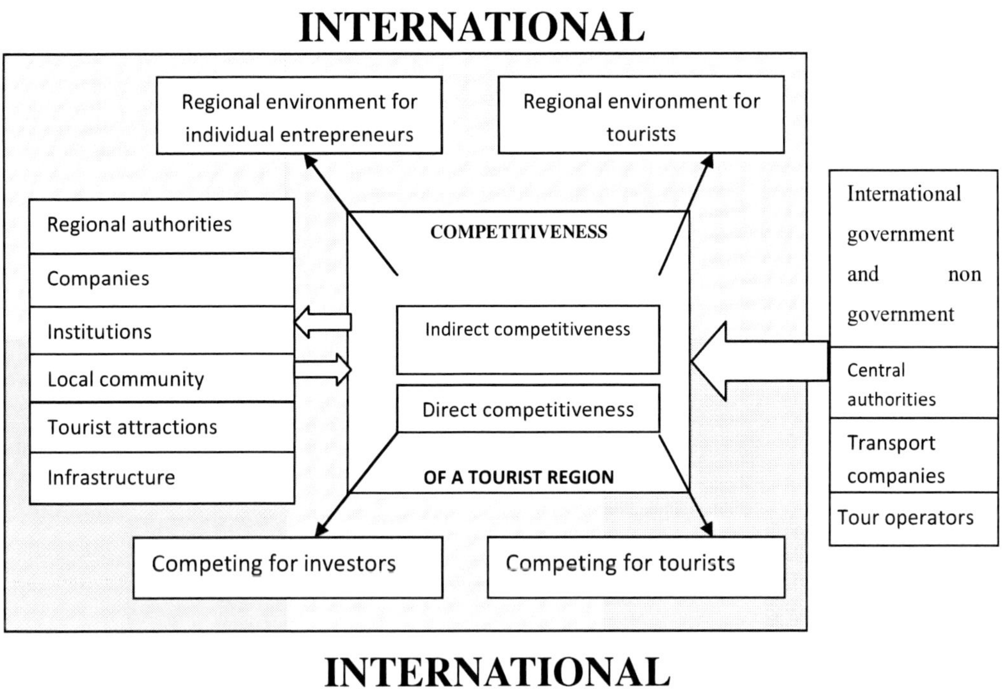

Figure 6.1. Competitiveness of a tourist region.

The competitiveness of a tourist region tends to be depicted as static and dynamic. Static refers to a certain moment in time and may be measured by the competitive position expressed by the participation on the trade market or the condition of the economic subjects of the region. The comparison of the competitive positions in the subsequent moments in time shows whether or not the given region has improved its position, in other words what was its competitive ability in that moment in time and whether it succeeded in using the full competitive potential to improve the competitive position and increase, sustain or balance the competitive domination as compared to other regions in the world.

As far as evaluation of the competitiveness of a tourist region is concerned, apart from general, universal competitive factors of a region one should also consider those that are important from the point of view of the possibilities of the development of the tourist function and are characteristic of tourism. It goes without saying that one of the most vital issues appears to be the problem of tourist product, it's shaping with the help of investments as well as using this product in the region with the help of strategic analysis (Nawrot 2006, p. 225). Considering the assumptions that have been put forward here it is worth mentioning that they do not fully cover the issue discussed they do however allow to create measures of competitiveness of a tourist region. They will refer most of all to four elements resulted from the systematic approach to the competitiveness of a tourist region:

- attracting tourists to the region,
- attracting investors to the region,

- creating the appropriate tourist offer in the region,
- creating appropriate environment to the existing entrepreneurs in the tourist region.

Bearing in mind assumed dimensions of consideration, the concept of a system of competitiveness of a tourist region points out two important aspects. First of all it refers to the process of competition as an immanent feature of contemporary spatial units and indicates its key elements with reference to the region of a trade character – tourist. Secondly it shows the importance of subjects participating directly and indirectly in the process of competition while creating the tourist product in the region. The efficient use of the given resources in the process of regional competitiveness may result in the success and strengthen the development processes in a broad meaning. Thus the tourist product of marketing, complex and international character should be considered as a starting point to enter the tourist market. We can say, that is the beginning in the process of regional management. In case of non urbanized areas of low level of development, with frail tourist structures the impact of development management should be put on creating a concept of regional tourist product. Because of the complexity of the issue all of the subjects concern in the system of competitiveness should be involved, namely: local governments, corporations, institutions and local community. It means that integrated approach in management process and economic policy is needed. In contemporary international relations based on knowledge based economy such an approach is crucial for tourism to be a factor of competitiveness of a region and influence the development processes.

THE INFLUENCE OF TOURISM ON AREAS OF LOW LEVEL OF DEVELOPMENT

The interdisciplinary and multispectral character of a tourist economy leads to the interdependence of its development to other sectors of economy. Tourism constitutes a stimulus for development processes as a sector of modern structure characterized for developed economies based on services and the inflow of information. These two aspects count for the fact that the incentives to intensify the development of tourism could be observed on one hand on areas of low level of development, economically underdeveloped, with traditional structure of economy, and on the other at the developed regions reinforcing and strengthening its economic functions. While considering that these days not only enterprises compete but also spatial units – regions, the outcome of reformation of its economic structure through the development of tourism should be the rise of competitiveness.

The importance of the development of service sector with dominant tourist function could be observed in the regions of low level of economic development through its influence on local economy. As a consequence the development of service sector leads to the development of information sector. So we can indicate here the effective path of development of underdeveloped areas from traditional model of the economy with the main share of agriculture, followed by manufacturing and services to the domination of service sector and information society specific for developed economies. The management of tourism development is thus economically reasonable and brings benefits in micro scale and at the regional level. It results also in the rise of competitiveness of a region as it changes its economic structure into more progressive and remunerative and thus flexible. However the question on prerequisites of development of tourist movement at particular areas should be raised. Worth considering are the possibilities of development and the character of tourist economy at the areas of low level of development, often of non urbanized, rural character, with the domination of agrarian function.

Tourism fulfills the certain function, included in the broad sense of a tourism function which could be defined as "social and economic activity of a place or an area which is directed to serve tourists and which a tourist destination plays in the system of national economy" (Kowalczyk, 2000, p. 37). Two dimensions could be identified in that respect, namely economic and social. The capacity of the later is broadly understood in general, so the particular functions infiltrate each other what in turn results from the definition of tourism in a broad sense tourism constitutes the entirety of spatial movement phenomenon connected with the free, temporal change of a place of residence, life environment while deeply entering the visiting environment (natural, cultural, social)" (Przecławski 1996, p. 30). Thus numerous social and economic dimensions could be identified important when considering the influence of tourism on development of areas of low level of economic development (Alejziak 2000, p. 2000; Gaworecki 2007; Gołembski 2002, p. 7-9; Wodejko 1997, p. 90-99):

- cconomic,
- ecological,
- educational,
- cultural,
- spatial,
- psychological,
- social.

The presented multidimensional character results in the multiplicity of functions played by tourism in socio-economic environment and which further influences the area of intense tourist arrivals what also refers to areas of low level of development. Due to the purpose, character and capacity of the chapter the consideration will be focused on economic function, having in mind the impact of the remaining.

Shortly referring to the economic function it should be pointed out that through the development of tourism and as a consequence followed by the inflow of capital resources the development of a region is provided. Through the involvement in tourist movement services the labor market is stimulated, the trade and services evolve and new tourist infrastructure of capital intensive character is built. The inflow of tourists enables the increase in the incomes of local society and the rise of the local budgets. Very often the local capital plays the crucial role in building the tourist infrastructure. The spillover effects for the local society are observed. The external inflow of capital provided by tourists leads to the multiplier effects, what additionally strengthen the process of economic development through tourism. However the come into being of above mentioned outcomes is only possible while reaching a certain level of the intensity of tourist movement, what means that achieving a success at regional arena of competition is necessary.

MANAGEMENT OF TOURIST FUNCTION DEVELOPMENT ON AREAS OF LOW LEVEL OF DEVELOPMENT

Agriculture and no urbanized areas may be able to attract a potential tourist due to their unique character and recreation functions what can constitute crucial factors of a stay of touristic nature. However the growth of tourist supply at the areas of low level of development, very often of rural character might be difficult from demand point of view, spatial character and can be contradictory to the agriculture economy. This situation may be observe in numerous polish regions. The development of tourist function at the areas of low level of urbanization, is combined especially from supply side with the remuneration of investment in tourist infrastructure, like hotels, gastronomy. In the regions of moderate tourist attractiveness it is however hampered because of demand respect (Nawrot and Zmyślony 2009a, p. 100). It happens thus that the economic importance of tourism might be inconsiderable, because of the ineffectiveness of locating tourist investments despite the tourist values of a place.

The tourist supply is characterized by exact location and spatial motionless. It refers to the immutability of tourist values which constitute the substructure of its creation. Furthermore the precise location of tourist qualities indicates their unique what implies that they cannot be replaced and that is why they are the main reason for tourist move. It means that the values offer by the rural areas cannot be sold without the necessity of attracting those interested in. However the tourist movement at rural areas, especially of agrarian character may constitute substantial problems at the stage of the realization an economic function of this character.

The development of tourist function at the area of low level of development faces numerous obstacles, what result from its multifunctional character. The economy of non urbanized regions, in general worse developed, mainly bases on agriculture or food processing. The scarce factors of production are used especially in preliminary stages of regional development and at the low level of per capita income. The competition of tourist function to other economic function which were accomplished in the given region is revealed. The possible conflicts can occur on the edge of tourism and other economic sectors what limits the development of tourist economy and its impact on regional competitiveness. A small number of economic functions at the rural areas dominated by agriculture have complementary character to the tourist function. What is more they are not the most important from economic point of view for the subjects functioning at the non urbanized areas. The situation of that kind occurs especially in the early stages of development of tourist region, when the benefits from the concentration of tourist movement are not spread widely. Thus the potential beneficiaries don't perceive themselves as those who should be interested in tourist movement development and its management.

It should be pointed out that at the rural areas of low level of development there is a dominance of tourist functions which are of substitution character to the main economic functions which is the agricultural function (Figure 6.2). The below presented figure may be a starting point for a precise interacting analysis and a search for substitution and complement relationships of the subject raised in the chapter and furthermore leads to a skillful management of development of those functions in order to raise competitiveness of a region in general.

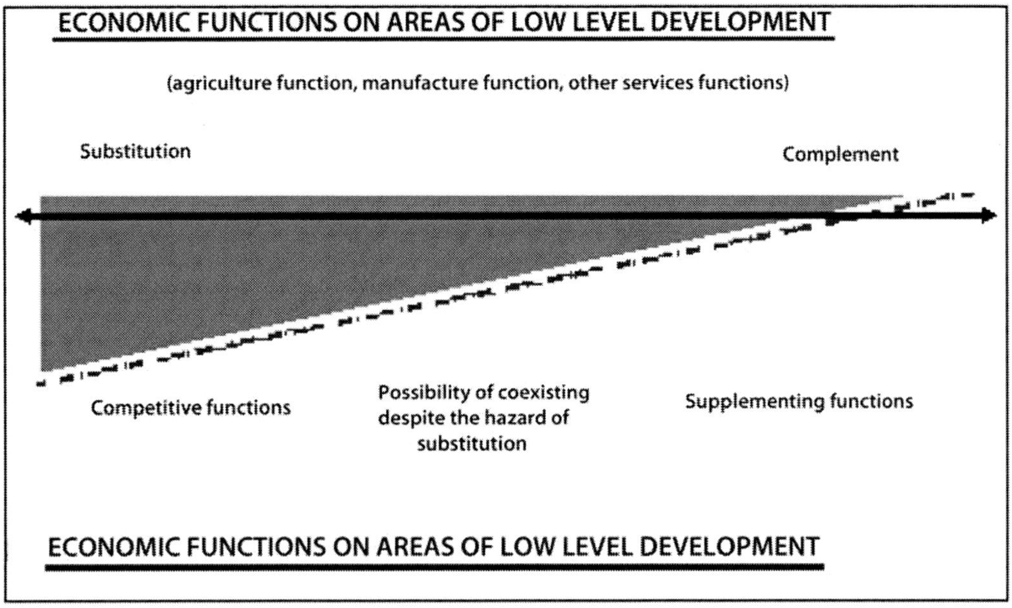

Figure 6.2. Tourist and economic functions on areas of low level of development – substitution and complement.

There is a question whether despite the above mentioned negative interaction the tourist function could constitute one of the substantial dimensions of non urbanized areas? It could be stated that it is as it refers to broadly understood regional policy, which encompass the issues of activating social and economic areas through tourism and thus equalizing regional disparities (Jędrzejczyk 2000, p. 35). Thus the character of rural areas should be taken into account especially indicating the dispersion of the demand and multifunctional of such a space. The substitution mechanism may be diminished through the enlarging of the beneficiaries of the development of tourist economy which can further stimulate the other traditional sectors of the economy in rural areas namely (Majewski and Lane 2001, p. 64-67): agriculture, gardening, fishering, forestry, handicraft, housing, transport, trade and services. Tourism may have significant impact on numerous sectors of economy, providing its share is at least significant2. The steps should be undertaken to develop tourism market from both the demand and supply sides. Simultaneously the influence on both sides seems to be crucial for effective development of tourist economy in the region in order to cope with the competition at the regional level. It is worth touching a few issues concerning the competitiveness at a trade level as the category which is not defined unequivocally and approved by the branch. The rise of the regional competitiveness of a tourist economy results in the increase in the competitiveness of a region as a whole and thus accelerates and strengthens the development processes, desirable by underdeveloped areas.

It should not be omitted that the process of competition at the regional level is of trade character and regards a tourist market. Thus if a tourist spends some of the maintenance in one tourist region the resources will not be spend in the other. It indicates the necessity for an effective management and the ability to compete. From the space point of view the tourist

[2] Assuming scale: dominant, significant, subsidiary, marginal.

spending is not the only merit – it is also important to consider the supply context in a broader sense.

Thus the increase in the competitiveness of the areas of agriculture character should be considered through the competition of a space with the presence of tourist function further perceived as a tourist region in systematic approach. The competitiveness of a tourist region is a complex issue what characterizes that kind of the categories at the mezzo economic level.

Economic Policy Implications for Stimulating Tourism Economy in Underdeveloped Areas

It is suggested that special attention should be paid to the basic categories of tourist market namely: tourist product, cooperation of the subjects of the tourist supply system, promotion and diversification of the regional offer. These categories are crucial in the management of tourist development and in the process of increasing the competitiveness, they should be perceived and analyzed as a whole. Several aspects refer to the process of building the competitive tourist product (Nawrot, Zmyślony 2009a, p. 107):

- broadly perceived and complex evaluation of natural, environmental, anthropological merits of a region,
- determinants of tourist investment rise in the region and decreasing its impediments, the previous analysis of a tourist supply in the region should be conducted – evaluation of the infrastructural and socio-economic resources,
- considering the possibility to develop special forms of agricultural tourism based on individual cultural and geographical values of a region,
- detail analysis of tourist demand undertaken on regular basis enabling to identify the demand, evaluate the situation, and proper programming of the tourist product – planning at the regional level leads to the increase in the tourist product,
- cooperation of subjects in the region in order to intensify the development of tourism and create the complex tourist product in the region, the assumptions should be included in planning documents, like a strategy of tourism development of a region, what may be a background to estimate investment needs at the given area,
- economic effectiveness of private investments, crucial for building the core of tourism economy.

The importance of tourism product complexity is crucial. Although tourists have different demands, impossible to be satisfied by the supply of individual producer, they perceive the stay as a whole, what may result in the situation when lack of sustaining one of them may influence the final evaluation of the tourist journey and possibility of resigning of future purchase (Niezgoda and Zmyślony 2003, p. 51). Tourist product in the region combine the numerous products, services and experiences and as a result proper tourist infrastructure and service is necessary, especially highly qualified and experienced human capital.

However the possibility of tourist product creation in the region is limited, so the management opportunities are restricted and process becomes more difficult. On one hand there are spatial barriers, what results from the capacity of a tourist region, on the other capital shortages in developing countries which limit the elasticity of investment decisions because of the cost of capital formation. Interdisciplinary character of tourism leads to the engagement of public and private sector and the market organizations. In the process of building the tourist product not only the level of investment but also its proper structure is important. The complex demand can only be sustain by proper and complementary supply. Not all of the investments are characterized by high profitability. The private investors will choose those with the highest possible rate of return. That is why the role of public sector is important in management of tourism development as a significant support in creating infrastructure crucial for tourist product in the region, but not always fulfilling the high return on investment criteria. There are however some disadvantages related to the investment activity of a public sector, connected with lower effectiveness, longer process of investment project and so called private investment washing (The World Bank 2003, p. 104). It will depend whether these are competitive to the private sector or complementary and supporting the development of the later. Nevertheless the public sector cannot be excluded. Tourism is an activity very much dependent on public sector – approximate half of the services used by tourist in a region is served by subjects financed through the local governments (Bordas, 2001, p. 38-41): road infrastructure, technical infrastructure, communal activity, administration and social services like security, health or education.

The individuals have limited potential in sustaining all requirements demanded by tourist in the region no matter of the character of activity, thus depending on the other tourist subjects, so in other words connected with them. As a result the existing tourist subjects in the region are equal no matter of the size, importance and prosecution and their investment activities complement each other. Thus the common efforts are required undertaken by the local governments, tourist enterprises and market institutions what may lead to the creation of a tourist product which will be competitive from a tourist point of view and simultaneously characterized by a complexity. Thus the above mentioned subjects complement each other in the creation of an environment for tourist product development. There is a question how these complementarities can actually lead to the complex product of high quality and sustaining the tourist expectations? The effectiveness of the cooperation depends on the possibility of all parts included to benefit and common goals should lead to the realization of individual purposes (Zmyślony 2008, p. 81). The region should be therefore perceived as a quasi-corporation, what enables to take advantage of the organization management theories. Very often both competition and cooperation could be observed.

The character of rural and agricultural areas requires the complement of other functions of recreation, educational, and social character (understood as an access for tourist attractions to locals, which are not tourist but in the leisure this kind of demand is congenial to tourist demand what could be used in order to rise the effectiveness of objects unable to hold on to tourist demand only). The agricultural areas should be prepared for the reception of new forms of tourism, especially of business character which opens new possibilities to use the potential of a country side. Openness for the new forms of tourism diminishes in the substantial way the occurrence of the seasonal phenomenon (i. e. educational tourism, business tourism, hunting). Obviously all those postulates face formal and legal obstacles resulted from the spatial management in different countries and thus cannot be put into practice easily.

Interesting form of tourism market support at agricultural areas is agro tourism which creates possibility to offer rooms by the farmers. The number of rooms to be offered is usually limited and gives the owner tax benefits. This could be perceived as a form of stimulating the entrepreneurship of the citizens the rural areas while raising their incomes. Supporting this kind of activities influences the local capital formation with reference to the service of tourist movement and furthermore builds the particular elements of the competitiveness of tourist supply based on internal resources only and changes the economic structure.

CONCLUSION

Conducted research leads to the general conclusion that tourism is not a perfect solution for equalizing development inequalities. However it doesn't mean that the positive aspects should be neglected, especially regarding rural and agricultural areas characterized by low level of development, where they create the opportunity to diminish the structural shortages, in the first place those of capital character. Furthermore, failing is not a crime but a lack of efforts is, so it is worth undertaking efforts in order to stimulate the development of tourist function and increase effectiveness of regional management. However it is not an easy process, on one hand due to the high level of competition in the sector and in substitution branches and on the other because of smaller possibilities of areas of low level of development. Besides at the rural areas of low level of development there is a dominance of tourist functions which are of substitution character to the main economic function which is the agricultural function. However the substitution mechanism could be diminished by enlarging the potential beneficiaries of the development of tourist economy which can further stimulate the other traditional sectors of the economy in rural areas. Taking the challenge to compete on international tourism market a special attention should be further paid to the basic categories of tourism market development, namely tourist product of the region, cooperation of the subjects of tourism supply, tourism investment, promotion and diversification of the regional offer, which in the process of shifting the competitiveness should be analyzed together what strongly indicates the complexity of a tourist product. Thus the steps should be undertaken to develop tourism market both from the demand and supply sides. Simultaneously the influence on both sides seems to be crucial for effective development of a tourist economy in the region in order to cope with the competition at the regional level. So, the background to manage the development of the tourist function in contemporary competitive environment is an approach trough the competitiveness of a tourist region as a complex system. It is fundamental in management process. The development of a region should be thus perceived through the main elements of that system. The rise of the regional competitiveness of a tourist economy results in the increase in the competitiveness of a region as a whole and thus accelerates and strengthens the development processes, desirable by underdeveloped areas. The efforts should be undertaken in this context, so the development of the tourist function, through the increase in the competitiveness of an area of low level of development results in the transformation into a region with the domination of a tourist function and as a result through the multiplier and spillover effects increase the level of social and economic development.

REFERENCES

Alejziak, W. (2000), 'Turystyka w obliczu wyzwań XXI wieku', *Albis,* Kraków.

Bordas, E. (2001), 'Improving public-private sectors cooperation in tourism: A new paradigm for destinations', *"Tourism Review"* 56 (3+4).

Dołęgowski, T.(2002), 'Konkurencyjność instytucjonalna i systemowa w warunkach gospodarki globalnej, *ZN Szkoły Głównej Handlowej w Warszawie nr 505',* Warszawa.

Dziembowska-Kowalska, J. Funck, R.H.(1999), 'Cultural activities: source of competitiveness in prosperity in urban regions', *Urban Studies,* 36 (8).

Gaworecki, W.W., (2007), Turystyka, wyd. V zmienione, Polskie Wydawnictwo *Ekonomiczne,* Warszawa.

Godlewska, H.Typa, M. (2002), Przestrzenne uwarunkowania konkurencyjności przedsiębiorstw, *Oficyna Wydawnicza Szkoły Głównej Handlowej w Warszawie,* Warszawa.

Gołembski, G. (ed.),(2002), 'Kompendium wiedzy o turystyce', *Wydawnictwo Naukowe PWN,* Warszawa-Poznań.

Gorynia, M., (ed.), (2002), 'Luka konkurencyjna na poziomie przedsiębiorstwa a przystąpienie Polski do Unii Europejskiej', *Wydawnictwo Akademii Ekonomicznej w Poznaniu,* Poznań.

Jędrzejczyk, I., (2000), 'Nowoczesny biznes turystyczny', Ekostrategie w zarządzaniu firmą, Wydawnictwo Naukowe PWN, Warszawa.

Kowalczyk, T. (2000), 'Geografia turyzmu, *Wydawnictwo Naukowe PWN',* Warszawa.

Krugman, P. (1994), 'Competitiveness: a dangerous obsession', *Foreign Affairs* 73 (2).

Krugman, P. (1996), 'A country is not a company', *Harvard Business Review* 74 (1).

Majewski, J. Lane, B.(2001), 'Turystyka wiejska i rozwój lokalny', *Fundacja Fundusz Współpracy,* Poznań.

Meethan, K. (2001), 'Tourism in Global Society', *Palgrave,* Hampshire – New York.

Nawrot, K. A. (2008), 'Determinanty rozwoju gospodarczego państw ASEAN, *Wydawnictwo Naukowe Scholar',* Warszawa.

Nawrot, Ł. (2006), Bezpośrednia konkurencyjność regionu turystycznego - istota i możliwości pomiaru, in: G. Gołembski (ed.), Turystyka w ujęciu podmiotowym i przestrzennym : człowiek - przestrzeń – przedsiębiorstwo, *Wydawnictwo Akademii Ekonomicznej w Poznaniu,* Poznań.

Nawrot, Ł. Zmyślony, P. (2009a), 'Międzynarodowa konkurencyjność regionu turystycznego'. Od programowania rozwoju do zarządzania strategicznego, *Wydawnictwo PROKSENIA,* Kraków.

Nawrot, Ł. Zmyślony, P. (2009b), 'Regiony turystyczne na międzynarodowej arenie konkurencji: programowanie rozwoju regionalnego czy zarządzanie przestrzenią zorganizowaną?, *"Folia Turistica"* 21.

Niezgoda, A. Zmyślony, P.(2003), 'Popyt turystyczny', *Wydawnictwo Akademii Ekonomicznej w Poznaniu,* Poznań.

Porter, M.E., (1990), 'The Competitive Advantage of the Nations', *MacMillan,* London.

Przecławski, K. (1996), 'Człowiek a turystyka – zarys socjologii turystyki', *Albis*, Kraków.

Rapacz, A. (ed.), (2004), Współpraca i integracja w turystyce w euroregionie Nysa w perspektywie członkostwa w Unii Europejskiej, *Wydawnictwo Akademii Ekonomicznej we Wrocławiu,* Wrocław.

Ritchie, J.R.B., Crouch, G.I., (2003), 'The Competitive Destination: A Sustainable Tourism Perspective', *CABI Publishing,* Wallingford.

The World Bank, (2003), Global Economic Prospects and the Developing Countries, Investing to Unlock Global Opportunities, *The World Bank,* Washington DC.

The World Competitiveness Yearbook (1999), (2000), *IMD,* Lausanne 2000.

Weiermair, K. (2001), 'The Impact of Membership in the EU upon Austria's Tourism Industry': Some Possible Lessons for Poland, materiały konferencyjne Forum Dyskusyjnego Tour Salon Gospodarka turystyczna w decydującej fazie negocjacji z UE - wyzwania i nadzieje, 26 października 2001.

Winiarski, B.(1999), Konkurencyjność: Kryterium wyboru czy kierunek strategii i cel pośredni polityki regionalnej? in: M. Klamut. (ed.), Konkurencyjność regionów, *Wydawnictwo Akademii Ekonomicznej we Wrocławiu*, Wrocław.

Wodejko, S. (1997), Ekonomiczne zagadnienia turystyki, *Wyższa Szkoła Handlu i Prawa w Warszawie,* Warszawa.

Zmyślony, P. (2008), Partnerstwo i przywództwo w regionie turystycznym, *Wydawnictwo AE w Poznaniu,* Poznań.

In: Development Management in the Twenty-First Century ISBN: 978-1-62100-699-2
Editors: Kartik Roy and Sandip Kar

Chapter 7

MANAGING THE GROWTH OF MEDICAL TOURISM IN INDIA BY PUBLIC-PRIVATE PARTNERSHIPS

Anita Medhekar*
CQ University, Queensland, Australia

INTRODUCTION

Medical tourism in India is a billion dollar and fastest growing healthcare service industry. Medical tourism involves traveling across the border nationally or internationally for urgent elective medical surgeries, cosmetic, dental and reproductive and other specialised treatments. This is a modern 'cost effective' term coined by healthcare and tourism industries across the globe, although the phenomenon is not new. People have been for centuries traveling within India, for medical healing to the ancient shrines and temples. Pilgrims and patients across the Mediterranean also travelled to ancient Greece to stay in the shrine of the healing god, Asklepios. Today a growing number of patients as tourist from developed countries such as UK, USA, Australia, Canada, and Europe are travelling abroad to developing countries like India, Malaysia, Thailand, and China with the main objective of obtaining immediate health care, plastic surgery, organ replacement, reproductive –IVF procedures including elective surgery and long-term care is gaining greater appeal in the globalised world with fewer barriers to travel. This trend is spreading fast due to the very high cost of elective medical procedures, lack or shortage of organ donors and above all long waiting lists in developed countries. India is the preferred choice in terms of low cost, no waiting period, climate, English language, exotic destinations, international and government accreditation and cultural affinity (Medhekar and Haq, 2010) .

Tourism sector in general and medical tourism in particular can play an important role in improving India's balance of payment position and foreign exchange reserve position. It is liberalization of the Indian economy that created a proper atmosphere for the growth of tourism. India cannot afford to overlook the capacity and capability of tourism to generate employment, reduce regional imbalance, improve the overall standards of living and earn

* A.Medhekar@equ.edu.au.

foreign exchange revenue. Tourism has become one of the world's largest service sector industries with enormous potential for further growth; however, it is sensitive to external factors, like terrorism, natural disasters, SARS virus and SWINE flu which can cripple the local economy at destinations in the developing countries (Medhekar 2005; Medhekar and Haq 2010).

According to Carrerra and Bridges (2006) at the international level, the health and medical tourism industry including medical tourism is sustained by 617 million individuals with an annual growth rate of 3.9% annually and worth US$513 billion. According to Bookman and Bookman (2007) economic impact of medical tourism in developing countries is significant, as nearly 272,000 medical tourists visited India for complex medical procedures in 2007, bringing in US$ 656 million in foreign exchange earnings. The health and medical tourism sector in India is growing fast compared to Thailand, Singapore, Malaysia, Pakistan and other Asian countries, as a popular destination of choice for patients from the developed as well as developing countries. The various private sector renowned hospitals providing world class medical procedures are: All India Institute for medical Sciences (AIIMS), Apollo Hospital, Birla Heart Research Centre, Christian Medical College, Tata Memorial Hospital, Apollo Cancer Hospital, and Institute Cardiovascular Diseases, Wockhardt, Fortis Healthcare and Max India. It is projected that India's medical tourism market is expected to generate over $ US2.5 billion in foreign exchange revenue by 2012 and US$ 3 billion by 2013 (RANCOS 2010).

India provides a wide range of medical procedures from simple to complex heart-cardiac surgeries, hip replacements etc and prospective patients can save 50 to 70 % of the cost of their treatment by choosing India as a medical tourism destination. On the other hand health tourism such as yoga, ayurvedic treatments which caters to physical, spiritual and mental healing of the body , mind and soul is also growing in the state of Kerala, with increasing demand not only from the affluent class in India but also from the foreigners as well as non-resident Indians. However, lack of efficient and ethical quality control, auditing of the hospitals, hospital accreditation system, asymmetric information and imperfect agency, bureaucracy and inefficient laws and regulation against corruption and malpractice in organ trade can be a big obstacle to the growth of medical tourism in India resulting in market and government failure in the absence of regulation.

Medical Tourism in particular require market and tourist friendly policies to position tourism as a major growth engine and to harness its economic benefits and multiplier effect for employment generation, stimulating social and economic development and poverty alleviation in an environmentally sustainable, responsible and ethical manner in India. It is important to have a re-look at the existing tourism policy and in particular medical tourism policy, and have a Public-Private Partnership (PPP) approach for its management (APEC 2002; GOI 2008), with a view to attract sizeable private investment in this emerging service export sector, position the states in the travel and tourism market and to promote certain regions in India as a medical and wellness tourism destination to locals and foreigners from developed countries. Thus the potential of medical tourisms as an important foreign exchange earner along with its multiplier effect in income generation, large employment creation, its ability in promoting economic growth and development and creating jobs which makes it a prime candidate for governmental focus and participation at all levels.

Moreover, it can be argued that for managing the growth of medical tourism in an efficient and effective manner public and private sector partnerships is essential between the various key stake holders for providing accredited, efficient, effective, equitable and good quality of health care for the long term sustainability of the medical tourism industry for the host country, given the increasing competition to maximise their participation in the global economy, as well as to guarantee quality of service, infrastructure needs, reasonable price, accreditation and handling of any legal disputes. Many countries such as Singapore, Malaysia, and Thailand, India also promotes medical tourism through government support and National Health Policy (NHP) reform of 2002 drafted by Prime Minister's advisory council on Trade and Industry, which treats this industry legally as an 'export sector' eligible for all fiscal incentives extended to export earnings. This chapter examines the management of the growth of medical tourism in India by public- private partnerships. Part one introduces the importance of medical tourism and its growth in India. Part two reviews the literature. Part three considers how the adoption of PPP policy is essential for the management and promoting the sustainable growth of medical tourism industry in India, to make India a globally competitive health care destination. Finally, part four provides some concluding discussion and comments regarding medical tourism policy development, implementation and management.

Medical Tourism in India

A developing country like India is not only a popular tourist destination but it is also emerging as a world class medical tourist market in the world, emphasised by world class technology-intensive medical equipment, highly qualified and experienced expertise of medical professionals, the cost-effectiveness of the medical procedures– and above all low cost medical-tourist package for foreigners along with recovery and rest in a five star medical-tourism resort for the patients, and accompanying family members. In 2009, on a global scale India ranked second to Thailand in medical tourism (IMT 2009). The most demanded treatments are heart surgery, knee and hip transplant dental care, IVF-reproductive-gender selection and cosmetic surgery (Ramesh 2005; Nagpal 2009).

Government of India (2003) budget for the first time announced to support trade in private sector medical tourism, (as an example of PPP) and promoting India to developed countries as a world class-high-tech healing destination for low cost medical treatment and procedures. Combining tourism with world class medical expertise became a government policy in 2003, when the Finance Minister Jaswant Singh, in his budget speech called for India to become a "Global Health Destination" (PC 2007; ESCAP 2009) in partnership with the private sector. For example, according to Financial Times (2-7-03) in April 2003, Madras Medical Mission, a Chennai-based hospital, successfully conducted a complex heart operation on an 87 year old American medical tourist at an approximate US $8000 (Euro 7,000 and Pounds 4,850) including cost of the airfare and a month's stay in the hospital for recovery. The patient claimed that "a less complex operation in USA would cost me a fortune".

Most of the Medical tourists travel to India given the advantage of English language, are from developed countries (USA, UK, Western/northern Europe, Middle east oil rich countries and the affluent expatriate Indian sub-continent Diaspora (Indian, Singaporean, and other nationals from developing countries) community living overseas, where not only the costs of medical invasive procedures and surgeries is very high along with long waiting period

(Adams 2006). Largest private healthcare chain of Apollo Hospital in Chennai (Madras) was started in 1983 and receives patients from Australia, Canada, UK, Germany, Mauritius, Seychelles, Maldives, Sri Lanka, Bhutan, Nepal, Oman, UAE, Bahrain, Qatar, Saudi Arabia, and East Africa. Apollo has branches all over the world such as Sri Lanka, Bangladesh, Ghana, Nigeria, Qatar and Kuwait. It opened its first branch in Oman with 100-bed super specialist hospital in 2006, with 300,000 expatriate Indians living in Oman (Medindia 2006; AMTA 2010).

The recent articles in Times of India by Nagaraj (2009) as well as numerous other websites (TravelBiz 2009; IMT 2009) based on a two year study by Deloitte International Healthcare research unit, ranked India 2nd in medical tourism in the world specializing in the areas of cardiac, neurological or orthopedic surgeries, next only to Thailand which focuses more on cosmetic surgery, but it spends only 1.2% of GDP on its own domestic health issues. In 2007, 450,000 thousand patients from foreign countries were treated in India, compared to Thailand's 1200,000. The study states that the key reasons for US, UK and other European countries patients to visit India are low cost, absence of waiting list, best quality treatment, globally accredited with JCI (Ramanna 2008; JCI 2010), clinical and para-medical talent, and third party intervention through health insurance.

India is increasingly focusing on highly specialised medical surgeries and treatments in the areas of orthopedics, joint replacement, neurosurgery and cardiothoracic, kidney transplant, eye, reproductive, vascular and spinal surgery, with a groundbreaking procedure known as hip resurfacing, an alternative to hip replacement that is more affordable and causes less post-operative stress. India's medical diversity is apparent given that robotic surgeries can be combined with alternative healing practices such as yoga, herbal, including ayurvedic treatments (IMT 2009; MTI 2009). Tourism in general and health and medical tourism (a sub-set of health tourism-see Figure-1) in particular can be used as a vehicle/engine of export-led growth of service sector following IT industry in India for providing employment opportunities for millions in India and its related supportive sectors. Medical tourism has a significant effect on the destination country's economy. Bookman and Bookman (2007) in-depth study of medical tourism in developing countries, noted that medical tourism brings foreign exchange to a developing country which trickles down throughout the economy in the form of employment generation, income, savings, investment, tax revenue, etc. Under the right conditions such as political, social and economic, the growth potential for medical tourism could be enormous. For example, in the next decade, medical tourism will do and earn foreign exchange for the Indian economy ten to twenty times more, what information technology in the 1990s did in terms of outsourcing from USA to India.

Various international medical tourism accreditation bodies such as: International Society of Quality in Health Care (ISQUAH) has approved India's accreditation process, National Accreditation Board for Hospitals (NABH) certification body, of the Indian Government. Further Joint Commission international (JCI), USA based accreditation body since 2002, and Trent International Accreditation Scheme (TIAS) evaluates hospitals all over the world (AMA 2008). NHP was drafted by Prime Minister's advisory council on Trade and Industry, and it states that "…the treatment of foreign patients/expatriates is legally an 'export' and the same is eligible for all fiscal incentives extended to export earnings…" (GOI 2003). Thus PPP at national, regional and international level is essential for the management of medical tourism sector.

Government of India has also realised the positive economic impact of medical tourism on the economy (GOI 2003 & 2008a). Tour operators of Medical Tourism are now connecting patients with hospitals which are internationally accredited providers of medical procedures. Since 2003, special Visa category was introduced. Medical tourism visa- (M-Visa) is granted to tourist travelling for Health and Medical Tourism related treatment to India, and this box has to be ticked in the landing card. All tourists travelling to India must have a valid passport and visa, and visas on arrival are not an option. India offers a variety of visas that are pertinent for medical tourism and must be obtained before travelling to (Chinai and Goswami 2007) India. a) A tourist visa is valid for six months from the date of issue. b) Medical (M) Visa, which is valid for up to one year or the length of treatment (whichever is less). In order to apply for an M visa a person must provide letters/documents explaining the details of treatment that are signed and stamped by the concerned hospital or doctor. c) Medical Escort Visa (MX) is provided to those who are accompanying a patient travelling to India for medical care on a medical visa. A close relative or a friend of the patient can apply for MX-Visa and be included in the application packet along with documents signed and stamped by the doctor or hospital. There should be a letter of declaration from the patient or immediate family member confirming the name of the escort/accompanying family member travelling with the patient 2010 (GOI 2003; Chinai and Goswami 2007; BWHO 2007).

Literature Review: Medical Tourism

Medical Tourism is one of the fastest growing niche healthcare industry worldwide (Huichinson 2005; Carrerra and Bridges 2006; Bookman and Bookman 2007; Herrick 2007; Ramírez de Arellano 2007; Healy 2009; Hopkins, Labonte, Runnels and Packer 2010; Lunt, Hardey and Mannion 2010; Medhekar and Haq 2010), where patients travel overseas to other developing or developed countries for the enhancement or restoration of the individual's health through medical intervention. There is paucity of academic literature and research in this area of study. People are becoming more aware of their health needs and healthy living. High health costs, long queues in developed countries, new technology and skills in destination countries, reduced transport costs, international accreditation, and internet marketing have all played a role in patients travelling to cheaper medical destinations overseas and combining it with leisurely or spiritual vacation for recovery such as India. Medical and health tourism as an academic and business concept is a new area of tourism that is probably an offshoot of special interest tourism and cultural tourism.

According to Connell (2006, p.1093), "the rise of medical tourism…it has become the central theme of tourism in an active rather than a passive sense. A new niche has emerged in the tourist industry….and it seems more useful to distinguish 'medical tourism' as one involving specific medical interventions. Medical tourism is a popular phenomenon where individuals travel long distances for surgery, dental and other medical treatments requiring intervention along with having a holiday". Medical tourism is a niche special interest tourism segment in the globalised health industry. Surgery can be added to existing six "Ss" of tourism, sun, sand, sea, and, sex, safari and spirituality (Connell 2006). Medical tourism, where patients travel overseas for operations, has grown rapidly in the past decade, especially for heart, cancer, liver transplant, hip-replacement, reproductive and cosmetic surgery.

Several Asian countries like Thailand, India, Malaysia and Singapore are dominant, and have sought to enter the market due to high-tech medical expertise and attractiveness of these countries (Connell 2006; Horowitz and Rosenweig 2007; Singh 2008; UNESCAP, 2008). This emergence of medical tourism can also be seen as a regional regeneration, rejuvenation and innovation for economic development and growth of India. Using medical tourism –as an export -led growth many socio-economic challenges and problems faced by India can be resolved, where there is decline in traditional industries (Hinings and Greenwood 1988; William and Shaw 1998). According to MTI (2009), Medical tourism can be broadly defined as provision of 'cost effective' private medical care in collaboration with the tourism industry for patients needing surgical and other forms of specialized treatment. This process is being facilitated by the corporate sector involved in medical care as well as the tourism industry - both private and public. Various on-line news articles use the two terms 'Medical or Health' tourism synonymously in India, which is a form of holiday - travel to another country, and mixes leisure, fun and relaxation together with wellness and covering a broad spectrum of medical services and healthcare procedures.

Further, the concept of healthcare tourism was explored by Goodrich and Goodrich (1991). Van-Sliepen (cited in Hall 1992, p.151) defines health tourism as, 'staying away from home, health as the most important motive and done in a leisurely setting.' Van-Sliepen has further identified health tourism market segments such as: sun and fun activities; healthy activities of sports tourism cycling golf, hiking; travel to a different climatic location for health reasons, travel to spa resorts for sauna, message etc and finally medical treatment (Smith and Puczko 2009). Health tourism which includes spa was examined by Williams, Andestad, Pollock and Dossa (1996); including Schofield (2004) who studied about health tourism in the soviet salt mines of Kyrgyztan, with the primary purpose of spa related relaxation benefit. Garcia-Altes (2005) used the term health tourism for all health related travel. Carrerra and Bridges (2006) also found that there was no existing academic empirical previous study on medical tourism in general. They conclude that there, "review of extant literature demonstrate the double-edged problem of a severely limited literature on both health and medical tourism and the lack of clarity regarding the two concepts" (p.452). Bookman and Bookman in (2007) provided a theoretical economic base to for the emerging global medical tourism industry in developing countries in their book called 'Medical Tourism in Developing Countries'. Heung, Kucukusta, and Song 2010), in their proposed integrated supply and demand model of medical tourism is yet to be empirically tested and validated for a particular destination, country or region within a country. Finally, a conceptual framework to understand the role of healthcare related internet sites in globalising medical tourism, which is the key driver in the growth of medical tourism. Finally, Lunt, Hardey and Mannion (2010), have provided a conceptual frame work to understand the role of internet advertising for globalising medical tourism. According to them, "A key driver in the medical tourism phenomenon is the platform provided by the internet for gaining access to healthcare information and advertising", (p.1). Patients search for medical tourism destination, cost comparison between countries for the type of surgeries, accommodation, read patient testimonials, accreditation and other things related to travel for medical tourism purposes.

Carrerra and Bridges (2006) have given the paucity of literature on this emerging area as well as ambiguity in the use of the two terms health tourism and medical tourism. (Carrerra and Bridges 2006, p.450) specified that under "health tourism, mobility applies to both patients and providers in recognition of the psychic benefits gained by medical professionals in participating in medical mission". A very clear definition of health-tourism is given by Carrerra and Bridges, (2006, p.449), Health Tourism is defined as "the organised travel outside one's local environment for the maintenance, enhancement or restoration of the individual wellbeing in mind and body".

A subset of this is medical tourism. Medical Tourism on the other hand is defined as "the organised travel outside one's natural healthcare jurisdiction for the enhancement or restoration of the individual's health through medical intervention" (p.449).

Thus the growth of medical tourism industry as macro-niche has also led to the emergence of new micro- niche specialised markets within the medical tourism industry, with different exotic-high tech destinations specializing in different types of treatments and procedures such as: invasive surgery (heart, cancer, hip and knee replacements), cosmetic surgery, reproductive treatment, dental treatment and diagnostic treatment.

Based on the extant literature review, the definitions and typology of health tourism a sub-set of which is health tourism is illustrated in Figure 7.1, which is developed for this study. Medical tourism can be defined as, when patients travel nationally or internationally for treatment involving state of the art technology and medical expertise that is invasive in nature. Whereas under health tourism, patient and the medical professionals, both travel nationally or internationally to gain emotional and psychic benefits for rejuvenation of body, mind, heart, soul and spirit, which is non-invasive in nature.

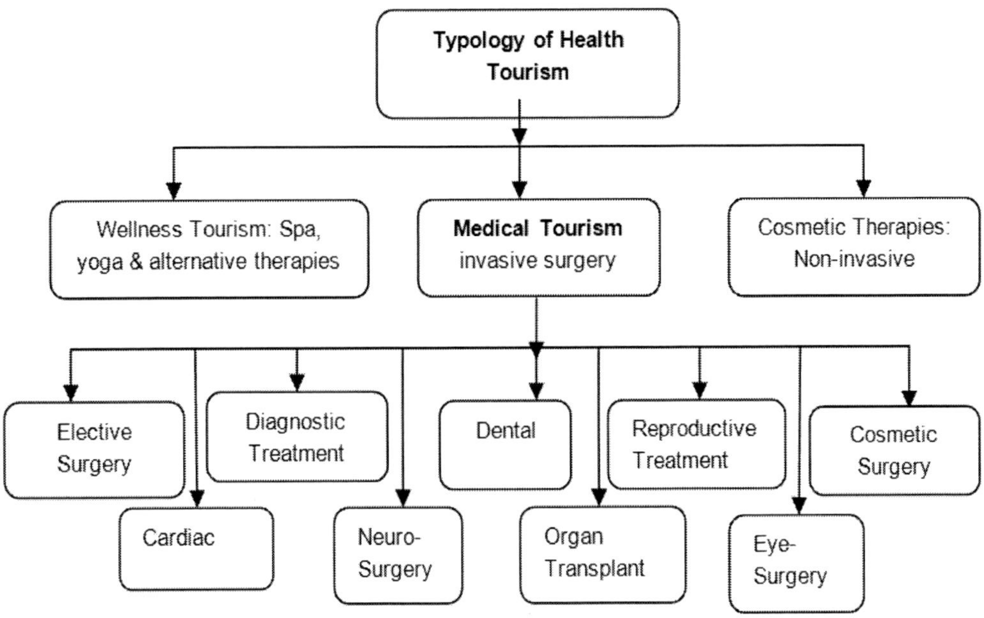

Figure 7.1. Typology of Health Tourism. Source: Developed for this study.

The rise of medical tourism emphasises the privatisation of health care, dependence on medical technology, uneven access to health resources and the accelerated globalisation of healthcare, health insurance and tourism by managing the growth of medical tourism by PPP at various public, private, regional and global level.

DEMAND FOR MEDICAL TOURISM

The world is in a healthcare crisis, given the ageing population, increasing cost of health care and long waiting period. Patients from developed countries are making choices and starting to travel to developing countries in search of health care which is of best quality and the most affordable medical care, combining with related tourism activity such eco-tourism and spiritual. More and more travel and tourism operators, hospitality industry, medical profession, universities offering medical qualifications, health insurance companies, employers, insurance claims payers, and health insurance agents are looking at health and medical tourism as the creative solution to the healthcare crisis. A recent report on Medical Tourism by World Tourism Organization (WTO 2009) stated that by 2017, over 16 million Americans could be travelling overseas for medical care. Table 7.1 compares the medical tourism cost for major medical treatments in six major countries. Patients make informed decisions based on cost, destination, reputation of the hospital and the whole medical tourism package.

Table 7.1. Medical Tourism Cost Comparison

Countries	Heart By pass	Hip Replacement	Knee Replacement	Hysterectomy
Australia	$33,340	$23,800	$20,089	$7,113
USA (US$)	$130,000	$43,000	$40,000	$20,000
India (US$)	$9,300	$7,100	$8,500	$6,000
Thailand (US$)	$11,000	$12,000	$10,000	$4,500
Singapore	$16,500	$9,200	$11,100	$6,000
Korea (US$)	$34,150	$11,400	$24,100	$12,700

Source: American Medical Association and Medi-bank Private (2008) (figures from 2006 / 2007 financial year.

According to a report by Deloitte (2007) in 2007, approximately 750,000 Americans travelled abroad for medical tourism which is expected to increase to 6 million by 2010, as more uninsured or underinsured Americans seek affordable healthcare alternatives in developing countries like India and Thailand. Extant literature review (Bookman and Bookman 2007; Carrera and Bridges 2006; Chanda 2007, CII and Mckinsey 2002; Deloitte 2007; Horowitz and Rosensweig; Hutchinson 2005) and numerous online medical tourism websites show that there are many reasons why people demand and travel to developing countries for medical treatment. The top ten reasons as clearly identified by Rakadiwa (2008) are: 1) Cost savings: nearly 50% or less in terms of destination and cost of the surgical procedure; 2) No waiting period: that is access to immediate medical care for patients who are tired of waiting in the queue for surgery as they cannot afford private medical care and insurance in their own country; 3) Excellent First World Quality of Care: many international providers choose to be accredited by organizations such as JCI, JCAHO and ISO or by their local accrediting bodies to demonstrate their commitment to quality; 4)World-Class Facilities: International providers offer luxurious accommodation, private spacious rooms, and access to hospitality services 24 hours and 7 days. The facilities are immaculate and there are no infections; 5) Access to Latest Technology: The technology and equipments used by the hospitals are the latest billion dollar robotic machines; 6) Surgeon Expertise: Most surgeons catering to international patients have either been educated or have received professional training at top medical schools in the US, UK or in other countries in Europe; 7) Personalized Service: Most medical tourists vouch for the genuine and excellent service that they receive from surgeons, nurses and other medical staff due to low staff to patient ratio making high level of personal care possible; 8) Longer Hospital Stay: One can have a longer hospital stay under the supervision of your surgeon, nurse, personal attendant and therapist; 9) Travel Convenience: The patient does not have to leave the comforts of home until the surgery is due and can access the Internet to find out about hospitals and surgeons, share your medical records online with them, book and plan your itinerary on the web; Finally 10) Tourism Opportunities: While the primary motivation for most customers is affordable surgery, the opportunity to visit and experience exotic cultures and destinations is an additional attraction if the surgeon allows.

MEDICAL TOURISM AND PUBLIC-PRIVATE PARTNERSHIPS (PPP)

The issue of public-private partnership (PPP) for medical tourism infrastructure development and management is critical given the growing worldwide demand for medical tourism to stimulate economic development in light of the increasingly high cost of provision of medical procedures needed by the people from other developed countries , long queues etc. It is important to have PPP between the government, and the private sector health industry as well as health and hospitality industry, including travel industry along with other specialised tourism segments, with can be packaged with medical tourism like health, spiritual, eco-tourism, cultural and historical and other natural retreats. A joint committee was formed by the Tourism Ministry and the Ministry of Health, thus combining tourism with world class medical expertise. The promotion of medical tourism became a government policy in 2003, when the Finance Minister in his budget speech, called for India to become a "global health destination". The 11th five year plan (2007-2012) also clearly emphasised the importance of the growth and development of medical tourism and support trade in health services by the private sector. Other initiatives taken by the government of India are: the introduction of Medical Visa (M-Visa), Medical Escort (MX) Visa, fiscal incentives for businesses involved in medical tourism as an export sector, holding international medical tourism trade fairs, 100% foreign direct investments in medical infrastructure facilities, and JCI accreditation for quality control (Ramanna, 2006; PC, 2007; GOI, 2008b; JCI, 2010).

This paper suggests that PPP enhances the competitive advantage of any industry and can be applied to medical and health tourism product through collaboration, and partnerships between the various stake holders: public (government and its departments and Government Business Enterprises), private hospitals and diagnostic clinics, local community, business organisations and international bodies such as (World Tourism Organisation (WTO), World Travel and Tourism Council (WTTC), Asia Pacific Economic Cooperation (APEC) , Asia Pacific Tourism Association (PATA) NGO and industry (APEC 2002; UNESCAP 2004; Bramwell & Lane, 2000). The Ministry of Public Affairs in British Columbia (1999) defines

PPP in the following terms: Public-Private Partnerships (PPPs) are arrangements between government and private sector entities for the purpose of providing investment in public infrastructure, community facilities and related services. Such partnerships are characterised by the sharing of investment, risk, responsibility and reward between the partners (cited in Schaeffer and Loveridge 2002, p.170). Public-Private Partnership defines cooperation between the public sector or government and the private sector. Partnerships are essential for planning, implementing and managing federal, state and local government tourism related infrastructure investment initiatives in regional economic development (Rosentraub and Joo 2009; Medhekar 2005; Selin and Chavez 1995; Augustyn and Knowles 2000).

It was a general belief that governments had failed in the provision of public goods and services and that the private sector would provide similar goods such as health of better quality at a lower cost and no waiting period. This led to privatisation initiatives around the world in major developed countries. But in many cases, privatisation without proper regulation and corporate governance resulted in private sector failure and the collapse of many large firms. Given these failures, PPP of a cooperative nature is often necessary for the provision of public goods and services including health and education to achieve economic goals and health related objectives. Sustainable PPP in medical and health tourism involves sharing of responsibilities, planning, accreditation, quality, product innovation, promotion, packaging, and marketing through ICT, undertaking financial risks, insurance, accountability and implementing various health and medical tourism packages (Montanheiro, Kuznik *et al.* 2003; OECD 1997; GOI 2008 a & b).

The key stakeholders in tourism management according to (Weaver and Lawton 2006, p.3) are the host communities and government, tourism industry, universities and educational institutions, NGO's, tourist and origin government. In case of medical tourism we can include other stake holders such as hospitals, medical practitioners, medical-health research institutes, pharmaceutical and medical equipment companies, insurance companies and finally hospitality, travel and tourism industry (Table 7.2).

According to the Confederation of Indian Industries study (CII and Mckinsey 2002), 150,000 medical tourist visited India in 2005, and by 2012, it will be growing annually at the rate of 30%. Federation of Indian Chambers of Commerce and industry (FICCI 2008) study also concluded that the health-care market along with health insurance is expected to grow by $69 billion by 2012. Therefore, public and private partnership (PPP) is very essential to support the growing worldwide global demand for health care and of medical tourism, as well as to guarantee quality of service, infrastructure needs, reasonable price, accreditation and handling of any legal disputes.

The key stakeholders in case of medical tourism are hospitals, medical practitioners, medical-health research institutes, pharmaceutical and medical equipment companies, insurance companies and finally hospitality, travel and tourism industry and the government at all levels. In India as elsewhere, what is required, is Public Private Partnerships (PPP) and private finance initiatives (PFI) in provision of latest world class medical infrastructure and qualified medical professionals for its long term sustainability, which underpin the economy's emerging and growing medical tourism sector, and maintain international competitiveness with Thailand, Malaysia, China along with other Asian economies as emerging markets for medical tourism.

Table 7.2. Stakeholders Framework in the Medical Tourism Industry

Supply Side	Category	Examples
	Resource, Infrastructure owners/Hospitals	Landholders, hospitals and medical centers, resort owners (public & private)
	Resource, infrastructure managers/Hospitals,	hospitals, medical and resort managers (public & private) Professional medical and non-medical staff, Accrediting bodies
	Providers of Medical Tourism related infrastructure	Construction, design, building, power, gas, water, waste treatment, road, hospitals infrastructure accommodation , pharmaceuticals
	Planning, development & control	Central, State and Local Government, ministry of foreign affairs &trade, private sector businesses, NGO, professional doctors, nurses hospital staff, regulatory body, accrediting bodies, e.g. JCI
	Deliverers of medical tourism related goods and services	Enterprise operators-hotels, airlines, hire cars, attractions, tour operators, travel agents, convention centers, restaurants, museums, and tourist events; e.g. trade & tourism fairs, religious events
	Tourism /Medical tourism Destination developers and marketers, advertisers	Tourism commissions, state and local government, Private sector Trade commission, tour operators, Airlines, hospitality-accommodation, local transportation,
	Employers & Employees	Medical specialist, Doctors, Nurses, Managers, hospitality, planning , communication, pharmaceutical, ICT, Finance, construction, insurance
Demand Side	Medical Tourist/ Domestic or International Patients	Domestic and international- health & medical tourists, medical package holidays, business travelers, backpackers visiting friends and relatives, conferences, cultural, spiritual eco-tourist.

Source: Developed for this study.

According to a study by Neelankhantan (2003) 150,000 foreign tourists visited India for medical tourism in 2002 and almost half of whom came from the Middle Eastern Arab countries and it was projected that by 2005 the number of medical will increase to 500,000. Health-related travel, initially promoted by individual medical facilities such as Bumrungrad International Hospital and Bangkok International Hospital, is now driven by government agencies, public–private partnerships, private hospital associations, airlines, hotel chains, investors and private equity funds, and medical brokerages (Turner 2007 and 2009). Moreover, it can be argued that public and private sector partnerships is essential between the various key stake holders (Table 6.2) for providing accredited, efficient, effective, equitable and good quality of health care for the long term sustainability of the medical tourism industry for the host country given the increasing competition to maximise their participation in the global economy.

Further partnership with Joint Commission International (JCI) which was launched in 1999 is the global arm of the US-based Joint Commission on the Accreditation of Healthcare Organizations (JCAHO) is essential for quality control and accreditation of the heath care facilities and hospitals. Since growing demand for medical tourism, JCI has accredited over 120 hospitals in Europe, the Americas, Asia, Africa, and the Middle East growing demand for a resource to effectively evaluate guarantee of quality and safety of the medical tourism product and service providers. Thus certification and accreditation by international accrediting bodies, guarantees and determines the quality of care and reputation of the medical institution and their medical professionals along with the demand for accredited hospitals by the patients. JCI's standards and qualifications are derived from an international consensus of achievable expectations for structures, outcomes, and processes for medical facilities. JCI works closely with partner hospitals- private and public, government agencies, health care providers, health insurance companies, patients, legal experts, medical consultants, and other major players in the larger health care industry to ensure the consistency and reliability of its accreditation process. Joint Commission International (JCI) approval is not the only accreditation available for medical tourism facilities; it is the most widely accepted medical tourism industry benchmark, besides Confederation of Indian industries (CII) accreditation for hospitals and India British standards Institute (BSI). Accreditation is very essential for patient information, rights of the patient & their families, quality of surgical service, protection from infection etc in the medical tourism industry to gain credible reputation due to increased demand for medical tourism (JCI 2010; IMTA 2010). The medical tourism industry in India took off with the approval obtained from Joint Commission International (JCI) and it is in process of giving accreditation to many hospitals across the major capital cities in the country since 2005 and to date have accredited 17 hospitals (FICCI 2008; JCI 2010; Sengupta and Nundy 2005).

DISCUSSION AND CONCLUSIONS

In recent years, India has seen a boom in its medical and technological sectors which in turn has created a burgeoning middle class and along with its advancing infrastructure has catapulted India out of its distinction as an underdeveloped nation and into the category of a developing nation along with Brazil, Russia, China and Argentina. Study on India's medical tourism sector in 2002, by Confederation of Indian Industry (CII), in collaboration with international management consultants, McKinsey and Company, outlined enormous opportunity and potential growth for this sector.

Indian Government in the 10th (2002-2007) and the 11th five year (2007-2012) plans clearly emphasised the importance of the growth and development of medical tourism to India (GOI 2003; PC 2007; GOI, 2008 a & b). It has taken measures not only to lower restriction on foreign direct investment but also to improve infrastructure facilities such as hospitality, accommodation, safety and security, roads and airport to smooth the arrival and departure of medical tourists from aboard (GOI 2008; BMHRC, 2009; Chinai and Goswami 2007; Chanda 2007). The numbers of foreign patients as medical tourists visiting India are growing at the rate of 30 per cent a year and it is projected by the Federation of Indian Chambers of Commerce and Industry (ICCI) that the health-care market in India will be worth around US$ 2.2 billion year, 5.2% of gross domestic product (GDP) by 2010, to between US$ 50 billion and US$ 69 billion, or 6.2% and 8.5% of GDP by 2020 (Chinai and Goswami 2007; CII and McKinse 2002; FICCI, 2008; Ernst and Young 2006).

India is a popular destination for medical tourists because its medical infrastructure and technology is on par with the United States, and many doctors are trained in the U.S. and/or England. JCI has accredited 13 hospitals in India which are scattered amongst the major state capital cities in India (Kolkata, Chennai, Punjab, Bangalore, Mumbai, New Delhi, Chandigarh, Hyderabad and Mohali) and 123 medical facilities and organisations across Asia, Europe, Middle East, the Caribbean and South America in late 2005-06 (JCI 2010; Forgione and Smith 2007).The leading players in the medical tourism niche sectors are the private hospitals such as Fortis, Apollo - partnered with Johns Hopkins medicine International and Wockhardt Group which is affiliated with Harvard medical International, who manage a total of 26 hospitals across the subcontinent. These hospitals are actively seeking foreign partners to promote medical tourism and collaborate and cooperate with tour operators like Thomas Cook and others in the hospitality resort business (JCI 2010; Ernst and Young 2006; FICCI 2008; Sengupta and Nundy 2005).

Among those with JCI accreditation, Apollo has four JCI accredited hospitals. Apollo is the largest healthcare group in Asia and they frequently collaborate with Johns Hopkins Medicine International. Official language being Hindi and English along with Urdu which is also widely spoken and understood, it is easy to target patients from all over the developed western countries as well as from South Asia, Africa and Middle Eastern Arab countries (FICCI 2008). Countries such as India have recognised that the Western world is faced with ageing population, long queues; high cost and thus are not able to provide timely and affordable medical care to its citizens. In, Australia, United Kingdom, Canada and United States it is not uncommon to wait for more than 6 months to one year, to be seen by a specialist after a referral is made. Additional time passes waiting for schedules tests and the test results. If there is a need for a surgical procedure, it could be several more weeks before surgery is scheduled. Non emergency medical attention may be extended for up to two years.

The Medical Tourism Council (MTC) is targeting several developed countries markets where millions are uninsured and cannot afford medical procedures in their own country. The patient can undergo medical treatment at a much more affordable price in India at cost which is 1/3 less than other Asian countries that are competing as the destination of choice for global medical tourists. The Medical Tourism Council is also doing heavy marketing campaigns to Western insurance companies. An increasing number of insurance companies are not only agreeing to overseas medical services, but are advocating that the patient obtain the less expensive services as a medical tourist. They are recognizing that outsourcing medical services to India will save tens of thousands of dollars in payouts, even if they need to pay airfare in addition to the medical bills (JCI 2010; GOI 2008b).

The Indian Finance Minister has also recognised that the opportunity exists to rebuild the infrastructure of the country to attract medical tourists, and generate foreign exchange revenue by medical tourism (GOI 2003; GOI 2008a). While the Medical Tourism Council of India is busy marketing, the government of India is working to ensure that first world medical facilities are built and that various international accreditations are secured for medical tourism industry. The revenue from medical tourism can then be used to provide a better standard of living, medical services to the citizens of India who are living in poverty and will provide over 40 million jobs to Indians (Deloitte 2007).

Due to increase in demand Indian universities are producing between 20,000 and 30,000 new doctors and nurses each year, designed to staff the state of the art hospitals providing medical tourism across the country. Many of the doctors who left India to study and work in developed countries are now returning to India to practice as top surgeons and specialists, to set up specialty clinics and hospitals on par with the best in the world. The medical tourists destined for India not only have a choice of destinations to choose from for medical treatment and recovery, but also visit exotic destinations for a relaxing holiday. Agra offers the medical tourist one the Taj Mahal one of the Seven Wonders of the World, Rajasthan borders the Thar Desert and has a history of romance and heroism. Goa offers golden sand beaches and palm trees, and Kerela the Venice of India with a networking of forty four rivers and the temples and beaches of south India Kerala in India, is a popular destination for tourism in general, but also for medical and health tourism, such as yoga, ayurvedic message, relaxation, cleansing, rejuvenation of body, mind, soul and spirit amidst the beautiful natural surroundings of mountains, forest, lakes and beaches.

The partnership between the government of India and Medical Tourism Council is not only essential to make India the number one destination choice in the global medical community but also for effective and efficient development, implementation and management of medical tourism industry policy. The low costs and high quality services, no queues, educated and experienced doctors, cutting edge technology, state of the art resort type hospitals and the beautiful vacation spots are all important factors to move India to the forefront of the global healthcare and medical tourism industry in the 21st century. This research will help in developing an understanding of the PPP between various stakeholders in context of an emerging global phenomenon of medical tourism industry and will have relevance for policy makers and healthcare managers as well as test the stakeholder framework empirically to further the knowledge.

REFERENCES

Adams, M. (2006), 'Rising popularity of medical tourism reveals deterioration of U.S. healthcare system'. http://www.newstarget.com/007097.html, (cited on 3-3-2010).

AMA. (2008), 'American Medical Association and Medi-bank Private, November'. 78, (10), pp. 38-43.

AMTA. (2010), 'The Asian Medical Tourism Association', http://www.health-tourism.com /medical-tourism/conference/

APEC (2002), 'Public and private partnerships for sustainable tourism': Delivering a sustainability strategy for tourism destinations; CRC for sustainable tourism, Asia Pacific Economic Cooperation (APEC) tourism working group: Terry De Lacy, Marion Battig, Stewart Moore, Steve Noakes 2002-July, Singapore.

ASEAN (2004), 'Plan of Action to Implement the ASEAN-India Partnership for Peace, Progress and Shared Prosperity', *ASEAN.* 2005: pp. 1-9.

Augustyn, M. M. and Knowles, T. (2000), 'Performance of tourism partnerships: a focus on York'. *Tourism Management,* 21, (4), pp. 341-351.

BMHRC (2009), 'Medical Tourism India: B.M. Birla Heart Research Centre', (BMHRC) http://www.medical-tourism-india.com/bmbirla.htm (viewed on Sunday 6-9-2009).

Bookman, M. Z. and Bookman, K. R. (2007), Medical Tourism in Developing Countries, New York, *Palgrave Macmillan,* July 2007.

Bramwell, B. and Lane, B. (2000), Tourism Collaboration and Partnerships – Politics, Practice and Sustainability, *Channel View Publications',* Sydney.

BWHO (2007), 'Bulletin of World Health Organisation, Medical Visas Mark growth of Indian medical tourism', http://www.scielosp.org/scielo.php?pid=S0042-96862007 000 300004&script=sci_arttext; 85, (3), (Cited on 7-3-2010).

Carrera, P. M. and Bridges, J.F.P. (2006), 'Globalisation and healthcare: understanding health and medical tourism', Expert Review of Pharmacoeconomics & outcomes research, Future Drugs, 7, (1), pp. 447-445.

Chanda, R. (2007), 'Foreign Investments in hospitals in India',: Status and Implications, India: Ministry of Health and Family Welfare and WHO Country office.

Chinai, R. and Goswami, R. (2007), 'Medical visas mark growth of Indian medical tourism', *Bulletin World Health Organisation,* 85(3), pp. 164-165.

CII and Mckinsey , (2002), 'Healthcare in India': The road ahead. New Delhi: *Confederation of Indian Industries & Mckinsey & Company.*

Connell, J. (2006), 'Medical tourism: Sea, sun, sand and … surgery', *Tourism Management,* 26, (6), pp.1093-1100, (cited on 4-10-09).

Deloitte (2007), 'Medical tourism: consumers in search of value', *Deloitte report.*

Ernst and Young (2006), 'Health Quotient: making ideas meet opportunities, Health Sciences India', New Delhi: *Ernst & Young, Private Ltd.*

ESCAP. (2007), 'Medical travel in Asia and the Pacific': Challenges and Opportunities Bangkok: United Nations Economic and Social Commission for Asia and the pacific.

FICCI (2008), 'Fostering Quality Healthcare for All', *Federation of Indian Chamber of Commerce and Ernst and Young,* New Delhi.

Financial Times (2-7-2003), 'Medical Tourism in India', http://www.medical-tourism-india.com/ (viewed on Monday 7-9-2009).

Forgione, D.A. and Smith, P.C. (2007), 'Medical Tourism and its impact on the US health care system'. Journal of Health Care Finance, 34, (1), pp.27-35.

Garcia-Altes (2005), 'The development of health tourism services'. *Annals of Tourism Research,* 32, (1), pp. 262–266.

GOI (2003), 'Government of India' (GOI) 2003 Health Sector in India, *Budget Papers.*

GOI (2008a), 'Eleventh Five Year plan (2007-12)', 1: Social Sector, New Delhi Planning Commission , Government of India, New Delhi, *Oxford University Press.*

GOI (2008b), 'Government of India (GOI) Public and Private Partnerships in India' Ministry of Finance, http://www.pppinindia.com/state-policy-andhra-pradesh.asp (cited on 14-9-09).

Goodrich, J. and Goodrich, G. (1993), 'Health-Care Tourism. In Management Tourism', S. Medlik, (editors), pp.108-114.Oxford: *Butterworth-Heinemann.*

Hall, C. M. (1992), 'Adventure, Sport and Health Tourism, in Special Interest Tourism', book edited by B. Weilwe and C. M. Hall, *Bellhaven Press,* London, pp 141-58.

Healy, C. (2009), "Surgical tourism and the globalisation of healthcare". *Irish Journal of Medical Science,* 178, (2), pp.125-127.

Herrick, D.M. (2007), 'Medical tourism: Global competition in healthcare', (NCPA Policy Rep. No. 304), http://www.ncpa.org/pub/st/st304, (cited on 3-3-2010).

Heung, V. Kucukusta, D. and Song, H. (2010), 'A Conceptual Model of Medical Tourism: Implications for Future Research'. *Journal of Travel & Tourism Marketing*, 27 (3), pp. 236-251.

Hinings, C.R. and Greenwood, R. (1998), 'The Dynamics of Strategic Change', Oxford: *Basil Blackwell.*

Hopkins, L. Labonte, R. Runnels, V. and Packer, C. (2010), 'Medical tourism today: What is the sate of existing knowledge'? *Journal of Public Health Policy,* 31, (2), pp.185-198.

Horowitz, M. D. and Rosensweig, J. A. (2007), 'Medical tourism-health care in the global economy' *The Physician Executive,* 33 (6), pp.24-31.

Horowitz, M. D. Rosensweig, J. A. Jones, C.A. (2007), 'Medical Tourism: Globalization of the Healthcare Marketplace'. *Medscape General Medicine,* 9 (4), pp. 33.

Hutchinson, B. (2005), 'Medical tourism growing worldwide', UDaily, http//:wwwudel.edu/PR/UDaily /2005/mar/tourism072505.html.

IMT (2009), 'India ranks 2nd in med tourism', http://www.medicaltourism.org/consortium.jsp?sect=consortiumdetail&id=6, (cited on 15-8-2009).

IMTA (2010), 'Indian Medical Travel Association', Towards Making India the Global Healthcare Destination, http://indianmedicaltravelassociation.com/Newsroom-Details.php?newsroom=56 (cited on 15-8-2009).

JCI (2010), 'International Society for quality in health Care', http://www.jointcommission international.org/ (cited on 3-3-2010).

Lunt, N. Hardey, M. and Mannion, R. (2010), 'Nip, Tuck and Click: Medical Tourism and the Emergence of Web-Based Health Information'. *The Open Medical Informatics Journal,* 4, pp.1-11.

Medhekar, A. (2005), 'Public private partnership for infrastructure development in India rail/road, Public and private sector partnership', editor, Montanheiro, England, *Sheffield Hallam University Press.*

Medhekar, A. and Haq, F. (2010), 'Marketing Indian Medical Tourism to Muslim Patients in an Islamic way, in the proceedings of the First International Conference on Islamic Marketing and Branding: Exploring Issues and Challenges', 29th-30th November 2010, Kuala Lumpur, University of Malaysia, pp.1-15.

Medical Tourism India (MTI), (2009), what is medical tourism? http://www.medical-tourism-india.com/what_is_medical_tourism.htm (viewed on Sunday 6-9-2009).

Medindia, (2006), 'Apollo to Open Super-specialty Hospital in Oman by Year-end', http://www.medindia.net/news/view_news_main.asp?x=11060, (cited on 3-3-2010).

Montanheiro, L., F. Kuznik, and Ochojski, A. (2003), 'Public and Private Sector Partnerships': Sustainable Success eds. England, *Sheffield Hallam University Press,* UK.

Nagaraj, N.M. (2009), 'India emerges 2nd in medical tourism race', in Times of India (March 27-2009, http://timesofindia.indiatimes.com/india/India-emerges-2nd-in-medical-tourism-race/articleshow/4321310.cms, (cited on 15-8-2009).

Nagpal, P. (2009), 'IVF Treatment according to Islamic Law in India, We Care Health Services-India', http://www.articlesbase.com/medical-tourism-articles/ivf-treatment-according-to-islamic-law-in-india-affordable-cost-1093191.html (cited 6-6-2010).

Neelankantan, S. (2003), 'India's global ambitions, *Far Eastern Economic Review'* 6 November 03.

OECD (1997), 'Conference on Partnerships in Tourism',: A Tool for Job Creation, http://www.oecd.org/document/49/0,3343,en_2825_503546_1932849_1_1_1_1,00.html (cited on 21-9-09).

Planning Commission (PC) (2007), 'Eleventh Five (5) Year Plan 2007-2012, Planning Commission India' http://planningcommission.nic.in/plans/planrel/fiveyr/welcome.html (cited on 7-7-2009).

Rakadiwa, (2008), 'Travel and Tourists', http://www.lartp.org/tourism-cares/top-10-reasons-why-medical-tourism-is-popular, (cited on 4-4-2010).

Ramanna, M. (2006), 'Medical tourism and the demand for hospital accreditation overseas', http://www.law.uh.edu/healthlaw/perspectives/2006%5C(MR)MedicalTourismFinal.pdf.

Ramesh, R. (2005), 'This UK patient avoided the NHS list and flew to India for a heart bypass. Is health tourism the future'? In The Guardian (1-2-2005) http://www.guardian.co.uk/uk/2005/feb/01/health.india (viewed on Monday 7-9-2009).

Ramírez de Arellano, A. B. (2007), 'Patients Without Borders: The Emergence of Medical Tourism'. *International Journal of Health Services,* 37(1), pp. 193-198.

RNCOS. (2010), 'Tourism Industry: Booming Medical Tourism in India New Delhi: Industry Research Solutions', *RNCOS E-Services* Pvt Ltd.

Rosentraub, M. S. and Joo, M. (2009), 'Tourism and economic development: Which investments produce gains for regions'. *Tourism Management,* 30, (5), pp. 759-770.

Schaeffer, P. V. and S. Loveridge (2002), 'Towards an understanding of types of public-private cooperation'. *Public Performance and Management Review,* 26, (2), pp.169-189.

Schofield, P. (2004), 'Health tourism in Kyrgyz Republic: The soviet salt mine experience; in New horizons in tourism, strange experiences and stranger practices'. T.V. Singh, editor, *Wallingford CABI Publishing:* 135–145.

Selin, S. and Chavez, D. (1995), 'Developing an evolutionary tourism partnership model'. *Annals of Tourism Research,* 22, (4), pp. 844-856.

Sengupta, A. and Nundy, S. (2005), 'The Private Health Sector in India'. *British Medical Journal,* 33, (1), pp. 1157-1158.

Singh, P.K. (2008), 'Medical tourism, New Delhi', India: *Kanishka Publishers.*

Smith, M. K. and Puczko, L. (2009), 'Health and Wellness Tourism, Butterworth', MA, USA: *Elsevier.*

TravelBiz, (2009), 'India ranks second in medical tourism'; Deloitte research, March 30-2009, http://www.travelbizmonitor.com/india-ranks-second-in-medical-tourism-deloitte-research, (cited on 15-8-2009).

Turner, L. (2007), 'First world health care at third world prices'. Globalisation, bioethics and medical tourism. *Biosocieties,* 2, pp.303-325.

Turner, L. (2009), 'Commercial Organ Transplantation in the Philippines'. Cambridge Quarterly of Healthcare Ethics 18, (2), p. 192.

UNESCAP (2008), 'Medical travel in Asia and the Pacific': Challenges and opportunities. Bangkok, Thailand: United Nations Economic and Social Commission for Asia and the Pacific http://www.unescap.org/ESID/hds/lastestadd/MedicalTourismReport09.pdf (cited on 3-3-2010).

UNESCAP, (2004), 'Major Issues in Transport, Tourism and Infrastructure Development': *Enhancing the Role of Tourism in Social and Economic Development and Major Initiatives of ESCAP:* 1-11.

Weaver, D. and Lawton, L. (2006), 'Tourism Management: Brisbane, Milton Queensland', *John Wiley and Sons*, Australia, Ltd.

Williams, A. and Shaw, G. (1998), 'Tourism and Economic Development: European Experience' (3rd Edition), Chichester: *Wiley.*

Williams, P. Andestad, G. Pollock, A. and Dossa, K. (1996), 'Health Spa Travel Markets: Mexican Long-Haul pleasure Travellers', *Journal of Vacation Marketing,* 3, (1), pp.11-31.

World Tourism Organization, (WTO 2009), Facts and Figures, The UNWTO World Tourism Barometer, http://unwto.org/facts/eng/barometer.htm (cited on 3-8-09).

In: Development Management in the Twenty-First Century ISBN: 978-1-62100-699-2
Editors: Kartik Roy and Sandip Kar

Chapter 8

TOURISM AS AN ENGINE OF SUSTAINABLE DEVELOPMENT IN ORISSA

Prakash Chandra Misra [*] ***and Nirmal Chandra Sahu*** [†]
Berhampur University, Orissa, India

INTRODUCTION

Tourism today has acquired wide social and economic dimension. The world travel and council (WTTC) has recognized it as one of the fastest growing industry. In fact, since the turn of the new millennium, tourism has emerged as the most promising and prosperous industry in the world because compared to all other industries it has got huge impact on economy, environment and society. In recent time tourism has been recognized as a sunrise industry because of its immense potentialities for employment generation and poverty alleviation. It has high employment multiplier effects with provisions for protection and preservation of natural and cultural resources especially in rural and remote areas. The present paper seeks to highlight the potentiality of tourism growth in Odisha with special thrust on Chilika Lake for sustainable development of tourism economy in the State. The published (secondary) data from the Statistical Bulletin of various years of the Department of Tourism and Culture of Government of Odisha have been extensively used for the purpose. The prime objective of undertaking such a study is to provide a better and greater knowledge of Chilika Lake and its natural and ecological attraction for the national and international tourist. The paper has been organized under six different sections. The first section is devoted for introducing the study by highlighting the objective, significance, methodology and the study plan. The second section provides a picture of the trend of tourism over last several years in the world and India. The third section depicts the development of tourism in odisha the trend of tourist arrival and their expenditures as well as the potentialities of the state in the tourism sector. Then section four describes the need for sustainable tourism in Odisha. Section five gives a clear picture of the prospects of eco-tourism in Odisha and the potentialities of Chilika

---

[*] Professor in Commerce; email: prakash755@rediffmail.com.
[†] Professor in Economics; email: nirmalcsahu@yahoo.com.

in particular. Section six being the last section it obviously concludes the various observations of our study in a nutshell and offers a few suggestions for development of community based participatory approach for eco-tourism in Chilka in particular and development of tourism in Odisha, in general.

TRENDS IN TOURISM

The justification for the success of tourism industry assumes significance for the following reasons.

- Tourism acts as a cementing force for National Integration and International understanding;
- Tourism induces for preservation of traditional life style, cultural expression and heritage of various habitations;
- Tourism helps to built a healthy national economy by creation of employment opportunities and earning of foreign exchange;
- It is the only smokeless industry which protects environment and promotes its conservation;
- It provides synergy for cultural assimilation;
- It broadens the knowledge of the people in relation to the happenings in different parts of the globe;
- It provides support to the local communities in the form of employment generation and poverty reduction.

In the record 'GLOBAL PARADEX' John Naisbrtt in association with WTTC highlights that tourism contributes 10.2% to world GDP, employee 10.6 percent of global work fore, largest industry involving 3.2 billion people accumulates 10.7 percent of global capital investment, accounts for 10.9 percent of consumer spending and generates 655 billion US dollar annually as tax revenue. The world tourism organization's (WTO'S) statistics indicated that the tourism industry's will continue to grow from strength to strength and will reach from 710 million at international tourist movement in the year 2000 to 1.5 billion by the year 2020.

The Indian Tourism industry is booming, with Indian State Governments promoting tourism and alluring foreign visitors to India. Many State Governments have devised new policies and offering attractive packages throughout the year. It is a fact that India has the potentiality to become the number one tourist destination in the world with the demand growing at 10.1 per cent per annum (WTTC – Prediction). At present the government spending on tourism is 153rd in the world with a share of only 0.9 per cent of its budget. On the other hand our neighbour China spends 3.8 per cent of its budget on tourism and ranks fifth in receiving the largest tourist arrivals (31.2 million) after France, US, Spain and Italy. India gets only 2.6 million tourists per annum on an average over the last 10 years.

The WTTC's Tourism satellite Accounting Research (TSAR) which measured tourism's share in the national economy in 160 countries over the world in the last 10 years, has found a global shift away from Europe to Asia and the Far East. According to WTTC study, while out bound tourism had grown over last ten years from 76 million to 179 (with the boom in the economy) the inbound traffic has remained almost static at 2.6 million arrivals.

Major attractions in India are the world's highest mountains, long coastline with excellent beaches, tropical forests and wild life, desert safari, lagoon back waters, ancient monuments, forts and palaces, adventure tourism and the Tajmahal. The tropical forests in Uttaranchal, Madhyapradesh, Karnataka, Odisha, Kerala and Rajasthan can be developed into major tourist attraction. Being located virtually midway between Europe and Far East, Europe and South-East Asia / Australia, India has strategic advantage. Since all international flights have to (out of necessity) fly over India the country can develop one or two international airports with the best of transit facilities, inducing passengers to have break-Journey and thery by facilitating visitors export.

Indian Scenario

India's performance in Tourism sector has been impressive. During the last ten years that is from 2000 to 2009 the country witnessed an increase in Foreign Tourist Arrivals (FTAs). Form 2.649 million to 5.108 million. Due to global slow down, terrorist activities, H1N1 influenza pandemic etc., the growth rate has fallen down by 3.3 percent in 2009 over the previous year. However the year 2009 has witnessed a contraction in global Tourism by 4.3 percent. Foreign Exchange earnings (FEEs) from Tourism increased from Rs. 15626 cores to Rs. 54960 cores over the same period. The growth rate in earnings in 2009 vis-a–vis 2008 was nearly 8.3 percent. (See Table 8.1)

Table 8.1. Foreign Tourist Arrival and Foreign Exchange Earnings during the Years 2000-2009

Year	Foreign Tourist Arrival (in No.)	% Change over Previous Year	Foreign Exchange Earnings (Rs. in Crore)	% Change Over Previous Year	Foreign Exchange Earnings (in Million US $)	% Change over Previous Year
2000	2649378	6.7	15626	20.6	3460	15.0
2001	2537282	-4.2	15083	-3.5	3198	(-) 7.6
2002	2384364	-6.0	15064	-0.1	3103	(-)3.0
2003	2726214	14.3	20729	37.6	4463	43.8
2004	3457477	26.8	27944	34.8	6170	38.2
2005	3918610	13.3	33123	18.5	7493	21.4
2006	4447167	13.5	39025	17.8	8634	15.2
2007	5081504	14.3	44360	13.7	10729	24.3
2008	5282603	4.0	50730	14.4	11747	9.5
2009	5108579	-3.3	54960	8.3	11394	(-)3.0

Source: Compiled from Statistics, Surveys and Studies Annual Report 2009-10, Govt of India.

A comparative study of the tourist arrival to India with that of world over a period of five years (from 2004 to 2008) reveals the facts that there is a consistent increase in arrivals, while the increase in case of world(over the same period) is form 761.4 millions to 924.0 million. Where as the same for India is form 3.46 million to 5.37 million respectively. The record of growth in world Tourist arrival over the period (2004 to 2008) is found to be 21.35 percent while the same for India stands at 55.20 percent. Again from the point of the share of India in world Tourist arrival it is noticed that the share has increased from 0.45 percent 0.58 percent over the period 2004-2008 (See Table 8.2).

Table 8.2. Tourism Scenario - World-India-Odisha

YEAR	WORLD (in millions)	INDIA (in million.)	ORISSA (in millions)	Share (India to World)	Share (Odisha to India)
2004	761.4	3.46	0.03	0.45	0.87
2005	803.0	3.92	0.03	0.49	0.77
2006	847.0	4.45	0.04	0.48	0.90
2007	903.0	5.08	0.04	0.56	0.79
2008	924.0	5.37	0.04	0.58	0.74

Source: Statistical bulletin 2008, Department of Tourism and Culture Govt of Odisha.

TOURISM IN ODISHA - AN INVESTIGATION

Geographically Orissa is situated in the Eastern region of the Indian subcontinent extending from 17.49′ N 22.34′ N latitude and from 81.29′ E to 87.29′ E longitude. It is bound by the Bay of Bengal in the East. It has got a total area of 1,55,507 sq. kms. The Tourism department of the Government Odisha has identified 315 centres of various district of Odisha as the tourist centers (as on 31st Aug., 2009). The tourist arrival to India and Odisha over a period of ten years starting from 1999 to 2008 has been depicted in the Table 8.3. In the year 1999 only 33101 tourists have visited Odisha which was only 1.40 per cent of the total tourist visit to India.

However in the year 2008, 43966 tourists have visited Odisha constituting only 0.82 Percent of the tourists visited to India. The tourist arrival in case of our country has recorded 227.54 percent of growth while for Odisha the growth is only 132.82 percent over the last ten years (1999 to 2008).

An analysis of the composition of total tourists visited to Odisha on the basis of domestic and foreign tourists, it is observed that nearly 99 percent are the domestic tourists and the rest only one percent are from foreign countries. The trend pertaining to this composition over the last seventeen years i.e. from 1992 to 2008 is presented in the table-3.

It is again observed that the state of West Bengal continued to be the major tourist generating State of Odisha contributing 875154 tourist (13.76% out of the domestic tourists of 6358445 during 2008 followed by Andhra Pradesh (3.47%), Madhya Pradesh (2.5%) and Chatishgarh (2.3%) respectively.[1]

Further on a country wise break-up foreign tourists visiting Odisha it is found that UK and France are the major tourist generating markets for Odisha during the year 2008 with 6373 and 4676 tourists respectively. Out of the total foreign tourists arrival of 43966, USA 4333, Germany 3787, Itally 3124, Japan 2358 have followed UK and France. This trend has been maintained over the last several years[2].

1 State wise break-up of domestic tourism visiting the State, statistical bulletin – 2008, Dept. of Tourism and Culture, Govt. of Odisha Pg. 9

2 Country wise break up of Foreign Tourist visiting the State Ibid pg.7

Table 8.3. Domestic and foreign tourists visited Odisha from 1992-2009

Year	Domestic	% Of Change	Foreign	% Of Change	Total	% Of Change	Share Of domestic Tourists as compared to the total Tourists (%)	Share of Foreign Tourists as compared to the total Tourists (%)
1992	24,71,346	--	26639.00	--	24,97,985	--	98.93	1.07
1993	25,38,875	2.70	24856.00	-6.70	25,63,731	2.60	99.03	0.97
1994	25,94,992	2.20	26024.00	4.70	26,21,016	2.20	99.01	0.99
1995	26,97,365	3.90	28201.00	8.40	27,25,566	4.00	98.94	1.06
1996	27,73,245	2.80	34303.00	21.60	28,07,548	3.00	98.77	1.23
1997	28,28,131	2.00	35081.00	2.30	28,63,212	2.00	98.77	1.23
1998	28,61,788	1.20	33.10	-5.60	28,94,889	1.10	98.86	1.14
1999	26,91,840	-5.90	25758.00	-22.20	27,17,598	-6.10	99.06	0.94
2000	28,88,392	7.30	23723.00	-7.90	29,12,115	7.20	99.18	0.82
2001	31,00,316	7.30	22854.00	-3.70	31,23,170	7.20	99.26	0.74
2002	34,13,352	10.10	23034.00	0.80	34,36,386	10.30	99.33	0.67
2003	37,01,250	8.40	25020.00	8.60	37,26,270	8.40	99.32	0.67
2004	41,25,536	11.50	28817.00	15.20	41,54,353	11.50	99.30	0.69
2005	46,32,976	12.30	33310.00	15.60	46,66,286	12.30	99.28	0.71
2006	52,39,896	13.10	39141.00	17.50	52,79,037	13.10	99.25	0.74
2007	59,44,890	13.40	41880.00	7.00	59,86,770	13.40	99.30	0.69
2008	63,58,445	6.90	43966.00	5.00	64,02,411	6.90	99.31	0.68

Source: Compiled from Statistical bulletin 2002 & 2008 Department of Tourism and Culture Govt of Odisha.

Table 8.4. Domestic Tourist visited to Odisha (Calendar Year-wise)

Year	Tourists of Odisha		Tourists of Other State/UTs in India		Total
	In No.	In % to Total	In No.	In % to Total	
1999	13,67,311	50.79	13,24,529	49.21	26,91,840
2000	14,13,956	48.95	14,74,436	51.05	28,88,392
2001	15,37,855	49.60	15,62,461	50.40	31,00,316
2002	17,03,002	49.89	17,10,350	50.11	34,13,352
2003	18,76,571	50.70	18,24,679	49.30	37,01,250
2004	21,56,986	52.28	19,68,550	47.72	41,25,536
2005	22,93,865	49.51	23,39,111	50.49	46,32,976
2006	26,99,654	51.52	25,40,242	48.48	52,39,896
2007	32,52,380	54.70	26,92,510	45.30	59,44,890
2008	38,46,512	60.49	25,11,933	39.51	63,58,445

Source: Compiled from Statistical Bulletin 2002 & 2008, Department of Tourism and Culture, Govt. of Odish.

On further analysis it is noticed that the domestic tourists those who have visited the tourist places of Odisha over the last 10 years (1999 to 2008) nearly 51.80 per cent (on an average) are from within the various parts of the state itself and the rest 48.16 per cent are from different states of our country. Table 8.4 provides the details of the composition of tourists of Odisha and tourists from the other States. However, it can be observed that in the last five years (2004-2008) there is a consistent increase in the flow of tourists within the state and the State tourists arrival has recorded a significant increase in the year 2008 by reaching the all time high of 60.49 per cent.

In flow of foreign exchange to our country in the rupee term has increased from 215625 crores in the year 2000 to 54960 crore in 2009 with an increase of nearly351.72 percent. Except two years i.e. 2001 and 2002 in all other years there is an increase of this flow over the previous years. In the term of Dollors also the same trend is observed with a deviation in the year 2009 where it has recorded a decline of 3.0 per cent (-3.0) over the previous year 2008 (Refer: Table 8.1).

An attempt is made to highlight the inflow of money to the State exchequer through tourist expenditure in Odisha. However it is very difficult to estimate the earnings of the State Government from tourism, because of the vastness and variety of sources. In spite of that an attempt is made to assess the same through a sample survey method. A tourist profile survey was conducted by the Department of Tourism, Government of Odisha during the year 1998-99. As per the findings of the survey an average duration of stay of a foreign tourist in the state was 10.6 days while for the domestic tourist it was 5.2 days. Similarly the average per capita daily expenditure by a foreign tourist was found out to be Rs.1119.00 where as it was Rs.644.00 in case of domestic tourist. While calculating the expenditure of the foreign tourist the expenditure on reaching and leaving the state were excluded.

In the year 2004-05 another survey of similar type was conducted by the same Odisha tourism department to find the changing profile of tourists. It was found that the average duration of stay is 12.7 days in case of foreign tourist and 3.9 days in case of domestic tourists similarly the average per capita daily expenditure in case of foreign tourist has gone up to Rs.1944 and Rs. 1275 for domestic tourist[1]. However, the details of the inflow of

[1] Statistical Bulletin, 2002 Pg. 9

money through tourist expenditure in Odisha since 1998 to the year 2008 can well be noticed from the Table 8.3. It is quite evident from the Table 8.3 that the expenditure of the domestic tourist has significantly contributed to the State exchequer by remaining almost above 96 Percent throughout and with an average of 96.85 per cent, leaving the balance of only 3.15 per cent to the foreign tourists. The same survey of 2004-05 reveals the fact that (i) the main purpose of visit of the foreign tourists is holidaying (71%) while for domestic tourist it is for holidaying, business and official (79%).

(i) The foreign tourists got the inspiration and motivation to visit Odisha by their friends and relatives (29%) and 23% out of their previous experience. On the other hand 57 per cent of the domestic tourists have gat motivation from their previous experiences.
(ii) out of the total tourists 22% of the foreign tourists and 72% of the domestic tourists are the repeat visitors i.e. before hand, they have already visited the State
(iii) out of their total expenses the foreign tourists spend 35% for accommodation , 18% for food and beverage,15% on shopping and 32% on Transport & sightseeing . While for the domestic tourists the expenses in respective heads are 29%, 19%, 22% and 30%[2].

It is again observed that the state of West Bengal continued to be the major tourist generating State of Odisha contributing 875154 tourists (13.76%) out of the domestic tourists of 6358445 during 2008 followed by Andhra Pradesh (3.47%), Madhya Pradesh (2.5%) and Chatishgarh (2.3%) respectively.[3] Further on a country wise break-up foreign tourists visiting Odisha it is found that UK and France are the major tourist generating markets for Odisha during the year 2008 with 6373 and 4676 tourists respectively. Out of the total foreign tourist arrival of 43966, USA 4333, Germany 3787, Italy 3124, Japan 2358 have followed UK and France. This trend has been maintained over the last several years[4] .

On further analysis it is noticed that the domestic tourists those who have visited the tourist places of Odisha over the last 10 years (1999 to 2008) nearly 51.80 per cent (on an average) one from within the various parts of the state itself and the rest 48.16 per cent are from different states of our country. Table – 4 provides the details of the composition of tourists of Odisha and tourists from the other States. However, it can be observed that in the last five years (2004-2008) there is a consistent increase in the flow of tourism within the state and the State tourism arrival has recorded in significant increase in the year 2008 by reaching the all time high of 60.49 per cent.

In flow of foreign exchange to our country in the rupee term has increased from 215625 crores in the year 2000 to 54960 crore in 2009 with an increase of nearly351.72 per cent except two years i.e. 2001 and 2002 in all other years there is an increase of this flow over the previous year. In the term of dellors also the same trend is observed with a deviation in the year 2009 where it has recorded a decline of 3.0 per cent (-3.0) over the previous year 2008 (Table 8.1)

---

[2] Statistical Bulletin, 2002 Pg. 16

[3] State wise break-up of domestic tourism visiting the State, statistical bulletin – 2008, Dept. of Tourism and Culture, Govt. of Odisha Pg. 9

[4] Country wise break up of Foreign Tourist visiting the State Ibid pg.7

An attempt is made to highlight the inflow of money to the State exchange through tourist expenditure in Odisha. However it is very difficult to estimate the earnings of the State Government from tourism, because of the vastness and variety of sources. In spite of that an attempt is made to assess the same through a sample survey method. A tourist profile survey was conducted by the Department of Tourism, Government of Odisha during the year 1998-99. As per the finding of the survey an average duration of state or a foreign of the survey an average duration of stag or a foreign tourist in the state was 10.6 days while for the domestic tourist it was 5.2 days similarly the average per capita daily expenditure by a foreign tourist was found out to be 21119.00 where as it was 644.00 in case of domestic tourist. While calculating the expenditure of the foreign tourist the expenditure on reaching and leaving the state were excluded[5].

In the year 2004-05 another survey of similar type was conducted by the same Odisha tourism department to find the changing profile of tourists. It was found that the average duration of state is 12.7 days in case of foreign tourist and 3.9 days in case of domestic tourist similarly the average per capita daily expenditure in case of foreign tourist has gone up to 1944 and 1275 for domestic tourist[6] . However, the details of the inflow of money through tourist expenditure in Odisha since 1998 to the year 2008 can well be noticed from the Table 8.5, as depicted below-

Table 8.5. Inflow of Money through tourist expenditure in Odisha since 1998 (Rs in crores)

Year (1)	Expenditure of Domestic Tourist(2)	Expenditure of Foreign Tourist(3)	Total (4)	(2) as % to (4)	(3) as % to (4)
1998	958.35	39.26	997.61	96.06	3.94
1999	901.44	30.55	931.99	96.72	3.28
2000	967.26	28.14	995.40	97.17	2.83
2001	1038.23	27.11	1065.34	97.46	2.54
2002	1143.06	27.32	1170.38	97.67	2.33
2003	1239.47	29.68	1269.15	97.66	2.34
2004	1381.56	34.18	1415.74	97.59	2.41
2005	2303.75	82.24	2385.99	96.55	3.45
2006	2605.54	96.63	2702.17	96.42	3.58
2007	2956.09	103.39	3059.48	96.62	3.38
2008	3161.73	108.54	3270.27	96.68	3.32

Source: Compiled from Statistical Bulletin 2002 & 2008, Department of Tourism and Culture, Govt. of Odisha.

It is quite evident from the table –5 that the expenditure of the domestic tourist has significantly contributed to the State exchanger by remaining almost above 96 Percent throughout and with an average of 96.85 per cent, leaving the balance of only 3.15 per cent to the foreign tourists. The same survey of 2004-05 reveals the fact that (i) the main purpose of visit of the foreign tourists is holidaying (71%) while for domestic tourist it is for holidaying, Business and official (79%).

[5] Statistical Bulletin, 2002 Pg. 16

[6] Statistical Bulletin, 2002 Pg. 9

(i) The foreign tourists get the inspiration and motivation to visit Odisha by their friends and relatives (29%) and 23% out of their previous experience. On the otherhand 57 per cent of the domestic tourists have get motivation from their previous experiences.
(ii) out of the total tourists 22% of the foreign tourists and 72% of the domestic tourists are the repeat visitors i.e. before hand they have already visited the State
(iii) out of their total experiences the foreign tourists spend 35% on shopping and 32% on Transport & sightseeing. While for the domestic tourists the expenses in respective heads are 29%, 19%, 22% and 30%.

NEED FOR SUSTAINABLE TOURISM

Sustainable development is not a fixed state of harmony but rather a process of dynamic change in which the exploitation of resources, the direction of investments, the orientation of technological development and institutional change are made consistent with future as well as present needs (WCED, 1987). It presupposes a development process which allows development to take place without degrading or depleting the natural capital, which make the development possible. This is generally achieved either by managing the resources so that they are able to renew themselves at the same rate at which they are used or switching from the use of a slowly regenerating resource to one which grows more rapidly. In this way, natural capital remains stable to support future as well as current generations. The main principles of sustainable development are:

- Ecological sustainability that development is compatible with the maintenance of essential ecological process, biological diversity and biological resources.
- Social and cultural sustainability, being compatible with the culture and values of people that strengthens community identity and ensures a development process, which increases people's control over their lives.
- Economic sustainability ensures that development is economically efficient and that resources are managed so that they can support future generations.

Realizing the negative aspects of the mass tourism culture of the early years of modern tourist development (1960-1995), a new tourism paradigm has emerged with clear emphasis on super segmentation of the tourism market. There is a growing realisation that despite having tremendous multiplier effects on income and employment generation, tourism may pose threats to the ecological balance and can easily destroy traditional value system of aboriginal communities. Tourism policy of India, 2002 strongly advocates this segmentation and Ministry of Tourism and Culture has already declared eco-tourism, cultural tourism and heritage tourism as special segments. The policy also envisages that a well coordinated private and public sector participation would bring forth the desired results.

Out of the six distinct categories[3], such as *recreational, cultural, sports/adventure, health, convention and incentive* tourism; *eco-tourism* basically comes in the category of recreational or leisure tourism. However, of late it has created its own brand under the head of environmental tourism. It refers to purposeful travel to areas of natural Nature to understand their natural and cultural history, and the environmental value for the human society. It has grown as a consequence of dissatisfaction, which arise on account of the inappropriate implementation of mass tourism. It is a process that does not alter the integrity of the ecosystem, while producing recreational opportunities. The term ecotourism was first coined by a Mexican environmentalist H'ector Leballos Lascurain in 1983. Initially the term was used to describe nature-based travel to relatively undisturbed natural areas with an emphasis on education. The concept has however, developed into a scientific approach to the planning, management and development of sustainable tourism products and activities. Ecotourism is nature based and ecologically sustainable. It conserves nature and it has negligible impact on the environment. The infrastructure required is very low and an educative component is also there. The visitors are able to understand the natural and cultural history of the area. But sometimes this acts as a secondary motive. In short, ecotourism has been conceptualised as nature based, ecologically sustainable and where local people are benefited.[4] Considering the growth and importance of ecotourism, the United Nations, celebrated the year 2002 as the "International Year of Ecotourism and Mountains" and promoted awareness programmes all over the world.

The Government of India published the ecotourism guidelines and policies in 1998, which are to be followed by the planners, tour operators, visitors and other agencies. The geographical diversity of our country and also the state of Orissa are the wealth of ecosystems. These ecosystems have become the major ecotourism resources of the country. These include mountains, reserve forests, flora and fauna, seas, lakes and rivers, caves waterfalls and hot water springs.

INTERRELATIONSHIP BETWEEN TOURISM AND ENVIRONMENTAL SUSTAINABILITY

The tourists normally look for natural environment in the form of land, water, plants and animals in a destination. Thus in the absence of an attractive environment, tourism industry cannot succeed. However, quality of tourism is also very important for the environment because[5] tourists may pollute the sites by causing air, water and noise pollution and by throwing junk (plastic and polythene) materials, may bring diseases (mainly sex related disease like AID), may not respect local religious sentiments, ridicule innocent behaviour and may make locals into caricatures. Several clear cut long-term and short-term policies[6] are necessary to improve the situation regarding the adverse impact of eco-tourism on environment.

Sustainable tourism development is a reaction to the unplanned growth of mass tourism. Sustainable development is now being recognized as an essential approach to achieving development goals without depleting natural and cultural resources or degrading the environment of a region, so that inter-and intra-generational equity and efficiency can be achieved. The strategy implies that the natural, cultural and other resources of tourism are for judicious use of future generations, while extending benefits to the present society. This approach to tourism planning is very important because most tourism development depends on attractions and activities related to natural environment, cultural values and historic heritage of areas. While planning tourism development, it is equally important that development should be integrated and should not deteriorate the existing environment, ecology and socio-cultural fabric for the sustenance of future generations. Ecology and economic dimensions of tourism are becoming more interwoven - locally, regionally nationally and internationally in a web of cause and effect. In the earlier approach to tourism, the tourism industry, environment and the community were interacting through give-take relationships, whereas the sustainable tourism approach looks at all the dimensions as the parts of the same integrated system, as shown in Figure 8.1. Sustainable tourism development connects tourists and providers of tourist facilities and services with advocates of environment with environmental protection and community residents and their leaders who desire a better quality of life. Through the cooperation and productive interaction of the tourism industry, environmental protectors and community all can benefit each other and achieve an improved quality of life of the community.

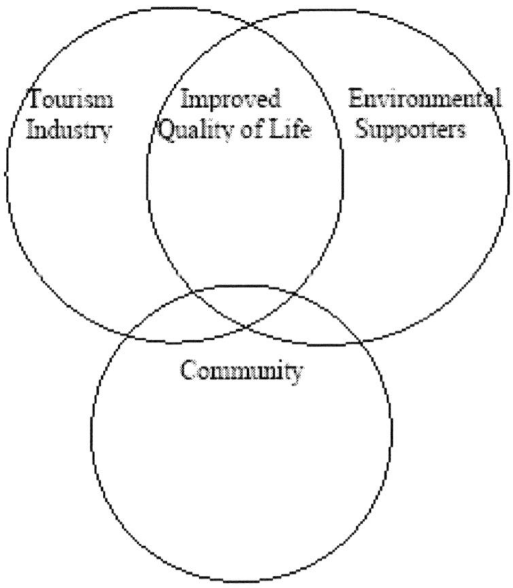

Figure 8.1. Sustainable tourism: An integrated approach of every thing in one place.

Since 1995 the WTO has categorically outlined the implementation of the principles of sustainable tourism popularly known as Agenda - 21 in this sector, working in collaboration with national tourism authorities, other inter-Governmental agencies and the private sector leadership. Sustainable tourism is defined as a model form of economic development that is designed to improve the quality of life of the host community, provide a high quality of experience for the visitor and maintain the quality of the environment on which both the host community and the visitors depend.

The benefits of sustainable tourism are manifold.

- It encourages an understanding of the impacts of tourism on the natural, cultural and human environments. It also encourages and helps to maintain and preserve historical sites and archaeological monuments.
- It generates local employment both directly in the tourism sector and indirectly in various support and resource management sectors.

- It stimulates domestic industries in forms of lodging facilities, restaurants, food facilities, transportation system, handicrafts, guide services etc.
- Generates foreign exchange for the country and attracts investments both domestic and foreign in to the local economy.
- Diversifies the local economy particularly in rural and remote areas where agricultural employment may be sporadic and insufficient.
- Seeks decision making among all segments and sections of society including local community, so that tourism and other resources users can co-exist. It incorporates planning and zoning which ensures tourism development appropriate to the carrying capacity of the ecosystem.
- It promotes productive and constructive use of land unsuitable for agriculture enabling large areas to remain covered with green vegetation through nature tourism.
- Cultural tourism ensures self-esteem of the local community and provides opportunity for greater understanding and interaction among people of diverse cultures and traditions. Thus it provides platform for ensuring national integration.
- Sustainable tourism monitors, assesses and manages the impacts of tourism both negative and positive by developing methods of environmental accountability and responsibility.

ECOTORISM IN ORISSA – A STUDY OF LAKE CHILIKA

Tourist Centres in Orissa

Orissa is known for its exotic tourist places. The various centres famous for tourist interest are: Bhubaneswar – a city know as Temple city, having Lingaraj and a set of temples to its credit. Puri is famous for the temple of Lord Jagannath and its beautiful Sea Beach. Other places of tourist interest are Konark, Nandan Kanan, Chilika Lake, Dhauli Buddhist Temple, Udayagiri-Khandagiri Ancient Caves, Ratnagiri, Lilitgir Buddhist Caves. Saptasjya scenic view of Hill Beds, Similipal National Park and Tiger project, Hirakud Dam, Duduma Water Falls, Ushakathi Wildlife Sanctuary, Gopalpur Sea Beach, Hari Sankar, Nrusinghnath, Taratarini, Taptapani, Bhitarakanika, Bhimakunda, Kapilash etc.

An Elaboration of Five Eco-Tourism Centres of Orissa

The state is having more than one hundred sites of ecotourism interest. Considering the time and space as a constraint only five ecotourism centres have been highlighted on the basis of case studies. Those are:

- Chilika Lake – A Wonder Creation of Nature: Nestling in the heart of coastal Orissa, Chilika is India's inland lake. Spread over 1,100 square kilometres, it runs along the borders of three districts of Puri, Khurda and Ganjam and finally joins the Bay of Bengal through a narrow mouth, forming and enormous lagoon of brackish water.

- Similipal – The Dreamland of Water: Thick and evergreen forests, extensive grassy lands and meadows, cloud kissing peaks, precipitous and sparkling waterfalls, meandering rivers, roaring tigers and trumpeting tuskers, fleeing deer and flying squirrels, talking myna and dancing peacocks et al. make Similipal a dreamland of Nature in the wilderness and an irresistible destination.
- Chandipur – Where the Sea Plays Hide & Seek: Unlike other beaches, the sea water here recedes away from the shore line about five km twice a day, an unusual phenomenon, rarely found anywhere. You see the sea literally vanishing before your eyes and also watch it coming back rhythmically at regular intervals, as if playing hide and seek.
- Bhitarakanika – A Wonder in the Wild: Widely acclaimed for its biodiversity in flora and fauna, it is the second largest compact mangrove ecosystem in India. It is also a Sanctuary and National Park.
- Gopalpur – A Popular Beach Resort: The deep and clear blue waters instantly provoke those who are good swimmers. The temptation of bathing here is irresistible. White surf splashing on the golden sand makes Gopalpur-on-Sea as one of the finest beaches on the eastern coast.

The Lake Chilika: A Bird's View

The Chilika lagoon is a land of unique and rare beauty stretching over Ganjam, Khurda and Puri districts. The international convention on "Wetland of International Importance" held at Ramsar recognised the lagoon as one of the important wetlands of the world in 1981. The sun is so happy to rise and set in riotous colours that it transforms each ripple to a sparkling diamond. It is located between the latitudes $19^{o}21^{/}$ and $19^{o}54^{/}$ N and longitude $85^{o}05^{/}$ and $85^{o}38^{/}$ E (Figure 8.1). It is famous for migratory and resident birds and rich varied aquatic life including the dolphin. The water spread area of the lake varies between 1165 sq.km. to 906 sq. km. during monsoon and summer season. A 35km long, narrow outer channel connects the main lagoon to the Bay of Bengal near the village Arakhakuda. This channel has become shallow and hence obstructs the flow of seawater and free movement of fish to and from the lagoon. Recently, the Chilika Development Authority has opened a new mouth near Sipakuda with a hope that the salinity and fish production will increase.

The major attraction of Chilika lagoon for the tourists and its natural beauty with the pleasure of boating, bird watching and cavorting dolphins, while the religious *Kalijai* and the mouth-watering delicious dishes, are incidental attraction. The important tourist spots of the Chilika lagoon are Barkul, Rambha, Nalabana Island and Satapada. Barkul is chosen as one of the tourist site for the study. It is situated on the southern end of the lagoon. The Orissa State Tourism Development has developed Barkul for recreation purposes owing to its scenic beauty. There is a *Pantha Niwas* at Barkul. The lagoon has immense potential for development of ecotourism.

Eco-Tourism Sites within the Lake Chilika

- Ramba Bay at the southern end of the lake with the group of islands including:
  - The Becon Island, with an architectural conical pillar (to put a light on the top) built by Mr. Snodgrass, the then collector of Ganjam of the East India Company, on a mass of rock in the Rambha Bay near Ghantasila hill. It has scenic water spread surrounded by the Eastern Ghat.
  - The Breakfast Island, pear shaped, known as "Sankuda island", with remnants of a dilapidated bungalow constructed by the King of Kalikote, has rare plants and is full of greenery with appealing flora.
  - Honeymoon Island, 5 km (3 mi) from Rambha Jetty, known as Barkuda Island, with clear waters has abundant red and green macro algae in the bed is also known for the limbless lizard, an endemic species found here.

- Somolo and Dumkudi islands, located in the Central and Southern sectors of the lake, in the backdrop of scenic Khalikote hill range, are inundated remnants of the Eastern Ghats with rich flora and fauna and also known for sighting of Irrawaddy Dolphins.
- Birds' island, located in the southern sector of the lake has huge exposed hanging rocks, are painted white due to folic acid of the droppings of the birds and is known for rich algal communities and few mangrove species and also migratory birds in winter.
- Parikud is a group of composite islands in the Garh Krishnaprasad Block for nature lovers and provides an avian spectacle during winter season
- Kalijai Temple located on an island is considered to be the abode of the Goddess Kalijai.This temple is located at a hill which is surrounded by the blue water bears. Local people of Chilika refer to goddess as the reigning deity of the lagoon.
- Satapada village, at the new mouth of the lake, provides a beautiful view of the Lake and also views of the Dolphins. Hundreds of boats here provide tours of the lake for tourists.
- Barunkuda, a small island situated near Magarmukh, mouth of the lake, has a temple of Lord Varuna.
- Nabagraha is an ancient deity located along the outer channel.
- Chourbar Shiva Temple is located near Alupatna village, along the outer channel.
- Manikpatna, located on the outer channel has historical evidence of a port which was used for trade with Far East and also has the Bhabakundeswar temple of Lord Shiva, an old Mosque whose entrance door is made of the jaws of the whale.
- Sand-Bar and Mouth of the Lake is a striking and un-explored stretch of 30 km (20 mi) of empty beach across the sand bar which separates the Lake from the Sea.

Tourism at Chilika - An Investigation

The concept of eco-tourism has been a tremendous success for the beautiful lake Chilika. Its enchanting sites including Rambha Bay, Somolo & Dumkudi Island, Bird's Island, Parikud, Maluda, Kalijai, temple, Chourbar, Siva temple, manikpatna etc., have been proved to be the great enchanting tourist places for both domestic and foreign visitors.

As per record, during the year 1992, the total tourist arrived to lake Chilika was near about 1.65 Lakh which was around 6.59% of the total tourist arrived to Orissa that further incresed significantly to 10.76% in the year 2002 thereby registering an upward trend (See Table 8.6).

Table 8.6. Share of Tourist Arrival to Chilika from 1992 to 2002

Year	Tourist arrival to chilika	Tourist arrival to Orissa	Share of tourist arrival to Chilika(%)
1992	164520	2497985	6.59
1993	282024	2563731	11.00
1994	229725	2621016	8.76
1995	201337	2725566	7.39
1996	223685	2807548	7.97
1997	249437	2863212	8.71
1998	266556	2894889	9.21
1999	225870	2717598	8.31
2000	273689	2912115	9.40
2001	322864	3123170	10.34
2002	369761	3436386	10.76

Source: Statistical Bulletin 2002, Department of Tourism and Culture, Government of Orissa and Personal Communication.

A site-wise split focusing on Rambha, Barkul and Satapada of Chilika Lake further revealed that the accumulation of domestic visitors acquired a considerable higher share in comparison to the foreign visitors that registered more than 99% of the total visitors over the years under observation (See Table 8.7).

Table 8.7. Site-wise Tourist Arrival to Chilika Lagoon from 1996-2008

Year	Chilika (Rambha)			Chilika (Barkul)			Chilika (Satapara)		
	Domestic (% to Total)	Foreign	Total	Domestic (% to Total)	Foreign	Total	Domestic (% to Total)	Foreign	Total
1996	20126 (99.36)	130	130	155210 (99.84)	255	255	47750 (99.56)	215	215
2001	47680 (99.77)	112	112	223590 (99.87)	285	285	50895 (99.41)	302	302
2006	70223 (99.51)	348	348	269100 (99.83)	445	445	95390 (99.15)	814	814
2007	72215 (99.82)	131	131	271300 (99.82)	493	493	133380 (99.37)	843	843
2008	73660 (99.82)	131	131	273200 (99.82)	500	500	141900 (99.40)	859	859

Source: Statistical Bulletin 2008, Department of Tourism and Culture, Govt. of Odisha.

Concluding Observations and Scope for Participatory Approach for Chilika

- Tourism is one of the fastest growing industries in the world. It has several local socio-economic multiplier effects.
- Growth of tourism has been impressive in India and Odisha during the last decade. All out efforts have been made to develop appropriate policies for the foreign and domestic tourists.
- However, realizing the negative aspects of the mass aggressive tourism culture, a new tourism paradigm has emerged with clear emphasis on super segmentation of the tourism market with eco-tourism, cultural tourism and heritage tourism as special segments.
- Eco-tourism refers to purposeful travel to areas of natural Nature to understand their natural and cultural history, and the environmental value for the human society.
- In Odisha there are 315 tourist centers (as on 31st Aug., 2009), which have attracted increasing number of foreign and domestic tourists in the recent years. The State is well-known for its exotic tourist places like Puri, Konark and Bhubaneswar, and at least five major eco-tourism sites, namely Chilika lake, Similipal, Bhitarakanika, Chandipur and Gopalpur.
- Chilika – a wetland of international (Ramsar) importance has several eco-tourism sites, including a bird sanctuary, a centre for watching dolphins, several small and large islands, and enormous scope for boating and water sport.
- The huge lagoon is surrounded by about 100 villages and a few urban centres, the people of which have been traditionally supporting the recreation activities. The cooperation of the people can be enlisted for protecting the environment and successful tourism planning for sustainable tourism development in the lake. The village community having the right type of resources, can gainfully develop eco-tourism and can bring about sustainable benefits to the community and the tourists.
- Tourism in Odisha is still a less-advertised activity. Air-link to the State and its other tourist destinations are inadequate. Hotel infrastructure needs manifold expansion. While several festivals, like Konark and Puri are attracting tourists from all corners of the world, a Chilika festival has not yet been programmed. The Chilka Development Authority, Tourism Department of the State Government and the local village community should engage in origanising a Chilika festival to create awareness on eco-tourism and generate socio-economic benefits for the people.

References

Bansal, S.P. and Gautam, P.K. (2002). 'Ecotourism by Community Involvement', Abstract, *International Workshop on Restoration of Chilika Lagoon, CDA, Bhubaneswar*: pp. 44-55.

Boullion, R. (1985), Planificacion del espacio turistico. *Editorial Trillas*, Mexico: pp. 9-20.

Kumar, R.B. (1999), Coastal Tourism and Environment. *APH Publ. Corporation*, New Delhi: pp. 5-10.

Lenka, S.K. (2002), 'Study material for certain course on Ecotourism', *IITTM, Bhubaneswar:* pp. 3-56.

Parida, B.B. (2002), 'Community based Tourism in Chilika'. Abstract, *International Workshop on Restoration of Chilika Lagoon, CDA, Bhubaneswar:* p. 43.

Rathakrishnan, L. (2001), 'Tourism infrastructure development and environment in Andaman and Nicobar Islands'. *Environment and People:* pp. 20-23.

Tantrigama, G. (1998), 'Carrying Capacity and Sustainability of Coastal Tourism in Hikkaduwa, Sri Lanka and Calangute, Goa, India'. *Tropical Coasts,* 5 (1), pp. 16-20.

In: Development Management in the Twenty-First Century ISBN: 978-1-62100-699-2
Editors: Kartik Roy and Sandip Kar

Chapter 9

SUSTAINABLE MANAGEMENT OF ECO-TOURISM TO BENEFIT GUJARAT

***Yogesh N. Vansiya*[*,1] and Subadra Ragothaman[†,2]**
[1] Assistant Professor, Mahadev Desai Gramseva Mahavidyalaya, Sadra, Gujarat Vidyapith, Nr. Income Tax Office, Gujarat State, India
[2] Professor & Head, Dept. of Economics, Veer Narmad South Gujarat University, Gujarat, India

INTRODUCTION

Tourism has emerged as an instrument for employment generation, poverty alleviation and sustainable human development. Tourism has been an important segment of the country's economy in terms of its contribution towards foreign exchange earnings, generation of additional income and creation of employment opportunities. With rapid advances in science of technology and the economic liberalization in India and consequential foreign investment opportunities tourism has acquired the status of an industry in all industrialized countries.

Tourism has been a major social phenomenon of the societies all along. It is motivated by the natural urge of every human being for new experience, adventure, education and entertainment. The motivations for tourism also include social, religious and business interests. The spread of education has fostered a desire to know more about different parts of the globe. The basic human thirst for new experience and knowledge has more become stronger, as technological advances are overcoming communication barriers. Progresses in air transport and development of tourist facilities have encouraged people to venture out to the foreign lands.

Tourism's importance, as an instrument for economic development and employment generation, particularly in remote and backward areas, has been well recognized the world over. Tourism can play an important and effective role in achieving the growth with equity objectives, which we have set for ourselves. Tourism is one economic sector in India that has

* yogesh.vansiya@gmail.com.
† subbiragurao@yahoo.com.

the potential to grow at a high rate and can ensure consequential development of the infrastructure at the destinations. It has the capacity to capitalize on the country's success in the services sector and provide sustainable models of growth.

Domestic tourism plays an important role in achieving the national objectives of promoting social and cultural cohesion and national integration. Its contribution to generation of employment is very high. Tourism has the potential to stimulate other economic sector through its backward and forward linkages and cross-sectoral synergies with sectors like agriculture, horticulture, poultry, handicrafts, transport, construction, etc. Expenditure on tourism induces a chain of transactions requiring supply of goods and services from these related sectors. The economic benefits that flow into the economy through growth of tourism in the shape of increased national and state revenues, business receipts, employment, wages and salary, buoyancy in central, state and local tax receipt can contribute towards overall socio-economic improvement and accelerated growth in the economy.

Tourism has also become an instrument for sustainable human development including:

- Poverty elimination.
- Environmental regeneration.
- Job creation.
- Advancement of women and disadvantaged groups.

ECONOMICS OF ECOTOURISM

Ecotourism has been proposed as a viable economic activity that can minimize negative human impacts on wildlife habitat and provide an incentive to preserve natural areas Ecotourism is a proxy market designed to align consumers' preferences for recreation with the protection of environmental assets. Because it does not necessarily address the direct protection of those assets, it is prone to market failure. Promoting ecotourism may actually distract from more appropriate means of environmental protection.

Tourism to natural areas has been touted for its potential to allow sustainable development of ecosystems and to provide incentives to preserve these areas instead of converting them to other uses. A particular variety, ecotourism, stresses minimal human impact on native ecosystems and cultures. Ecotourism is demonstrating some promise as profitable and relatively non-damaging form of economic enterprise.

Tourism is evidently a large industry with potential for growth. Rising income also has increased the demand for environmental amenities (Randall 1987). Touted as a low-impact alternative to traditional tourism (Eadington and Smith 1992; Roxe 1998), ecotourism has been called "responsible travel that conserves natural environments and sustains the wellbeing of local cultures" (Ecotourism Society in Wheat l998:10). The stated purposes of ecotourism are to raise the public's awareness of the environment, to sensitize travelers to nature and its - processes, and to reduce negative impacts of human activities on natural areas (Sirakaya and McLellan 1998)

Recreation is one of the benefits of protecting natural areas. Others include habitat protection, biodiversity preservation, soil formation, nutrient recycling, and control of water and air pollution (Dixon and Shennan 1991).

Protected areas can provide resilience and stability in ecosystems and maintain numerous natural services (Heywood and Watson 1995; Perrings 1995; Tumer *et al.*, 1995). The values of these amenities must be weighed when considering actions that affect the conservation of natural areas (Weisbrod 1964; Knltilla 1967; Dixon and Sherman 1991).

Returns to ecotourism have encouraged the preservation of elephant (Elaphas indicus) habitat in Thailand (Dixonand Shennan, 1991, McNeely and Dobias 1991) and protection of wildlands on Mount Kinju, South Korea (Lee *et al.* 1997).

Ecotourism has been seen as aiding in the conservation of primate habitat in Zaire, harp seal (Pagophilus groenlandicus) habitat in Labrador, and Costa Rican rainforest (Farrell 1992). Ideally, providing ecotourism is consistent with providing other, complementary ecosystem functions (Dixon and Sherman 1990).ln this way, conservationists hope that ecotourism is proxy market for those other items of value, including wildlife conservation.

The ecotourism market itself may contain negative externalities-costs imposed on others and ignored in the operation of market exchange.

The existence of negative externalities does not mean that ecotourism is necessarily detrimental. Indeed ecotourism is likely to be less damaging to the environment than alterative industries like agriculture mining, timber and urban development (Poirier 1997) Nevertheless negative externalities must be recognized in assessing and designing ecotourism programs

Based on its amazing increase and inarguable contribution to economy and society as well as its important role in environment conservation, the tourism industry has been regarded as an efficient development strategy that keeps a balance between improving the living standards of people and maintaining the sustainable use of resources for the future. It is also widely acknowledged that local participation in tourism is critical and is hardly implemented in reality, although often advocated in principle.

Tourism, for example, is supposed to involve the process of consultation, decision-making, or program implementation (Mam Kosal 1996). It has been observed that the indigenous people are just involved in labor-based tasks or providing services in most destinations.

It is a common knowledge that tour operators receive most of the benefits from tourism and leave the local resources exploited, and the local people poor. Such a financial "leakage" gives little incentive for the locals to maintain their environment on which tourism depends.

On the other hand, as tourism is growing around the world, environmental and social impacts are immediate concerns. Negative impacts such as environmental pollution and enormous waste management problems, the violation of human rights, commoditization of cultures, etc., have affected many indigenous peoples around the world.

Given their knowledge, local wisdom, and sense of ownership, the local people immediately become the best protectors of the resources on which the industry relies.

As ecotourism is being implemented around the world, there is a growing international agreement that it should be community-based.

In other words, the key to assessing tourism's potential for improving environmental conservation and community well-being is the direct involvement of the local communities and the promotion of linkage between conservation and enterprise development.

Some Socio-Economic and Environmental Benefits of Ecotourism

- Tourism revenue generated can be channeled in to the management of the protected areas
- Tourism could generate local employment, both directly from the tourism sector and from various support and resource management sectors.
- It could stimulate local industry i.e., hotel, restaurants, transport systems souvenirs and guide services. It generates foreign exchange.
- It diversifies the local economy, particularly in rural areas where agricultural employment may be sporadic or insufficient
- It could benefit local people by stimulating development and improvement in support, infrastructure of service i.e. local transport, communications and water and energy systems.
- It serves as an effective educational tool for visitors.

The Following Points Must Be Considered While Implementing Eco-Tourism

a) The scale of development should be appropriate for the local community.
b) Roads should be placed in a manner so as to minimizing intrusion on the environment.
c) Measures should be taken during construction to minimize negative effects on the environment.
d) Construction on the facility should use locally available material and blend with the surroundings.
e) Energy sources should be environmentally sound and suitable.
f) Appropriate technologies should be employed for the treatment of organic and other wastes.
g) Local communities should be involved in planning, construction and operations.

Tourism has proved to have negative impact as well as the positive ones. It is criticized for contaminating indigenous culture. This takes the form of changing values, resulting in social maladies like drug addiction etc. The movement towards eco- tourism is at once a threat and an opportunity to create more sustainable tourism by diverting tourist traffic to ensure the carrying capacity of any destination is not exceeded and by planning for regeneration of natural resources. The local communities need to be educated to deal with the negative impact of mass tourism.

Indian Tourism

Tourism in India has grown substantially over the last three decades. Foreign tourist arrivals during 1997 were 2,374,094 as compared to 2, 2867,860 in 1996, an increase of 3.8 per cent. India's share in the world tourist market at the end of 1996-97 was 0.39 per cent.

Foreign exchange earnings in the same year were estimated at Rs. 10,418 crore and for 1997-98 it was Rs. 11,264 crore. Thus tourism has become one of the largest foreign exchange earners of the country. At the same time domestic tourism's contribution to the generation of employment is very high.

The year 2006 has been a highly successful year for India. For the fourth successive year, India witnessed a positive growth in foreign tourist arrivals, reaching a level of 4.43 million against 2.38 million during 2002. The growth rate of 13.04 percentages during 2006 was achieved over 2005 and the share of India in world tourism is expected to be around 0.52 per cent. Foreign exchange earnings has reached US$ 6569.34 in 2006 and marked an increase of 14.63 per cent over 2005 (US $ 5730.86). In absolute rupee terms, the increase in foreign exchange earnings during the year 2006 was Rs. 4431.31 crores over 2005. Tourism is the third largest net earner of foreign exchange next to garments, gem and jewellery industry, recording earnings of US $6569.34 million in 2006 (Rs. 29603.56 crores). India's share in the total global tourist arrivals and earnings remained quite insignificant at 0.52 per cent of the world arrivals and the percentage of share of tourism receipts for 2006 was 0.90 per cent. The following table gives an idea of foreign tourist in India.

Table 9.1. Foreign Tourists Arrival to India (In millions)

Year Arrivals % Change		
2002	2.38	(-) 6.0
2003	2.73	(+) 14.3
2004	3.46	(+) 26.8
2005	3.92	(+) 13.2
2006*	4.43	(+) 13.0
Growth in 5 years i.e., 2006 over 2001: 86%		

Source: Ministry of Tourism.

The Tourism satellite Account for India has brought out that tourism's contribution to GDP of the country has been 5.9 per cent in 2003-04, while employment in tourism sector both direct and indirect, has been 41.8 million in the same year, which accounts for 8.78 per cent of total employment in the country. Though the growth in tourism in India has been impressive, India's share in global tourist arrivals is quite insignificant. However, earning per tourist is highest for India compared to neighboring countries. It is universally acknowledged that the tourism resources of India have the potential to generate significantly higher levels of demand from the domestic and international markets, and if exploited intelligently in a manner, it can prove to be the engine of growth for the economy.

Another important feature of the industry ,which is of significance to India, is its contribution to national integration, preservation of natural as well as cultural environments and enrichment and heritage properties and helps the survival of arts forms, crafts and culture. Over 382 million domestic tourist visiting different parts of the country every year return with a better appreciation of the cultural diversity and understanding of the people living in different regions of the country.

Table 9.2 and Chart 1 & 2 give an idea about the growth and hence the importance of tourist activity in India.

Table 9.2. Domestic Tourism in India

Year	Domestic Tourist Visits	% Change
2002	269.6	14.0
2003	309.0	14.6
2004	366.2	18.5
2005	382.1	4.3
2006*	432.0	13.0
Growth in 5 years i.e., 2006 year over 2001:82.9% (end of 9th plan to end of 10th plan) *Predicted		

Source: ministry of Tourism.

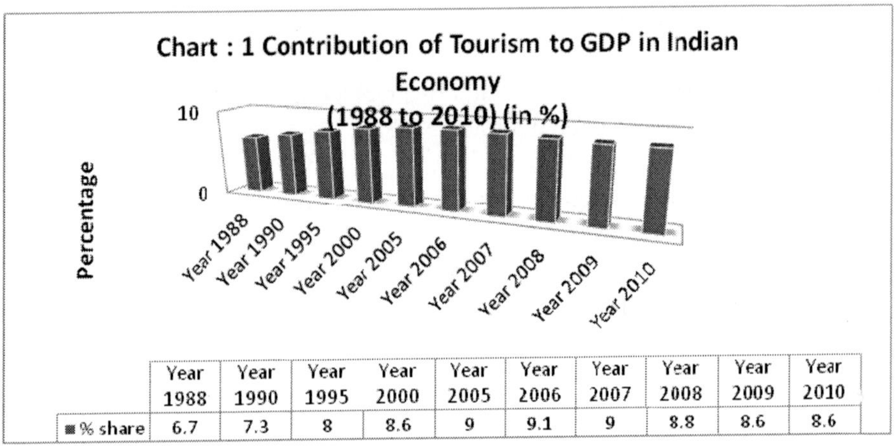

Chart 1. Contribution of Tourism to GDP in Indian Economy.

It is clear that tourist's activities are gaining in importance in the economy. The contribution of 8 per cent to the GDP is significant. Tourism activity if developed can provide opportunities for the development of backward regions of the economy.

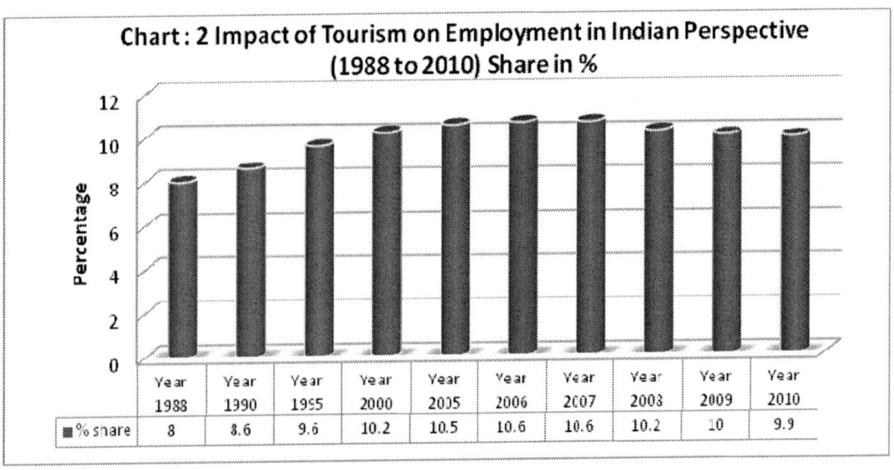

Chart 2. Impact of Tourism on Employment in Indian Perspective.

The positive impact of tourism on employment is indicated in the above table. Since the employment related to tourism does not demand high skilled labor, it can provide opportunities to the absorption of labor in India.

GUJARAT TOURISM - WESTERN TIP OF INDIA

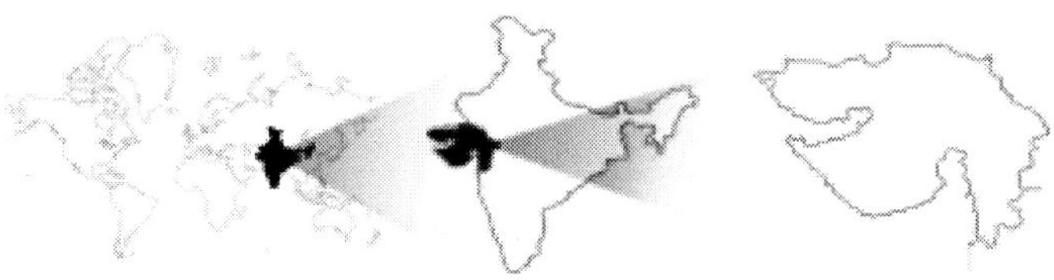

Gujarat has undertaken extensive efforts to develop tourism activities and to attract greater number of tourists. With the celebration of festivals like Navaratri Mahotsav, Patangotsav, Sharadotsav and Rannotsav, the State intend to put the rich culture of Gujarat and its various places of pilgrimages on the world map

Gujarat has immense potential to become a major tourist destination. Its historical monuments represent the great religions of Asia Hinduism, Buddhism, Jainism, Islam, Zoroastrianism and Sikhism.

In Gujarat total flow of tourist in the year of 2006 – 07 was 12.34 million. It has recorded a growth of 15 percentages over the previous year. Growth of 18.5 percentages was observed in the tourist flow from foreign countries during 2006-07, with a number of more than 2 Lacs foreign tourists in 2006-07 and around 1.75 Lacs in 2005-06.

Gujarat is a land which has the best eco tourism opportunities. Eco friendly recreational avenues like boating, camping and picnic spots are favorite recreational outings for local as well as tourists in Gujarat. Gujarat cities have magnificent gardens which are maintained in natural settings, enhancing their exquisite beauty with fountains and fountain shows.

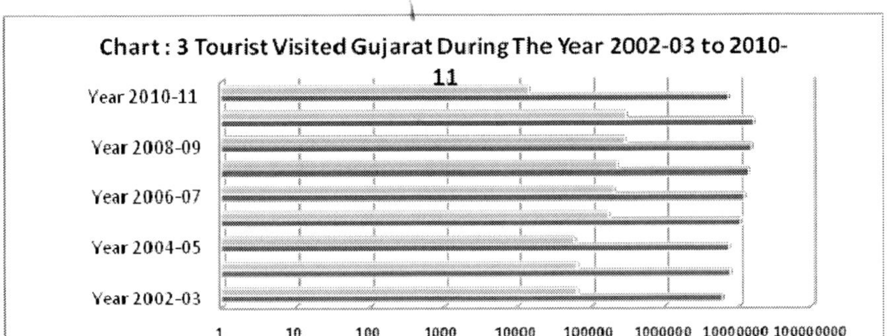

	Year 2002-03	Year 2003-04	Year 2004-05	Year 2005-06	Year 2006-07	Year 2007-08	Year 2008-09	Year 2009-10	Year 2010-11
Foreigners/NRI Tourist	65094	65107	59987	173122	206729	228976	294739	309702	14512
Total Domestic Tourist	6100123	7915487	7552026	10505755	12136599	13894055	15512794	16701545	7471353

Chart 3. Tourist Visited Gujarat during the Year 2002-03 to 2010.

Chart 3 explains the flow of tourists in Gujarat. This tourism activity in Gujarat has shown continuous upward trend since2002-03.In terms of both domestic tourists as well as foreign tourists. This is an encouraging trend and provides ground for the development of Eco-Tourism at Dangs.

KEY INITIATIVES UNDERTAKEN BY THE GOVERNMENT[1]

More than 2000 fairs and festivals are celebrated in the State such as Navratri, Uttaranyana / Makar Sankranti, Sharad Poornima, Mahashivaratri melas, Tarnetar Fair, Kvant Fair, Chitra Vichitra Fair, Dangs Durbar, etc. The Gujarat Government has created successful events like Rann Utsav, Modhera Dance Festival, International Kite Festival, Vibrant Gujarat, etc.Infrastructure development and basic amenities are strengthened since 2006 with an annual budget of INR100 crore. Tourism department has rationalised various taxes like the luxury tax, entertainment tax, sales tax etc.

The government of Gujarat has also provided infrastructure support to promote tourism. Tourism Corporation of Gujarat Ltd (TCGL) has selected 37 destinations for integrated tourism development. In last 2 years more than 600 projects in 300 tourist destination have been taken up with a cost more than USD 24 million. 35 Pravasi Path of international standards has been taken up in Gujarat, involving an investment of USD 19 million. Tourism year budget have been increased from USD 7 million to USD 24 million. This provision is continued in the new 5 year plan.

PROSPECTS OF DEVELOPING DANGS AS ECO-TOURISM SPOT AND THE PROFILE OF DANGS

Dangs is a mountain range in western part of India which is inhabited by tribals. Properly planned eco-tourism can change the fortunes of people in remote and less developed regions. Eco-tourism is open to various interpretations, criteria, such as benefits for local people, support for conservation, low scale development, low visitor volume and educational experience; suggest that if tourism develops in these regions as an eco-tourism centre, it can bring various economic benefits to the local population. Dangs is a tribal district located in South Gujarat region. The Bhil, Konkana, Varli, Kotwaliya, Kathodi and Gamit are the major tribal groups of Dang. This district shares its border with the state of Maharastra and is covered with high hills and dense forest. The district comprises of 311 villages and one taluka. The total population of the Dangs as per 2001 census is 186729. The district headquarter is Ahwa. The reserved forests in Dangs are amongst the richest forests in the state. Rich wildlife, gardens, ropeway, sunrise point and echo point are some to the main tourist attractions in Dangs. In Dangs agriculture is the main source of livelihood. 85 percentage of the population is either a cultivator or employed as an agricultural labour. Animal husbandary and Bamboo cutting are the other economics activities in the district. There are approximately 100 small scale industries in Dangs e.g. farm based industry,

* http://www.vibrantgujarat.com/focus-areas/tourrism.aspx.

Bamboo furniture etc. Firewood accounts for fuel requirement of 915 of the households, which is mostly collected from the forest. In the Dangs there is high pressure on the land, since the majority of the land is forestland (59 per cent) and only a limited amount of land is available for agriculture purpose. 66 per cent of the agriculture land in the district is situated on slopes, with uneven terrain. Of the total cultivable land only 13 percentages is irrigated. The whole Dangs district has very limited opportunities for irrigation due to limited amount of flat land. The cropping pattern of the Dangs is conditioned to rain fed nature of agriculture land and lack of irrigation. Most of the cultivation is being done during monsoon and the farmers take only one crop. Major food crops and frits produced in the district are rice, ragi, kharsani, tuver, groundnut, mangoes, custard apple and others. The agriculture production pattern is slowly changing from traditional course grains like ragi, kharsani and tuver to rice. Ragi is the main crop in the Dangs district. Tourism in Dangs can be analysed as follows. The district having rich forests, few small and large waterfalls beautiful landscapes and tribal culture which account for huge influx of tourist in the district Saputara, in south Dangs the only hill station of Gujarat, on Surat – Nashik high way also known as Abode of serpentsm, is a hill resort on a plateau of the sahyadri range of mountains. This offers rich wild life for tourist. Saputara Museum Contains interesting Information about the pography and anotheroplogy of Dangs. Hatgarh fort situated 60 km from saputara was built by Maratha leader Chhatrapati Shivaji and is a beautiful piece of architecture. There are around 20 small and big water falls in the district. Gira Fall is the most picturesque sight in the district Vansda. National park in Dangs, harbors large mammals including the leopards, Hyena, Jungle cat macaques and barking Gardon situated at Waghai is also attractive place for tourists. Due to dense forest in Dangs, various types of plants are available and it will be used in medicine and it will be a great potential for medical tourism.

TOURIST ACTIVITIES IN DANGS; A PRELIMINARY SURVEY

We have taken Dangs as a case study to 1.) Find out the impact of tourist activity on the development of the region. 2.) To find out the effect of tourism on the income of the local residents. 3.) To find out how many local people take up tour related jobs. The tourist arrival at Dangs has consistently increased since 2000 and this shows that Dangs is an important tourist attraction in Gujarat. The year 2009-10 had recorded tourist arrival of 1,86,944 persons at Dangs district. The impact of tourism at Dangs district is analysed based on the survey undertaken. Based on the data collected the following picture emerged. The results are presented in three sections namely (1) The view of local people on tourism (2) The tourist view point on tourism development (3) The view point of businessman associated with tourism at Dang district.

Local People and Tourism Development in Dangs District

A Survey of the local residents in Dangs was undertaken to find out the impact of tourism on their economic life. Though their level of education was not high most of them were literates.

People of Dangs have a strong realization of the importance of tourism in improving their economic status. Tourism gives a boost to their revenue earning capacity since the tourists buy the local products. Though tourism gives opportunity for the employment our survey has revealed that out of the people whom we have surveyed only 38.2 percent were lucky to get tour related jobs. Relating employment with education, it can be said that with more training and education tourism can bring more tour related jobs.

If government gives more priority to development of eco-tourism at Dang district it will help in the employment generation.

It has also been observed that seasonal employment has increased to a larger extent as compared to regular employment. This is because mountain tourism is seasonal and people tend to avoid those places during rainy season.

The survey has also revealed that 82.4 percentage local people have a strong feeling that after tourist development their income has increased. We also find from our sample survey that 38.2 percentage of family got employment at tourist place itself. The survey result also indicates that 91.2 percentages of tourists purchase local products and this has resulted in the improvement their economic conditions. In Dang district 76.5 percentage of local people have expressed satisfaction with the tourism development. It is observed that 17.6 percentage tourists purchased local crops which are their special crops when they visited the Dang district. This result also indicates that tourism helps to improve local economy.

It has been observed that after tourist spot development the cropping pattern has changed slightly. The agricultural production pattern is slowly changing from traditional coarse grains like ragi, kharsani, and tuver to rice and many people started cultivating medicinal plants. It indicates that in Dang district if we develop medical tourism then many local people can benefit.

Dangs district forests have resources for medicinal plants, such as Mardasingi (Helicteres ixora) and Baheda (Tecome stans microcarpa). Besides these, Sag (Tectona grandis), Khakro (Butea monosperma), Umbero (Ficus racemora), and bamboo trees are also present.

The encouraging finding of our survey is that local people have experienced an increase in their income due to tourist activities. The average annual income reported in the survey in Rs. 25789. Tourism has a potential to bring development it backward region. There is a strong case to develop Dangs as an eco-tourism center in Gujarat.

Further based on our survey it can be said that people of Dangs have not experienced negative impact of tourism so far. Mostly the local people are engaged in basic agricultural activities. Very few have taken up the cultivation of medicinal plants for commercial purpose. There is a need to train them on these aspects so that –they can benefit by cultivating medicinal plants which grow in their surroundings.

However people of Dangs have shown clear awareness about the necessity to protect the environment. The residents have given a strong opinion that usages of plastics need to be prevented in order to save the environment. The local residents can be involved directly in the development of ecotourism center at Dangs as they are aware of the necessity to protect the environment.

The preliminary survey on the tourists who arrived at Dangs revealed some interesting findings. Dangs has recorded tourists mainly from India. International tourists are occasionally touring this place. To promote this place as Eco- Tourist centre a lot of initiatives either from the government or through private-public partnership are required.

Tourist activities have taken a momentum since 2000 in this place. The government's policy of providing "Leave Travel Concession "has a positive impact on tourism here. Apart from people employed in government services, the majority of the tourists here are business people or traders.

Special feature of Dangs tourism is that the medicinal plants and herbs are purchased by tourists. There must be special efforts to be taken if these products are to be commercially traded. This will clearly bring advantages to the local population.

The Tourists' View Point on Tourism Development at Dangs

Since Dangs district is selected by Gujarat government as an eco-tourism spot, it is necessary to take an interview of the tourists who have visited this place. The respondents gave different reasons for choosing Dangs as their tourism place. The main objectives to visit Dangs were to enjoy forest, to visit hill station for fresh air and to buy some medicinal plants. The government can consider these reasons for their plan in developing the eco-tourism at this place. Travel & Tourism demand is continuously rising in Dangs district.

The tourist's opinions on the type of facilities to be developed in this local area are recorded based on research survey. The observations show that various facilities like infrastructure, educational, banking are required in this place. If government, NGOs or others insinuations take up this work properly then more people will benefit from eco-tourism. Government also can implement select schemes for tourism development in Dang district like,

- Scheme for eco-tourism
- Scheme for Market Development
- Scheme of Assistance for Large Income Generating Project
- Scheme for to highlight local Product
- Scheme for developed Medical Tourism or Health care Tourism
- Scheme for Transportation Development and others

Tourist say that if Dang district economy is to grow as eco-tourism centre then it is necessary to develop the following facilities like Hotel, Transport, Medical, Drinking and Others facility.

The Sunset point - Ahava, Naladana Dev (Borakhal), Shabarimata Praishtha at Subir, Pampa Lake, Gira Falls(Girmal Shingana), Botanical Garden (Vadhai), Shiv temple (Chikhli), The Forest of Mahalkot - Mahal , The Fort of Roop Gadh (Kalibel), Maya Devi(Bhenshkatri) and others spots has vast opportunity for eco-tourism. Dangs district has more potential to develop various type of tourism, and for this the role of government is important. Public private partnership has a major role in this development program.

The observations of tourist after they completed their tour prorgamm are recorded and it is to be mentioned here that their expectation and their experience matched almost perfectly. The tourists enjoyed the clean environment and they benefited a lot in knowing about the medicinal plants (based of forest) and the visit to the tribal people was a life experience. The various types of expenditure of tourists will help in the growth of the local economy and also help to improve the standard of living of the locals.

The tourists, it is observed, have greatly enjoyed and benefited from their experience at Dangs. For many of them Dangs appeared as an important eco-tourism center with a lot of potential.

The View Point of Businessman Associated with Tourism at Dang District

The Businessmen / traders/ tour operators possess/ or acquire the knowledge regarding tourism and tourist activities of the place in which they operate. The business people are the important stakeholders in tourist activity. Their opinion is considered as important for evolving a suitable strategy for the tourism development. The opinion of business people also reveal that with a balanced approach Dangs can develop as an important tourism centre.

The other important suggestions from the businessman regarding the infrastructure facilities are worth noting. It is necessary to give importance to the development of banking, transport, electricity and basic requirements if sustained tourism activities are to be developed in this area. In this tribal area women are seen participating in tourist related services. This is also the trend witnessed in other important tourist center in south Asia like Thailand, Indonesia and other places. Almost 53 per cent of them were from backward groups. However their educational background is not encouraging. Hardly 30 per cent reached higher secondary level and above.

Most of the people employed in tourist activities are from this region. It is strongly felt that for the development of tourist place the local people must have participatory role.

Conclusions and Recommendations

For sound ecotourism in a mountain range, there must be a participatory and a humanist efficiency, environmental friendliness and a humanistic philosophy and management. More specifically one can consider the following measures:

1) Make ecotourism more sustainable. This requires that mountain communities should invest in mechanisms that allow them to monitor development over time in the environment, in the economy and in social and cultural aspects with strict regulation and visitor use limits.
2) Reduce dependency and increase diversity Dangs is an important place for becomes these are lot of medicinal plants and herbs. As tourism matures linkages must established with medical tourism so that local people can participate and learn about medicinal plants and their commercialization.
3) Restructure and reform existing governmental and nongovernmental institutions. Successful ecotourism will hinge on the implementation of national policies and strategies formulated in consultation with local stakeholders. They can implement the ideas in their respective areas.

4) Provide access to training, communications and funding. Training in meal preparations, lodge management should expand to include local people. Further, training to create awareness of the potential harmful effects of tourism will give social benefits. Local products need to be packed as per the modern requirement. Training on these aspects is essential.

If Dangs as a mountain region is to take advantage of ecotourism, efforts must be focused on developing long term plans and policies necessary for successful implementation. Ecotourism in Dangs has a huge potential and if planned well there can be sustained development of one of the backward region of the state and this will uplift the down trodden tribal population.

REFERENCES

Alain de Janvry, Marcel Fafchamps and Elizabeth Sadoulet. (1991), Peasant Household Behavior with Missing Markets: Some Paradoxes Explained, *Economic Journal* (1101), pp. 1400-1417.

Blangy, S. and Wood, M.E. (1993), Developing and Implementing Ecotourism Guidelines for Wildlands and Neighboring Communities. In Ecotourism: A Guide for Planners and Managers, edited by Kreg Lindberg and Donald E. Hawkins (The Ecotourism Society).

Ceballos-Lascuram, H. (1996), 'Tourism, Ecotourism, and Protected Areas: The State of Nature Based Tourism Around the World and Guidelines for its Development', (Gland Switzerland IUCN).

Dangs District profile and Socio-Economic review 2006-07.

E. Boo (1990), 'Ecotourism: The Potentials and Piyfalls' 1 and 2 (Washington D.C World Wildlife Fund).

Eadington, W. and Smith, V. (1992), 'Introduction: The emergence of alternative forms of tourism. In V. Smith and W. Eadington (eds) Tourism Alternatives Potentials and Problem in the Development of Tourism (pp.1-13). Philadephia: *University of Pennsylvania Press.*

Eadington, W.R. and Redman, M. (1991), 'Economics and tourism', *Annals of Tourism Research,* 18(1), pp. 41-56.

Honey, M. (1999), 'Ecotourism and Sustainable Development: Who Owns Paradise?' Washington D.C.: *Island Press.*

Isaacs, J. C. (2000). 'The Limited Potential of Tourism to Contribute to Wildlife Conservation', *Wildlife Society Bulletin,* (28), pp. 61-69.

Lindberg, K. (1991), 'Polices for Maximizing Nature Tourism's Ecological and Economic Benefits' (Washington. C.: World Resource Institute).

Maharana, I.,.Rai, S.C. and E. Sharma, (2000), 'Valuing Ecotourism in a Sacred Lake of Sikkim Himalaya, India,' *Environmental Conservation* (27), pp. 269-277.

McNeely. J.A. and Dobias, R.J. (1991), 'Economics incentive for conserving biological diversity in Thailand', *Ambio,*20(2):86-90.

Poirier, R. (1995) 'Tourism and Development in Tunisia.' *Annals of Tourism Research* (22), pp. 157-171.

Sirakaya, E. and McLellan, R.W. (1998), 'Modeling Tour Operators' Voluntary Compliance with Ecotourism Principles: A Behavioural Approach. *Journal of Travel Research,* 36 (3), pp. 42-54.

Taylor J. E. and Adelman, I. (1996), 'Village Economies: The Design, Estimation and Use of Village wide Economic Models', *Cambridge University Press,* Cambridge.

Thomas Reardon and Steve Vosti, (1997), 'Poverty-Environment Links in Rural Areas of Developing Countries, in Sustainability, Growth, and Poverty Alleviation : A Policy and Agro ecological Perspective', ed. Steve Vosti and Thomas Reardon (Baltimore: *John Hopkins University Press*).

Websites: http://gujenvfor.gswan.gov.in/wildilife/eco-torism.html,
http://www.ecoindia.com/education/what-is-ecotourism.html,
http://www.gidb.org, http://www.gujarattourism.com,
http://www.tourisminidia.com

In: Development Management in the Twenty-First Century ISBN: 978-1-62100-699-2
Editors: Kartik Roy and Sandip Kar

Chapter 10

ENVIRONMENTAL OVERSIGHT IN INDIA

Lawson R. Smith
School of Commerce & Law, Central Queensland University, Australia

INTRODUCTION

In a smooth running democracy with a comprehensive set of environmental laws, regulations and management systems, an accountable and responsive administrative system not to mention real respect for the rule of law, a set of super-added fundamental inalienable human rights in relation to the environment, would seem to be of largely symbolic, political value. However, the potential role of human rights extending to the environment, is most apparent where federal and state governments, such as in India, have failed to set up and adequately fund the necessary administrative and managerial systems to implement and enforce their environmental laws. Out of desperation, aggrieved parties have taken their plaints to India's superior courts which on an ad hoc basis have sought to ameliorate the evident *enforcement-gap* by expansively interpreting and enforcing basic constitutional rights such as the "right to life" as extending to the right to live in a non-polluted environment.

In the hands of India's enlightened responsive judiciary, where both market and government failure has occurred in respect of the provision of environmental goods (clean air, water and land) a set of such environmental rights as trumps is unarguably of real value. However, in any country, having to resort to the courts to redress serious environmental "bads" is at most a second best substitute for life in a civil society that attaches high value to the environment and funds its government agencies accordingly, besides having long run adverse institutional and constitutional effects in relation to the (non) separation of legislative, executive and judicial powers of the state.

CIVIL SOCIETY AND SUSTAINABLE DEVELOPMENT

This paper examines, with reference to the novel Indian situation, aspects of the ecological-economic interrelationship between individuals and the environment, and whether this can usefully be couched in terms of fundamental inalienable human rights within the context of sustainable human development, premissed as it is on the environmentally sustainable development imperative since, 'perhaps the biggest challenge of our times is the task of achieving a transition to sustainability' (Kasemir *et al.* 2003, p.3) achievable only by co-opting all societal sub-systems however resistant within a whole-of-society partnership. The topic can usefully be approached with reference to the basal issue of the entrenchment of fundamental inalienable rights in the primary constitutional enactments of sovereign states, as well as in international environmental law. There are clear advantages and disadvantages attached to such an enterprise. To recap, in a democracy with an array of responsive, environmental rules plus managerial-administrative systems, fundamental human rights vis-a-vis environment values would be symbolic, political value. But in the hands of an enlightened responsive judiciary, in a country such as India where systemic market and government failure occurs, a set of such *rights as trumps* is unarguably of real utility. Nonetheless having to resort to the courts to redress serious environmental externalities or "bads" is a remedy of last resort and poor partial substitute for life in a civil society that attaches high value to preventing, 'the overuse and abuse of "environmental goods" including clean air, water and wildlife by controlling access and use' (Cole 2002, p.xi) despite the ongoing developmental imperative, and adequately funds its government agencies so that environmental laws and regulations are well promulgated and enforced against both public and private sector entities.

The remainder of this paper is structured as follows. Section two briefly surveys the growing linkage and eventual merger between human rights, environmental rights and sustainable development by the early 1990s. Then section three provides an overview of India's then mediocre economic growth and even worse environmental record. In section four, the failure of effective environmental remedies in India is examined leading to the inevitable conclusion that - applying Hart's (1961) criteria – at that juncture, India didn't have a functional legal system in environmental law matters. Section five considers the response of India's entrepreneurial, activist judiciary – principally the superior courts – in the face of government failure vis-a-vis the environment. This is followed in section six by a critical appraisal – on legal and political economy grounds – of that judicial activism and then, with concluding comments in section seven.

INCLUSION OF ENVIRONMENT IN THE HUMAN RIGHTS AGENDA

In a global community that since World War II has been concerned with advancement of the notion of fundamental human rights beginning with the *Universal Declaration of Human Rights* and the *Genocide Convention* (Abella 1999) then proceeding across a seemingly ever–expanding horizon, it is not surprising, given the parallel expanding pre-eminence afforded environmental issues, the two should eventually merge to create the composite concept of environmental rights. In 1972, the *Stockholm Declaration on the Human Environment* expressly recognized the linkage between human rights and environmental protection, stating in Principle 1 that:

> Man has the fundamental right to freedom, equality and adequate conditions of life, in an environment that permits a life of dignity and well-being … (United Nations 1972)

Since 1972, there has in effect been a three-way merger between notions of environmental rights, human rights and human development, with minimum environmental values being seen to underpin or facilitate achievement of the range of personal capabilities, well-being and freedoms (Sen 2000) that are necessary for individuals and societies to achieve personal and collective gains in human development, and which is only possible where minimum levels of human rights are recognized and enforceable:

> ... all of these claims are aimed at securing the freedoms of the persons involved - to do this or that - in one way or another. In this way, human rights are also ultimately grounded in the importance of freedoms for human lives. (UNDP 2000, p.20)

The United Nations Commission on Human Rights has – as one might expect - continued to champion that merger as evidenced by its 1994 *Draft Declaration of Principles on Human Rights and the Environment* (based on a five year study presided over by Special Rapporteur Ms Ksentini) Principle 1 of which states that: 'Human rights, an ecologically sound environment, sustainable development and peace are independent and indivisible' (United Nations Commission on Human Rights 1994).

In contrast however, the 1992 *Rio Declaration* signalled a clear departure from an over-extended human rights approach, with Principle 1 of Agenda 21 stating that: 'Human beings are at the centre of concerns for sustainable development. They are entitled to a healthy and productive life in harmony with nature' (United Nations 1992, p.1).

This was, as Birnie and Boyle (2002, p.252) observe, 'indicative of continuing uncertainty and debate about the proper place of human rights law in international law', with the principal objections against an autonomous human environmental rights including, 'uncertainty, anthropocentricity and redundancy' (p.256).

That trend continued with the 1998 Aarhus Convention generally avoiding rights-terminology but rather focusing on substantive and procedural environmental rights by requiring the parties to, 'ensure that members of the public have access to information, are allowed to participate and have access to judicial review' (Ebbesson 2002, p.1).

Nonetheless, while the merits of the merger of human rights, environmental concerns and human development continues to be a hotly contested issue (see eg. Dias 1999; UNDP 2000; Birnie and Boyle 2002, Chapter 5; OHCHR 2002), the connexion of human rights and the environment is now entrenched to various degrees in subnational, national and international environmental law provisions, statutes, constitutions, regional, bilateral and multilateral conventions and treaties. First, 'at the national level, the right to a healthy environment (or a related formulation) has been formally recognised in most national constitutions enacted since 1992' (OHCHR 2002, p.3).

And secondly:

> Generally, global and regional treaties since 1991 contain at least some reference to public information, access to remedies .... [however] ... In general, global treaties have not included specific reference to the environment or environmental rights. In contrast, even prior to the Rio Conference, regional instruments contained provisions on environmental rights. (Shelton 2002, pp.3-4)

Examples of such environmental provisions include the following.

- In the USA, there are some 30 state constitutions with environmental provisions, 18 of those being explicit. For example, the 1776 Constitution of Pennsylvania was amended in 1971 with section 27 providing that: 'The people have a right to clean air, pure water, and to the preservation of the natural, scenic and aesthetic value of the environment …'
- In Latin America, the 1853 Constitution of Argentina was amended in 1994, similarly providing in section 41(1) that: 'All inhabitants are entitled to the right to a healthy and balanced environment fit for human development in order that productive activities shall meet present needs without endangering those of future generations; and shall have the duty to preserve it.'
- The 1990 Constitution of Mozambique mandates in Article 37 that: 'The State shall promote efforts to guarantee the ecological balance and the conservation and preservation of the environment for the betterment of the quality of life of its citizens.'
- The 1996 Constitution of the Republic of South Africa recognises, in section 24 of its Bill of Rights that: 'Everyone has the right to an environment that is not harmful to their health or well-being.'
- The Constitution of the Socialist Republic of India was amended in 1977 to include Article 48A which states that: 'The State shall endeavour to protect and improve the environment and to safeguard the forests and wildlife of the country.'
- In the 1992 Rio Declaration, Principle 1 declares that: 'Human beings are at the center of concerns for sustainable development. They are entitled to a healthy and productive life in harmony of nature.'
- the European Union, whose December 2000 Charter Of Fundamental Rights Of the European Union in Article 37 espouses a fundamental right to environmental protection (European Union 2000, p.17):

A high level of environmental protection and the improvement of the quality of the environment must be integrated into the policies of the Union and ensured in accordance with the principle of sustainable development.

Moreover, general human rights provisions in constitutions such as India's, have been afforded an expansive interpretation so as to extend to the protection of minimum environmental values. Judicial activism of India's Supreme Court in a series of seminal cases dubbed public interest litigation (PIL) – but better described as "social action litigation" (Baxi cited in Sathe 2003, p.203) - beginning with *Mullin v. Union Territory of Delhi* AIR 1981 SC 746, saw Article 21 of the Constitution of India which states, 'No person shall be deprived of his life or personal liberty except according to procedure established by law', creatively expanded to encompass, inter alia, an implied right to minimum environmental standards. Such standards were considered a prerequisite to Indian citizens enjoying the right to live with human dignity and a quality of life beyond that of "mere animal existence". But whether the Article 21 principle of "human rights and decency" extends for example to permit the banning of beauty contests is a moot point: *Chandra Raja Kumari v. Police Commissioner Hyderabad* AIR 1998 AP 302 (cited in Pandey 2001, p.209).

India's Economic and Environmental Record

It is well recognized that the state's primary linkages are to the economy and that the state is the primary vehicle – via 'social steering' (Musters *et al.* 1998, p.244) - for making and implementing public environmental policy (Mercuro *et al.* 1994). In other words, 'it is the role of government to intervene to correct environmental failures of markets and economic growth' (Wiener 2000, p.1). Unsustainable environmentally destructive behaviour comprises human population growth, over-consumption of natural resources and pollution of air, water and land (Bazeman and Hoffman 1999). The transition to ecologically sustainable development worldwide has been too slow and with the main long-run dangers being not limited resource stocks but ecological degradation – land, air and water pollution comprising the most pervasive negative externalities (Baumol and Oates 1994, pp.11-12) due to, 'the fragility of self organized natural cycles' (Ayres 1998, p.198). Good environmental policy intervention is required, amongst other things to correct *market failure* including negative externalities—where the price of goods and services doesn't include their adverse environmental impact.

Indeed, the 2006 Stern Review observed that climate change was resultant upon the greatest market failure of all. The key questions which the Stern Review (Stern 2006) addressed were: what were the risks of climate change, on whom did the adverse impacts fall, what were the mitigation options and what would they cost. These translated into three critical policy issues: for mitigation what kind of incentive structures and policies will be most efficient and equitable; for adaptation, what approaches are appropriate and how should they be financed; and how can approaches for both mitigation and adaptation work at an international level (Stern 2006, p.3). Elevating environmental concerns to the lofty level of a fundamental right against society-at-large and government agencies in particular, is one thing. The ability of a society to uniformly deliver on such a promise is quite another, especially when a raft of contemporaneously enacted environmental laws had clearly failed to effect the requisite decoupling of economic activities (let alone secure poverty reduction above the low pre-1991 "Hindu rate of growth") from environmental degradation.

In sum, until the 1990s, the Socialist Republic of India adhered to a perverse autarkic, market-socialist approach to economic management that produced lacklustre gains in economic growth (Smith 2001) at a very high cost in environmental degradation in a laissez faire 'grow now clean up later' approach common in Asia (ESCAP Secretariat 2000, p.2) but a particularly poor trade-off and arguably the worst of both worlds in India's case (Hediger 2000; Pargal and Mani 2000; Stuligross 1999). Since 1950, life expectancy has nonetheless increased from about 28 to 60 years and sustained economic growth since 1990 has boosted per capita GDP by 2002 to (PPP) US$ 2,840, as measured by the 2003 *Human Development Report* (UNDP 2003). This however represented mediocre comparative progress, with India's 2003 ranking of 127 pushed down by sizeable countrywide (including gender-related) variation and poor health indicators reflecting under-nutrition, poor health services and high mortality rates (highest among the poor and rural caste populations) exacerbated by outdoor and indoor air pollution related diseases and premature deaths (Smith 2000; UNEP 2001 GAIA 2002; World Bank 2002).

It has been estimated that 60 per cent of Calcutta's residents have air pollution related diseases (GAIA 2002, p.5). Rapid increases in industrial activity, urban population growth, transport, energy demands and motor vehicles in addition to indoor household air pollution from use of unvented biomass fuel, has led to very high levels of urban pollution – with almost 70 per cent being vehicular pollution. For example, compared with the US annual particulate matter (PM10) standard of 50 ug/m3 – and a US wide average of less than 30 ug/m3 - in New Delhi for the July 2000 to July 2001 period, the mean respiratory suspended particulate matter was 204 ug/m3 (World Bank 2002, p.1). There was also the discovery by scientists of a colossal haze of air pollution about the size of the USA covering the Indian Ocean during winter time, 'composed of several kinds of minute byproducts from the burning of fossil fuels for industry and transportation' (Stevens 1999, p.18).

As a consequence, there were an estimated 50,000 -300,000 premature deaths per annum in India caused by outdoor air pollution. In addition, indoor air pollution levels some 10-50 times higher caused a further 400,000-550,000 million premature deaths with young children and adult women being most at risk so that, 'on a risk factor basis, the burden of dirty air at the household level lies only behind dirty water ...and poor food ... the largest two risk factors in India in the early 1990s' (Smith 2000, p.1392). Thus while particulate matter pollution in the west has generally fallen sharply since 1950 reducing related mortality rates, it had risen sharply in urban India - New Delhi in particular - which has indeed undercut India's overall gains in human prosperity (see Lomborg 2001, Chapter 15).

In the midst of India's mediocre growth with high environmental degradation phase, Indian governments enacted an array of environmental legislation which if adhered to by the public and private sectors alike - ignoring the problematic non-compliant small-scale private sector (Stuligross 1999) - would have achieved a noticeable reduction in emission levels and natural resource degradation. However, that has not been the case. The eminent Indian environmental lawyer Divan (2000, p.4) cites the Indian Supreme Court as having lamented that the burgeoning body of environment law, 'has, unfortunately, not resulted in preventing environmental degradation which, on the contrary, has increased over the years.'

In light of successive Indian governments having failed to adequately address the issue, the United Nations Environment Program in its report *State of the Environment India 2001*, specifically addressed vehicular-sourced urban air pollution. It noted that existing schemes and programs were not being effective and outlined a 10 point practical strategy for the effective management of urban air pollution, 'that reduces both emissions and congestion, using a mixed set of instruments, which are dictated by command and control, and/or the market-based principles' (UNEP 2001, p.109).

FAILURE OF EFFECTIVE ENVIRONMENTAL REMEDIES

The judicial activism of India's Supreme Court and State High Courts with respect to development of novel environmental remedies did not occur in an autopoietic vacuum. It transpired as an innovative response to the evident shortcomings – collectively comprising government failure (see Wolf 1993, Chapters 3-4) - of existing legal remedies combined with chronic systematic failure by the leading government agencies to function properly and to devise and enforce relevant planning procedures, legal rules and regulations relating to the all-important impact of economic activities on environmental values. While it is a truism that legal environmental remedies are a poor substitute for good planning and legal compliance in the first instance, India had a wide array of common law based and statutory civil and criminal procedural rights and remedies available to those suffering physical, property or financial damages caused by industrially sourced pollution and environmental degradation. Briefly stated, the main rights and remedies were as follows.

- The Indian Code 1860 had a number of public nuisance offences relating to air and water pollution, with individuals having the right to make a Police complaint that if sustained should lead to a successful prosecution.
- Relatedly, the existence of a public nuisance was the basis of three distinct, concurrent sets of procedural rights. Section 133 of the Code of Criminal Procedure 1973 by which an individual or group could obtain an order from a Magistrate for the removal of a public nuisance A civil remedy whereby if an individual had suffered special damage then in addition to the grant of a conditional order under criminal law, damages and an injunction (preventing continuance of the nuisance) is obtainable. And section 91 of the Code of Civil Procedure 1908 which allowed individuals, with leave of the court, to institute proceedings for a declaration as to their rights, a mandatory injunction or similar relief with respect to incidents of public nuisance.
- As in other common law countries (Australia and New Zealand, UK and USA), a number of general civil tort actions - nuisance, trespass and negligence – were available, by which on satisfying certain requirements as to proof of causation and quantum of damages etc., individuals and classes of individuals can obtain a financial award for past damages against a defendant or class of defendants, as well as injunctive relief to prevent ongoing damages (Anderson 1998, pp.204-206; Divan and Rosencranz 2001, pp.87-111).

Besides these essentially private law means by which environmental values could be protected, India had enacted more than two hundred laws effecting environmental protection in some manner, with there being a bout of legislative activity in the 1980s following the industrial catastrophe at Bhopal in 1984. The main legislative enactments included:

- The Factories Act 1948;
- The Mines and Minerals (Regulation and Development) Act 1957;
- The Water (Prevention and Control of Pollution) Act 1974;
- The Water (Prevention and Control of Pollution) Cess Act 1977;
- The Forest (Conservation) Act 1980;
- The Air (Prevention and Control of Pollution) Act 1981;
- The Environment (Protection) Act 1986;
- The Public Liability Insurance Act 1991;
- The National Environment Tribunal Act 1995;
- The National Environment Appellate Authority Act 1997; and

- Environmental Impact Assessments and Environmental Management Plans have been required since 1994 for new projects (Jaswal and Jaswal 2000; Modak and Biswas 1999, Chapter 1).

These were essentially public acts that by a somewhat obsolete, high cost and ineffective (see Baumol and Oates 1994, Chapters 12-14) "command and control" prohibition and licencing system, sought to control the location of industry and set emission standards to technically specified levels under an administrative system undertaken, e.g., by the much beleaguered Central and State Pollution Control Boards. For example, section 7 of the *Environment (Protection) Act 1986* provides that:

> No person carrying on any industry, operation or process shall discharge or emit or permit to be discharged or emitted any environmental pollutant in excess of such standards as may be prescribed.

A breach of the *Environment (Protection) Act 1986* exposed the individual, corporation or government department liable under sections 15-17 to a range of compliance orders, fines and imprisonment of up to five years - subject to the usual "due diligence" defence. Of some interest, section 19(b) of the Act provided a private right of prosecution for non-compliance with the Act on giving 60 days notice of the alleged offence to the authorities and of the intention to lodge a private prosecution. However, this was a somewhat flawed remedy with the upshot that there hadn't been a single private citizen-based prosecution. The Air and Water Acts contained similar provisions allowing for private prosecutions, but also had a poor record of successful citizen-initiated prosecutions.

In contrast, the *Public Liability Insurance Act 1991* and *National Environment Tribunal Act 1995* comprised more effective regimes with of no-fault liability standards that provided industrial accident victims with summary remedies and speedy claims-processing machinery operating on a mostly decentralized district basis, with few defences available to the owners of a hazardous facility (Divan and Rosencranz 2001, pp.132-133).

Nonetheless, collectively these general common law and specific statutory provisions relating to the specification of minimum environmental standards and their private and public enforcement were ineffective. Principally, this was due to the aggregate effects of flaws in their design, procedural constraints and shortcomings and most importantly, the abject failure of public agencies in dissemination and enforcement of public environmental laws, resulting in a massive *compliance and enforcement gap* (on responsive environmental regulation see: Ayres and Braithwaite 1992; Gunningham and Grabosky 1998). On one approach, chronic failure here had occurred due to India's political-administrative agencies collectively comprising a classic Myrdal-type "soft state" which is, 'not capable of implementing policies that go against the interests of the bureaucracies or powerful groups in society' (Martinussen 1997, p.226). In this context, the *soft Indian state* was a composite of inadequate funding, lackadaisical commitment by the executive to environmental issues vis-à-vis economic growth and the status quo, corruption, agency incompetence and lack of resilience in the face of industry (including the public sector) hostility to being forced to bear the costs of regulatory compliance.

In marked contrast to the situation in other common law countries where the tort law actions in nuisance, trespass and negligence were the main private remedies in relation to "environmental wrongs", their following failings in the Indian legal system, meant that Indian litigants weren't able to exploit their potential. First, the legacy of the British Colonial era in which disputes were resolved via public law and administration rather than private litigation. Second, long delays in obtaining legal remedies, e.g. from 1950 and 1985 it took some 17 years on average to obtain final judgment in tort cases before the Supreme Court. Third, the complex uncodified case law based system of private tort law remedies was somewhat daunting to Indian lawyers better versed in Statute-based remedies. Fourth, the level of damages awarded was generally low, failing to act as a deterrent against polluting companies. Fifth, archaic procedural constraints that were a significant barrier to tort-based litigation. Sixth, unlike other common law countries, the Indian government still had the benefit of the archaic nineteenth century *immunity doctrine* based on the 1861 *Peninsular & Oriental Steam Navigation v. Secretary of State for India* case that gave government agencies extensive immunity from liability for civil wrongs relating to their ownership or occupation of property etc. And seventh, as elsewhere, reliance on environmental tort remedies in India had some inherent limitations (Anderson 1998, pp.200-201; 207-209). Consequently, although the law of torts seemed well suited to tackling environmental externalities in India such as industrial pollution, as Anderson (1998, p.201) rightly concluded, 'the overall impact of tort in abating environmental degradation has been minimal.'

In addition, as adverted to above, government agencies had an exceptionally poor record for enforcing most legislation including Air, Water, Environmental and Forestry Acts. The State and Central Pollution Control Boards (PCBs) in particular, attracted sustained criticism. As Rosencranz and Jackson (2003, p.3) observed, 'due to a chronic lack of funding, the Boards have been relatively ineffective, and as of 1997, no one has ever been jailed for polluting the environment.' However, such failings of the PCBs should be viewed in the context of successive governments privileging economic growth over environmental integrity. For example, in 1997, the Finance Ministry of the United Front Government gave a directive that new small businesses would be exempt from environmental regulation. While the succeeding BJP Government was apparently been little different, 'the most coherent interest of the coalition is to keep business booming' (Stuligross 1999, p.3). Anderson (1998, p.202) levels the following broad based criticisms at the PCBs:

The monitoring and implementation of environmental standards under such legislation is inconsistent and haphazard. The Pollution Control Boards are generally under funded and overburdened with routine record keeping. Although many of the administrators are highly trained, their work is frequently impeded by political interventions on behalf of particular polluters. Apart from some important exceptions, the Boards tend to be chaired by short tenure political appointees with no practical experience in the area of environmental management, leaving technical staff unsupported and demoralized. Since many major industries - including coal, petroleum, electricity, iron and steel, agrochemicals and heavy machinery - are mainly in the public sector, they are not likely to be prosecuted by a Board consisting of government nominees.

Shaman (1996, pp.8-9) noted similar failings of the PCBs, typical of which was that while the Water Act was enacted in 1974, 'by 1988 the state of Bihar had not set up a laboratory for testing water and air samples and not also received appropriate authorization from the Central Board to institute proceedings under the Water Cess Act 1977.' However, the Central Pollution Control Board subsequently became more pro-active in pollution control. It reported that in 2001-2002:

> … special thrust was given to nation-wide pollution prevention plan, particularly with reference to combating vehicular pollution, pollution control in 17 categories of highly polluting industries, implementation of action plans for restoration of environmental quality in critically polluted areas, noise pollution control, municipal solid wastes and hazardous wastes. (Central Pollution Control Board 2002, p.12)

The general non-compliance by industry and non-enforcement by officials of environmental legislation, makes the question moot, with reference to Hart's (1961) two minimum and sufficient conditions for the existence of a legal system, whether India actually had a functional legal system in operation in this era with respect to environmental rules and regulations. On an empirical basis, there seemed at best only a weak correlation between environmental law requirements and prescribed behaviour. This should have provided grounds for serious disquiet in the world's largest democracy that formally adhered to the rule of law. Hart's (1961, p.113) two minimum and sufficient conditions for a legal system are as follows.

- Those rules of behaviours which are valid according to the rule of recognition must be generally obeyed. This does not require that private citizens have to internally accept the primary rules and the rule of recognition, just that from whatever motive they obey them. Although, in a healthy society the rules will be obeyed from the "internal" viewpoint.
- That officials must accept and apply its rules of recognition, criteria of legal validity, as well as rules of change and adjudication. And that these must be:

> … effectively accepted as common public standards of official behaviour by its officials ... and [who] appraise critically their own and others deviations as lapses ... Evidence for the existence of a legal system must therefore be drawn from two different sectors of social life ... that the rules recognised as valid at the official level are generally obeyed. (p.113)

Admittedly, Hart distinguished the matter of legal validity of a rule from the notion of its efficacy, meaning, 'the fact that a rule of law which requires certain behaviour is obeyed more often that not, it is plain that there is no necessary connexion between any particular rule and its efficacy' (Hart 1961, p.100). Such disconnexion was perhaps never in greater evidence than in Indian environmental law.

Response of India's Activist Judiciary

As adverted to in the first section of this paper, the potential role of human rights principles extending to the environment is most apparent where federal and state governments such as in India failed to establish and adequately fund the necessary administrative and managerial systems to implement and enforce their environmental laws. Aggrieved parties, could then so the argument runs take 'the last resort of the oppressed and bewildered' (Justice Goswami in *State of Rajasthan v. Union of India* (1977) 3 SCC at 592 as cited in Rosencranz and Jackson (2003, p.12) via the public interest litigation route to the superior courts (the state High Courts and the Supreme Court) and articulate arguments for an expansive interpretation and enforcement of basic Constitutional rights such as the Article 21 "right to life" as extending to include minimum environmental standards in relation to the air, water and land. The question arose therefore as to how India's superior courts effected a paradigmatic shift in the efficacious availability of remedies and procedures in relation to blatant environmental wrongs that the relevant government agencies failed to take notice of and respond to. They did so in a responsive evolutionary process – principally in association with an entrepreneurial, autonomous judicial agency expansion (see Breton 1996, Chapter 3) into collective or public interest litigation - the effect of which, 'changed the character of the judicial process from adversarial to polycentric and adjudicative to legislative' (Sathe 2003, p.235). That entrepreneurial expansion of legal remedies in response to a large unmet public demand for public sector sourced environmental goods from other government agencies, proceeded principally by:

- An expansion of their writ jurisdiction.
- The allowance of public interest litigation with an associated radical expansion of the willingness of the courts to engage in ongoing administrative-type supervision of remedies (often over a period of years) besides the wholesale relaxation of existing locus standi restrictions on standing to sue.
- Permitting class actions to proceed, on an expansive interpretation of the *Code of Civil Procedure 1908*.
- Circumventing the obsolete, repressive *Official Secrets Act 1923* by deriving the right to know relevant government-sourced information from Article 19(1)(a) of the Constitution of India concerning the fundamental right to freedom of speech and expression, and Article 21 - the right to life and personal liberty. Of these four, judicial innovations relating to the writ jurisdiction and public interest litigation are particularly noteworthy.

First, regarding their writ jurisdiction, the Supreme Court and state High Courts exploited their empowerment under Articles 32 and 226 of the *Constitution of India* to issue directions and a range of prerogative writs (types of judicial orders) in order to provide speedy, cheap and simple environmental remedies to litigants, in substitution for the raft of more cumbersome, slow and ineffective private remedies they would otherwise have to pursue to address the systemic failings of government agencies in environmental and other matters. For instance, the prerogative writ of mandamus could be issued against a public agency to mandate its performance of some statutory duty such as providing basic public health infrastructural services or to enforce emission standards against some non-compliant industrial polluter.

Secondly, the technical barriers to (environmental) justice were dramatically reduced by a liberalised Supreme Court whereby in matters of public grievance, the traditional requirements for litigants to have a sufficient legal interest (be a person aggrieved and therefore have adequate legal standing or *locus standi*) beyond that of the general public were radically truncated. Not only was the right to sue extended to the poor and oppressed suffering socio-economic or environmental injustices, they were allowed "representative standing" (another person e.g. a public minded lawyer could act on their behalf). In addition, in matters of broad public interest (public interest litigation) where historically, no individual had legal standing to petition the courts for judicial review of even patently egregious or abusive exercises of executive authority, the Supreme Court granted such rights to any individual citizen in his/her own right - now referred to as "citizen standing" (Divan and Rosencranz 2001, Chapter 4).

Such innovative procedures were put to sterling use in the environmental arena, with the judiciary having progressively assumed, ‘a pro-active role of public educator, policy maker, super-administrator and more generally, amicus [the friend of] environment. The judicial initiatives do not derive from any particular statute but have grown from the court's constitutional obligations’ (Divan 2000, p.3). These procedural innovations were instrumental in the courts developing a range of substantive general legal environmental principles which collectively have empowered the victims of pollution against non-compliant polluters and governments hitherto unwilling to pro-actively commit the necessary public resources to pollution prevention and planning, environmental law enforcement including the precautionary principle and ensuring that victims are compensated for any pollution-induced damages suffered.

Meanwhile, the extensive involvement of India’s superior courts in administering its notions of environmental justice continued apace. For example, during 1999 the Supreme Court delivered some 22 environment related judgments and orders, the various state High Courts delivered 21 environment law decisions and the redoubtable environmental lawyer M. C. Mehta himself having filed 10 legal actions (Jariwala 2000, pp.15-16).

Political Economy Critique of Judicial Activism

Whilst skeptics and critics of an activist Indian judiciary readily conceded that their contribution with respect to freeing up environmental litigation had effected clear human and legal rights as well as environmental gains, they nevertheless asserted that the sustainability, economic, legal and philosophical merits of such a radical contribution to procedural remedies and substantive environmental legal principles remained open to conjecture. In this section the activism and entrepreneurship of India’s superior courts is critically appraised on various legal and political economy grounds.

First, the inter-connected doctrine of the separation of powers and concept of the rule of law. While Locke (1690) in his *Two Treatises of Government*, wrote on the separation of the legislative and executive powers of a commonwealth and adhered to existing views regarding the balancing of power, as Laslett (2002, p.120) notes in Locke’s view:

> … the judiciary was no separate power, it was the general attribute of the state …. [so that] … the proper functioning and just exercise of these powers … is done by the concept of trust, which applies to the legislative in its fullest force, but also to the executive and federative.

Rather, it was Montesquieu drawing on Locke amongst others and his familiarity with and admiration of the Constitution of England, who in his 1748 *The Spirit of the Laws*, ‘developed a genuine doctrine of separation of powers’ (Neumann 1949, p.lx). This advocated a clear separation of the (third) judicial power in the machinery of the state or government from legislative and executive powers in order to best secure the life and liberty of the subject:

> In every government there are three sorts of power: the legislative; the executive in respect of things dependent on the law of nations; and the executive [i.e. judicial] in regard to matters that depend on the civil law ... When the legislative and executive powers are united in the same person, or in the same body of magistrates, there can be no liberty; because apprehensions may arise, lest the same monarch or senate should enact tyrannical laws, to execute them in a tyrannical manner. Again, there is no liberty, if the judicial power be not separated from the legislative and executive. Were it joined with the legislative, the life and liberty of the subject would be exposed to arbitrary control; for the judge would then be the legislator. Were it joined to the executive power, the judge might behave with violence and oppression. (Montesquieu 1949, pp.151-152)

Since Montesquieu, variant models that imperfectly separate the legislative (law enacting) and executive (law enforcing) powers of government but better quarantine its judicial (adjudicative) powers have formed the basis of workable constitutional settlements and enactments including India's 1950 Constitution. While as Allars (1990, p.35) notes the pure version of Montesquieu's doctrine involves three propositions, it is the third proposition, 'the personnel of one branch of government should not be members of any other branch exercising any of the functions of that other branch ... [that] ... is probably the most fundamental and is designed to protect individual liberty by the dispersion of power.' However Allars (1990, p.35) adds the important rider that, 'the third principle must be supplemented by a positive doctrine of checks and balances in order to provide a theory about control by one branch over another in the form of checking, of securing accountability.'

Secondly, in a political economy extension of the doctrine of separation of powers and associated doctrine of checks and balances, Breton (1996, pp.71-72) cogently argues that since there is invariably some overlapping in the activities of government centres of power, the separation of powers in contemporary democratic practice means rather, 'the separate, singular, and distinctive authority (power in the singular) possessed by these centres of power ... [and that] ... the authority of a centre of power cannot easily be taken away from it and abolished.' The concept of the rule of law – is its variant versions – to the effect the government must be by law and not arbitrary decree, articulates elements of the construct of the separation of government powers as well as the importance of internal checks and balances. A modest version of the rule of law (a composite of six propositions) includes the proposition that, 'individuals [and institutions] having legal authority to apply or enforce norms should do so correctly and consistently and should be accountable for their compliance with legal standards applicable to their decision' (Allars 1990, p.15). Thus, the judiciary acts as an important autonomous centre of power which ensures that laws enacted and enforced are valid with reference to the existing legal system – that is, an authoritative source and list of primary and secondary rules - and which the relevant agencies can be required to recognize and enforce at the instigation of any citizen or group recognized by the courts as having the necessary locus standi or standing to sue (Hart 1961). Moreover, as Breton (1996, pp.321-325) elaborates in a refutation of the Landes and Posner thesis that as a matter of design, judiciaries behave as if they are colluding with the legislature, that judiciaries are in fact designed as, 'independent, autonomous and balanced centres of power that can and do check other centres of power, including legislatures.' What then is judicial power? The nature of judicial power and decision-making – which ought not to be exercised by the legislature or executive – can be defined as follows (Allars 1990, pp.36-37):

> .... a process of inquiry concerning the law as it is and the facts as they are, followed by an application of the law as determined ... [so that] ... the end to be reached in the process of judicial decision-making must be an act which entitles and obliges the persons between whom it intervenes, to observance of the rights and obligations that the application of law to facts has shown to exist ...

Because it generally comprises a secondary or residual checking and balancing function vis-à-vis more extensive and better resourced centres of government, the judicial centre(s) of autonomous power is generally regarded as the weakest organ of government — though this view is moot. As Australian High Court Justice McHugh (2004, p. 1) writing extra-judicially noted, this 'weakest organ' view originates with the revolutionary American, Alexander Hamilton writing in 1787–88. Hamilton asserted that 'the judiciary is beyond comparison the weakest of the three departments of power' since it had, 'no influence over either the sword or the purse' and 'could take no active resolution whatsoever', so that it had to, 'depend upon the aid of the executive arm even for the efficacy of its judgments' (cited in McHugh 2004, p.1). However - with special relevance and application to India's pro-active, interventionist judiciary - Justice McHugh (2004, p.2) contested Hamilton's view, correctly asserting that it overlooked three developing aspects of the judiciary's strengths:

> The first is the frequency with which the judiciary has been called on to exercise the power of judicial review and declare legislative and executive acts void and of no effect. The second is the importance of the social, economics and political issues that courts—especially federal courts—must decide. The third is the underpinning of the judiciary's strength by public confidence in its integrity, impartiality and capacity.

Relevantly, Sathe (2003, Chapter 7) argues that the expanded role of India's superior courts – public interest litigation especially – arose in response to government lawlessness, corruption and abuse of power and that the legitimacy of the courts and judicial activism arose from the faith of the Indian people in their ability to withstand public pressure, to be impartial and objective. Employing Breton's (1996) exegesis of the positive effects of competition between autonomous centres of power in a compound government, India's superior courts (a non-elected centre) responded to the utility loss Indian citizens suffered from the chronic failure of elected centres of power to produce the array (quality and quantity) of public and private type goods and services (e.g. effective regulations to ensure clean air, water and land, an accessible justice system etc) - many of which government had a monopoly over – they demanded and expected supply of at the aggregate tax price (the budget) which they bore. In sum, Indian citizens were paying a premium price for the (non) delivery of an array of very inferior public-sector delivered and mediated goods and services and which in the environmental arena resulted in a polluted environment hazardous to individual capability and well being. Breton (1996, p.95) cogently argues that:

> Because centres of power [elected and non-elected] seek the consent of constituencies of citizens, because these grant consent in amounts that vary with the volume of characteristics offered, and because that volume is obtained by making use of checking instruments, centres

> of power compete with one another to produce and deliver, through concessions and compromises, a vector of characteristics that meet the preferences of citizens and, through that channel, forge Wicksellian links between taxprices and the valuation of goods and services provided.

Thus as far as the average Indian (especially urban resident) citizen was concerned, on a whole-of-government basis, the expansion of the non-elected autonomous judicial centre of power via various entrepreneurial means (i.e. judicial creativity) and coercive-cooperative devices to obtain the necessary resources in order to deliver an augmented array of legislative, executive and regulatory services that elected centres were unable to deliver for a variety of reasons, to employ Breton's (1996, p.84) terms while, 'zero-sum for centres of power ... [is] ... positive-sum for citizens. Competition in politics as in economics, is beneficial in the sense of generating a surplus for citizens.'

Nonetheless, the "strong version" of Breton's thesis of compound governments and the virtues of intragovernment competition between elected as well as non-elected autonomous centres of power has intrinsic constraints and arguably cannot be deployed for example in the Indian case to sanction and give carte blanche to - on a long run basis and by way of permanent equilibrium shift - the judicial activism of its superior courts. Legislative, executive and judicial powers in the modern state are distinctive and non-substitutable except perhaps at the margins. Breton arguably envisages an otherwise tolerably well functioning compound government in which competition exists vis-à-vis the efficient delivery of a dynamic set of goods and services, not the exceptional case of one autonomous centre of power (e.g. the judiciary) feeling duty bound – on a long run but ad hoc basis - to expand and deliver services it does not have a comparative or competitive advantage in, to redress the partial or total failure of other centres – despite their statutory duty - to deliver those services.

Breton (1996) adheres to the separation of powers doctrine and advocates, as noted above, especially the independence of the judiciary. In exercising what are demonstrably legislative and executive powers under the guise of judicial entrepreneurship and activism, India's superior courts are – despite their best intentions and endeavours - reintegrating government powers and in the process, amongst other undesirable consequences, depriving citizens of the potential for independent judicial review of that exercise. The superior courts also suppress standard political processes in doing so – including concession and compromise – and which is frequently buried in the internal machinations and reports of ad hoc delegated committees set up by the courts and also the potential for critical debate since in those matters encompassed within judicial proceedings, otherwise permissible public criticism can be deemed contempt of court. For example, criticism of the role and decisions of India's Supreme Court in relation to a big dam project led to the celebrated Indian author and political activist Arundhati Roy, facing contempt charges.

Furthermore, notwithstanding evident systemic failure by government agencies and centres of power, it is somewhat ironic and perhaps akin to hypocrisy (the homage that vice pays to virtue) for India's superior courts to have felt bound to remediate such failings when, 'ordinary civil and criminal justice systems are in a chaotic condition. Justice is expensive, time-consuming and over-technical ... [and] ... the legal aid system in India is most unsatisfactory' (Sathe 2003, p.301-302).

Thirdly, there are by way of numerous examples, clear constraints as to how far judges can arrogate to themselves what are patently legislative and executive/administrative functions without jeopardizing to some degree the reputation of the superior courts within the international and domestic legal fraternities if not the public-at-large.

One case that clearly illustrates this point is *M. C. Mehta v. Union of India* AIR 1992 SC 382 in which the renowned environmental lawyer and environmentalist persuaded the Supreme Court to issue detailed orders requiring: (i) the media to broadcast environmental programs; and (ii) educational authorities to include environmental material in secondary and tertiary courses. The "decision" (executive order) of the Supreme Court is objectionable on various procedural and substantive legal grounds including the non-representation of all those parties with legitimate interests at stake as well as the common sense objection of the Supreme Court having no particular knowledge or expertise in pedagogical and commercial media matters. However the principal objection to the order issued was that on any understanding of the separation of powers doctrine and the rule of law, the Supreme Court was evidently usurping first, legislative powers of the Indian Parliament in formulating what was tantamount to a regulation. And secondly, the Union Government's executive powers in issuing or promulgating the order. A similar action if undertaken by an inferior tribunal with quasi-judicial powers or a magistrate's court would presumably have speedily attracted, on application by the relevant attorney-general, the issuance of a prerogative writ invalidating its purported order and a judicial rebuke for having so clearly exceeded its jurisdictional mandate.

But perhaps the best example of such ill-advised albeit well-intentioned incursion into legislative and executive/administrative territory was provided by the notorious Delhi air pollution case, ongoing since 1985 when the redoubtable M.C. Mehta initiated public interest litigation proceedings against the Union Government of India, 'charging that existing environmental laws obligated the government to take steps to help reduce Delhi's air pollution in the interests in public health' (Rosencranz and Jackson 2003, p.5). After interminable delays, on 28 July 1998, the Supreme Court issued a direction that to remediate that city's chronic air pollution problem, by 31 March 2001 the entire fleet of city buses was to be converted to the single fuel CNG mode. However, *M. C. Mehta v. Union of India* 1998 SOL Case No. 339 reveals that bargaining about the original order was already occurring by September 1998 and similar directives from 1996 to shut down small polluting enterprises operating illegally in residential areas of Delhi.

The Supreme Court's lack of comparative advantage vis-à-vis the regular government agencies usually charged with the design and implementation of environmental policy in a complex socio-economic and political milieu also requiring resolution of technical issues and policy choices, was most starkly evident here. There seems little evidence that if charged with such a project and made responsive to public opinion and consent, the relevant agencies would not have performed the task more quickly and at least equally as well on any objective criteria. Especially since social steering through public policy intervention is highly problematic so that policy evaluation typically reveals flaws in the policy's rational foundation (van den Knapp 1995). As Raskin *et al.* (1999, p.x) rightly observe, 'there are no blueprints for a transition to sustainability, what is required is the refinement of goals over time in the light of additional information and events in a spirit of adaptive management.' Although as it happens, the choice of a single fuel CNG was justifiable on economic and environmental grounds (at least according to the Bhure Lal Committee), the development of a schedule for completion once again was an act of administrative policy formulation and implementation with purely legal matters relegated to a subsidiary facilitative role. Moreover, in stark contrast with the 18 years of litigation in the Delhi air pollution case, under public sector management of one sort or another, as Rosencranz and Jackson (2003, p.13) observed, 'construction of the multi-billion dollar Delhi subway system remains on schedule and on budget. By subcontracting most of the work to private firms ... major civil projects can apparently be completed efficiently, without any element of compulsion by the Court.'

Moreover, it was evident in the Delhi pollution case that the Delhi Government and private transport firms were on occasions, less than cooperative. Also, when it became evident that the 31st March 2001 deadline could not be met, in a series of cases that basically comprised haggling exercises, subsequent grants of extensions were rationalized on various grounds including hardships being faced by school children. In sum, the prestige and reputation of India's Supreme Court was potentially jeopardized by this ill-advised excursion into the byzantine business of government administration and their assumption of the role of bus fleet managers and ad hoc issuers of temporary dispensational permits: *M. C. Mehta v. Union of India* 2001 SOL Case No. 212; *M. C. Mehta v. Union of India* 2001 SOL Case No. 248. Axiomatically therefore on a whole-of-government basis, as Rosencranz and Jackson (2003, p.14) note, the Supreme Court's involvement and rulings in the Delhi pollution case, 'had harmful institutional and constitutional consequences ... likely to impede capacity building in the pollution control agencies, and thereby to compromise the development of sustained environmental management in India.'

CONCLUDING COMMENTS

As Divan (2000) rightly explained it, India's superior courts were no substitute for a well-performing well-financed executive/administrative branch of government. They were both not designed for nor should they have been engaged in the ongoing management of cases (often for decades) tantamount to assuming oversight of the task of departmental administration of environmental laws and regulations. And as Divan (2000, p.6) further posited, whilst the superior courts admirably stepped into the breach as a super-agency, 'court-administered implementation can at best supplement, not replace, the formal agency-dependent enforcement mechanism.' Moreover, the scope of the resultant environmental rights - as is the case of many legal principles – were necessarily vague and poorly defined, 'thus leaving both businesses and environmentalists uncertain how far their rights and duties extend' (Anderson 1998, p.11).

What was evidently necessary, was remedial legislation clearly articulating environmental standards, rights and duties (i.e. substantive rights) and correlative procedural rules mandating rights of court access enabling enforcement of those substantive environmental rights. That is, procedural rights to the judicial system enabling enforcement of hard-edged "black-letter" substantive rights. In the 1994 *Final Report of the UN Sub-Commission on Human Rights and the Environment* by the Special Rapporteur Mrs Ksentini, particular attention was devoted to the importance of procedural rights (cited in Cameron and Mackenzie 1998, p.132).

To sum up, fundamental politico-democratic grounds existed – despite the evident systemic failings of Indian's political processes - for opposing the continuing over-extensive incursion of India's superior courts into environmental policy formulation and administration. As Campbell (1999, p.13) cogently argued:

> ... there are strong grounds for asserting a democratic version of the rule of law which gives electorates and their elected representatives the overwhelming dominant role in law making. This is only in part because courts are not likely to arrive at morally better conclusions, and only in part because the processes of self-determination are as important as their outcomes ... Add to these the difficult task of making good laws and you not only overload the system, but produce a confusion of law-making, law-identification and law-application which undermines at least two of the reasons for having the rule of law, namely to curb the self-interest of legislators and to enable citizens to know the standards by which their conduct will be judged should they come into conflict with the state.

REFERENCES

Abella, R. S. (1999), 'Human Rights and the Judicial Role', AIJA Annual Oration in Judicial Administration, viewed 1 October 2001, http://www.aija.org.au/Rabella.htm.

Allars, M. (1990), 'Introduction to Australian Administrative Law', *Butterworths,* Sydney.

Anderson, M. (1998), 'Human Rights Approaches to Environmental Protection: An Overview' in A. Boyle and M. Anderson (eds) Human Rights Approaches To Environmental Protection, *Clarendon Press Oxford,* Chapter 1.

Ayres, I. and Braithwaite, J. (1992), 'Responsive Regulation: Transcending the Regulation Debate', *Oxford University Press,* Oxford.

Ayres, R. U. (1998), 'Eco-Thermodynamics: Economics and the Second Law', *Ecological Economics,* 26 (2), pp.189-209.

Baumol, W. J. and Oates, W. E. (1994), 'The Theory of Environmental Policy', 2nd edition, *Cambridge University Press,* Cambridge.

Bazeman, M. H. and Hoffman. A. J. (1999), 'Sources of Environmentally Destructive Behaviour'Individual,Organizational and Institutional Perspectives', *Research in Organizational Behaviour,* 21, pp.39-79.

Birnie, P. and Boyle, A. E. (2002), 'International Law and the Environment', 2nd edition, *Oxford University Press,* Oxford.

Breton, A. (1996) 'Competitive Governments: An Economic Theory of Politics and Public Finance', *Cambridge University Press,* Cambridge.

Cameron, J. and Mackenzie, R. (1998), 'Access to Environmental Justice and Procedural Rights in International Institutions', in A.Boyle and M. Anderson (eds) Human Rights Approaches To Environmental Protection, *Clarendon Press Oxford*, Chapter 7.

Campbell, T. (1999), 'Judging in a Democracy, Judicial Conference of Australia', viewed 1 October 2001, http://www.law.monash.edu.au/JCA/Campbell.htm.

Central Pollution Control Board, (2002), Annual Report 2001-2002, viewed 4 February 2004, http://www.cpcb.delhi.nic,in/ar2002/ar-2.content.htm.

Cole, D. H. (2002), 'Pollution and Property': Comparing Ownership Institutions for Environmental Protection, *Cambridge University Press,* Cambridge.

Dias, A. (2000), 'Human Rights, Environment and Development': With Special Emphasis On Corporate Accountability, Human Development Report 2000 Background Paper, viewed 1 October 2001, http://www.undp.org.hdro/Dias2000.html.

Divan, S. (2000), 'Judicial Juggernaut: Environment Protection Through Indian Courts NELA National Conference' 6-8 September 2000, Freemantle, Western Australia.

Divan, S. and Rosencranz, A. (2001), 'Environmental Policy and Law in India: Cases, Materials and Statutes', 2nd edition, *Oxford University Press,* New Delhi.

Ebbesson, J. (2002), Information, Participation and Access to Justice: the Model of the Aarhus Convention, Background Paper No. 5, Joint UNEP-OHCHR Expert Seminar on Human Rights and the Environment, viewed 6 February 2004, http://www.unhchr.ch/environment/bp5.html.

ESCAP Secretariat, (2000) Review of the State of the Environment in Asia and the Pacific, viewed 1 October 2001, http://www.unescap.org.mced2000/so1.html.

European Union, (2000), 'The Charter of Fundamental Rights of the European Union', viewed 6 February 2004, http://www.europarl.eu.int/charter/default.en.html.

GAIA, (2002), 'Air Pollution: A Detailed Report', viewed 6 February 2004, http://www.ess.co.at/GAIA/CASES/IND/CAL/CALpollution.html.

Gunningham, N. and Grabosky, P. (1998), Smart Regulation, Clarendon Press, Oxford.

Hart, H. L. A. (1961), 'The Concept of Law', *Oxford University Press,* Oxford.

Hediger, W. (2000), 'Sustainable Development and Social Welfare', *Ecological Economics* 32 (3), pp. 481-492.

Jariwala, C.M. (2000), 'Environmental Justice: The Directions and Outcome', *Indian Journal of Environmental Law,* 1 (1), pp.15-30.

Jaswal, P. S. and Jaswal, N. (2000), 'Environmental Law: Environmental Protection, Sustainable Development and the Law', *Pioneer Publications,* Delhi.

Kasemir, B. Jäeger, C and Jager, J. (2003), 'Citizen Participation in Sustainability Assessments', in B. Kasemir, J. Jager, C. Jaeger and M. Gardner (eds) Public Participation in Sustainability Science: A Handbook, *Cambridge University Press,* Cambridge, Chapter 1.

Laslett, P. (2002) 'Introduction' in P. Laslett (ed) John Locke: Two Treatises of Government', *Cambridge University Press,* Cambridge.

Locke, J. (1690, 2002), 'Two Treatises of Government, with an Introduction' by Peter Laslett, *Cambridge University Press,* Cambridge.

Lomborg, B. (2001), 'The Skeptical Environmentalist: Measuring the Real State of the World', *Cambridge University Press*, Cambridge.

Martinussen, J. (1997) Society, State and Market: A Guide to Competing Theories of Development, *Zed Books* Ltd, London.

McHugh, M. (2004), 'The strengths of the weakest arm', Australian Bar Review, 25, viewed 8 May 2005, http://www.hcourt.gov.au/speeches/mchughj/mchughj_2july04.html.

Mercuro. N. Lopez. K. and Preston, K. (1994), Ecology, 'Law and Economics', University Press of America, New York.

Modak, P. and Biswas, A. K. (1999), 'Conducting Environmental Impact Assessment in Developing Countries', *United Nations University Press,* Tokyo.

Montesquieu, Baron de ([1748], 1949) The Spirit of the Laws, Translated by Thomas Nugent, with a Introduction by Franz Neumann, 2, *Hafner Press*, New York.

Neumann, F. (1949), 'Introduction" in Baron de Montesquieu, The Spirit of the Laws', Translated by Thomas Nugent, 2 Vols, *Hafner Press,* New York.

Office of the United Nations High Commissioner for Human Rights, (2002) Meeting of Experts On Human Rights and the Environment – Conclusions, Joint UNEP-OHCHR Expert Seminar on Human Rights and the Environment. Viewed 6 February 2004, http://www.unhchr.ch/environment/conclusions.html.

Pandey, J. N. (2001), 'Constitutional Law of India', 37rd edition, Central Law Agency, Allahabad.

Pargal, S. and Huq, M. (1997), 'Inspections and Emissions in India': Puzzling Evidence on Industrial Water Pollution, PRD Working Paper No. 1810, The World Bank Policy Research Department, Washington DC.

Raskin, P., Gallopin, G., Gutman, P. Hammond, A and Swart, R. (1998), 'Bending The Curve: Toward Global Sustainability', Polestar Series Report No. 8, Stockholm Environment Institute, Stockholm.

Rosencranz, A. and Jackson, M. (2003), 'The Delhi Pollution Case: The Supreme Court of India and the Limits of Judicial Power', Columbia Journal of Environmental Law 28 (2), pp.223-254, viewed 6 February 2004, http://www.lexis.com.

Sathe, S. P. (2003),' Judicial Activism in India', 2nd edition, *Oxford University Press,* New Delhi.

Sen, A. (2000), 'Development as Freedom', Alfred A. Khopf Inc, New York.

Shaman, D. (1996), 'India's Pollution Regulatory Structure and Background', New Ideas in Pollution Regulation (NIPR) The World Bank Group, Washington DC, viewed 6 February 2004, http://www.worldbank.org/nipr/india/india-back.html.

Shelton, D. (2002), 'Human Rights and Environment Issues in Multilateral Treaties' Adopted between 1991and 2001, Background Paper No. 1, Joint UNEP-OHCHR Expert Seminar on Human Rights and the Environment, viewed 6 February 2004, http://www.unhchr.ch/environment/bp1.html.

Smith, K, (2000), 'National Burden of Disease in India from Indoor Air Pollution', Proceedings of the National Academy of Sciences, 97(4), pp.13,286-13,293, viewed 6 February 2004, http://intl.pnas.org.

Smith, L. R. (2001), 'Reform of India's State-owned Enterprises 1991-1997': Reincarnation and Rejuvenation or Disingenuous Disinvestment?, in L. Montanheiro and M. Spiering (eds) Public and Private Sector Partnerships: The Enterprise Governance, *Sheffield Hallam University Press,* Sheffield, pp. 511-524.

Stern, N. (2006), 'Stern Review on the Economics of Climate Change': LSE Presentation, viewed 5 November 2007, http://www.hmtreasury.gov.uk. Stevens, W. K. (1999) 'Enormous Haze Found Over Indian Ocean', The New York Times 10 June, pp.28-29.

Stuligross, D. (1999), 'The Political Economy of Environmental Regulation in India' Pacific Affairs, 72 (3), pp. 392-406.

United Nations Commission on Human Rights, (1994), 'Human Rights and the Environment.' viewed 7 February 2004, http://www.unhchr.ch.

United Nations Development Program, (2000), 'Human Development Report 2000', *Oxford University Press,* New York.

United Nations Development Program, (2003), 'Human Development Report 2003 Millennium Development Goals': A Compact Among Nations To End Human Poverty, viewed 7 February 2004, http://hdr.undp.org/reports/global/2003.

United Nations Environment Program, (2001), 'State of the Environment India 2001', viewed 7 February 2004, http://www..rrcap.unep.org/reports/soe/Indiasoe.cfm.

United Nations, (1972), 'Declaration of the United Nations Conference on the Human Environment', viewed on 7 February 2004, http://www,unep.org.

United Nations, (1992), 'Rio Declaration on Environment and Development', Viewed- 7 February 2004, http://www.un.org/esa/sustdev/documents/agenda21/index.htm.

van den Knapp, P. (1995), 'Policy Evaluation and Learning, Evaluation' 1 (2), pp.189-216.

Wiener, J. B. (2000), 'Towards Sustainable Governance, Policy Matters' Paper No. 8, AIE-Brookings Joint Centre for Regulatory Studies, Washington DC.

Wolf, C. (1993) 'Markets or Governments: Choosing between Imperfect Alternatives', 2nd edition, *The MIT Press,* Cambridge MA.

World Bank, (2002), 'What Do We Know About Air Pollution'? South Asia Urban Air Quality Management Briefing Note No. 4, The World Bank, Washington DC, viewed 7 February 2004, http://www.worldbank.org/cleanair/global/publications/uaqm_pubs.htm.

In: Development Management in the Twenty-First Century ISBN: 978-1-62100-699-2
Editors: Kartik Roy and Sandip Kar

Chapter 11

CLIMATE CHANGE AND ITS IMPACT ON POVERTY IN DEVELOPING COUNTRIES

Dhulasi Birundha Varadarajan
Senior Professor and Head, Department of Environmental Economics, School of Economics, Madurai Kamaraj University Madurai-625021, Tamil Nadu, India

INTRODUCTION

Climate change is a serious risk to poverty reduction and threatens to undo decades of development efforts. Currently over 1 billion people -two thirds of them women - live in extreme poverty on less than US$1 a day .This figure rises to 2.8 billion if a standard of US $ 2 a day is used (OECD 2001). The adverse impacts of climate change will be most striking in the developing nations, because of their geographical and climate conditions, their high dependent on natural resources and their limited capacity to adapt to a changing climate. Climate change is projected to reduce poor people's livelihood assets for example health, access to water, homes and infrastructure. Climate change caused disasters lead to production losses, damage to infrastructure and health crisis. Lower growth rates from climate change could also reduce fiscal revenues. The stern review projects potential losses of 1.2 percent of GDP in 2050, rising to 2.8 percent of GDP by 2100 with losses in developing countries.

In developing countries like India, climate change could represent an additional stress on ecological and socio economic systems that are already facing tremendous pressures. With its huge and growing population, a 7500 km long densely populated and low laying coast line and an economy that is closely tied to natural base, India is considerably vulnerable to the impacts of climate change (DOD 2002). Lonergan S (1998) estimates that India's climate could become warmer under conditions of increased atmosphere carbon di oxide. The average temperature change is predicted to be in the range of 2.33^0C to 4.78^0C with a doubling in CO_2 concentrations. It is also likely that there will be an increase in the frequency of heavy rainfall events in south and southeast Asia (Lalm. Cubasch U et al 1995). Climate change has had an effect on the monsoons too. Subtle changes have already been noted in the monsoon rainfall patterns by scientists at IIT, Delhi. To them, India will experience a decline in summer rainfall by the 2050s, summer rainfall accounts for almost 70 percentage of the total annual rainfall over India and is crucial to Indian agriculture. Apart from monsoon rains, India uses perennial rivers, which originate and depend on glacial melt-water in the Hindukush and Himalayan ranges. Rising temperatures will also contribute to the raising of snowline, reducing the capacity of this natural reservoir and increasing the risk of flash flooding during the wet season. Increased temperatures will reduce the total duration of crop cycle by inducing early flowering, thus shortening the grain fill period. The shorter the crop cycle, the lower the yield per unit area (Green peace world wide 2006).

POVERTY AND INEQUALITY

The first millennium development goal target – halving the proportion of people living in extreme poverty – will be met well ahead of the proposed 2015 deadline if the observed trend continues: the proportion of people living on less than 1.25 dollars a day fell to 26 percent in 2005 (Chen and Ravallion 2008). This implies some 400 million people are now in extreme poverty and more. Over the same period, global child mortality rates have dropped form 106 to 83 deaths per thousand live births and life expectancy has increased by three years (UNDP, 2007).Close to half the world's population (48 percent) is still in poverty, living on less than 2 dollars a day. Nearly a quarter of the world's people – 1.6 billion –do not have access to electricity (IEA, 2007) and one in six people don't have access to clean water (UN 2008). Life expectancy in sub-Saharan Africa in 2005 was lower than 15 years earlier a well below the World's average (UN 2006). Around 10 million children under five still die each year form preventable diseases such as respiratory infections, measles and diarrhea (UN 2008). Large inequalities remain within countries: in developing countries, child mortality rates in the bottom quintile are typically as high as in the top quintile (Gwatkin *et al.*, 2007). Global estimates of poverty that take into account the increase in food prices might show a reversal of the steady decline in poverty rates of the previous few years. The development process can also be affected by policy response to climate change particularly poorly designed. The over all impact on poverty depends on the structure of the economy but higher food prices are usually associated with an increase in poverty rates (Ivanie and marlin 2008).

VULNERABILITY

Vulnerability to climate change is a socially and spatially variable phenomenon which may change over the course of time. It is conceptualized in many different ways in climate change literature and is determined by a wide range of factors. Many scholars in recent climate change literature suggest separating vulnerability into social and bio physical vulnerability (Cutter 1996, Brooks 2003). According to Brooks (2003) social vulnerability exists within a system independently from the external hazards and is therefore not a function of the frequency and severity of a given type of hazard but of factors which are incorporated within a human system, for example poverty and inequality, marginalization, literacy, food entitlement health and so forth. In sufficiency of income assets or wealth is one of the most important determining factors of socio economic vulnerability of rural people. Climate change is likely to further aggravate the situation of poor peoples, especially those living in places that are susceptible to natural disasters, and will consequently further limit their ability to cope with or recover from shocks (DFID 2004).

Furthermore, climate change is expected to have negative impacts on efforts for poverty eradication and to challenge the attempts made to reach the Millennium Development Goals (MDGs).

HEALTH AND NUTRITION

Communities which are already suffering from bad health conditions and malnutrition are to be more vulnerable to climate change impacts. As a result of their prevalent poverty and marginalization they often have very limited access to mainstream health services, health prevention and promotion programmes and, in case they do have access to such services, they are often culturally in appropriate (Montenegro and Stephens 2006). The IPCC report (2007b) predicts that climate change will further weaken the health status of millions of people.

The World Health Organisation (WHO 2003) estimated that in the year 2000 climate change was responsible for approximately 2.4 per cent of world wide diarrhoea, and six per cent of malaria in some middle income countries. WHO (2003) further suggests that of the vector borne diseases, malaria is the one which is more sensitive to long term climate change. Assuming a global temperature increase 2.3^{0}C the number of people at risk of malaria in climatic terms would rise about 3.5 per cent or several hundred million.

On 2004, an estimated 790 million people suffer from nutritional deficiency (DFID 2004). This situation is expected to aggravate with climate change, especially in low-latitude countries where the overall crop productivity is expected to decrease (IPCC 2007a).

Food insecurity and malnutrition will affect the overall health status of million of people with implications for infant mortality and child growth and development. Groups which are most at risk from malnutrition or even famines include rural dwellers especially those living in marginalized areas, pastoralists, urban poor people, refuges and displaced people (DFID 2004).

Bio physical vulnerability highly depends on the intensity and frequency of hazards. According to IPCC working group I report (2007a) the type, frequency and intensity of extreme events including heat waves, floods and droughts are going to change. The IPCC report (2007a) projects that it is likely that areas affected by drought will increase during the 21st century and that it is very likely that the frequency of heavy rainfalls will increase over most areas during 21st century.

Floods and droughts can lead to serious health impacts especially vulnerable regions. Floods facilitate the proliferation and spread of infectious diseases as well as respiratory and disrrhoeal diseases. Droughts can boost concentrations of pathogens in water resources as pathogens multiply at increased rates in less available water (DFID 2004).

Persistent droughts may also lead to an increase in forest fires and desertification and as a consequence to a lack of fuel wood. A lack of firewood and safe water could prompt these communities to take their children especially girls, out of school, in order to help their mothers to complete these tasks.

Food Security

Climate change may affect food systems in several ways ranging from direct effect on crop production (e.g changes in rainfall leading to drought or flooding, or warmer or cooler temperatures leading to change in the length of growing season), to changes in markets, food prices and supply chain infrastructure. Initial research in the Indo-Gangetic Plan (IGP) has used more integrated approach to define the vulnerability of the region's food systems due to Global Environmental Change (GEC). In the western IGP, food systems are more vulnerable to issues related to the availability of water, excessive irrigation has lead to rising water tables, rapidly increasing costs of pumping and shortage of drinking water. In eastern IGP, resource poor farmers, who have very limited options to cope with and recover from external stresses, are most vulnerable to environmental changes such as rising sea-level, and climate change and climate variability leading to increased risk of flooding (Gregory *et al.* 2005).

Vulnerability is also determined by the degree of dependence on natural capital and exposure to multiple stressors. Welfare losses associated with climate change are likely to be much greater for poor countries and poor people, worsening intra-and international inequality. The intersection of poverty with old age, gender disadvantage and ethic minority status can leave people particularly exposed to shocks and unequipped with the human, social and physical capital necessary for recover (World Development Report 2010).

Impacts

Climate change will add many stress faced by developing nations as well as poor people in such countries and could reverse recent progress. Both the Developing countries as well as developed countries are the biggest CO_2 emitters. This is clear from Table 11.1.

Table 11.1. North and South: The Biggest CO_2 Emitters

Country	Co2 Emissions (Kilotons)	CO2 Emissions (Tons Per Capita)	GDP per Capita Current US $
China	5,005,687	3.9	2,517
India	1,341,761	1.2	973
Mexico	437,630	4.3	8,346
South Africa	436,641	9.4	5,719
Brazil	331,486	2.8	7,023
United States	5,877,677	20.6	44,594
Japan	1,284,376	9.8	34,348
Germany	892,545	9.8	34,979
Canada	593,063	20.0	43,191
United Kingdom	551,998	9.8	45,060

Note: CO_2 emissions per capita data are for 2004, from World Bank's World Development indicators on line. GDP per capita data is for 2007, from UNCTAD (2008).

Studies point to projected decreases in agricultural productivity in the poorest regions in the world, corresponding inequalities between poor and rich countries (Cline 2007, Dinar *et al.* 2008). Resulting food insecurity combined with increased food, energy and transport prices, has already and will continue to some region. Malnutrition rates are likely to increase. Other health outcomes are also likely to worsen. The total number of people exposed to malaria, dengue and unsafe food and water will increase as temperatures risk. The world health organization (WHO) estimates that 1, 50,000 deaths can already be attributed to climate change annually (WHO, 2006). Floods and droughts will be more severe with climate change. Droughts have immediate harmful impacts on poverty rates and economic growth, but also long-lasting effects on lifetime earnings and health (Dercon and Hoddinrott 2004). Other extreme events such as cyclones are likely to increase in intensity and security. Nordhous (2006) estimates that warming related increases in hurricane wind speed will result in additional damages of 8 billion dollars per year in the US alone. The increased variability in the weather patterns will create an extra burden for people with out access to insurance, credit markets or social protection.

Indian climate is dominated by the south-west monsoon, which brings most of the region's precipitations. It is critical for the availability of drinking water and irrigation for agriculture. Rice and wheat yields could decline considerably with climate changes (IPCC 1996; 2001). Kumar and Parikh (1998) show that economic impacts would be significant even after accounting for farm-level adoption. The loss in net income at the farm level is estimated to range between 9 percentage to 25 percentage for the temperature rise of 2°c to 3.5°.Sangli, Mendelsohn and Dunar (1998) also attempt to incorporate adaptation options while estimating agricultural impacts. They calculated that a 2°c in mean temperature and a 7 per cent increase in mean precipitation would reduce net revenues by 12.3 percentages for the country as a whole.

While Saseendran et., al have reported decrease in rise yields by 3 to 15 per cent under a scenario of 1.5°c rise in temperature and Lal et al, have reported that yields of soybean in India would vary between -22 to 18 percentage under different climate scenario's considering +4° c change temperature 20 and 40 percentage change in precipitation.

ADAPTATION

Rural livelihoods are subject to multiple shocks and stress that can increase household vulnerability. Climate variability is one of the pervasive stresses that individuals and communities in rural areas have to cope with (Lesotho Gina Ziervogel 2003). Seasonal climate forecasts provide an indication of how variable the rainfall might be compared to past years and is therefore considered as information that could help to prepare for and adapt to climate variability (Goddard *et al.* 2001, O'Brien and Vogel 2003).

The growing evidence of global environmental change and increased climate variability demands that adaptation options, adopting capacity and ways to reduce risk should be prioritized (Rayner and Malone 1998, Kelly and Adger 2000, Smit *et.al.* 2000). Because climate is only one stress on livelihoods, the impact of seasonal forecasts requires assessing not just agricultural activities that might change in response to forecasts, but the multiple dimensions of rural livelihoods that constrain the uptake of information, have secondary effects and determined the systems ability to handle future stress (Yohe and Dol 2002).

Development of human society has involved a continuous process of adopting to changing stresses and opportunities changes in climate variability and mean values will bring additional complicating to many especially those dependent o food system that are particularly vulnerable to additional stresses.

Rural people are highy connected to their land, not only through the livelihoods but also through spiritual bonds. However, in many cases land tenure and access rights of people are not legally recognized (IFAD 2003).

As a consequence, their land and resources are often exploited and encroached by outsides with the implementation of projects related to the clean development mechanism (CDM) or the reduced emissions form the deforestation in developing countries (REDD) and as a result of the increasing demand for bio-fuels there are fears that the land rights of rural people will be increasing by contested or violated (Mirjam Macchi 2008).

This insecure situation further accumulates the already challenging situations ofmany of these people and may result on severe implications to their vulnerability and capacity to adopt. So it is crucial to protect land leisure and access rights of local people and to reward them for the goods and services their lands provide (Salick and Byg 2007).

MANAGEMENT POLICIES

Policies that are to be managed to tackle climate change will also affect growth, equity and sustainability with the direction of the impact determined by how the policies are designed. Such policies include internationally drawn carbon labeling of traded goods, bio fuels and carbon sequestration forests, domestic implementation of green growth strategies and associated price changes in global and local market.

The process of climate change includes dangerous and irreversible effects. Adherence to the precautionary principle in order to avoid catastrophic risks requires stabilization of global atmosphere concentrations at levels at least as low as 450-550 ppm co_2 e. Mitigation policies will increase demands on water and in some cases land – as they lead to more calls for afforest ration and reforestation, bio-fuels and non-fossil fuel energy sources (hydro electricity and nuclear), even as many countered will need to allocate more resources to food production.

Many potential solutions to individual resource management problems exist. Some of the solutions are institutional such as adaptive management, better monitoring and better enforcement of regulations. Some are economic such as removing subsidies that encourage over exploitation of resources or finding incentives for large scale private investment in conservation. Some involve new technologies namely bio-technology for the production of crop varieties more resistant to climate related stresses.

The approaches available to manage risks and reduce vulnerabilities both ex-ante and ex-post are early warning systems, community based and national disaster risk management schemes, indigenous adaptive strategies, migration and income diversification, weather linked insurance and social safety nets.

Historical approaches provide a useful starting point to address peoples risk and vulnerabilities. Public policy needs to encourage such approaches and strategies where they have proven to be effective, strengthen, scale them up or help to reduce there costs where appropriate, and strengthen institutions and mechanisms for adoption where existing ones prove inadequate.

CONCLUSION

Climate change will exacerbate poverty and inequality and compromise the advance of human rights and social justice for the poorest and most vulnerable. Evidence shows that the poor are very vulnerable to exactly the sorts of climate shifts, policy interventions, and other shocks that will be engendered by climate change.

Developing countries overriding priorities are increased prosperity and the sustainable reduction of poverty and inequality. In the longer terms, their goals cannot be achieved without managing climate change. But policies to lack climate change must factor in the reality that sustainable development faces many other immediate and dramatic challenges.

The future policy architecture will need to go well beyond narrowly defined environmental sustainability concerns and address fundamental shifts in the way countries achieve growth and well being. The establishment of the UNFCCC laid the foundation for global action on climate change. The Kyoto protocol has set limits to GHG emissions in industrialized countries and through its innovative market instruments, spurred cost-effective mitigation in developing countries as well.

Thus to prevent climate changes with dangerous welfare consequences, all countries will need to mitigate emissions of green house gases, under the guiding principle of common but differentiated responsibilities, with attention to the need for continued poverty reduction.

REFERENCES

Brooks, N. (2003), 'Vulnerability to environmental hazards. *Progress in Human Geography'* 20.

Chen, S. and M. Ravallion. (2008), 'The Developing World is Poorer than We Thought, But No Less Successful in the Fight against Poverty.' *Policy Research Working Paper* 4703, World Bank, Washington, DC.

Cline, W.R. (2007), 'Global Warming and Agriculture: Impact Estimates by Country'. Washington, DC: Center for Global Development and Institute for International Economics.

DFID (2004), 'Key sheets on climate Change and Poverty'. http://www.dfid.gov.uk/pubs/flies/climagechange/keysheetssindex.asp

Dinar, A., R. Hassan, R. Mendelsohn, J. Benhin.(2008), 'Climate Change and Agriculturein Africa: Impact Assessment and Adaptation Strategies'. London: Earthscan; Pretoria, South Africa: Center for Environmental Economics and Policy in Africa (CEEPA).

DOD(2002), 'Annual Report 2001/02, New Delhi': Development of Ocean Development.

Goddard L, Mason S J, Zebiak S E, Ropelewski C F, Basher R and Cane M A (2001), Current approaches to seasonal to interannual climate prediction, *International Journal of Climatology* 21 1111-52.

Green peace world wide (2006), 'Climate change and its possible impact on India' WWW. Green Peace org. India.

Gregory P J Ingram J S I and Brklaich (2005), Climate change and food security, philosophical transaction on line, *Journal of the Royal Society,* 360, pp. 2139-2148.

Gwatkin, D., S. Rutstein, K. Johnson, E. Suliman, A. Wagstaff, and A. Amouzou. (2007). Socio-Economic Differences in Health, Nutrition and Population within Developing Countries: An Overview. *Country Reports on Health, Nutrition, and Population Series.* Washington, DC: World Bank.

IEA (International Energy Agency). (2007), *World Energy Outlook (2007): China and India Insights. Paris: OECD / IEA.*

IPCC (1996), 'Climate Change 1995: Impacts, Adaptations and mitigation of climate change' – scientific technical analysis.

IPCC (2007a), 'Climate Change 2007: The Scientific Basis', Working Group I. Contribution to the Intergovernmental Panel on Climate Change Fourth Assessment Report. *Cambridge University Press, Cambridge.*

IPCC (2007b), 'Climate Change 2007 Impacts, Adaption and Vulnerability', The working Group II Contribution to the Intergovernmental Panel of Climate Change Fourth Assessment Report, *Cambridge University Press,* Cambridge.

IPCC(2001), 'Climate Change 2001:Impacts, Adaptation and vulnerability', *Summary of policy makers,* pp. 103.

Ivanic, M. and W. Martin. (2008), 'Implications of Higher Global Food Prices for Poverty in Low-Income Countries', *Policy Research Working Paper* 4594, World Bank, Washington, DC.

Kelly, P. M. and Adger, W. N. (2000), 'Theory and practice in assessing vulnerability to climate change and facilitating adaptation Climatic Change', (47), pp. 325-52.

Kumar, K. and Parikh,(1998), 'Climate Change impacts on Indian Agriculture: the Ricardian Approach In measuring the impact of climate Change on Indian agriculture' ed by A. Dinar et al, *World Bank technical paper* No:42.

Lal M Cubasch U Voss R Waszkewitz J (1995), 'Effect of transient increase in greenhouse gases and sulphate aerosols on monsoon climate', *Current Science* 69 (9): pp752-763.

Lesotho Gina Ziervogel and Rebecca Calder (2003), 'Climatic Variability and rural livelihoods assessing the impact of seasonal forecasts', *Area,* 35, (4), Dec 2003, pp 403-407.

Lonergan, S.(1998), 'Climate warming and India, In measuring the impact of climate change on Indian Agriculture', edited by A Dinar, et al. Washington DC: World Bank (*World Bank Technical Paper No.402*)

Mirjam Macchi ,(2008), 'Indigenous and Traditional Peoples and Climate Change',Issues Paper, *ICUN Publication,* March 2008.

Montenegro R A Stephens, C.(2006), 'Indigenous Health 2 Indigenous health in Latin America and the Carribbean'. *Lancet* (367), pp. 1859-69.

Nordhaus, W. (2006), 'The Economics of Hurricanes in the United States', *NBER Working Paper* 12813. Cambridge, MA.

O'Brien K L and Vogel C (2003), 'A future for forecasts'? in O'Brien K L and Vogel Ceds Coping with climate variability: the use of seasonal climate forecasts in southern Africa Ashgate, Burlington pp. 197-211.

Rayner S and Malone E L eds (1998), 'Human choice and climate change 1 Batelle Press', Columbus.

Salick,J. Byg.A.eds.(2007), 'Indigenous peoples and Climate Change'. A Tyndall centre Publications.Tyndall centre for Climate Change research, Oxford.

Smit B, Burton I, Klein R J T and Wandel J (2000), 'An anatomy of adaptation to climate change and variability Climatic Change', (45), pp. 223-51.

UN (United Nations) 'Department of Economic and Social Affairs, Population Division. (2006). World Population Prospects': The 2006 Revision. New York: United Nations.

UN (United Nations) Department of Economic and Social Affairs. (2008), 'The Millennium Development Goals Report 2008', New York: United Nations.

UNDP (United Nations Development Program). 2007. Human Development Report 2007/2008. Fighting Climate Change: Human Solidarity in a Divided World. New York: UNDP.

WHO (2003), 'Climate change and Human Health – Risks and Responses', Summary Available at: http://www.int/globalchange/publications/cchhsummary/en/.

WHO (World Health Organization)(2006), WHO/UNEP Health and Enviromcnt Linkages Initiative. Geneva: WHO. Website accessed September 2008. Available at: http://www.who.int/heli/risks/climate/climatechange/en/index.html

World Development report(2010), 'Development in a changing Climate', *Concept note, world bank publication.*

Yohe G and Tol R (2002), Indicators for social and economic coping capacity - moving toward a working definition of adaptive capacity Global Environmental Change 12 25-40.

In: Development Management in the Twenty-First Century ISBN: 978-1-62100-699-2
Editors: Kartik Roy and Sandip Kar

Chapter 12

SUSTAINABLE MANAGEMENT OF CLIMATE CHANGE EFFECTS DURING RECESSION

Robert Scott Gassler*
Professor of Economics, Vesalius College of the Vrije,
Universiteit Brussel, Brussels, Belgium

INTRODUCTION

Even though the greatest crisis faced by humankind in this century – and perhaps the greatest of all time – is that of climate change, the most urgently-felt crisis in the US and elsewhere at the moment is the current recession. It is thought by some that addressing the former must wait until after addressing the latter. The fallacy of this reasoning is of course that global climate change is a very long-run problem that requires continuous action to address it, through thick and thin, whether there is a recession on or not.

Contrary to the way economists are used to thinking, nature does not react to prices. She reacts to the *quantity* of CO_2e[1] in the atmosphere. Any solution to the climate-change problem has to start with a constraint on quantity. There are of course tremendous microeconomic problems in implementing such a constraint (or set of constraints), but we should first consider the prior questions of whether such a constraint is feasible and how it can be incorporated into a macroeconomic view, one which stresses the avoidance of unemployment as well as of inflation.

THE PROBLEM

The economic problems associated with global climate change are: open access, lack of governance, externalities, and public goods. The economic problems associated with the

* rsgassler@vub.ac.be.

[1] CO_2e refers to carbon-dioxide equivalent gases. Use of that measure reduces all such gases to a single quantitative measure (UN.IPCC, 2007).

economic crisis are lack of governance, uncoordinated lending, and consequent collapse of the housing market and thereby of consumption and investment.

Open access is to be distinguished from common-property resources. Common-property resources (or common-pool resources as in the case of petroleum in the ground) are governed by rules and conventions developed over time by the people involved: governance systems for Mongolian grasslands and Nepalese water have been documented by Elinor Ostrom (Economic Governance 2009). Open-access resources are those which have not yet been subject to a successful governance procedure, whether establishment of property rights by a government or development of customs and rules through tradition or negotiation. The ozone layer is now under the jurisdiction of a governance process; the dumping of CO_2e into the atmosphere and oceans is not.

The problem is similar with the external costs of pollution which is under only partial global governance (O'Neill 2009). Each country has developed a mixture of taxes, regulation, and auctions to cause firms to internalize the externalities. Since these policies are uncoordinated at the global level, their effectiveness is dubious.

The international regime itself, such as it is, has public-good characteristics (Keohane 1984), though regimes and other governance procedures should probably be classified elsewhere (Gassler 2003, Chapter 4. I would place them under the heading of "economic system: transactions" rather than "public goods"). The international regime is weak in its ability to respond to the economic crisis. At the global level, the World Bank, IMF, etc., were unable to prevent the housing bubble from expanding and bursting, though some blame must be shared with the leaders of the economics profession, who failed to see what was going on. The lack of a strong governance structure however contributed to the slow, confused initial responses to the crisis as it unfolded. Policies had to be designed at the national level, even as the crisis spread across the planet.

Indeed, even at the national level, governance was weakened, partly for ideological reasons: the deregulation movement of the last generation was inspired at least as much by doctrine as by evidence. As with previous crises, this failure of the principal-agent relationship between depositors and regulators led to a prisoner's dilemma for financial institutions, as each one raced to keep up with the reckless lending practices of the others lest they lose profits to them (Milgrom and Roberts 1992, pp.166-176.). When the market finally collapsed, so did consumption and investment demand (Blanchard, Giavazzi, and Amighini 2010, Chapter 20).

The two crises thus hold some characteristics in common. Both are examples of lack of proper governance structure and conduct which results in free riding, which in turn results in catastrophic climate change in the one case and global recession in the other.

THE SOLUTION

How do we go about overcoming these two crises? The first thing we need to do is decide what our goals are. To most economists, the most important goal is to promote allocative efficiency. Distributional equity is logically next, though some economists shy away from it, believing erroneously that it involves more normative judgments than the decision to privilege efficiency. Third is macroeconomic stability, the important aspects of it being full employment and price stability these are described in Musgrave (1959). Daly (1996) adds a fourth, economic scale, meaning the size of the GDP that the ecology can sustain. There are others (a comprehensive list is given in Gassler 2003, Chapter 4) but for present purposes scale is the most important goal in the very long run, and stability is the most important one in the short run.

Taking the goals in scrambled order, the scale Daly means is in relation to the environment in which the global economy is embedded. Comparative economists have modeled this since the 1970s (Koopmans and Montias 1971), though for different purposes. The economy is part of a societal system that includes individuals with their tastes and preferences; technology in the form of knowledge in the heads of those individuals (and in what Kenneth Boulding refers to as their "prosthetic devices:" libraries, and now the internet), and resources. The last refers to land, labor, capital, and other factors of production such as energy. "Land" rather awkwardly includes the natural environment or ecosystem, from which humans ultimately extract all the other resources. The planetary ecosystem includes the human societal system, which in turn includes the economic system. A circular-flow diagram of the economic system would rightly include an arrow from the left showing the sources of the resources extracted for the economy and an arrow to the right showing the sinks for the items excreted by the economy (Harris 2006, Ch.7; Daly, 1995).

The problem is that the scale of the economy has grown too large for the natural environment to sustain it. (I would say that it has also grown too large for the societal environment to sustain it, for reasons different from Schumpeter (1950), but that is a subject for another time.) The economy is extracting too many inputs from its sources; it is depleting them too fast (Meadows et al., 1972; Gautier 2008). It is also excreting too much waste into the sinks; it is building them up too fast (UN.IPCC 2007; Stern 2007, 2008). So the first goal is to reduce the scale of economic activity to one compatible with the planet's environment. The only real way to do that is to severely restrict the amount of CO_2e that is extracted from the land, and thereby to severely restrict the CO_2e that is excreted into the atmosphere and oceans.

The policy must be to limit the amount of CO_2e emitted into the atmosphere in any given year (UN.IPCC 2007). Thus a quota is more consistent with the underlying science. Whatever the mechanism for achieving it, the important thing is the quantity of emissions, not the price, or the ratio to GDP, or the quantity per capita. Sustainable development implies a reduction in extractions from the environment, and global climate policy implies a reduction in excretions into the environment. Just as a limit on the amount of labor implies a limit on the GDP that can be produced (full-employment GDP), so does the limit on the amount of CO_2e imply a limit on the GDP that can be produced.

Allocative efficiency is a goal only for economists; for others it is a means. Neoclassical and ecological economists tend to agree that once the maximum allowable CO_2e is established, any of an array of policies can be used to enforce the restriction. Eco-taxes, regulation, and simply auctioning off the carbon all have their advantages and drawbacks.[2] It is not so clear how to reduce other extraction from the sources, except to use the same instruments.

[2] For the first two, see any textbook on microeconomics or environmental economics. For the latter see the literature on mechanism design (e.g.,Maskin, 2008). Unfortunately that literature has not percolated into the textbooks, except for, e.g., McGuigan, Moyer, and Harris (2008).

Whether this in itself would significantly reduce unemployment is unclear, since firms might be able to substitute other inputs as well. In any event, these methods, while enforcing the scale of economic activity, also achieve the goal of allocative efficiency.

Regardless of the mechanism by which the carbon is allocated (see below on efficiency), the price of natural resources with high carbon content will rise relative to other inputs, including labor. Daly points out that all production uses some materials, but this policy would reduce the carbon use overall. Production shifts from carbon-intensive to labor-intensive, and the GDP shifts from plastic toy fighter planes and to old-school kites.

The time scales in question here are immense compared with the usual situations faced by economists doing benefit-cost analysis. Any given year that we examine could be so far in future that no one knows whose descendants are whose. Thus the relevant consideration in analyzing social welfare is the welfare of the people in the period in question, not the intertemporal tradeoffs with people long dead. Frank Ackerman (2004) makes the argument. We do better to assume a veil of ignorance. Therefore a discount rate is rather odd in this context. Fortunately, in setting climate policy, a discount rate is not necessary. We need to set the quantity of pollutants that the ecosystem can tolerate now in order to mitigate and adapt to climate change, and then provide the economic mechanism for allocating that quantity in the usual way.

From the negotiations on climate change, it is clear that any policies at the global level must address distributional questions. They are difficult, and there is no clear consensus among economists on the subject as there is for efficiency, but it appears to be impossible to mitigate or adapt to climate change on a major scale without addressing them. This is as it should be, since allocation is not the be-all and end-all of public policy or even of economics.

A neoclassical approach would stress the form of the social welfare function and the achievement of efficiency. Boulding renames the famous contract curve the "conflict curve," since an allocation on the curve can be changed only if the individuals engage in conflict. His solution is relevant here: redefine the problem to include another variable, like fringe benefits in a bargaining session about wages. That puts the players off the curve so they can negotiate for mutual gain. There may be creative ways that climate negotiators can make progress by introducing new variables into the bargain. Moreover, perhaps as long as some growth continues, the rich can buy off the poor and still have some left for themselves.

Other approaches may not be quite ready for policy-making. The happiness research implies that growth and riches do not always lead to greater well-being, but the theoretical basis for their claim is shaky (Johns and Omerod, 2008). The research on Stone-Geary utility functions that got the former discoverer the Nobel Prize some years ago is still more or less theoretical, though like game theory it can still guide our thinking. Perhaps John Rawls (1971) or Amartya Sen (1999) can be of help. Certainly there should be consideration for making sure that everyone has a claim on the necessities of life before we talk about how to conserve them as the resources to produce them decline. There is one thing on which we should all agree: those who are not responsible for climate change or recession should not be the ones disproportionately penalized for them, nor should those who are responsible be rewarded. It should also be mentioned that redistribution is compatible with all traditions in economics, from Austrian[3] through neoclassical to radical.

[3] http://voices.washingtonpost.com/ezra-klein/2010/07/hayek_on_social_insurance.html

In each case, there should be two levels of assistance: national and personal. Among nations, there should be technology transfer, debt forgiveness, and targeted aid for environmental projects. The first would shift out aggregate supply in the long run, and the second and third would shift out aggregate demand in the short run. Within nations, to the extent possible, there should be unemployment compensation and other safety-net provisions, but also perhaps adjustment assistance like the US's Trade Adjustment Assistance Act or the Swedish active labor-market policy. Can this be justified on neoclassical grounds? Yes, as a way for the winners (or losers of less) to compensate the losers (or losers of more). Moreover, since in some cases actual survival is at stake, these measures are necessary, since death is not part of a Pareto optimum (Koopmans 1957, second essay). Nor is it part of the definition of success in any other tradition in economics.

The last goal is stablization, tackling the recession directly without interfering with the other policies. Fortunately there is little conflict among them. As said earlier, setting limits on carbon inputs leads firms to substitute labor for carbon where possible, maybe increasing employment. Taxes and other policies induce firms to switch to environmentally-friendly inputs and outputs, which may involve increased investment. Redistribution of income from rich to poor will increase consumption demand, helping reduce unemployment. Monetary and fiscal policies to stimulate demand therefore have less to do than otherwise. What remains is re-introduction of public supervision of the financial sector to prevent another bubble. National governments seem to have finished the new programs of financial bailouts and rewritten the rules of the game. If they have done enough without encouraging moral hazard, then we can move on. Thus, re-regulation of the financial sector and the oil industry to prevent bubbles and spills and mechanism design to auction chunks of carbon would move the system closer to the production-possibility frontier. A proper stabilization policy implies that there is no tradeoff between environmental considerations and employment.

The bad news is that to be completely effective, this has to happen all over the world. The good news is that to be somewhat effective, it needs only to start somewhere and spread.

What is the overall effect on social welfare? A rise in the price of CO_2e leads to a shift in demand away from CO_2e-intensive goods and services. If some of those other goods and services are noneconomic – such as the color of a sunset or the pleasure from seeing enlightenment in the faces of one's students – there is no, or less, welfare loss. Redistribution toward the poor might move the economy to a higher level of social welfare as well.[4] None of these is a sure thing, but none is ruled out either.

The important thing to remember, though, is that the choice is not between continued growth in GDP and welfare on the one hand, and some green nightmare on the other. The choice is between continued growth in GDP and welfare that leads to catastrophe on the one hand and continued growth in GDP and welfare that leads to a green solution on the other. The status quo is not an option. The Stern report claims the choice is between a 20% decline in GDP on the one hand, and a 5% decline on the other, but even those numbers do not necessarily correspond to proportionate declines in welfare.

In sum, set limits on carbon inputs. Firms will substitute labor and perhaps increase employment and investment. Redistribute income from rich to poor: that will increase political stability and raise consumption demand, again increasing employment. Pursue

[4] Tol (2010) argues that inequality aversion by rich countries is growing and is separable from risk aversion and time discounting.

monetary and fiscal policies that stimulate aggregate demand to fight recession. Re-introduce public supervision of the financial sector and adequate governance of climate policy at both national and global levels. If we do these things we will have fought climate change and recession at the same time, and won.

OBSTACLES TO POLICY MAKING

In order to design and implement policy, one must take into account more of the complexities of social behavior than the simple models imply. The models show us the goals in their clearest form, but the realities of policy must be messier. There are at least three obstacles to the success of any reasonable plan to fight climate change and recession: international coordination, regulatory capture, and ideology.

The first set of obstacles is the problem of international coordination (O'Neill 2009, Chapter 4). As mentioned above, climate policy is uncoordinated at the global level: the UN Environmental Program, the World Meteorological Organization, their creature the International Panel on Climate Change, the World Bank, the WTO, and the non-UN organizations such as the OECD, G-8, and EU have varying degrees of commitment to solutions. As long as each country has its own climate policy, there is a free-rider problem, and as long as the international community's institutions are fragmented, there is danger that a strong solution will not emerge. Countries can engage in a race to the bottom by loosening regulations concerning carbon emissions or by ignoring international agreements even after signing them. Firms with little sense of corporate social responsibility[5] can move to areas with lower taxes, less stringent regulation, etc., making the excuse that they have an "obligation to their shareholders."[6]

As with other free-rider problems, it is difficult for an economist to distinguish between (a) an individual who genuinely does not desire a good from (b) an individual who understates preference for the good in order not to pay for it. How many corporate-sponsored "skeptics" actually believe the problem is real but think that by delaying the solution for a year or more they can pocket more profits in the short run? How much influence do they have over governments and media?

There is some hope in the attempts so far to overcome the coordination problem: from the agreements controlling CFCs to the fits and starts of the Copenhagen conference, there seems to be a willingness on the part of some nation-states to stop being free riders and just get on with solving the problem. The role of nonprofit organizations, aka civil society, in these efforts has only begun to be explored in the social-science literature. Elinor Ostrom's work should give us inspiration.

---

5 The growing literature on varieties of capitalism shows that firms in Europe have more of such a sense than those in the US, for example.

6 It is rather puzzling that firms privilege one factor of production over another. One does not have to be Adam Smith or Karl Marx to notice that capital is no more indispensible to production than labor. My own answer, based only on introspection, is that the bias toward capital is related to the fact that owners of that factor are more numerous at the men's clubs of the nineteenth century or the country clubs of the twentieth and twenty-first than, say, owners of labor or even land. Therefore the managers, who control the decisions of the firm, are more likely to meet them and want to get along with them socially. This is a matter that merits further research, I think, perhaps by economic sociologists.

The coordination problem also exists with respect to the recession. The fundamental problem here though is the fact that countries can be free riders on other countries' policies. If a large country cuts taxes, increases government expenditures, and/or increases the money supply, it risks bigger deficits and rising price level, but it gains a recovery from the recession. If a small country waits for the large country to move first, its exports to the large country increase, so it gains a recovery from the recession without risking a bigger deficit or higher price level. The prisoner's dilemma thus works here as well. Nonetheless here has been some success in coordinating monetary and fiscal policies, though opposition to what are clearly appropriate stimulatory actions is rather strident.

The second obstacle in each case is big-business politics, whether lobbying or regulatory capture (Stigler 1971; Mueller 2003). In climate policy, we saw for eight years a US administration captured by the oil industry. It is not so clear under Obama. In the case of the recession, regulatory capture has been written into the charter of the Federal Reserve System since its inception (Gassler 2003). There are exceptions however: viz. the case of the Federal Communication Commission (Brodsky 2010). One sees hope here.

The third obstacle is ideology, whether political or religious (Rose-Ackerman 1996, Kelman 1987). It is used of course as the handmaiden of politics, but it has an independent existence of its own. The public and secular universities and professional scientific societies exist to pursue truth, even if their members, being for the most part human, have preconceptions about what that truth might me. Many religious universities, think tanks, and odd societies have other goals. Examples include Calvin College (2010), the Cato Institute (2010), and the Association of American Physicians and Surgeons (2010). When the preconceptions are written into the mission statement or obvious from the website, one can be fairly certain that the organization is serious about them.

Herman Daly propounds a strange view of religion and its relation to attitudes toward the environment (*Beyond Growth*, Chapter 15). He claims that one must be religious to care about the environment, since if we believe that we are in God's image, then we must exercise stewardship over what has been entrusted to us. The non-religious claim is that, if we are only one species, why worry about our own extinction?

As much as I admire Daly's work, I think he is wrong on this. To see why, draw a matrix. The columns are "environment yes" and "environment no" and the rows are "religious" and "other." The upper left cell is Daly's view, and the lower right the one he attributes to the non-religious. However, there are two other cells. Take the upper right one. Religious people could (and as we know, often do) take the view that the future of the planet is in God's hands, so there is no need to worry; alternatively, they could say (and again often do) that these are the "end times" so once more there is no need to worry. This is true of West Asian religions (Judaism, Zoroastrianism, Christianity, and Islam), and of the South Asian ones (Hinduism and Buddhism) as well.[7] In the lower left cell we have the view that, yes we are only one species, but Nature has no values, only humans have values, so we must look out for the welfare of our own species.[8] Be that as it may, we see clearly that religious ideology is important in the politics of climate change policy.

---

[7] Some religions, such as the Aztec or Bahá'i, have no eschatology in the sense used here; their adherents could perhaps be placed in either cell.

[8] Ironically, I heard this best stated by Kenneth Boulding, a Quaker like Daly.

So is political ideology, or, as we should perhaps call it here, economic ideology. From its origins in the work of such economists as Milton Friedman, Friedrich Hayek, and James Buchanan, the hyper-individualism and consequent market fundamentalism have all the elements of a rigid ideology. That ideology can be seen in the background of some of the attacks on climate science. In its incarnation as "climate skepticism" we see it beating a gradual but belligerent retreat. First it was "there is not enough research." Then after two decades of IPCC, it became "the science is not settled." Then after the fourth IPCC report it was, "who cares about consensus anyway: they were wrong about alchemy," and "they have to agree in order to get grants from the elite of the profession." Now finally it is "I found a mote in the IPCC report's eye," and "someone at the University of East Anglia doesn't like me."

In macroeconomics, there is an alarming tendency to ignore the lessons of the Keynesian revolution and return to the self-destructive attempts to balance the budget while revenues keep falling rather than increase demand to reach full employment. Sometimes there is not even an attempt to justify it by claiming that there will be not enough lenders to support the deficit. The creators of the mainstream economics that ignored the causes of the recession now ignore the cures.

Again there is hope in the economics profession as well as the public at large. For one thing, the history of economics is much richer than the recent dominance of market fundamentalism would suggest. Many of the great economists of the past, including Léon Walras (1896, 1898), would have been fine with the idea of limiting resource use. Indeed this paper triangulates (Nelson, 2000) from neoclassical,[9] modern, and heterodox approaches alike.

Public policy debates tend to lag behind developments in economics, and in this case the economics profession has spent the better part of a generation emerging from market fundamentalism. Let us hope that the new trend will seep into the public consciousness before it is too late.

IMPLICATIONS FOR DEVELOPMENT MANAGEMENT

There are several implications we can draw from this analysis so far. The most important one is that business is not simply a player in the game, memorizing the rule book and accepting the referee's decision without question. Business influences the making and amending of the rules and therefore cannot claim to be the poor innocent victim when arguing for their relaxation. Leaders of all sectors of society – business, government, labor, religion, charity, and so on – must take seriously their moral duty to help the society run more

[9] Landreth and Colander (2002) make a distinction between neoclassical economics and modern economics. The former was born in 1874 with the publication of Léon Walras's Element of Pure Economics and began to lose hegemony a hundred years later to several new approaches: behavioral economics, public choice, game theory, and transaction-cost theory to name a few. For lack of a better name, Landreth and Colander call these approaches "modern economics."

smoothly. Adam Smith said businesspeople are not to be trusted;[10] management needs to prove him wrong.

The fields of business ethics and corporate social responsibility assume greater importance. The idea that people in general and businesspeople in particular do and should consider the ethical implications of their actions is an old one in economics. Recall that Adam Smith wrote two books, one of which (1759, 1790) explicitly claims that people have a natural sympathy for others. The other and more famous one (1776), written and revised at the same time, should be read along with the first and its lesson put in context: within a society as civilized as 18th-century Scotland, businesspeople can be as selfish as they want, since the rules of social interaction preclude such tactics as, say, killing ones competitors. Socialists such as Mill and Walras considered that income distribution was obviously within the jurisdiction of (political) economists, and Pareto's concept of optimality should be considered as a first step in defining social improvements beyond mere market transactions.

But should businesspeople *per se* worry about such things during their hours of work during the week, or should they wait until worship services to consider matters beyond mere profit? We know now that "profit maximization" occurs only under strict assumptions in economic models and that "efficient allocation" and "equitable distribution" result only under a similarly strict set of assumptions[11]. Veblen (1921), Berle and Means (1932), and even Schumpeter (1942) knew better: they thought of corporations not as mere economic machines, but also as political organizations. The market is embedded in a wider society (Polanyi 1944; Boulding 1953, 1978; Gilpin 1987; Granovetter 1985). If the society influences the market, then it can set up the conditions for its success and correct for its failures (Gassler, 2003, Chapter 5); but if the market influences the society, that cannot be good (Galbraith 1958, Chapter 11; Mueller 2003, Chapter 15). The same people participate in both, which means they must be mindful of the overall effects of their actions no matter which institution they are participating in.

In management studies, the interrelation between business and society has been studied in many ways. The University of Texas at Austin recently started a new Department of Business, Government, and Society, reviving a field that had fallen on hard times. It remains to be seen what they do with it. More of interest and to the point, the Bainbridge Graduate Institute recently started with an MBA program in "sustainable business," taking seriously the notion that businesspeople should think about such things themselves without waiting around for governments to compel them.

This would move the US away from the US variety of capitalism and closer to the European one, as John Mikler describes them (2009). In comparative economics (Gardner, 1998) we have known for a long time that, as the political scientists say, there are different "varieties of capitalism" (Hall and Soskice 2001, Chapter 1). US firms fight government regulations – or bend them to their will – and claim to be waiting for consumers to tell them what they want through the market. European firms are more likely to have worked with the government to formulate regulations in everyone's interest and to take the initiative in leading

---

[10] Smith (1776), Book V, Chapter I, Part III, Article I, contains the passage on how corporations are not to be trusted because they are not careful with other people's money. Book I, Chapter X, Part II contains the passage about how meetings of businesspeople turn into conspiracies against the public.

[11] Arrow and Debreu, 1954. What the Austrians sometimes appear to believe appears by magic the neoclassicals specified quite precisely.

the market toward some improvements. It is pretty clear that the world would be better off with the latter approach. It is difficult to imagine, for example, customers pressuring the local grocery store in Brussels into putting doors on their coolers for lettuce and orange juice, for example. Yet the stores did just that this year, saving energy and helping the environment.

The general implication here is inescapable: regardless of what the hard-core market fundamentalists argue, people must act through all institutions – families, businesses, governments, nonprofit organizations – to effect ethical and environmentally friendly changes. This is not empty rhetoric or "airy-fairy" moralizing. This is what we need to have happen now.

Conclusion

To summarize, this paper makes several arguments. First, in setting climate policy, a discount rate is not necessary. Any given year that we examine could be so far in future that no one knows whose descendants are whose. Thus we do better to assume a veil of ignorance.

Second, distribution counts, at national and global levels. Redistribution is compatible with all traditions in economics, from Austrian through neoclassical to radical.

Third, a proper stabilization policy implies that there is no tradeoff between environmental considerations and employment.

Fourth, in setting global climate change policy, quantity restrictions are better than taxes.

Fifth, the relevant consideration in analyzing social welfare is the welfare of the people in the period in question, not the intertemporal tradeoffs with people long dead.

Likewise we need not worry about risk, since we are looking at a time span in which just about everything can and will happen.

The short-term problem is that there are not enough jobs in the world economy for the people who are willing and able to work. It is a short-term problem due to the recession. The solution is coordinated monetary and fiscal policy to stimulate demand and bring the economy to full employment again.

The policy implication is clear: First, impose a Daly constraint on CO_2e extractions and emissions. Second, increase demand through coordinated fiscal and monetary policy. Third, redistribute income through international aid and technology transfer and national welfare state programs. Finally, re-regulate banks and carbon producers and auction off the carbon allowed.

The results would be: Scale decreases to a more appropriate level in the very long run. Stability is reached in the short run: Unemployment decreases for several reasons: the shift from carbon to labor inputs, the stimulative fiscal policy, and the unemployment-insurance safety net. Inflation remains low through monetary policy. Equity is achieved by coordinating the attack on climate change to achieve as close to a Pareto improvement (Hicks-Kaldor would be better) as possible – by making the transfers, not just calculating them. Efficiency is achieved by pursuing the other goals, well, efficiently.

The very-long-term problem is that the global economy is growing too big for the environment in which it is embedded. It is a very-long-term problem because the global climate is warming due to increases in CO_2e from industrialization. The solution is coordinated climate-change policy to limit CO_2e emissions severely everywhere on the planet, redistribute the costs toward the wealthy while encouraging development in poor countries, and adjust our thinking away from believing that growth of GDP means anything more than growth of GDP.

Is imposition of a Daly constraint feasible and compatible with fighting recession? It is feasible in principle, though that is only the beginning of the solution. It is compatible with fighting recession, since it leads to substitution of labor for carbon.

REFERENCES

Ackerman, F. and Elizabeth A. Stanton (2010), 'The social cost of carbon', real-world economics rev(53), 26 June, pp. 129-143, http://www.paecon.net/PAEReview/issue53 /AckermanStanton53.pdf .

Ackerman, Frank (2004) "Priceless Benefits, Costly Mistakes: What's Wrong with Cost-Benefit Analysis?" Post-Autistic Economics Review, (25), 18 May, pp. 2-7, http://www.btinternet.com/~pae_news/review/issue25.htm

Ackerman, Frank and Ian J. Finlayson (2006), 'The Economics of Inaction on Climate Change: ASensitivity Analysis', *Global Development and Environment Institute Working Paper* No. 06-07. October.

Arrow, Kenneth J, and Gerard Debreu (1954), 'Existence of an Equilibrium for a Competitive Economy', *Econometrica,* (22), pp. 265-90.

Baumol, William J. (1978), 'Economic Theory and Operations Analysis', 4th edition, Englewood Cliffs, New Jersey: Prentice-Hall.

Bergson, Abram (1938), 'A Reformulation of Certain Aspects of Welfare Economics', *Quarterly Journal of Economics,* 52, February, pp. 310-334.

Berle, Adolph A. and Gardiner Means (1932), *The Modern Corporation and Private Property.* New York, Macmillan.

Blanchard, Olivier, Francesco Giavazzi, Alessia Amighini (2010), *'Macroeconomics: a European Perspective Financial Times'/Prentice Hall.*

Boulding, Kenneth E. (1952), 'Welfare Economics', in Bernard F. Haley (ed.), A Survey of Contemporary Economics, II, ed, Bernard F, Haley, Homewood, Illinois: Irwin for the American Economic Association, pp. 1-34.

Boulding, Kenneth E. (1953), 'The Organizational Revolution: A Study in the Ethics of Economic Organization'. New York: *Harper and Brothers.*

Boulding, Kenneth E. (1956), 'General Systems Theory: The Skeleton of Science', Management Science, 2, 197-208, reprinted as Buckley, Walter (ed) (1968), *Modern Systems Research for the Behavioral Scientist: A Sourcebook,* Chicago: Aldine, Ch. 1, pp 3-10.

Boulding, Kenneth E. (1978), 'Ecodynamics: A New Theory of Societal Evolution', Beverly Hills.

Boulding, Kenneth E.(1966), 'The Economics of the Coming Spaceship Earth' in Henry Jarrett (ed.) (1966), Environmental Quality in a Growing Economy: Essays from the Sixth RFF Forum, Baltimore, Maryland: Johns Hopkins Press for Resources for the Future, pp. 3-14, reprinted in Kenneth E. Boulding (1968a), Beyond Economics: Essays on Society, Religion and Ethics, Ann Arbor: *University of Michigan Press,* 274-287 and in Kenneth E. Boulding (1971), Collected Papers, Fred R, Glahe, (ed.), Boulder: Colorado Associated University Press, II, Ch. 26.

Caldwell, Bruce J. (1993), 'Introduction', in Caldwell, Bruce J. (ed), *The Philosophy and Methodology of Economics, Aldershot: Elgar,* 3, l, I, ix-xxxiv.

California: Sage. Brodsky, Art (2010) 'The Uncommon Courage of the Federal Communication Commission', The Huffington Post, June 23. http://www.huffingtonpost.com/art-brodsky/the-uncommon-courage-of-t_b_617275.html

Calvin College. http://www.calvin.edu/about/identity.htm accessed 16 October 2010.

Cato Institute. http://www.cato.org/about.php accessed 16 October, 2010.

Coase, Ronald (1960), 'The Problem of Social Cost', Journal of Law and Economics, (3), pp. 1-44.

Colander, David, ed. (2006) Post-Walrasian Macroeconomics: Beyond the Dynamic Stochastic General Equilibrium Model Cambridge: *Cambridge University Press.*

Daly, Herman (1996), 'Beyond Growth: The Economics of Sustainable Development', Beacon Press. Economic Governance: The Organization of Cooperation. "Popular Information". Nobelprize.org.29 Jun 2010.
http://nobelprize.org/nobel_prizes/economics/laureates/2009/info.html

Galbraith, John Kenneth (1958), 'The Affluent Society. New York: Houghton Mifflin'.

Gardner, H. Stephen, (1998), 'Comparative Economic Systems', second edition, Fort Worth, Texas: Dryden.

Gassler, Robert Scott (2003), 'A Framework for Heterodox Economics', Economics for the Future: Celebrating 100 years of Cambridge Economics, Cambridge (UK), September, poster session. www.econ.cam.ac.uk/cjeconf/delegates/gassler.pdf

Gassler, Robert Scott (2003), Beyond Profit and Self-Interest. Cheltenham: Edward Elgar.

Gassler, Robert Scott (2007), 'Socialism without an Auctioneer: Walras as a Heterodox Economist', European Association for Evolutionary Political Economics, Porto, November 1-3.

Gautier, Catherine (2008), 'Oil, Water, and Climate: An Introduction', Cambridge: *Cambridge University Press.*

Gibbons, Robert (1997), 'An Introduction to Applicable Game Theory', *Journal of Economic Perspectives,* 11(1), Winter, pp.127-149.

Gilpin, Robert (1987), 'The Political Economy of International Relations'. Princeton: *Princeton University Press.*

Goosse H., P.Y. Barriat, W. Lefebvre, M.F. Loutre and V. Zunz, (2010), 'Introduction to climate dynamics and climate modeling', Online textbook available at http://www.climate.be/textbook (March 19) .

Granovetter, Marc (1985), 'Economic Action and Social Structure: The Problem of Embeddedness;' *American Journal of Sociology* 91 (3), pp. 481-510.

Hall, Peter A., and David Soskice, eds. (2001), 'Varieties of Capitalism: Institutional Foundations of Comparative Advantage'. Oxford: *Oxford University Press.*

Harris, J. (2008), 'Ecological Macroeconomics: Consumption, Investment, and Climate Change' Global Development and Environment Institute, *Working Paper* No. 08-02, July.

Harris, Jonathan M. (2006), 'Environmental and Natural Resource Economics A Contemporary Approach', Second edition. Boston: *Houghton Mifflin.*

Heinzerling, Lisa, and Frank Ackerman (2002) 'Pricing the Priceless: Cost-Benefit Analysis of Environmental Protection' Georgetown Environmental Law and Policy Institute.

Holt, Richard P.F., Steven P., and Clive L. S., eds. (2009) Post-Keynesian and Ecological Economics: Confronting Environmental Issues. *Cheltenham: Elgar.*

Johns, Helen and Paul Ormerod (2008) 'The unhappy thing about happiness studies', real-world economics review, (46), 20 May, pp. 139-146, http://www.paecon.net/PAEReview/issue46/JohnsOrmerod46.pdf

Kelman, Steven, (1987), 'Public Choice and Public Spirit', *The Public Interest,* (87), Spring, 80-94.

Keohane, Robert O.(1984), 'After Hegemony: Cooperation and Discord in the World Political Economy', Princeton, New Jersey: *Princeton University Press.*

Koopmans, Tjalling C. (1957), 'Three Essays on the State of Economic Science', New York: *McGraw-Hill.*

Koopmans, Tjalling C. and John Michael Montias (1971), 'On the Description and Comparison of Economic Systems', Ch. 2 of Alexander Eckstein (ed.) (1971), Comparison of Economic systems: Theoretical and Methodological Approaches, Berkeley: *University of California Press.*

Landreth, H., and David C. C. (2002), 'History of Economic Thought'. Boston: Houghton Mifflin.

Maskin, E. S. (2008), 'Mechanism Design: How to Implement Social Goals', February. Revised version of his Nobel lecture.

McGuigan, James R., R. Charles Moyer, and Frederick H. deB. Harris(2008), 'Managerial Economics: Applications, Strategy and Tactics'. 11th ed. Cengage.

McKibben, Bill. (2010), 'How the Mountain of Climate Change Evidence Is Being Used to Undermine the Cause', 27 Feb. http://www.alternet.org/environment/145838 /how_the_mountain_of_climate_change_evidence_is_being_used_to_undermine_the_ca use

Meadows, Donella H., Dennis L. Meadows, J. Randers, and W.W. Belnews (1972), 'The Limits to Growth'. New York: *Universe Books.*

Mikler John. (2009), 'A Varieties of Capitalism Approach to Disaggregated Authority and Climate Change', *5th ECPR General Conference*, Potsdam, Germany.

Milgrom, P. and John R. (1992), 'Economics, Organization, and Management. London': *Prentice-Hall.*

Mueller, Dennis C. (2003), 'Public Choice III. Cambridge': Cambridge *University Press.*

Musgrave, Richard A. (1959), 'The Theory of Public Finance: A Study in Political Economy', New York: *McGraw-Hill.*

Nelson, Julie A. (2000), 'Confronting the Science/Value Split: Notes on Feminist Economics, Institutionalism, Pragmatism and Process Thought', European Association for Evolutionary Political Economy, Berlin, 2-4 November 2000. Later published in the *Cambridge Journal of Economics* 27, (1), 2003, pp. 49-64.

Nordhaus, William D. (2007), 'A Review of The Stern Review on the Economics of Climate Change', *Journal of Economic Literature,* 45, September, pp.686-702.

O'Neill, Kate (2009), 'The Environment and International Relations'. Cambridge: Cambridge University Press.

Oreskes, N. (2004), 'The Scientific Consensus on Climate Change', *Science,.* 306,3 December, p.1686.

Oswald, A. (1999), 'A Nontechnical Introduction to the Economics of Happiness',December. http://www2.warwick.ac.uk/fac/soc/economics/staff/academic/oswald/intro.pdf

Polanyi, K. (1944), 'The Great Transformation', Boston: *Beacon Press.*

Rawls, J. (1971), 'A Theory of Justice. Cambridge', Massachusetts: *Harvard University Press.*

Rose-Ackerman, S. (1996), 'Altruism, Nonprofits, and Economic Theory', *Journal of Economic Literature,* June, 34(2), pp.701-728.

Royal Swedish Academy of Sciences. Economic Sciences Prize Committee. (2009), 'Economic Governance: Scientific Background on the Sveriges Riksbank Prize in Economic Sciences in Memory of Alfred Nobel 2009'. Stockholm: the Academy, 12 October.Samuelson, Paul Anthony [1947] 1971 Foundations of Economic Analysis, *Harvard University Press*, reprinted New York: Atheneum.

Schumpeter, Joseph A. (1950), 'Capitalism, Socialism and Democracy, New York': *Harper.*

Sen, A. (1999), 'Development as Freedom', New York: *Anchor.*

Smith, A. (1759), The theory of moral sentiments. http://en.wikisource.org/wiki/The_Theory_of_Moral_Sentiments London: A. Millar, (1790), http://www.econlib. org/library/Smith/smMSCover.html

Smith, A. (1776), 'An Inquiry into the Nature and Causes of the Wealth of Nations'. http://www.gutenberg.org/files/3300/3300-h/3300-h.htm

Stern, N. (2008), 'Richard T. Ely Lecture: The Economics of Climate Change,' American Economic Review: Papers & Proceedings, May, 98:2-37.Stern Review on the Economics of Climate Change [2007] http://www.hmtreasury.gov.uk/independent_reviews/stern_review_economics_climate_change/stern_review_report.cfm

Stigler, George J. (1971), 'The Theory of Economic Regulation', *The Bell Journal of Economics and Management Science,* 2 (1), pp. 3-21.

Tol, Richard S. J., "Modelling the costs of emission reduction: different approaches," *Pacific and Asian Journal of Energy.* 10(1): pp. 1-7.

Tol, Richard S.'International Inequity Aversion and the Social Cost of Carbon,' *Climate Change Economics,* 1(1), 2010, pp.21-32.

United Nations. Intergovernmental Panel on Climate Change. *Climate Chan*ge (2007). *Synthesis Report*. http://www.ipcc.ch/

Veblen, T. (1921), 2001 The Engineers and the Price System. Kitchener, Ontario: Batoche Books. http://socserv2.mcmaster.ca/~econ/ugcm/3ll3/veblen/Engineers.pdf

Walras, L. (1898) 1992 Etudes d'economie politique appliquée: Théorie de la production de la richess sociale. Paris: *Economica.*

Walras, L. [1874] (1988) Éléments d'Économie politique pure, ou Théorie de la Richesse sociale. Paris: Economica, (édition compare des éditions de 1874, 1889, 1896, 1900, 1926 (et de l'édition de l'Agrégé de 1938) augmentée de la traduction des notes de William Jaffé dans Elements of Pure Economics, 1954. Publié avec le concours du Centre Nationale des Lettres). (Auguste et Léon Walras : Œuvres économiques complètes, VIII). Translated as Leon Walras [1874] 1977 Elements of Pure Economics: Or the Theory of Social Wealth, translated from the French by William Jaffé, Homewood, Illinois: Irwin,(1954), reprinted Fairfield, New Jersey: Augustus M, Kelley.

Walras, L.(1896) 1990 Etudes d'economie sociale: Théorie de la repartition de la richess sociale. Paris: Economica.

Welsch, Heinz (2009), 'Implications of happiness research for environmental economics', *Ecological Economics,* (68), pp. 2735-2742.

In: Development Management in the Twenty-First Century ISBN: 978-1-62100-699-2
Editors: Kartik Roy and Sandip Kar

Chapter 13

GREEN DEVELOPMENT IN ENVIRONMENT AND CLIMATE CHANGE CRISES IN THE ASIA–PACIFIC: A STRATEGY IN MINIMIZING THE IMPACT

Manoranjan Mohanty*
Associate Professor, Development Studies,
The University of the South Pacific, Suva, Fiji

INTRODUCTION

The contemporary world is facing serious economic and environmental crises. It is a climate –stressed world today. The global crises are affecting all societies and economies, but more the poor countries in the 'majority' world. The ongoing triple 'F' (financial, food and fuel) crises are likely to exacerbate poverty and inequality. Population growth, environmental degradation, resource depletion and scarcity, water and energy crises, and climate change are compounding the challenges to sustainable economic growth. Achievement of the Millennium Development Goals (MDGs) particularly in regards to poverty alleviation and environmental sustainability remain the greatest challenge especially in the Asia and the Pacific region. Navigating towards sustainable development remains an enormous task. Sound environmental and development management are the key issues in this task.

The synergy between environment and economy are more pronounced now than ever before. The emphasis is more on a low- carbon development or 'green development' rather than CO_2 emission reductions. The 'black' vs. 'green development' debate draws much of world attention today. 'Green development' has emerged as an alternative development strategy, a livelihoods approach, and also a mitigation strategy to climate change. 'Green growth' is an approach to achieve sustainable development and is gaining momentum. Green growth policy not only emphasizes an ecologically sustainable economic progress through a low-carbon economy, but also a socially inclusive development (UNEP 2008b). It emphasizes the need to improve the ecological efficiency of economic growth. Green energy development

* mohanty_m@usp.ac.fj.

is a crucial link between energy-economy and development and has potential for achieving a green development on a sustainable way. It is argued that improving energy efficiency (EE) can lead to a low-carbon economy and help reducing green house gas (GHGs) emissions. Development of renewable energy sources and green energy technologies are the pathways in achieving sustainable 'green energy' development. 'Green economy' and 'green growth' aim at a low -carbon or low-fossil-fuel development that will increase energy efficiency (EE) and in turn, an eco-efficiency of economic growth.

The questions arise: How does climate change affect development and affected by development? How can climate change and sustainable development be integrated? How to transform social and economic infrastructures and manage development towards a low - carbon economy? How carbon emission reductions be made without compromising economic growth? How can green development strategy help achieving eco-efficiency and minimizing the climate change impact?

The aim of the paper is to examine the concept of 'green development' as an alternative development strategy, and mitigation strategy and an approach to achieve sustainable development in amidst global environmental and climate change crises and to explore pathways for a low-carbon development in the Asia and the Pacific region.

The following sections are divided into different parts. The First part brings out theoretical linkages between environment, climate change and development, and 'green development' as an alternate sustainable development model and a strategy in lowering the impact of climate change. Second section gives a brief account of the current climate change scenario and emerging issues. The Third part deals with 'green growth' and 'green economy' concepts and 'green energy' and 'green technologies' as pathways to green growth and their prospects especially in the Asia and the Pacific region. The final section focuses on environmental and developmental management and policies and the institutional capacity-building initiatives in the Asia and the Pacific region in achieving a low-carbon development.

ENVIRONMENT, CLIMATE CHANGE AND GREEN DEVELOPMENT: THEORETICAL LINKAGES

Climate change is a part of global environmental change which is caused due to the global changes: social, demographic, economic and political. Development and climate change are closely intertwined in a multidimensional, dynamic, and complex two-way relationship. Their relationship is linked through environmental change, energy consumption and waste generation. Generally speaking, higher the level of development, greater is the energy consumption and in turn, higher is the GHGs emissions leading to global warming, the prime cause of climate change and sea level rise. 'Green' verses 'black' economic development views draw much of world attention today in the face of climate change. Green economic development model based on green energy, green technologies and green business is growing in importance vis-a-vis fossil-fuel based 'black' economic model. The linear growth model 'grow now and clean up later' is unsustainable (UNEP 2005a:1). Rather there is a need for a 'clean up and grow' approach to achieve sustainability.

The debate between 'hard energy' and 'soft energy' path in development continues in energy –development discourse. The traditional approach of a hard energy is based on the assumption that the mass energy use will lead to better development. This involves burning of inefficient fossil-fuels, nuclear power and other conventional energy sources. The soft energy path on the other hand is based on the assumption that energy is a means to social ends and it involves efficient use of energy sources and reliance on 'soft energy technologies' such as solar, wind, geothermal and bio-fuels. Renewables and non-conventional energy are the more efficient and soft energy sources that have potential for 'green growth'.

On the one hand, population growth, and poverty alleviation in the 'majority' world demand fast economic growth. On the other, the current high-carbon, 'black' economic development processes generate GHGs and contribute to global warming and consequently, the climate change. The processes and strategies of carbon emission reductions are expensive and the 'majority world' cannot afford for them. The countries in the developing world are thus caught in the basic dilemma how to reduce carbon emissions without compromising economic growth and development? There has thus been a search for alternative development model which can achieve both.

How Does Climate Change Affect Development?

Climate change undermines development and aggravates poverty. The extreme climate events such as cyclone, flood and droughts make significant economic, social and sectoral loss due to water contamination, (surface and underground water), salt water intrusion, infrastructure damages: road and transport, and tourism. Climate change affects food security and livelihoods of people, and reinforces poverty and malnutrition. Extreme climate change events and environmental effects cause population movements and migration of people to higher and secured grounds especially towards cities, and substantially contribute to growing urbanization. An increasing urbanization lead to growing demand for energy and higher energy consumption and GHGs production. Urbanization is also responsible for organic wastes dumping and air pollution thus contributing significantly to emission of methane and carbon dioxides to atmosphere. Methane from solid waste disposal sites contributes 3-4 per cent of anthropogenic GHG emissions (IGES 2010: xxvi). The extreme weather events cause vector -borne and water – and food-borne diseases and affect human health, which adversely affect productivity and efficiency of labour and in turn, the development in a country. Diseases and poor health due to climate change events also demand more social welfare spending, cutting down development budgets. In addition, huge adaptation and mitigation spending by the governments for minimizing climate change drains out substantial resources and hamper development.

Concept of Green Development

The concept of sustainable development is highly contested and seems to be less achievable. 'Green development' has emerged as an alternative development paradigm, a mitigation strategy to climate change and aim at achieving sustainable development. Friberg and Hettne (1985) explored green development paradigm that opposes developmentalism (cited in Adams, 1995b:94). It is an 'endogenous development' model (ibid). According to Adam (1995a: xvii) Green development "tries to bridge two important gulfs. The first is between environmentalism and development and the second between armchair theory and practice". Greening the whole process of development amidst environment and climate change and crises and managing carbon emissions through a low-carbon development through 'green growth' by promoting 'green economy', 'green industry', 'green investment', 'green business', 'green cities', 'green infrastructure', 'green housing' and 'green building' and so on, all aiming at increasing energy efficiency (EE) and a low-carbon development. This in turn is likely to enhance an eco-efficiency of economic growth that can help achieve a sustainable development. As Adam (1995a: xvii) said the "greening of development calls for a fundamental reassessment of development itself". He further said there was a need for reform the development process by imposing 'sustainable development from above' through ecological modernization, as well as the potential for achieving 'sustainable development from below' (ibid).

A transition to 'green economy' is underway and green technological and low-carbon revolutions are taking shape. A green economy entails green energy generation based on renewable energy sources and substituting fossil-fuels and conserving energy for its efficient use.

Green growth has emerged as an approach to sustainable development and it has potential for "eco-efficiency or minimizing environmental pressure while maximizing economic benefit, the key principle of sustainability" (UNESCAP 2008:11). A sustainable use of 'ecosystem goods and services' are critical to long- term economic and social viability (UNEP 2005b). To improve the eco-efficiency of the economic growth, there is a need to improve the eco-efficiency of production and consumption patterns of society. According to the Johannesburg Plan of Implementation, the approach aims to harmonize economic growth and sustainable use of environmental resources by "fundamentally changing the way in which societies produce and consume" (ibid). Green growth can be achievable by "developing and capitalizing on synergies between economic growth, social development and environmental protection" (ibid).

Eco-efficiency of economic growth is the main focus. Improving energy efficiency can enhance eco-efficiency of economic growth and it is one of the "most cost-effective mitigation options" (UNESCAP, 2009: 79). The ecological efficiency can be achieved through green energy development and their linkages are shown below:

Green energy energy efficiency economic efficiency ecological efficiency.

Steps to improve eco-efficiency involve adopting a process or technology that reduces the amount of water or energy required to produce a good or service (ibid). Green energy and clean technologies are crucial links between energy-economy and development and have potential for achieving a sustainable green development. Development of renewable and alternative energy sources and green energy technologies is the pathways in achieving sustainable energy development and thus a green growth.

CURRENT CLIMATE CHANGE SCENARIO AND EMERGING ISSUES

The Intergovernmental Panel on Climate Change (IPCC) has already established that climate change is real and universal, and it is largely a human–induced phenomenon. Climate change has been caused by greenhouse gas emissions from energy intensive human economic activities based on fossil-fuels (coal, oil and natural gas) burning. The economic growth processes are heavily dependent on oil consumption and the global economic and environmental crises are partly due to heavy dependence on oil. Oil dominates the world energy regime accounting for about 34 per cent of total world energy consumption today (Wikipedia 2011 b). All efforts should be made to reduce the oil dependence and to enhance non-fossil-fuel and clean energy use? Fossil fuels still account for about 86 per cent of total global energy consumption (ibid). With just 15 per cent of the world population, rich countries account for 45 per cent of CO_2 emissions (UNDP 2008: 42).

Global warming is the main concern. In the last century, the average global surface temperature has increased by 0.74 degree Celsius and by the end of the century it could rise 2 or 3 degree Celsius or even as much as 6 degree Celsius (UNESCAP 2009: 73). Since 1993, the sea level has been rising at a rate of about 3 millimetres annually- a major threat to coastal areas and many Pacific Island countries (ibid). Even small islands in the pacific and the Maldives could disappear due to rise in sea level if the worst scenario of climate change occurs (ibid:71).Global temperature increase of 3-4 degree Celsius could result in 330 million people being displaced through flooding (UNDP 2008:9). The "increase in the surface temperature especially in Asia and the Pacific is much higher than the global average...so is the impact" (UNESCAP 2009:73). Besides other this has implications for melting of mountain glaciers and river flooding in the region. Himalayan glaciers for example, are shrinking at an average of 10-60 metres annually; some are retreating by 74 metres a year and may melt entirely by 2035 (ibid). According to the United Nations Department of Economic and Social Affairs (2009):

> Climate change is an inevitable and urgent global challenge with long-term implications for the sustainable development of all countries.... While climate change will know no boundaries, poor and developing countries, particularly the LDCs, will be among those most adversely affected and least able to cope with the anticipated shocks to their social, economic and natural systems. The International Panel of Climate Change, IPCC projects that by 2080, millions of people will be displaced due to sea-level rise, with densely-populated and low-lying countries, like many SIDS, facing the greatest threat from storm surges and rising seas.

The food-fuel crises debate continues. The food crisis reflected through dramatic increase in food grain prices, is affecting millions of people. This crisis burdened developing countries by over $324 billion in 2007 (UNEP 2008c:1). The food and fuel crises together have put 950 million people worldwide at risk of hunger and malnutrition (ibid). About two billion people globally do not yet have electricity, oil or gas to cook food and for daily living (UNEP 2008a). Currently, some 2.5 billion people depend on biomass (UNDP 2008:44). There has been severe stress on water resources as well due to climate change. One billion people in the Asia-Pacific region could be affected by water stress (UNESCAP 2009:74).

The environmental and climate change crises however provides opportunities for cutting GHGs and achieving a low- carbon development. As the Secretary-General Ban Kid-moon once said "...climate change is not only posing serious global threat but is generating a "world of opportunities" (ibid). The 'Global Green New Deal' promoted by the Secretary-General of the United Nations provides a way forward towards a low-carbon development path (UNEP, 2009:71).

GREEN GROWTH AND GREEN DEVELOPMENT STRATEGY

In 2005, 52 Governments from Asia and the Pacific convened at Seoul at the Fifth Ministerial Conference on Environment and Development (MCED), they moved beyond sustainable development rhetoric and pursue a path of 'green growth' for achieving environmentally sustainable economic growth (UNESCAP 2008:5). In June, 2009, OECD also adopted Green Growth Declaration acknowledging that 'green' and 'growth' can go hand in hand and it was adopted to help countries to promote economic growth while reducing GHG emissions (OECD, 2009).

Green development is a strategy towards a low-carbon growth and sustainable development. The rationale behind green development is to promote sustainable economic growth while reducing GHGs by increasing energy efficiency. Green development is likely to help mitigating 3'F' (financial, food and fuel) crises and a strategy to climate change mitigation. Green economy concept is fast emerging in contrast to the 'black' economy model based on fossil-fuels. It includes green energy sources based on renewable energy to substitute for fossil fuels and energy conservation for efficient energy use to achieve ecological efficiency. The basic principles of greening growth are: quality of economic growth, eco-efficiency of economic growth and environmental sustainability (UNEP, 2008b: 8).

UNEP introduced Green Economy Initiative that encourages investments in environmental assets and green production (UNEP 2011). The Initiative aims at greening national economies by reshaping and refocusing policies, investments and spending towards a range of sectors such as green technologies, renewable energies, water services, green transportation, waste management, green buildings and sustainable agriculture and forests (UNEP 2009).

Global Green New Deal (UNEP 2008a) was introduced to generate transition in terms of economic returns, environmental sustainability and job creation. It identified six priority sectors that include: clean energy and clean technologies including recycling rural energy, renewables and sustainable biomass; sustainable agriculture, organic agriculture; ecosystem infrastructure; reduced emissions from deforestation and forest degradation (REDD) and sustainable cities planning, transportation and green building (ibid).

The green growth paths can be achieved by: adopting sustainable consumption and production (SCP) practices, undertaking green businesses, promoting sustainable infrastructure, Green Tax and Budget Reform (GTBR) and green investment in natural capital (Green Growth 2005a). There is a need for greening business at all levels of economy in order to create an enabling environment for more green jobs; adapt to the impacts of climate change; support new markets for sustainable products; improve the use of natural resources, and to reduce environmental degradation caused by business activities (ibid). Green business is defined as "enterprises which consider environmental protection as an essential component of their long-term business objectives, both by promoting eco-efficient production activities and by marketing sustainable products and services" (ibid). Emphasis has been placed on sectors with high potential for creation of 'green job' – the employment that contributes to protecting and preserving the environment and identifying how these activities can accelerate the transition to green growth. A new industry sector is building up around climate change covering renewable energy (wind, solar, wave and bio-fuels), carbon trading, carbon offsets, technology development, carbon capture and sequestration and disaster insurance (IGES 2010:2). Along with a 'green technological' revolution, a kind of 'green industrial revolution' is also taking shape in the world today.

Natural capital is considered as both ecosystem goods (raw materials) and services that make the earth habitable by stabilizing the global climate, cleansing the water and air, pollinating agricultural crops and storing nutrients in soils (UNESCAP 2008:40). Transforming business practices to restore investment in natural capital is key to long-term environmental sustainability. Investment on natural capital is likely to expand environmental carrying capacity. Investment in clean technologies and 'natural' infrastructure such as forests and soils are the challenges for real growth, and combating climate change (UNEP 2008a).

GREEN ENERGY

Green energy' is the main tool for achieving an efficient energy development in order to achieve the ultimate goal of 'green economy' and 'green growth' or a 'smart growth' for an efficient and low-carbon economy. This is likely to lead to an 'efficient ecology' and in turn, an environmental sustainability. Renewable energy sources have potentials for 'green energy' development and achieving green growth and low-carbon development. Green energy and renewable energy are used synonymously.

Renewable energy (RE) is growing in its importance worldwide (see Table 13.1). The main advantages of renewable energy sources are that they provide energy security, they are non-polluting, inexpensive, and available locally, more environmental-friendly and can reduce oil dependence and help achieving green growth. In 2008, renewable energy accounted for about 19 per cent of the world's energy consumption (Wikipedia, 2011b). By the early 2010, there were more than 100 countries which enacted some type of policy target and /or promotion policy related to renewable energy, an increase over 80 per cent in number or up from 55 in the early 2005 (REN21 2010:9).

There are three generation renewable/green energy technologies: first, second and third. First-generation technologies include for example, hydropower, geothermal, and biomass combustion. Second generation technologies are solar heating and cooling, solar photo-voltaics, and wind power. The third generation technologies include biomass gasification, bio-refinery, geothermal, and ocean/marine energy (tidal, waves, and ocean thermal differences) (Wikipedia 2011a).

The 'new' renewable energy include solar energy (solar photovoltaic and solar hot water), wind, biomass, small hydro projects, hydrogen, bio-fuels, and geothermal energy sources are growing in importance. The capacity of wind power, solar PV, solar hot water and bio-fuels have increased significantly over the years, the solar PV capacity has grown the most, nearly three times between 2007-2009 (Table 13.1).

The green investment has expanded substantially. It amounts to about US$ 1.3 trillion per year (UNEP, 2011:31). Investment in clean energy assets (excluding large hydro) was $ 29.5 million in the first quarter of 2010 (REN21, 2010:29). Worldwide, jobs in renewable energy industries exceeded 3 million in 2009, of this, bio-fuel industry accounted for half, wind power 0.5 million, solar PV and solar hot water 0.3 million each (ibid:34). Investment in 'new' renewable energy capacity was $ 150 billion in 2009, about 44 per cent growth since 2007 (see Table 13.1).

Table 13.1. Selected Global Renewable Energy Growth indicators

Global Indicators	2007	2008	2009	% Change 2007-2009
Investment in new renewable capacity (annual) billion USD	104	130	150	44. 2
Existing renewables power capacity, including large-scale hydro (GWe)	1,070	1,140	1,230	78.5
Existing renewables power capacity, excluding large-scale hydro (GWe)	305	280	305	0.0
Wind power capacity (existing)	94	121	159	69.1
Solar PV capacity (grid-connected) (GWe)	7.6	13.5	21	176.3
Solar hot water capacity (GWth)	126	149	180	42.9
Countries with policy targets for renewable energy use	68	75	85	25.0
Bio-ethanol	50	69	76	52.0
Biodiesel	10	15	17	70.0

Source: Wikipedia, 2011a.

Bio-Fuels

Bio-fuels, a form of 'new' renewable energy and bio- energy are attracting more global attention today than ever before. This is mainly due to the fact that bio-fuels have significant potential for reducing GHG emissions, and are potential substitute for fossil fuels, inexpensive source of energy, have high energy value and the most efficient energy source. Bio-fuels as energy sources have disadvantages as well. Among others, bio-fuels cause deforestation and soil erosion, food shortages leading to food insecurity, food and fuel price rise and have adverse impacts on water sources.

Bio-fuels are derived from biomass and organic wastes and include both bio-ethanol and bio-diesel. Bio-fuels are made from agricultural feed stocks, vegetable oils and animal fats using conventional technology (IGES 2010:106). Bio-ethanol is blended with gasoline or petrol and produced by fermenting sugars. The feed stocks used in production of bio-ethanol include sugarcane, corn, wheat, and sugar beets (ibid: 107). Sugar and jatropha based ethanol have the most potential to reduce GHG emissions (ibid). The USA and Brazil, the leading countries in ethanol production, accounted for about 88 per cent of global ethanol production in 2009 (REN 21, 2010:24). Bio-diesel on the other hand is blended with petroleum diesel and produced from vegetable oil or animal fats. The feed stocks to produce bio-diesel mainly include palm oil, coconut, and soya beans. Table 13.2 shows a comparison of feed stocks used in bio-fuels, their potential for GHG (CO_2) emission reductions, the Net Energy Value (NEV) and the countries where they are produced.

Table 13.2. Comparison of Bio-fuel Feed Stocks, Country of Production, GHG Emission reduction and Net Energy Value (NEV)

Feedstock/fuel	Country	% CO_2 emission reduction	NEV (MJ/L)
Corn ethanol	USA	2-23	5. 89
Cassava	Thailand	63	22.38
Cassava	China	-	15.14
Sugarcane	Brazil	80	41.34
Oil Palm	Malaysia	60	37.45
Jatropha	India	80	5.26
Jatropha	Thailand	-	3. 82
Coconut	Philippines	60	31.72

Source: Institute for Global Environmental Strategies (IGES), 2010: 107.

ASIA - PACIFIC CONTEXT

Asia –Pacific region is home to 60 per cent of the growing world population and the region accounts for 40 per cent of the global economy (UNEP 2005a). The region is becoming the hub of production and causing considerable impact on the ecological carrying capacity of the region (UNEP 2005b). Climate change is the potential threat to the region. Pacific island countries (PICs) are the most vulnerable to the climate change threat and there has been increasing concern especially in the low lying atoll states such as Kiribati, Marshall Islands, Tokelau and Tuvalu and the low-lying areas of other Pacific Island countries. Climate change, climate variability and sea level rise are not just an environmental issue, but also an economic, social and political issue for PICs (WWF 2003).

The energy consumption varies widely in Asia and the Pacific region. As Table 5.3 shows in 2007, the percentage share of fossil fuel to total primary energy supply was very high in Malaysia (95 per cent), China (87 per cent), Korea (82 per cent), and India (70 per cent) compared to Singapore (5 per cent). Pollution (air and water) is one of the major concerns in the region. Death rates due to air (indoor and outdoor) and water pollution are higher especially in South Asian countries, China and Papua New Guinea (see Table 13.3). China is the first country to assess the price of its pollution which was US$ 64 million in 2004 (UNEP 2005 a: 13). Another concern is access to clean sources of energy especially, electricity. Living without electricity affects many dimensions of human development (UNDP 2008: 43) and thus undermines economic growth. The proportion of population without access to electricity remains high in several Asia and the Pacific countries e.g. Bangladesh (59 per cent), Pakistan (40 per cent), and Indonesia (36 per cent) (see Table 13.3).

As elsewhere, green energy or renewable energy sources are gaining importance in the Asia-Pacific countries as well. The percentage of renewable energy was relatively higher in Singapore (95 per cent), Sri Lanka (55 per cent), Philippines (43 per cent) and Indonesia (31 per cent) in 2007 (see Table 13.3). China, India, and South Korea continue to increase their commitments to renewable energy (REN21, 2010:9). A sizable volumes of fuel ethanol and biodiesel are produced in China, India, Malaysia and Thailand (ibid, 24-25).

The ecological footprints, a measure of human demand on the earth's ecosystem remain low in Asia and the Pacific countries varies between 0.5 to 4 hectre per capita with an exception of Singapore where the value is 35 hectre per capita (Table 13.3). A carbon footprint, a subset of ecological footprint, is an important measure of GHG emission. It is defined as the total GHG (greenhouse gas) emissions caused directly and indirectly by an individual, organization, event or product (UNDP 2008: 43). In general, poorer the country, lower is the carbon footprint. The carbon footprint of the world's poorest 1 billion people on the planet is around 3 per cent of the total footprint (ibid: 43).

Table 13.3. Energy Supply and Ecological Footprint in selected Asia and the Pacific Countries

Country	% share to primary energy supply, 2007		Ecological foot print of consumption (hectares per capita), 2006	% Population without Electricity 2008	Death rate due to pollution (indoor and outdoor, and water) (per million people) 2004
	Fossil fuel	Renewable energy			
China	87	13	1.8	0.6	693
Rep. of Korea	82	1	3.7	-	150
Indonesia	69	31	-	35.7	505
Malaysia	95	5	-	0.7	60
Thailand	-	-	-	0.6	345
Philippines	57	43	-	13.8	322
Singapore	5	95	34.7	0. 0-	262
Bangladesh	66	34	-	59.3	821
India	70	29	0.8	34.2	954
Pakistan	63	37	0.7	39.8	896
Sri Lanka	45	55	0.9	23.4	
Fiji	-	-	3.7	-	0
PNG	-	-	1.7	-	737
Solomon Isl.	-	-	1.7	-	433

Source: UNDP, 2010. PNG: Papua New Guinea.

Green Growth and Sustainable Development Declarations in Asia and the Pacific

Several environmental and sustainable development Initiatives have been taken in the Asia and the Pacific. These include: the Barbados Programme of Action for the Sustainable Development of Small Island Developing States (1994), Phnom Penh Regional Platform on Sustainable Development for the Asia and the Pacific (2001), Bali Strategic Plan for Technology Support and Capacity-building (2004), the Mauritius Strategy for Implementation of the Programme of Action for the Sustainable Development of SIDS (2005), the Regional Implementation Plan (RIP) for Sustainable Development in Asia and the Pacific, 2006-2010 which was adopted by the Ministerial Conference on Environment and

Development (2005), Cebu Declaration on East Asian Energy Security (2007) and Bali Action Plan, 2007.

The Seoul Initiative Network on Green Growth (SINGG) was taken in 2005 with a vision on achieving environmentally sustainable economic growth in the Asia and the Pacific region by promoting effective environmental policies (Green Growth 2005b). To achieve this goal, the Seoul Initiative has identified three targets: improving eco-efficiency for environmental sustainability, enhancing environmental performance and promoting the environment as an opportunity for economic growth and development (ibid). Green Growth strategy was included in the Regional Implementation Plan (RIP) for Sustainable Development in Asia and the Pacific, 2006-2010.

Similarly , Manila Declaration on green industry in Asia was adopted in September 2009 that reaffirm commitment to Rio Declaration on Environment and Development and the provisions of Agenda 21 , World Summit on Sustainable Development , in particular Johannesburg Plan of Implementation and the Declaration provided framework for action (UNIDO 2009).

Green Growth Initiatives in Asia and the Pacific Countries

The Republic of Korea is the leading country in the world today with much of emphasis on green growth. The country has strong commitment to 'greening' the economy. The country launched a 'Green New Deal' in 2009 as a means of stimulating job creation and revitalizing the economy (UNEP, 2009: 7). South Korea has designed its 'green stimulus' package around 4 per cent of GDP to direct growth along a low–carbon path and to be implemented between 2009-2012 (ibid). The Republic of Korea is world's leading country in terms of 'green stimulus' per capita followed by Japan, China and United States (ibid: 12). The country is expected to create around 1 million green jobs (UNESCAP, ADB and UNDP, 2010: 51). The President of Republic Korea Lee Myung–bak is pushing a "low-carbon, green-growth" policy aimed at lessening South Korea's dependence on fossil fuel and promoting the development of substitute energy sources, such as solar and wind power, and other technologies enhancing energy efficiency (UNESCAP, 2010). The President once remarked, "Green growth is not a matter of choice but a requirement that we must fulfill by all means for our future survival" (UNESCAP, 2009:70).

South Korea has a "five-year green growth plan," announced in July 2010, that aims to spend nearly107 trillion won ($87 billion) on several projects to reduce emissions and develop cutting-edge technologies and other areas (UNESCAP 2010). The country has made huge green investments that include energy conservation in villages and schools ($ 5.8 billion), forest restoration ($1.7 billion), water resource management ($ 690 million) and river restoration ($ 10 billion) (UNESCAP, ADB and UNDP 2010:51). The Secretary-General of the United Nations, Ban Ki-moon, emphasized "investing in the green economy is not an optional expense. It is a 'smart investment' for a more equitable and prosperous future" (UNESCAP 2009: 71).

The Republic of Korea has also introduced a Framework Act for Low Carbon Green Growth in 2010 to establish a "comprehensive legal framework of relevant policies to foster the development of green technology and industries, to create new green jobs, to respond to climate change, to control energy targets, to promote a green lifestyle for citizens and to promote sustainable development" (UNESCAP 2010).

China has introduced a Resource Saving Society Initiative which was implemented through the National Five-Year Plan (2006-2010) (ibid). China has invested about $140 billion for promoting renewable energy that employs around 1 million people (UNESCAP ADB and UNDP 2010:51). China's 'green stimulus' is about US$218 billion (UNEP 2009:3). China has also announced some national measures in pursuit of green growth that include promoting improvement in technological processes and scientific research for energy efficiency and recycling technologies, improving energy consumption management, developing new tools and mechanism such as energy efficiency labeling (UNEP 2005b).

India is not lagging behind in its green growth strategies. In India Economic Summit in 2009, the Prime Minister Dr. Manmohan Singh said "the historic accumulation of CO2 is not the result of what we have done, but is the consequence of 150 years of industrialization in the major developed countries of the world...Our strategy is not just to deliver rapid growth, but to deliver rapid and inclusive growth..." (World Economic Forum 2009).

The Indian Ministry of New and Renewable Energy (MNRE) has been promoting renewable energy technologies and efforts have been made to increase the contribution of renewable energy in the total energy mix (Government of India 2010). New and renewable energy sources such as solar energy including solar photovoltaic (SPV), wind, biomass, small hydro projects, hydrogen, bio-fuels, geothermal energy have been promoted by the Government. In 2007, renewable energy sources accounted for 29 per cent of India's total primary energy supply (see Table 16). India is fifth worldwide in total existing wind power capacity and is rapidly expanding many forms of rural renewables such as biogas and solar PV (REN21, 2010:9). India, which ranked sixteenth in 2009 in biodiesel production has increased its production more than 100-fold to over 130 million litres (ibid: 25). Remote Village Electrification and National Biogas Programme are the two renewable energy programmes for rural applications in the country (Government of India, 2010). The Ministry plans to undertake electrification (primarily lighting) of villages in paddy growing areas through gasification of rice husk. In urban areas, the primary focus is on solar water heating systems and construction of green building (ibid). Power generation from Municipal Solid Waste (MSW) is in progress in India especially in Karnataka and Delhi (ibid).

The Government of India has implemented a Scheme-"Energy Efficient Solar/ Green Buildings" with the main objective to promote the widespread construction of energy efficient solar/ green buildings in the country (Government of India 2010:5). A National Rating System named GRIHA (Green Rating for Integrated Habitat Assessment) has been developed in the country to 'rate' a building on the degree of its greenness (ibid).

Other countries in the region such as Philippines for example has promoted green growth strategies through its waste minimization activities such as recycling, composting, management of medical waste, raising institutional capacity building especially in Cebu city (UNEP 2005b). Similarly, the Royal Government of Cambodia has embarked on the development of a 'National Green Growth Roadmap' in January 2009 which aims to contribute to the national economic development policy and mainstream environmental sustainability into development plans (Green Growth 2010). Many Pacific Island countries such as Vanuatu, Samoa, and New Caledonia have been successful in developing coconut oil as bio-fuel. Prospects do exist in Fiji for ethanol bio-fuels from sugar cane, cassava, and bio-fuels from coconut oil.

Solid Waste management in reducing GHGs and energy resource recovery from waste are critical concerns. Several Asia and the Pacific countries such as China, India, Indonesia, Thailand and Philippines have undertaken national waste policies and legislation regarding Municipal Solid Waste management (IGES 2010: 143-145).

ENVIRONMENTAL MANAGEMENT AND POLICIES

Climate change is a global problem and seeks global mitigation. Development, especially green development is a key to climate policy. Climate change is a development and environmental management challenge. Developing countries now emphasize more on green development or low-carbon development, rather than CO2 emission cuts. There has been little success in Clean Development Mechanism (CDM) that aim at GHG emission reductions. The Clean Development Mechanism is an arrangement under the Kyoto Protocol allowing industrialized countries with a green house gas reduction commitment to invest in projects that reduce emissions in developing countries as an alternative to more expensive emission reductions in their own countries (IGES 2010:81). Traditional environmental management pursues reactive policies but in order to achieve sustainable development, a paradigm shift is needed towards more preventive policies (UNEP 2005a). These policies need to integrate ecological principles into development. The environmental management needs to improve eco-efficiency of production and consumption. Climate change mitigation calls for transforming to a low- carbon energy society and economy. The Green Growth policy seeks to harmonize economic growth for poverty reduction and improved well-being with environmental sustainability, while improving the eco-efficiency of economic growth. Green development therefore, calls for best environmental management practices. The four pillars of green growth management are identified as: green tax and budget reform (i.e. eco-tax reform), sustainable infrastructure, greening business and sustainable consumption (UNESCAP 2008:18). Carbon offset or the mitigation of carbon emissions through the development of alternative projects such as solar or wind energy or reforestation, represent one way of managing environmental carbon footprint. Reduced emissions from deforestation and forest degradation (REDD) is high on the international climate change agenda and it is considered to be a low-cost option for reducing GHG emissions (IGES 2010: xxv). Some best practices and policy responses that are adopted in Asia and the Pacific countries towards environmental management and sustainable development pathways are worth mentioning. These include for example, Thailand's policy of 'self sufficiency economy', China's concept of 'circular economy' and 'resource saving society', India's 'knowledge economy', Bhutan's 'gross national happiness' development model and the green growth paths as followed by Republic of Korea, China, Philippines and India (UNEP 2005a).

Green Infrastructure

The built- environment in some countries is responsible for up to 40 per cent of total energy use (UNEP, 2008a). A green or sustainable infrastructure system is one that "facilitates a higher-quality delivery of housing, transport, energy, water, waste and sanitation services, with less use of resources, to support social and economic development in an integrated, eco-efficient and inclusive manner" (Green Growth 2005a).

Green Cities

Cities that are tomorrow's 'habitat for humanity' need to be converted to 'green cities' with ecological friendly 'green building' and 'green infrastructure'. Cities now account for 75 per cent of energy consumption and 75 per cent of carbon emissions (UNEP 2011: 11). Green cars are on the make as well. In 2008, Thailand approved the plans by Toyota Motor, Mitsubishi Motors and Tata Motors to build fuel-efficient eco-cars in the country (UNEP 2008c). South Korea has built fuel-efficient and lower emission green car as well. Efforts are to be made to convert cities towards a zero-carbon city. To become a zero carbon city, a modern city must collectively reduce GHGs to zero and all practices that emit GHGs must cease (Wikipedia 2011c).The world's first zero-carbon city is Masdar City in the Gulf emirate of Abu Dhabi which started its construction in 2008 (ibid).The city is being designed to be powered entirely with renewable energy, including solar power. A zero-carbon city is a renewable–energy-economy city.

Green Building

Buildings consume more than 40 per cent of total energy use globally (Government of India 2010) and over 90 per cent of all electricity use in certain countries (UNEP 2008b). Buildings are responsible for about 75 per cent of GHGs, mainly CO2 emissions (UNESCAP 2008:29). Converting into green building is an important environmental management option and a climate change mitigation strategy. A green building has potential for reducing GHGs more quickly and cheaply than other means and slowing down global warming. It can increase materials, water and energy efficiency as well. It is estimated that green building design can reduce energy and water use by human settlement by more than 30 per cent over the life time of the structure (ibid:28).

Policy Dilemma

Climate change policy however has received less attention in the Asia and the Pacific and there is an absence of national policy framework for adaptation (IGES 2010:2). This is mainly because of at least three reasons: Firstly, the countries have currently pressing economic development and poverty reduction priorities aiming at achieving Millennium Development Goals and climate change issues are given less priority. Secondly, there are too much uncertainties exist on climate change outcomes, so countries are unwilling to invest on adaptation programmes. Finally, different developing countries view climate change differently. Low lying Small Island Developing States (SIDS) or countries with vast floodplains (like Bangladesh) for example, view their situation in a perspective of potential victim of sea level rise (ibid) and they expect a global mitigation process and international assistance for adaptation.

There is wide range of 'known unknowns' of climate change outcome (UNDP 2008:36). The 'known unknowns' surrounding rising sea levels are a particularly striking example of threat facing the whole of humanity (ibid: 37). Uncertainties regarding future climate change impacts at the national and local levels and lack of relevant information necessary for adaptation planning are major obstacles to the development of effective adaptation actions (IGES 2010:45).

INSTITUTIONAL CAPACITY-BUILDING

Governments across the region need to institute legislation and polices to encourage the greening of businesses. Developing countries in general and Asia-Pacific region in particular, have low level of energy efficiency (EE) and limited capacity for resources and development of new green technologies (UNDP, 2008:12). Low levels of energy efficiency in developing countries are currently a threat to climate change mitigation efforts (ibid). There is a need for transforming this threat to opportunities.

Countries in Asia and the Pacific have introduced policies that indirectly affect GHG mitigation and adaptation (IGES, 2010:22). Countries have also created new institutions to address climate change for example, the Bureau of Energy Efficiency in India, a National Climate Change Committee in Cambodia, India, and Malaysia, a climate Change Steering Committee in Laos, Greenhouse Gas Management Organization in Thailand, Presidential Task Force on Climate Change in Philippines, and a national Climate Change Programme in China (IGES, 2010:23). Several countries in the region have developed their energy policies and plans to promote green development measures for instance India, Malaysia have set their renewable energy targets, Indonesia and South Korea have developed Climate Change National Action Plans (ibid). Malaysia has instituted tax incentives for energy efficiency and initiatives for mainstreaming energy efficiency in its development Plans (ibid).

CONCLUSIONS

Today, it is a climate–stressed world. Climate Change greatly undermines development, and environmental sustainability. Climate change is a development and environmental management challenge. The reduction of GHGs emissions as mitigation strategy of global warming and climate change remain expensive in the developing countries and jeopardize their economic growth and development. 'Green development', a 'low-carbon' development has emerged as an alternative development paradigm, a mitigation strategy to climate change and an approach to achieve sustainable development. The 'majority' world need 'green' development, not CO2 emission cuts to fight climate change. Development of renewable energy sources (solar, wind and bio-fuels) and green energy technologies are the pathways in achieving sustainable 'green development. 'Green economy' and 'green growth' all aim at a low -carbon development that will increase energy efficiency (EE) and in turn, an eco-efficiency of economic growth. The 'grow now and clean up later' is unsustainable growth model, there is rather a need for 'clean up and grow' approach to achieve sustainability. Green investments in clean technologies and 'natural' capital can enhance green jobs and achieve green growth. Along with the 'green technological' revolution, a kind of 'green industrial revolution' is taking shape in the world today.

The Asia and the Pacific countries are vigorously pursuing green growth and green development strategies. The Republic of Korea is the leading country in the world today with much of its emphasis on green investments for achieving green economy and green growth. China, India, Philippines and Thailand are following the green path as well. In order to achieve sustainable development the green policies need to integrate ecological principles into development. There is a need for integration of sustainable production and consumption into national development plans and policies. A holistic and multi-disciplinary approach is required to understand and integrate energy production and consumption, environment and climate change. Above all, there is a need for strengthening regional and international co-operations in promoting 'green growth' and 'green development' strategies for achieving green and sustainable society.

REFERENCES

Adams, W. M. (1995a), 'Green Development: Environment and Sustainability in the Third World', London: *Routledge.*

Adams, W. M. (1995b), 'Green Development Theory: Environmentalism and Sustainable Development', in Crush, J. Eds. Power of Development. London: Routledge, pp.87-99.

Government of India (2010), '*Annual Report 2009-10,* New Delhi': Ministry of New and Renewable Energy.

Green Growth (2005a), Green Growth Paths, Accessed from www.greengrowth.org/ggtracks.asp on 15 March 2011.

Green Growth (2005b), Seoul Initiative Network on Green Growth, Accessed from www.greengrowth.org/seouls.asp on 15 April 2011.

Green Growth (2010), National Ministerial Roundtable on Green Growth Roadmap Summary Report, Accessed from http://www.greengrowth.org/download/2010/Final-Summary_Report_of_National_Ministerial_Roundtable_on_Green_Growth_Roadmap.pdf on 15 April 2011.

Institute for Global Environment Strategies (IGES) (2008), 'Climate Change Policies in the Asia-Pacific': *Re-Uniting Climate Change and Sustainable Development, Kanagawa, Japan: IGES White Paper.*

OECD (2009), Declaration on Green Growth Accessed from http://www.oecd.org/dataoecd/58/34/44077822.pdf on 10 April 2011.

Rees, W. E. and M. Wackernagel, (1994), 'Ecological Footprints and Appropriated Carrying Capacity: Measuring the Natural Capital Requirements of the Human Economy', in Jansson, A. et al, Eds. Investing in Natural Capital: *The Ecological Economics Approach to Sustainability,* Washington DC: *Island Press.*

REN21 (2010), Renewables (2010),: 'Global Status Report, Paris'*: Renewable Energy Policy Network for the 21st Century (*REN21).

UNDP (2008), Human Development Report 2007/2008: Fighting Climate Change: Human Solidarity in a Divided World, New York: United Nations Development Programme.

UNDP (2010), Human Development Report (2010), 'The Real Wealth of Nations: Pathways to Human Development', New York: United Nations Development Programme.

UNEP (2005a), Sustainable Development Pathways, Accessed from www.rrcap.unep.org /nsds/pub/SUSTAINABLE DEVELOPMENT PATHWAYS.pdf . on 5th April 2011.

UNEP (2005b), Green Growth in China, the Republic of Korea and the Philippines, Accessed from http://ekh.unep.org/files/GREENGROWT-FV.pdf. on 5th April 2011.

UNEP (2008a), 'Global Green New Deal' - Environmentally-Focused Investment Historic Opportunity for 21st Century Prosperity and Job Generation. Accessed from www.unep.org/Documents.Multilingual/Default.asp?DocumentID=548&ArticleID=5957 &l=en on 2April 2011.

UNEP (2008b), 'Green Growth, Accessed from http://www.greengrowth.org/ on 18 April, 2011.

UNEP (2008c), 'Towards a Green Economy Flyer' Accessed from http://www.unep.org/pdf/TowardsGreenEconomy-Flyer.pdf on 4 April 2011.

UNEP (2009), 'Global Green New Deal': An Update for the G20 Pittsburgh Summit, UNEP, Accessed from www.unep.ch/etb/publications/Green Economy/G20policybriefFinal.pdf. on 10 April 2011.

UNEP (2011), 'Towards a Green economy: Pathways to Sustainable Development and Poverty Eradication': *A Synthesis for Policy Makers,* France: UNEP.

UNESCAP (2008), 'Greening Growth in Asia and the Pacific', Bangkok: UNESCAP.

UNESCAP (2009), 'Climate Change Challenge: Re orienting development towards greener and sustainable growth' Chapter 3, in *Economic and Social Survey of Asia and the Pacific: Addressing Triple Threat to Development,* New York: UNESCAP, pp.71-90.

UNESCAP (2010), Green Growth Initiatives in and Beyond the Region, Accessed from http://www.greengrowth.org/gg-initiative.asp on April 3, 2011.

UNESCAP, ADB and UNDP (2010), Achieving the Millennium Development Goals in an Era of Global Uncertainty: Asia- Pacific Regional Report 2009/10, Bangkok: UNESCAP, ADB and UNDP.

UNIDO (2009), Manila Declaration on Green Industry in Asia, Accessed from http://www.unido.org/fileadmin/user_media/Services/Green_Industry/Manila_declaration .pdf on 10 April 2011.

United Nations (2009), Sustainable Development in Small Island states, Department and Economic and Social Affairs. Accessed from http://www.un.org/en/development/desa/climate-change/index.shtml

Wikipedia (2011a), 'Renewable Energy' Accessed from http://en.wikipedia.org/wiki/Green_economy. Viewed on 5 April 2011, Wikipedia (2011b), 'World Energy Consumption' Accessed from http://en.wikipedia.org/wiki/World_energy_consumption, Viewed on 10 April 2011.

Wikipedia (2011c), 'Zero-carbon City', Accessed fromhttp://en.wikipedia.org/wiki/Zero-carbon_city on 19 March 2011.

World Economic Forum (2009), 'India Economic Summit Report: India's Next Generation of Growth', Accessed from https://members.weforum.org/pdf/India/India09_report.pdf on 12 April 2011.

WWF (2003), 'Climate Change in the Pacific', Suva, Fiji: WWF South Pacific Programme.

In: Development Management in the Twenty-First Century ISBN: 978-1-62100-699-2
Editors: Kartik Roy and Sandip Kar

Chapter 14

THE IMPACT OF CLIMATE CHANGE ON POVERTY REDUCTION: UGANDA'S EXPERIENCE

Jamil Serwanga *

Lecturer of Economics, Department of Economics and Development Studies, Faculty of Arts and Social Sciences, Islamic University in Uganda, Mbale, Uganda

INTRODUCTION

The paper looks at the impact of climate change on poverty reduction, drawing practical experiences from Uganda. Generally the paper aims at analyzing the effect of climate change on poverty reduction in Uganda analyzing how the negative and positive impacts of climate change on poverty reduction have been managed through the various policy options and orientations by the concerned government organs such as the ministries of Environment and Natural resources and Agriculture Animal and Fisheries among others. Individual efforts to adapt to climate change by the poor sections of the population, is also considered in this paper.

Uganda located in the East African region, along the equator is expected to enjoy a good climate, suitable for various agricultural practices that form the core sources of income for both the country and the nationals especially the rural dwellers – whose major source of income is agriculturally based activities that include farming and animal keeping. This position was experienced especially during the 1960s. However the current scenario is totally different given the erratic climatic variations. Such a climatic condition has made most Ugandans mainly the peasant farmers to face high levels of poverty. This is because of the fact that due to the global climatic changes the country's seasons are changing into erratic seasons that have made the agricultural activities to be more costly and unprofitable for the peasant farmers. Under this condition the peasant farmers are unable to afford the cost of transformation and modernization of their agricultural activities and processes in order to withstand the erratic climate changes and reduce on the high poverty levels caused by climate change at international, regional, national and local levels.

* sjjamil@yahoo.com.

The agricultural sector in Uganda presents a key factor in the general improvement of economic performance, increased incomes and rising living standards of rural household as well as in ensuring food security and poverty reduction. The importance of the agricultural sector is captured in one of the key national development goals that is "To ensure food security for all Ugandans and to increase household incomes through increased exports of high value agricultural products" (Uganda National Water Development Report 2005:2) The full attainment of this goal has been however hampered by the erratic weather conditions experienced in most parts of the country thence exacerbating the poverty incidences in the country and more so in the rural areas among the peasant farmers and pastoralists .

It must be noted that agriculture is one of those sectors which are most sensitive to climate change. Therefore climate change is expected to have profound impacts on the agricultural activities and other water resource based activities (Donaghy, Eheart, Herrick and Orland, 2006:79). Efforts must be put forward in order to improve the performance of the agriculture sector in relation to the climate change, in order to reduce the number of people living below the poverty line.

In Table 14.1 the share of the agricultural sector in Uganda's GDP is presented. It is clear that agriculture's share in GDP is still high putting the sector in a critical position in the fight against poverty in the country.

Table 14.1. Sector Share in Total GDP at Current Price (%)

Sector	2003/04	2004/5	2005/06	2006/07	2007/08	2008/09
Agriculture	23.8	25.1	24.1	22.3	21.2	23.7
Industry	22.9	23.5	22.8	51.1	25.6	24.2
Services	47.4	45.4	47.2	47.0	47.3	46.4

Source: Uganda Government (2010), NDP 2010/11-2014/15.

Considering economic forecast, Uganda's GDP growth rate over the National Development Plan (NDP) period is projected at an average of 7.2 per cent per annum. With this growth rate the nominal per capita income is projected to increase from United States Dollars (USD) 506 in 2008/09 to about USD 850 by 2014/15. It is also expected that during the same period the proportion of people living below the poverty line will decline to a level from 31% in 2005/06 to about 24.5% in 2014/15 above the Millennium Development Goal target of 28% (Government of Uganda 2010: ii) This is premised on an improved agricultural sector performance – since it is the biggest employer of people in the rural areas (in most less developed countries – Uganda inclusive).

Table 14.2. Uganda GDP Growth Rate 1997/98-2007/08

Financial Year	GDP Growth Rate
1997/98-2000/01	7.2
2001/02-2003/04	6.8
2004/05-2007/08	8.0

Source: Uganda Government (2010), NDP 2010/11-2014/15.

The GDP growth rate (Table 14.2) made the percentage of population living below the poverty line decline from 56 percent in 1993/93 to 44 percent in 1997/98 and to 31 percent in 2005/06, the percentage is projected to go down to a level of 24.5% by 2014/15 (Government of Uganda, 2010:ii). However, the 31 percentage of the population below the poverty line is still high. This is against an absolute number of 8.4 million Ugandans living below the poverty line and 7 million trapped in chronic poverty – mainly widows orphans, unemployed, youths, elderly the plantation workers and people with disabilities (Uganda Government 2010:276).

Documentary reviews and analyses have been made in order to ascertain the impact of climate change on poverty reduction and what the government of Uganda is doing at policy formulation and implementation level, to minimize the negative effect of climate change. Individual farmer's adaptation strategies to climate change have also been presented and discussed in this paper.

Elements of Climate Change and Adaptation in Uganda

Climate change is understood as, permanent changes in the mean climatic conditions of the global environment with such changes invariably causing serious impacts on ecosystem, natural resources and socio-economic development of people (IPCC 1998) as quoted by Agwata (2006:216). In consideration of climatic records recurrences of above-normal and below-normal conditions leading to episodes of drought, floods and severe storms, cold or hot spells and other extreme events also form integral components of climate of a given place (Agwata 2006:216). Climate change is considered to pose a number of serious threats on the social and economic development of various communities and countries of the world (Agwata 2006:216).

However the magnitude of the impact of climate change on the socio-economic development of communities and countries vary from community to community and from country to country depending on the level of development of such communities and countries in terms of climate adaptation mechanism. It is argued that more developed countries will suffer differently form less developed countries the consequences of climate change.

Adaptation has been most of the time understood as the antidote to mitigation. In this case mitigation places much emphasis on human capabilities to revert human-induced environmental trends. And on the other hand adaptation implies adjusting to climate change in order to reduce vulnerabilities of society and ecosystems (Ruth, Donaghy and Kirshen 2006:15).

Uganda's Variable Climate

Climate change, which is a term used to describe a gradual shift in one or more climatic elements from a long-term norm, manifests in Uganda in the form of global warming and climate variability. According to (Uganda National Water Development Report 2005:2) climate in Uganda, with particular reference to rainfall, has been erratic since early 1990s. The incidence, duration and amount of rainfall have all exhibited abnormal departures from long-term means. While rainfall in some years was far short of long-term means thereby causing droughts, in other years it was excessive and produced catastrophic floods. The heaviest rains in recent years were recorded in 1994 and were associated with the El Niño phenomenon. The rains led to sharp rises in lake levels, widespread flooding, washing away of roads and bridges, extensive soil erosion and landslides. For instance in Lake Kyoga, rising water levels caused detachment of previously firmly anchored floating papyrus swamps. The freed swamps drifted downstream and collected at the outlet of the Nile from the lake, causing a near total blockage there. The blockage cause a further rise in lake levels and led to partial inundation of marginal homesteads and farmlands, the spread of water-borne diseases and disruption of economic activities around the lakeshores. As water levels above the blockage continued to rise, levels (in the Nile) below the blockage dropped significantly. The blockage was cleared in 2001 through dredging with equipment provided by Egypt, a Nile riparian. The government in 2000 set up a programme "The Mitigation of Lake Kyoga Floods" aimed at alleviating the economic hardships brought upon the local communities in Kyoga basin by the floods and lake level rise. The recent Soroti floods of 2007 and Bududa landslides of 2010 provide a clear manifestation of the impact of climate change on the general socio-economic conditions of the vulnerable people in Uganda.

Further evidence from the (Uganda National Water Development Report – 2005) reveal that in additional to the variability in rainfall amounts has been the confusing shifts in season since the early 1990s, with heavy rains falling in the months expected to be dry and persistent desiccating sunshine experienced in the months that are normally wet and cold. Since Uganda's agriculture is heavily dependent on rainfall, the erratic variation in season have caused an increase in frequency of food and water shortages in the country, with the worst hit area being the dry cattle corridor that stretches from the Uganda-Tanzania border to Karamoja region. Death of livestock from lack of water in the corridor has been common and has forced traditional pastoralists to migrate with their herds during hard times to neighboring districts or game reserves causing more problems to the neighboring communities. In Karamoja and Teso regions, for example several deaths from starvation have been recorded in recent years. This means therefore that Pastoralism is a highly sensitive agricultural activity to climate change, implying that where there is no rain , there will be no pasture, and hence death of animals a variable asset to the pastoralist such as the Karamajong in the north eastern part of Uganda. This climatic variability has caused more poverty in the affected areas.

It is further reported that Uganda as a country experiences two annual rainfall maximas between March to May and September to November. In the drier parts of the country – (Karamoja region), rainfall between the two maximas is not strikingly different thereby producing a unimodal type of distribution. These parts of the country are characterized by one long dry season followed by one long wet season. In the rest of the country, rainfall has a bi-modal (twin-peaked) pattern with a pronounced dry season between the two rainfall maximas.

Climate change as linked to climate variability would be considered to imply a change in climate that persists for decades or longer, arising from human activity that alters the composition of the atmosphere (i.e., greenhouse gas emissions). Climate change also means natural variations in the climate that are not caused by greenhouse gas emissions (e.g., it rains more in some years and less in others) Pettengell (2010:10). Climate variability is becoming a major issue of concerned in the field of development economics mainly with regard to rural development and particularly with the rural poor (Oxfam, 2010:7). Climate change in different parts of the world has been linked to the global warming phenomenon.

For governments in developing countries Uganda included struggling with multiple problems, climate change comes as an added and largely poorly understood complication. Climate change is often viewed as an environmental issue that is peripheral and sometimes in competition with the goals of development. Despite the crippling economic and social implications of climate change, many countries continue to be represented by environment or meteorological departments at international negotiations, which hold limited power at the national level. In many countries, development and finance ministries are still not entirely engaged, or even convinced that they need to be engaged. Yet development budgets are being overstretched by numerous national crises in which climate change is playing a role Pettengell (2010:12).

In connection to the above argument the ideal climate for agricultural development and poverty reduction in reference to Uganda from a general point of view, as according to Todaro and Smith (2003:92-93), is that,

> "Almost all developing countries are situated in tropical or subtropical climate zones. It has been observed that the most economically most successful countries are located in the temperate zones. The dichotomy cannot simply be attributed to coincidence; it must bear some relation to special difficulties caused directly by differing climatic conditions. It is undeniable that the extremes of heat and humidity in most poor countries contribute to deteriorating soil quality and the rapid depreciation of many natural goods. They also contribute to the low productivity of certain crops, the weakened regenerative growth of forests, and the poor health of animals. Finally, and perhaps most important, extremes of heat and humidity not only cause discontent to workers but can also weaken their health, reduce their desire to engage in strenuous physical work, and generally lower their levels of productivity and efficiency."

Given the above experiences by Todaro and Smith (2003), Uganda also included among the developing countries located in the tropical climate zones experiences the identified negative consequences of climate change putting forward difficulties to the reduction of poverty in the country. With continued climate variability families and communities find it harder to predict the ever-changing inconsistent weather and as a result families end up selling their property and thence became more vulnerable to risks emanating from climate variability (Oxfam 2009:11).

VULNERABILITY TO CLIMATE CHANGE

Vulnerability to climate change is something that occurs differently to different people living in different environmental conditions and confronting different social, economic, political and institutional challenges (Oxfam 2010:7). Likewise the vulnerable categories of people in different regions and communities are struggling with how to understand the aspect of climate variability and obtain or identify new patterns and establish what responses they need to able to be move beyond reacting and coping to adapting to new realities and being resilient (Oxfam 2010:8)

A dilemma therefore already exists in the sense that people who are already poor and marginalized are already overburdened in addition to climate change and if no serious action is taken poverty will only increase to higher levels instead of being reduced, forcing the already poor people to be more vulnerable to climate change in all dimensions of human life. This is premised on the fact that, intensified climate change culminates into water shortage, food insecurity and it is also observed that with climate variability the workload of women and girls will increase tremendously as there will be fewer options to find alternative ways of survival hence increasing poverty incidences in the area.

PERCEPTIONS AND TRENDS OF POVERTY IN UGANDA

Poverty reduction is one of the Millennium Development Goals (MDGs). And at the international level the World Bank is committed to reduce the incidence of poverty through out the world. This is based on the background that in 2002, about half of the world's population subsisted on less than $2 a day. About 44 percent of the all household in Africa, and 33 percent of people in South Asia lived below the $1-a-day poverty line – World Bank (2006) as quoted by World Bank (2008:2).

Uganda is one of the poorest countries of the world where more than 80% of the population live in rural areas and depend on agriculture for their livelihood. Uganda's agricultural sector is characterized by the following features; it is mainly rain fed, and activities done using basic simple technologies, mechanization is too minimal and the land is highly fragmented. These features plus more have made the participants in the agricultural sector mainly the farmers and pastoralists to be more vulnerable to climate variability. The wide spread poverty in Uganda, mainly in the rural area is mainly explained by the low productivity in the agricultural sector and the productivity is worsened by recurring drought as agriculture in Uganda is basically rain – fed (World Bank 2008:2).

Generally, poverty has been understood from two major dimensions, that is absolute poverty and relative poverty. Under absolute poverty an individual or household is found to be incapable of accessing the basic needs of life throughout the 12 months of the year. And the basic needs of life considered in this case include food, safe water, shelter medical facilities and education. Regarding relative poverty an individual or household will be poor relative to others (Serwanga 2006:18). Poverty is a multidimensional phenomenon. "Thus effective strategies to manage it should be premised on conceptualizing it not only as lack of income or shortfall in the expenditure required to achieve a certain minimally acceptable living standards but also as lack of capabilities that individuals require in order to live meaningful and valued lives in societies" (Kessy and Aiko 2008:11). Persistent poverty with all its manifestations such as discounting the future, low investment rates and degradation of the environment – natural resources is considered to cause growing environmental problems and consequently a growing need to the examination of potential interventions from all the stakeholders mainly the governments and the civil societies.

PERCEIVED CAUSES OF POVERTY IN UGANDA

From a general perspective, Serwanga (2006:18) points out the causes of poverty from a theoretical point of view where some people are of the view that poverty is God given, other explain the causes of poverty from the culture of poverty thesis – that is some people are poor because of their ways and values of life. Additionally, it is pointed out that poverty to some individuals and households is explained by the Neo-classical Marginal Distribution Theory. Under the theory of the Neo-classical Marginal Distribution it is observed that access to the factors of production will determine someone's capability to access the benefits from the available factors of production. Any individual or household without access will be rendered poor. According to the structuralist theory some people are poor because of the prevailing social stratification which determines the distribution of material, and economic and political power in the society.

Additionally the causes of poverty especially in low developed countries like Uganda include low agricultural productivity because of extended drought, inadequate access to input, low levels of technology used in the agricultural activities, limited access to credit, poor infrastructural development more so the road network which inhibit easy access to the market by the peasant farmers (Serwanga 2006:22; Kessy and Aiko 2008:11).

According to Okori, Emuria and Ojuman (2002:12-14), the main causes of poverty in the context of Uganda are perceived to be the political and social upheavals such as insecurity, insurgency and cattle rustling that affected some regions mainly between 1985 and 1993. HIV/AIDS pandemic has also been singled out as another cause of poverty in Uganda. In the rural areas of Uganda communities look at the causes of poverty in terms of poor crop yields, physical impoverishment due to old age, lack of farming implements, non-ownership of livestock, limited access to produce markets and social services. While in the urban areas, the major cause of poverty is unemployment and low payment against increasing cost of living against big family sizes in terms of dependants.

LINKAGE BETWEEN CLIMATE CHANGE AND POVERTY

Climate change definitely has influence on the incidences of poverty in a given community. For example it observed that poor people are generally the most vulnerable to climate change. This is due to the fact that poor people live in areas which are prone to climatic hazards such as drought, floods and cyclones and they have little capacity to adapt to the shocks emanating from climate change related hazards. Additionally the poor are more vulnerable to climate change because they live and depend on the ecosystem services and products for their survival. The survival is in terms of subsistence farming and fishing, fuel and construction materials (Agwata 2006:218). This implies that change in climate will automatically affect the welfare of the poor people and more likely the effect would be negative and in form of reduced food supplies and income caused by loss of opportunities because of climate change.

Given the linkage between poverty and environment (climate change) the World Bank in 2006 provided $81.4 billion (in form of loans and grants) as aid to poor countries to improve the environment – leading to predictable climate changes, this was expected to assist in poverty reduction. The funding was based on the fact that proper environment management will greatly contribute to poverty reduction in many countries. And from research findings it is indicated that poor countries are much more dependent on natural resources as assets than the rich countries. In the same manner, the ratio of people to forested land is more than 3 times higher in low-income than in high income countries. Likewise, changes in environmental management can have two major impacts on the household welfare in both short and medium terms. In the first place better environmental management can change the return to assets and consequently improve on the ability of the households to move out of poverty (World Bank 2008:2).

Further theoretical explanation of the linkage between climate change and poverty indicate that climate change can increase the variability of returns from the agricultural based economic activities. For example, greater variation in the rainfall patterns is likely to increase the variability of crop yield. New disease vectors are also likely to emerge from climate change making the households more vulnerable to exogenous shocks, such as floods, storms and drought among others that can wipe out household assets and thence contribute to loss of life and property (World Bank 2008:6). These occurrences obviously would lead to more poverty incidences in the area under consideration

Negative impacts of climate change related to hazards include, malnutrition and famine, dependence on food aid and imports that reduces economic growth of the countries affected. Other impacts include loss of infrastructure and disruption of economic activities, disease outbreak and displacement of population. The ecological impact of climate change include, land degradation, desertification, loss of natural habitats, and change in the biodiversity, increased soil erosion and silting of rivers, dams and coastal ecosystem (Agwata 2006:217).

Uganda's Experience with Impact of Climate Change and Poverty Reduction

A number of people are expected to fall below the poverty line as a result of problems associated with climate change, disasters and illness (Uganda Government, 2010:276).

The question at this level is - what is being done by the different stakeholders mainly the government and the individuals to appropriately manage the impact of climate change on poverty reduction among the vulnerable people in the country? It is clear that policy makers in developing countries like Uganda are facing challenges of how to define, refine and redefine policies and strategies to deal with poverty under conditions of climate change.

Major climate change related disasters faced in Uganda between 1997 and 2010 include the following as according to the Uganda Government (2010:276) during the following episodes;

(i) During the following years (1998, 1999, 2002, and 2005), about 625,000a people were affected by drought and famine
(ii) It is also reported that 700,000 people were affected by the floods of (1997, 2007)
(iii) The Bududa land slides of 2010 - the most recent case of land slide in the country are reported have affected more than 2,053 people.

It is generally reported that drought, floods, landslides, windstorms and hailstorm contribute to 70% of natural disasters in Uganda annually and destroy an average of 800,000 hectares of crops and cause economic losses equivalent to 120 billions Uganda shillings a thing which exacerbated poverty levels especially in the rural areas (Uganda Government2010:295). It is against this scenario that a full ministry of Disaster Preparedness is in operational to manage the negative effects of climate change.

Meteorological parameters are important ingredients in the management of climate change and weather variability. However it is found out that in Uganda the quality of meteorological information is below the expected standard (Uganda Government 2010:301). For example, out of the 9 meteorological stations needed for quality meteorological parameters only 6 are in place. Further more it is reported that Upper Air, Radar and Pilot Balloon are missing. This means that inappropriate adaptation strategies for climate change are designed and hence putting less impact on poverty reduction emanating from the negative climate changes across the country.

Observation stations are also not to the required number as per given type within the defined specific zones. In Table 14.3 a summary of the types of zones and the expected observation stations and the available observation stations is presented. What is revealed is that there is no zone with the required observation Stations.

Table 14.3. Types of Zones and the expected and available Observation Stations in Uganda

SN	Type of Zones	Expected Observation Stations	Observation Stations Available	Percentage of Available Observation Stations
1	Agro-Meteorological Zones	20	4	20.0
2	Climatological Zones	110	18	16.4
3	Hydrometeorological Zones	20	2	1.0
4	Synoptic Zones	16	12	75.0
5	Isohytic Zones	600	65	10.8
6	Satellite Zones	4	1	25.0

Source: Uganda Government (2010) NDP -2010/11-2014/15.

Connected to the above, Pamela Komujuni from the Department of Disaster Management, Relief and Refugees in Uganda is quoted to have said that: 'We used to plan on needing to deliver food relief two years out of every five, now it's every year. We also need early warning so that we can advise farmers when and what to plant. This will have an effect on our budget.' Pettengell (2010:12).

What Is Being Done to Minimize the Negative Impact of Climate Change on Poverty Reduction in Uganda

Generally studies on impacts of climate change on poverty reduction have different assumptions which include; changes in cultivars, planting and harvest dates, crop mix, use of irrigation (Kaiser 1999), as quoted by Antel, Capalbo and Paustian (2006:129) It is pointed out that climate change may have many positive and negative, direct and indirect impacts on environment, economic and social systems and those impacts vary across space, time and various segments of an economy and society. To date climate change debates have concentrated on direct negative impacts of climate change on current generation (Ruth, Donaghy and Kirshen 2006:13).

Climate change adaptation must therefore reduce vulnerability both by reducing exposure to climate risk and through addressing existing and emerging inequalities of power and assets that would otherwise make adaptation impossible. Successful adaptation to climate change means people becoming increasingly able to make informed decisions about their lives and livelihoods in a changing climate (Pettengell, 2010:10, Ruth, Donaghy and Kirshen, 2006:13). It is also pointed out that the distribution of the economic impacts of climate change across regions with more and less favorable resource endowments is likely to depend on the ability of the farmers in those regions to adapt to climate change (Antle, Capalbo and Paustian 2006:156). Due to the differential effects developing countries like Uganda are to surfer more from the economic impacts of climate change, as well as being the least able to adapt to new climatic conditions (McGuigan, Rynolds, and Wiedmer 2002:3; Siwar, Alam, Murad and Al-Amin 2009:318)

It is observed from the five year, National Development Plan of Uganda for the period 2010/11-2014/15 that the Government of Uganda has put up key interventions to deal with and minimize the negative effects of climate change on the socio-economic welfare of the masses. The interventions generally include;

(i) Provision of emergency shelter
(ii) Relief food and water supply delivery
(iii) Emergency medical care
(iv) Farm inputs

More adaptive measures have in addition been proposed and implemented as it is indicated in the National Development Plan 2010/11-2014/15 with a major component being increasing accessibility to water for production. This is expected to lead to an increase in the acreage under irrigation from the current level of 14418ha to 22,000ha. Additionally the government of Uganda through the (NDP of 2010/11-2014/15), is expected to increase the supply of water for livestock watering in the cattle corridor from the current 36% to 50% and those out side the corridor from 21% to 30%. The increase is also considered as one of the major components in the development of the rural industries. This is aimed at enhancing the development of agro-processing industries in the rural areas. This is a major strategy to deal with climate change involving the diversification of activities in those areas most heat by the climate variability in form of drought. The above strategies are expected to lead to an increment in the agricultural (crop and animal) productivity. The challenge that is likely to inhibit the success of the strategies would be the poor management of the funds allocated to such activities Uganda Government 2010:295). A number of strategies have been suggested and developed to manage the effects of climate change on poverty reduction in Uganda, (Okori Anthony, Margaret Emuria and Paul Ojuman, 2002:9-10). These strategies include district water committees.

Conclusions and Recommendations

From the above presentation a number of conclusions and recommendations can be deduced and these recommendations can be used for further empirical tests for the effectiveness and feasibility of the different climate change adaptation strategies to deal with the impact of climate change on poverty reduction in Uganda.

In line with the ideas reviewed and presented in this paper, Oxfam (2010:41-42) when analyzing climate change in Ethiopia, recommended that the international community and governments of developing countries could put into action the following activities in their management of the impacts of climate changes on the socio- economic conditions of the vulnerable people. The recommendations are at both national and community levels.

In the first place the government of Uganda should strengthen and increase investment in climate research and disseminate information to increase awareness of climate change and its impacts especially among the farmers and pastoralists. Strengthen cooperation among policymakers, nongovernmental organizations, research institutions, and the media. In this case universities should play a major role (Serwanga 2006: 30)

Increase meteorological station density and make climate information available in an accessible format to farmers and pastoralists through methods such as radio broadcasts and mobile phones. The Uganda National Development Plan 2010/14-2014/15 provides for this and what is needed is the commitment of the various stakeholders especially the Uganda Meteorological Department and the National Research Institutions such as National Agricultural Research Organization (NARO). The findings from these institutions are expected to lead to new crop varieties and livestock species that are more tolerant to drought.

Strengthen the capacity of policymakers and institutions to effectively use climate information for development planning and to make informed decisions that consider climate risk, change, and variability. Ensure civil society and community participation, especially women's groups, both in formulating climate change policies and in integrating climate change into development priorities. Ensure priorities and investments address the gendered impact of climate change.

Building on the National Adaptation Campaign to, prepare and implement the national framework for guiding climate change adaptation and mitigation. This framework should also be integrated with the National Development Plan. The current PASDEP for 2005/06 – 2009/10 mentions climate change in passing only twice. Since climate change negatively impacts poor people the most, the next strategic framework for 2011 – 2016 should invest in economic activities to make them more resilient to greater climate variability and change.

Recognize pastoralism as a viable mode of production and way of life. Develop a land use policy in harmony with traditional land use systems.

Provide seasonal precipitation forecasts as part of a revitalized extension package that includes access to basic agricultural technologies, such as plows, new crop varieties, and fertilizers, as well as access to information, improved market linkages, and credit and insurance schemes.

Support agro-ecological practices for adaptation and mitigation.

Diversify rural livelihoods through the promotion of non-agricultural sectors to reduce pressure on land and avoid further fragmentation of agricultural lands.

Address environmental degradation by drawing on community-based experiences and mechanisms.

Invest in social protection mechanisms to give vulnerable communities quick support in times of crisis. Connect these protection mechanisms to longer-term development actions.

At the Community Level investment in livelihood opportunities and risk management strategies for poor farmers and pastoralists and other vulnerable people is necessary in the management of the impact of climate changed in regard to poverty reduction.

Prepare long-term adaptation plans based on the sharing of best practices through community participation, civil society engagement, and the participation of academic and research institutions, with regular monitoring to identify promising practices for scaling up.

Build on what farmers and pastoralists are already doing to adapt to climate variability and change. Investigate these practices further for their sustainability and impact on poverty and inequality, and potential for replication or enhancement.

Invest in new forestation programs, reforestation, and sustainable management of the remaining forests. Ensure that management systems guarantee a return to the communities that manage the resource — the only way to ensure genuinely sustainable use of forests and woodland. The Uganda National Forest Authority (NFA) and Uganda National Environment Management Authority are to spear head these activities.

The use of agro-forestry systems as an economically feasible adaptive strategy to protect crop plants from extremes in microclimate and soil moisture should be promoted. The Uganda National Agricultural Research Organization (NARO) is expected to be at the center of this activity/strategy.

In case of pastoralist Communities for example the Karamajong in the North Eastern Part of Uganda improved livestock, market linkages, and livestock health services should be done. Improved access to feed and water for both livestock production and household consumption should also be an integral part in the strategy to deal with the impact of climate change on the poverty levels amongst the pastrolists. The Karamoja Development program is to be strengthened in this regard.

At international level it is argued that more developed countries have the responsibility to help developing countries like Uganda and others adapt to climate change. The more developed countries need to reduce their emissions and provide substantial financial support for adaptation (Oxfam 2010:41). In case of Uganda, socio-economic development where poverty eradication is still a big problem there more need of foreign assistance is needed to help its people adapt to climate change. Otherwise the new climate changes are expected to make more Ugandans to live below the poverty line.

REFERENCES

Agwata Jones F. (2006), 'Mainstreaming Climate Change: Issues in the Attainment of the Millennium Development Goals', in *The Role of African Universities in the Attainment of the Millennium Development Goals,* Nairobi, Kenyatta University.

Anderson Jock R. (2002), 'Environmental Issues and Farming in Developing Countries Rural Development Department', Washington, DC The World Bank.

Antle J, Capalbo S, and Paustian J (2006), 'Ecological and Economic Impacts of Climate Change in Agricultural Systems: An Integrated Assessment Approach', in Regional Climate Change and Variability, Impacts and Responses, Northampton MA, Edward Elgar, pp 128-160.

Donaghy K, Eheart W, Herrick E and Orland B, (2006), 'An Integrated Assessment of Impacts of Predicted Climate Change on the Mackinaw River Basin' in Regional Climate Change and Variability, Impacts and Responses, Northampton MA, Edward Elgar pp 79-127.

Elepu Gabriel (2008), 'Poverty and its Reduction in Uganda' in Out of Poverty: Comparative Poverty Reduction Strategies in Eastern and Southern Africa, Mkuki na Nyota Pulishers, Dar es Salaam, pp 33-55.

Kessy Flora and Aiko Rose (2008) 'The Evolution of Poverty Reduction Strategies in Tanzania' in Out of Poverty: Comparative Poverty Reduction Strategies in Eastern and Southern Africa, Mkuki na Nyota Pulishers, Dar es Salaam PP 10-32.

McGuigan Claire, Rynolds Rebecca and Wiedmer Daniel (2002), 'Poverty and Climate Change': Assessing Impacts in Devloping Countries and the Initiatives of International Community, London School of Economics Consultancy Project, The Overseas Development Institute.

Okori Anthony, Margaret Emuria and Paul Ojuman (2002), Uganda Participatory Poverty Assessment Process, Soroti District Report, Soroti District.

Oxfam (2008), 'Turning up the Heat: - Climate Change and Poverty in Uganda, Oxfam, Oxford

Oxfam' (2010), The Rain does not come on time Anymore, Poverty, Vulnerability and Climate Variability in Ethiopia Oxfam International.

Pettengell Catherine (2010), 'Climate Change Adaptation', Enabling People living in Poverty to Adapt, Oxfam GB April 2010.

Republic of Uganda (2004), 'Poverty Eradication Action Plan 2004/5-2007/8', Ministry of Finance, Planning and Economic Development, Kampala.

Republic of Uganda (2010), 'National Development Plan 2010/11-2014/15', Ministry of Finance, Planning and Economic Development, Kampala.

Ruth Matthias, Donaghy Kieran and Kirshen Paul (2006),(Editors), Regional Climate Change and Variability, Impacts and Responses, Northampton MA, Edward Elgar.

Serwanga Jamil (2006), 'The Role of Universities in the Existing Strategies for Eradicating Extreme Poverty and Hunger in Uganda' in The Role of African Universities in the Attainment of the Millennium Development Goals, Nairobi, Kenyatta University.

Siwar Chamhuri, Alam Md. Mahmudul, Murad Md. Wahid and Al-Amin Abdul Quasem (2009), 'A Review of the Linkages between Climate Change, Agricultural Sustainability and Poverty in Malaysia' in *International Review of Business Research Papers*, 5 (6) November 2009 Pp 309-321.

Todaro M.P and Smith S.C (2003), 'Economic Development' 8th Edition, Boston, *Addison Wesley Uganda National Water Development Report* – 2005.

World Bank (2008), 'Poverty and the Environment', Understanding Linkages at the Household Level, Washington DC, The World Bank.

In: Development Management in the Twenty-First Century
Editors: Kartik Roy and Sandip Kar
ISBN: 978-1-62100-699-2

Chapter 15

MANAGEMENT OF INDIA'S ANTI–POVERTY PROGRAMME: A REVIEW

Anita Medhekar[1] *and Kartik Roy*[2,*]
[1]Central Queensland University, Australia
[2]Research Professor, Auckland Institutue of Studies St Helens (AIS), Auckland, New Zealand

INTRODUCTION

Poverty alleviation or "Garivi Hotao" has been consistently used by all political parties in India as a policy item in development management and policy implementation agenda during election campaign. After the election is over, this item is thrown into back burner until political necessity requires political party leaders to bring it back into forefront election manufesto. Unfortunately however, there has neither been any attempt to define clearly the wider concept of poverty nor any attempt to correctly estimate the number of poor who according to the proper definition of poverty can be considered as poor. The measures undertaken by the government of India have aimed to alleviate economic poverty of poor families living '*Below the Poverty Line*' (BPL) income by such measures of targeted income distribution as providing BPL income families with essential food and fuel at subsidized prices as well as creating income earning employment opportunities for BPL households for a specified duration of time during a year. Such a policy is similar to "Dole for Work" policy or "Dry Dole" schemes which were implemented by the British Raj in India and continued by the Nehru Government up to the 1960s (Roy, Blomqvist & Clark 2012).

However, under targeted income distribution policy, it would require an enormous amount of Government expenditure and other state resources to transfer one percent of income from the richest percentile group of households to the poorest percentile group of households. Even then, this one percent increase in income of the poorest percentile group of households would not make a significant difference to their current standard of living. Moreover due to presence of endemic corruption in the governance machinery in charge of

* kartikr@ais.ac.nz, kcroy20@gmail.com.

administering the distribution of income actual transfer would significantly be less than one percent. It is precisely for this reason that economists have advocated growth promotion policies for management of development projects which, if properly implemented, will generate employment for BPL families. China which also implemented through local communes some schemes of targated distribution of goods and services for poor families was able to bring several hundred million people out of poverty primarily by achieving consistently over more than two decades, high rate of economic growth (exceeding 10 percent per annum) which created hundreds of millions of jobs for China's unemployed labour force (Roy, Blomqvist & Clark 2012). Today the share of BPL population in China's total population is almost Zero. Unfortunately, however successive governments in India have never implemented such high growth oriented economic policies. For the current "Dole for work" scheme, which we have dwelt on in this paper to achieve results, it is necessary to have a correct estimate of number of households living below poverty line. But such an estimate is unlikely to be arrived at in Indian society where households tend to understate their annual income to field agents of the National Sample Survey Organisation (NSSO). Hence it is within these above noted constraints that we comment on the Mahatma Gandhi Poverty Alleviation Programme.

The world has recognised India's commitment to economic liberalisation and globalisation being pursued since 1991 economic crisis. Firstly, it was economic liberalisation and reforms, rather than controls that created a proper atmosphere for economic growth of India and secondly, India cannot afford to overlook and neglect the capacity and capability of its poor, to generate employment, reduce regional imbalance, alleviate poverty and improve the overall standard of living of the poor in the rural-regional, remote areas, hilly and mountainous regions, including the urban poor (CFPR 1983; Cassen & Joshi 1996; Lal 1999; IFAD 2001; MHDC 2000). It is important to have a diverse basket of industries supporting the employment opportunities in small and medium enterprises (SME), which is essential to harness economic benefits and multiplier effect flowing from employment generation, stimulating socio-economic development and poverty alleviation in an environmentally sustainable manner through the *National Rural Employment Guarantee Act* (NREGA) introduced on the 2nd of February, 2005, and has recently been renamed as *Mahatma Gandhi Rural Employment Guarantee Act* (MGNREGA) on 2nd October, 2009 (Wikipedia 2009).

MGNREGA is a uniquely democratic and transparent anti-poverty employment act, and revolutionary in its promise of inclusive growth, e-governance, right to work, dignity of labour and a rational participatory relationship of the worker with the state (Roy & Dey 2009; MGNEGRA 2009). Apart from providing livelihood to millions of households since 2006-2007, MGNREGA has become a significant vehicle for promoting good governance and for strengthening grassroots democratic processes and implementing mechanisms that strengthens transparency and accountability at every step of the delivery of program, and for the citizens to raise their voice regarding various problems such as regeneration of India's depleting natural resource base and directly engage with the state (MGNEGRA 2009; PC 2008, TIE 2006).

One of the overarching goals for the developing countries in the Millennium Development Goals (MDG's) is to end poverty by 2015, "international fight against underdevelopment, hunger and poverty" (DFRSA 2005; UNDP 2009). Alleviation of Poverty (both economic and institutional) by implementing anti-poverty programmes is a long term goal of Government of India (PC 2009; IFAD 2001). Poverty alleviation has made some progress in the form of trickle down effect of the growing middle class, increasing stress on education program, reservation of seats in government jobs for the underprivileged, economically weaker members of the society and empowerment of women are some of the various factors which will contribute to alleviating poverty (MHDC 2000; Roy & Blomqvist 2004). Government of India has accelerated its pace of anti-poverty programs and strategies since the implementation of National Rural Employment Guarantee Scheme (NREGS) implemented in 200 districts by 2006. Additional 130 districts were added during the year 2007-08 (Jaffer 2009; PC 2008; MGNREGA 2009) in recent years by mobilising greater Central Government budget resources, creating time frames for quantifiable, deliverables and linking with Millennium Development Goals global frameworks of action, which provides a benchmark approach for addressing many development and global issues (UNDP 2009). The seriousness and urgency of these anti-poverty programs, policy and resource commitments to poverty alleviation are in a single legislative Act of MGREGA, which strengthens livelihood security through time bound guaranteed wage employment which is the basic right of any human being. MGNREGA, with its 'Rights Based' framework, is a paradigm shift from all other past development programmes that were traditionally supply driven, but now the implementation of this law is supported by a Central Government budget based on demand for employment, and the way the citizens engage with the state in a democratic manner, the management of this poverty program is yet to be critically evaluated.

The first MDG's of 'Eradicating Extreme Poverty and Hunger' aims at reducing the proportion of people whose income is less than $1 between 1990 and 2015 by half (UNDP 2009; DFARSA 2005). India's 11th Five Year Plan (2007-2012), has reiterated the country's commitment to the MDG's, and has set socio-economic targets for inclusive growth and development to end poverty by 2015. These include, reducing the headcount ratio of consumption poverty by 10 percentage points, increase the real wage rate of unskilled workers by 20 percent, and creating 70 million new work opportunities for 300 million Indians who are living in extreme poverty. The poor people face absence of basic capabilities and necessities to function efficiently and effectively in the society with the lack of access to public infrastructure and employment opportunities. A majority of poor earn their livelihood through unskilled, casual manual labour and exploitation of the natural resource base. This dependence makes them more vulnerable to crises such as, climate change stress, natural disaster, ill-health (e.g. swine flu virus of 2009), all of which adversely impact on their employment opportunities and reduce their ability to move out of the vicious circle of poverty trap. Indian Planning Commission designed programs under MGNREGA, to directly attack poverty to provide self-employment among the poor, provide wage employment during the lean agricultural season, and address minimum needs such as nutrition, health, housing, education sanitation and mortality rate (Dantwala 1985; Hirway 1985; Ravallion 1991, Ravallion & Subbarow 1992; Tendulkar 1998; Allen & Thomas 1997). This chapter is structured as follows.

The first part gives an overview of poverty in India. Second part discusses critically the Five year plans, development and management of various anti-poverty programs and policies implemented by the Indian Government. Part three focuses on the development and management of Mahatma Gandhi National Rural Employment Guarantee Act (MGNREGA) and the National Rural Employment Guarantee Scheme (NREGS) under the acts. Part four, discusses the general overall benefits of (MGNREGA) with reference to states and finally some critical discussion and conclusions are provided.

POVERTY IN INDIA

Poverty can be defined as a social phenomenon in which a section of the population is unable to meet its basic necessities of life and is deprived of minimum standard of living giving rise to mass poverty in India and in many developing countries. Poverty can be defined in absolute or relative terms. Absolute poverty occurs when income and expenditure are below the poverty line, which means that it is not even possible for a person to purchase minimum quantities of food to survive. Whereas relative poverty, takes into account the income distribution of the population in different percentile groups and a comparison is made with the top 10 percent of population with the bottom 10 percent of population's standard of living. India has the world largest number of poor people in any country after China. In 1951, population census recorded 363.2 million people living in India (Dandekar 1998; Mehta 1997). Given the population of just over one billion in 2009, approximately 350 million are living below the poverty line, of which 75 % live in rural areas and more than 40 % of population is illiterate being the main cause of poverty (Agarwal 1996; Datt & Sundharam 1997; Ahluwalia & Little 1998). According to Kuznets hypothesis, inequality is likely to worsen in the early stages of development before it declines, as per capital income rises gradually to reach the levels of developed countries (Solow 1994; Todaro & Smith 2008). In the last decade from 1998-2008, economic prosperity in terms of GDP growth rate in India has been impressive but with growing inequality (ADB 2003; MGNREGA 2009; Roy and Blomqvist 2004; UNDP 2009). Thus economic growth has not eliminated or alleviated absolute poverty in developing countries (Fields 1991; Findlay & Wellisz 1994; Squire 1993; Allen & Thomas 1997).

Three causes of poverty have been given by Elesh (1973): (a) ideology of individualism (b) Culture or subculture of poverty which describes the way of life of poor people and (c) Social structure as cause of poverty accepted by the liberals and sociologists. Poverty is perceived in terms of poverty line, which explains what is actually needed for health, efficiency, social and work participation, nurturing of children and maintaining dignity self respect with dignity (Becker 1966). In India, poverty line is drawn one basis of a per capita daily intake of 2,400 calories for the rural and 2,100 calories for the urban areas. On the basis of this the monthly per capita consumption expenditure is calculated (Sagar 1990). The planning commission in 1997 March adopted the Lakdawala Committee 1993, methodology to measure incidence of poverty in India during the Ninth Five Year Plan (1996-2000) after a period of three years.

The Tenth Five-Year Plan (2002-2007), targeted 8% annual growth, in the employment-intensive sectors, so that there is equal distribution of income to sustains the pace of reducing poverty ratio by 5 percent and by 15 percent by the end of the Eleventh -plan in 2012(ADB 2003; NREGA 2009). In India 230 million were living in poverty during the eighth plan from 1991-1995. This constituted 27% of total population. In the same year the numbers of people in rural areas were estimated to be 168.6 million, which accounted for 28.2 percent of rural population, as compared to urban population of 42.2 million, which is 19.3 percent of the urban poor population living in poverty (Agarwal 1996; Tendulkar & Jain 1995).

Development and Management of Anti-Poverty Programmes under Five Year Plans

The Government of India has adopted a pro-poor multifaceted development strategy that promotes economic growth and also addresses the needs of the poor by ensuring their basic right to work. Indian Planning Commission was established by the Government of India in 1950 (PC 2008). The First Five Year Plan was implemented in April 1951-1956, to rectify the effects of Second World War and 1947 Partition of India and it aimed to solve problems within agriculture and irrigation sectors, investing 44.6% of the total planned budget. The aim of the Second-Plan (1956-61) was to achieve industrialisation by investing in basic and heavy industries, creating jobs and promoting greater equality in income and wealth to establish socialist pattern of society. The Third-Plan (1961-66) goal was to have self sustained growth in income, agriculture sector, basic industries, (steel, power and chemicals) employment creation, and decentralisation of economic power to the states and at local/regional level. The Fourth-Plan (1969-74) aimed at increasing Gross Domestic Product by 5.5%, reducing economic instability, inequality in income distribution and achieving social justice with equity. Prime Ministers cash program and employment guarantee program was also introduced in Maharashtra (1972-73) which was effective in preventing famine and dealing with short-run income variability (Ravallion 1991 & 1992).By the end of the Fifth-Plan (1974-79), it was realised that the benefits of growth did not trickle down to the poorest of poor due to wars and inflation, thus giving rise to unemployment.

The Fifth-Plan thus focussed on removal of poverty (Garibi Hatao), creating jobs, removing regional imbalance, minimum wage law was introduced, export promotion and attaining economic self-sufficiency (Ahluwalia 1978; Ahuja 1997). However, with the change in the Central Government, rolling yearly plans were introduced from 1978-80, without any significant improvement in socio-economic conditions, except increase in food production due to the success of Green Revolution. The Sixth-Plan (1980-85), was formulated taking into account the failure of the previous plans in removal of poverty besides promoting economic growth; reduce unemployment, price stability, inequality in the distribution of income and wealth, technological self sufficiency and control of population growth (Tendulkar & Jain 1995). The Seventh-Plan (1985-90) focussed on employment and the eighth plan (1991-95) on poverty reduction and 3% increase in employment each year by implementing Jawahar Rozgar Yojna (JRY). Sectors like education, health, family planning, employment, welfare got a larger slice from the Central Governments budget (Bagachee 1987; Ahuja 1997; Dutt & Sundharam 1997; Dutt & Ravallion 1998; PC 2008).

The Eight-Plan (1992-97) was implemented after the 1990 financial crisis resulting in devaluation of rupee, dismantling of the Licence Raj, and reduction in trade barriers. By the end of the plan it did not show much progress in term of the benefits of growth tricking down to the poorest of poor in the rural areas and to the weaker sections in the society, hence the Ninth- plan (1997-2000), was implemented under such circumstances and lot had to be done to restructure and liberalise the economy (PC 2009) besides public-private partnerships and private finance initiatives are essential to solve the social-economic problems of poverty, illiteracy, unemployment, child labour, and infrastructure deficit (Medhekar 2005; 3iNetwork 2002). The Tenth-Plan (2002-2007) aimed to increase the growth of Gross Domestic Product (GDP) to 10% by creating market friendly environment for private and foreign investors, improve corporate transparency and infrastructure, reduce poverty ratio by 5% and increase literacy rate by 75% by the end of 2007. The current Eleventh-Plan (2007-2012), has the key objective of increasing agriculture sectors contribution to GDP by 4% per year create 70 million new employment opportunities under MGNREGA, schemes to alleviate poverty with an overall GDP growth of 10% by the end of the plan, which is yet to be seen and evaluated.

In 1970s and 80's various wage employment programmes were introduced such as: Food For Work Program (FWP) (1977-78) and Integrated Rural Development Programme (IRDP-1978-79) which was credit based poverty alleviation program to empower women (Roy & Blomqvist 2004), National Rural Employment Programme in 1980-88 and Training of Rural Youth for Self Employment (TRYSEM), The Rural Landless Employment Guarantee Program (RLEGP) in 1983 and Jawahar Rozgar Yojna in 1989, which were very significant for creating employment in rural areas and for urban poor (Khanna 1996; Datt & Sundharam 1997;Tendulkar & Jain 1995). Since economic liberalisation in 1991, it was realised that most of these employment programs were not backed up by sufficient resources for the poor to reap the benefits. Although Central and State Governments intervention was recognised for employment generation, under liberalisation it was critical to do away with control, regulation and licence raj, mobilising private sector investment and involvement and encouraging partial or full privatisation and competition in monopolistic markets (Sagar 1990; Agarwal 1996; Datt & Sundharam 1997; Lal 1999; MHDC 2000; Roy & Blomqvist 2004; Medhekar 2005).

The Ministry of Rural Development has a gamut of targeted programmes from providing direct employment, self employment, social security, housing, building rural infrastructure and manage land resources to alleviate poverty. The safety net systems used in the past were PDS, IRDP, JRY, and sustained form of self employment through programs like Swaranjayanti Gram Swarozgar Yojana (SGSY), Self-help Groups (SHGs), National Skills Development Mission (NSDM) under public-private partnership model for developing human capital in rural unemployed youth were, merely to compensate the poor for short-run ill-effects of liberalisation and reforms (Khanna 1996; MHDC 2000; PC 2008; Medhekar 2005; MGNREGA 2009).

Mahatma Gandhi National Rural Employment Guarantee Act

Federal Government formulated the National Rural Employment Guarantee Act (NREGA) in 2005. It was a paradigm shift from earlier *supply side programmes* to fight poverty to *demand side schemes,* renamed as Mahatma Gandhi National Rural Employment Guarantee Act (MGREGA) on 2nd of October 2009. With its legal framework and human rights-based approach, MGNREGA provides employment to those who demand it. Announced on 7th of September 2005 MGREGA aims at "enhancing livelihood and security of the household in rural areas of the country by providing at least one hundred days of guaranteed wage employment in every financial year to every household whose adult members volunteer to do unskilled manual work" (MGREGA, 2009). The Act covered 200 of the country's poorest and most backward districts in its first phase which became the 'human face' of India's United Progressive Alliance (UPA) government's reform agenda, an anti-poverty programme was launched nationwide on February 2, 2006 and was extended to 330 additional districts in 2007-2008 and the remaining rural areas have been notified from April 1, 2008.

The MGNREGA, Act is also a significant vehicle for strengthening decentralisation and deepening the processes of democracy by giving a pivotal role to local governance bodies, that is, the Panchayai Raj Institutions. The Scheme is sponsored by the Ministry of Rural Development, Government of India. Unique features of the Act include, time bound employment guarantee and wage payment within 15 days, provide incentive-disincentive structure to the State Governments for providing employment as 90 per cent of the cost for employment provided is borne by the Federal Government or payment of unemployment allowance at their own cost. The Act also mandates 33 percent workplace participation for women (PC 2009; MGNREGA 2009).

See Table 15.1 (MGNREGA 2009), which illustrates the total employment generated under MGNREGA schemes since implementation.

Table 15.1. Total Employment Generated Under MGNREGS

Employment provided to households	3.34 crores
Total – person days in crores	133.32 crores
SC	40.19 = 30.15%
ST	29.1 = 21.83%
Women	68.02 = 58.02%
Others	64.02 = 48.02%
Total Works Taken up	25.98
Total Works Completed	7.08
Work in Progress	18.9 Lakhs

Source: MGNREGA 2009.

The Central Government contributed Rupees 5,500 crores, which was funded by the merging of the two programs Sampoorna Grameen Rozgar Yojana and the Food-for-Work Programme. The law envisages coverage of all of India's 600 districts within five years. The Central Government has already pledged 90% of the funds required for the scheme's implementation. The remaining 10% is expected to come from the states' coffers. Under the scheme, if a State Government fails to provide employment, within 15 days of an application, the applicant will have to be paid an unemployment allowance. As some states have their own Minimum Wage Acts, the MGNREGS Act 2005, enables the Central Government to fix a minimum wage of no less than Rupees 60 per day (TIE 2006; Jaffer 2008; MGNREGA 2009; PC 2009). Through short term employment, these programmes provide income transfers to poor households during critical times such as lean agricultural seasons and enable consumption smoothening. Over time, this will facilitate the transition of the village economy from subsistence to self-sustenance by increasing agricultural productivity and creating durable assets for regeneration of the natural resource base. The infrastructure development will not only lead to market and supply chain linkages and but also create further employment opportunities generated under NREG Scheme. See Table 15.2 (MGNREGA 2009) which provides an example of MGNREGA employment schemes statistics for various vulnerable groups in 2009 in the selected states of Jammu and Kashmir in the north to Maharashtra in the west, Assam in the east and Kerala in the south west of India.

Table 15.2. MGNREGA Four Selected State-Wise Statistics

State	Jammu & Kashmir	Maharashtra	Assam	Kerala
Employment provided to households	1,08348	13,16021 lakhs	11, 42992 lakhs	4,74909 lakhs
Total – person days in lakhs	33.76	219.35	303.82	81.41
SCs	1.91(5.685)	47.35 (21.59%)	32.01(10.54%)	15.93 (19.57%)
STs	6.26 (18.53%)	82.62 (37.66%)	102.9 (33.875)	5.89 (7.24%)
Women	1.19(3.53%)	87.13 (39.72%)	91.5 (30.12%)	67.99 (83.51%)
Others	25.58(75.79%)	89.38 (40.75%)	168.91(55.6%)	59.59 (73.19%)
Total Fund	107.14 crores	546.85 crores	711.53	314.16 crores
Expenditure	38.44	216.39 crores	403.48	118.94 crores
Total Works Taken up	9090	17365	12691	34120
Total Works Completed	2646	4658	2920	23407
Work in Progress	6444	12707	9771	10713

Source: MGNREGA 2009.

BENEFITS FROM NREGS UNDER MGNREG ACT

Benefits of NREGS under the MGNREG Act are numerous and not just limited to enhancing economic and social, potential of supplementing income through wage earnings, savings and investments, financial inclusion, providing employment on demand to households, but also has many multiplier effects which are now visible in terms of building social and physical capital, democratic process which is transparent and accountable, augmenting household income, savings and investment, pro-poor climate change policy and sustainable development meeting the numerous MDGs.

Firstly, *Social Capital* is built under, MGNREGA and the most vulnerable group can help build capabilities and articulate and demand employment needs and negotiate their rights to escape the poverty trap. Nearly 33.9 million households were provided employment in 2007-08, and nearly 26 million households have worked under MGREGA for 952.7 million work days. The legislation has also had a positive impact on the socio-economic empowerment of women mandating at least 33 percent participation for women. These efforts are extremely wide ranging. They include the creation of a digitised monitoring system, on site roll verification, proactive disclosure of all records and conducting regular social audits.

Secondly, MGNREGA projects have built *Physical Capital* and have enhanced productivity of land and regeneration of natural resources and food security in most states, through water harvesting, ground water recharging, improve moisture content, soil erosion, micro irrigation and increased access to markets and services, reducing distressed migration to urban areas, supplementing household incomes with increased women workforce participation ratio through rural connectivity.

Thirdly, it has strengthened *Democratic Processes*, and built local capacity at grassroots level for planning and decision making and encouraged transparency and accountability in grass root democratic process. MGNREGA has effectively used technology Management Information System (MIS), which is one of the largest data bases of rural households in the world, through their engagement in MGNREGA job cards. MIS makes transparency intrinsic to MGNREGA by placing all critical variables such as wage payments, number of days of employment provided and works under execution online for easy public access, encouraging the transfer of local solutions and best practices through an online knowledge network system. Currently 400 district programme coordinators are members of this network. The network also links up with Civil Society Organisations improving delivery of services such as initial experiments in the use of smart cards for wage payment to MGNREGA workers in remote rural villages.

Fourthly, MGNREGA schemes have helped the vulnerable poor in *augmenting household income, savings and investment* to escape the poverty trap by providing legal guarantee of 100 days of work in a given financial year and a basic minimum wage of Rupees 75 to Rupees 80, in 2008-09. All wage payments are made and disbursed through bank and post office accounts of the workers. Workers under MGNREGA are also provided with health insurance along with smart cards and biometric signatures for wage payments to workers under MGNREGA project.

Fifthly, MGNREGA has strengthened natural resource management by developing and implementing *'Pro Poor Climate Change Policies,* such as afforestation, regenerating natural resources like grasslands, drought and flood proofing, water conservation and harvesting systems and help the poor to cope with climate change impact which will increasingly affect the poor who are most vulnerable to it by reducing access to drinking water, negatively affecting the health of poor and posing a real threat to food security (Richards 2003). Among the poor, vulnerability may also vary, as some groups are lacking in the financial, social, and political means of securing alternative livelihoods less exposed to risk than other groups. Women, for example may be constrained by social and cultural structures that place them in inferior social positions, limiting their access to income, education, public voice, and survival mechanisms (MHDC 2000; Roy & Blomqvist 2004; UNDP 2009).

MGNREGA integrates responses to climate change adaptation measures into strategies for poverty reduction to ensure sustainable development. It strengthens capacity to cope with current climate variability and extremes and to adapt to expected future climatic conditions. Climate change policy and mechanisms can also generate income for small and marginal farmers and investment flows including transfer of technology for rural communities. It is seen that only 3-4% of carbon trading is sourced from agriculture, land use, land use change, agro-forestry and forestry. Efforts are directed in using the unique identity of MGNREGA workers, its ongoing works, detailed documentation and records, MIS systems and advanced ICT to streamline measurement, financial flows to benefit rural communities from carbon trading. *Finally*, it has tried to implement the MDG's of sustainable development and poverty reduction and established an Untied Fund for Local Area Planning to encourage convergence for sustainable development processes through social audits. MGNREGA is the first ever law in context of employment generation linked to poverty alleviation, developed and implemented internationally, and its primary goal is to guarantees wage employment at an unprecedented scale to addresses causes of chronic poverty like drought, deforestation, famine and soil erosion, so that the process of employment generation is maintained on a sustainable basis (MGNREGA 2009; WTO 2004; PC 2008; WB 2004).

DISCUSSION AND CONCLUSIONS

The Government of India has recognised since independence that alleviation of poverty is its long-term objective. However, poverty alleviation cannot be left to five year plans alone. The various five year plans (1st to 8th Five year plan) have not achieved much in terms of alleviating poverty, as the unemployment programs were not well targeted; there was paucity of revenue for infrastructure programs and employment creation in rural areas and lack of political will and commitment (Dandekar 1998; Medhekar 2005; Roy, Blomqvist & Clark 2012). A direct action taken by MGNREGA, the buzz word for Indian politicians, along with right to work and dignity of labour, participatory relationship with the government and various anti-poverty schemes and programs which are demand driven is growth inclusive. MGNREGA emphasis should be on the "power of people (BPL poor people) and the power of place (rural areas)" besides to ensure what is enshrined in the MGNREGA that economic growth is inclusive and reaches the poorest, weakest and the most vulnerable in the society. It has given rural poor people the right to demand work, re-established their dignity and respect, ensure their economic and democratic rights and entitlements, create labour intensive infrastructure projects and finally to build human capital empower the rural poor population, which will lay the foundation for sustainable economic growth.

Livelihood and workforce participation of the marginalised groups such as: Scheduled Castes and Tribes and Other Backward Classes and Minorities groups and the Women in the society are also ensured under MGNREGA. A lot more needs to be done to study and evaluate the management, implementation and efficiency and effectiveness of these programs state wise. It is important to further research MGNREGA and examine what works, what doesn't work, under what conditions and what are its costs and benefits, and most importantly, what lessons can be drawn from each of these programs for enhancing our understanding of the impact of MGNREGA, to generate employment for BPL groups and alleviate poverty, as well as the political will and commitment at the state level in context of its democratic, accountability and transparency processes.

Over the last two years, management of the poverty program and implementation trends vindicate the basic objective of the Act, which is to provide employment and reduce poverty significantly. MGNREGA also has provided constitutional sovereignty in the form of transparency and accountability which is woven in the daily interaction of people with the government and allows any person to monitor and report the delivery of the schemes under MGNREGA. However, this transparency and accountability for all states is still to be properly evaluated. The total expenditure of schemes and workers 94% of total accounts is required to be posted on MGNREGA official website, with every transaction revealed in detail (MGNREGA 2009; Roy and Dey 2009).

The question is whether India will be able to follow the path of anti-poverty programmes as developed and implemented by Malaysia, Vietnam and Indonesia, where opportunities are created for the poor people to benefit from liberalisation and reform process in terms of infrastructure development and social security safety nets, in order to meet the MDG's by 2015. Agriculture sector (land reforms) and social security (employment prospects) should be treated jointly as an anti-poverty measure, through ownership of physical assets and investment in human and physical capital for the poor. The impact of MGNREGA on the rural population, workforce and cost is still to be examined, in terms of energising people, mobilising resources and empowering the marginalised rural people as a group to take action and delivering the goods and services as promised under the act and much more in the future.

According to World Development Report by World Bank (2009), MGNREGA programs and schemes of the UPA government are a policy barrier to poverty alleviation, economic development and internal mobility, which prevents communities to fully capture the benefits of labour mobility and migration (WSJ 2009; PTI 2009). World Development Report further explains how internal mobility is essential as way out of poverty requires shifting populations from villages to cities. The process of migration should be encouraged, according to the World Bank. Migration is overlooked as a force in economic development due to negative attitudes held by the government and ignorance of the benefits of population mobility (World Bank 2009; UNDP 2009). Economic benefits of migration are not usually recognised by policymakers. MGNREGA has increased rural employment and watershed developments to improve agricultural productivity and development of small and medium towns mainly to reduce or prevent migration of population from rural to urban areas and cities. These policies prevent local communities to fully capture and capitalise on the benefits of labour mobility. Further in the State of Punjab and Madhya Pradesh, implementation of MGNREGA, job schemes have created a wage-floor for unskilled rural workers, causing a rise in agricultural wage from rupees 58 per day in 2005-06 to rupees 91 in 2009. Farm costs have increased as a result of decrease in labour supply, and glaring irregularities and corruption have been reported in the implementation of the scheme in the Bundelkhand region, state of Uttar Pradesh (EPW 2009; WSJ 2009; TIE 2009).

According to Work Bank 2009 report, decentralised scams have become the norm for MGNREGA scheme across the various states and the hard earned money of the poor is being siphoned off by a corrupt administration, contractors and ruling class nexus (World Bank 2009; WSJ 2009; TIE 2009). The World Bank research in 2009 reported that MGNREGA has not provided urban centric development as its schemes are blocking rural migration to urban cities. The WDR 2009 proposes that concentration of economic activity is inevitable and usually desirable for economic growth. MGREGA thus retards rural-urban migration. Its is important to note that, this old Lewis model of growth based on a dual economy (Todaro & Smith 2008) has had its share of criticism even from within the capitalist framework—be it the human capital framework theory or from theories of market fragmentation or even the capability approach of Nobel Laureate Amritya Sen from the 1960s (Wiebke & Sen 2005; Nussbaum 2000; Nussbaum & Sen 1993). If we follow the World Bank's suggestion, then the wages will be lower in the rural areas, the rural welfare programmes will be downsized under MGNREGA thus allowing the rural poor to desperately migrate into the urban areas, resulting in exploitation of the urban poor. Notably, it only suggests this model for domestic markets and not for international labour markets. World Bank (2009) report also recommends to have special economic geographical transformation based on three dimensions, that is *higher density* of population for the growth of cities, which means using the scarce resources intensively; secondly *shorter distance* to where work and economic opportunities are available and lastly *fewer the restrictions and barriers* between countries economic borders, greater is the flow of goods, services, labour, capital and ideas across borders by taking advantage of economies of scale, specialisation and trade as seen in European Union (World Bank 2009) .

It's almost 6 years to the 2015 deadline to achieve the Millennium Development Goals (MDG's). However the measures to fight poverty and hunger have begun to slow as a result of the global food crises including the global financial crisis, which has resulted in a sluggish and even negative economic growth in developed countries. Despite many successes, overall progress has been too slow for most of the targets to be met by 2015 in the developing countries (UNDP 2009). Finally India's anti-poverty program names after the father of nation Mahatma Gandhi (MGNREGA) is not immune from this global crisis and has a long way to go, to not only guarantee employment for the first 100 days under the Act, but empowering poor people by providing them with continuous training and skilling (while not working). Elimination of poverty is not only a question of economics (raising income, equal distribution, and investment), but is a social and political issue related to socio-political awareness of people to the causes and consequences of poverty, and how anti-poverty programs can bring awareness, with dignity and respect for the millions living in poverty, in India. One can only hope that the Indian politician's passion for renaming streets and programs after the Father of the Nation-Mahatma Gandhi, will have some miraculous impact on the MGNREGA to not only remove corruption within the system, but also policy makers and management goal to meet the overarching MDG's to end poverty by 2015.

REFERENCES

3iNetwork (2002), India Infrastructure Report 2002: Governance Issues for Commercialization, New Delhi: *Oxford University Press.*

ADB (2001), 'Asian Development Outlook', Hong Kong: *Oxford University Press.*

Agarwal, A. N. (1996), 'Indian economy: problems of development and planning', 22nd revised edn, New Delhi: *Wishwa Prakashan.*

Ahluwalia, I. J. and I. M. D. Little (eds) (1998), 'India's economic reform and development: essays for Manmohan Singh', 3rd edn, New Delhi: *Oxford University Press.*

Ahluwalia, M. S. (1978), 'Rural Poverty in India: 1956-57 to 1973-74', *Journal of Development Studies,* 14, (3), April.

Ahuja, R. (1997), Social Problems in India, Second edn, New Delhi: *Rawat Publications.*

Allen, T. and A. Thomas (1997), 'Poverty and Development in the 1990s, London, United Kingdom': *Oxford University Press.*

Asian Development Bank (ADB) (2003), 'Competitiveness in Developing Asia. *Asian Development Outlook',* (ADB), New York: *Oxford University Press.*

Bagachee, S. (1987, January 24), 'Poverty Alleviation Programmes in Seventh Plan: *An Appraisal', Economic and Political Weekly,* Bombay.

Becker, H. (1966), 'Social Problems: A Modern Approach, New York': *John Wiley and Sons, Inc.*

Cassen, R. and V. Joshi (1996), India: 'The Future of Economic Reform, India, Delhi': *Oxford University Press.*

CFPR (1983), Population, Poverty and Hope, Centre For Policy Research, (CFPR), New Delhi: *Utpal Publishing House.*

Dandekar, V. M. (1998), 'Agriculture, Employment and Poverty, in The Indian economy': Recent Development and Future Prospects, Lucas, R.E.B. and Gustav, F.P. (Eds), New Delhi: *Oxford University Press* .

Dantwala, M. L. (1985), 'Garibi Hatao: Strategy Option', Economic and Political Weekly, Bombay, 2, March, 16.

DFARSA (2005), 'Cape Town Ministerial Communiqué', India-Brazil-South Africa (IBSA) Dialogue Forum, viewed 2/10/05 2005, http://www.dfa.gov.za/docs/2005/ibsa0311.htm, (cited on 9-9-09).

Dutt, R. and K. P. M. Sundharam (1997), 'Indian Economy, 36th revised edition', New Delhi': S. *Chand & Company* Ltd.

Dutt, G. and M. Ravallion (1998), 'Farm Productivity and Rural Poverty in India', *Journal of Development Studies,* 34, (4), pp. 62-85.

EPW (2009), 'Survival of Agricultural Labour in Punjab': *A Burning Questions, Economics and Political Weekly,* 18 July 2009.

Elesh (1973), 'Poverty Theories and Income Maintenance: Validity and Policy Relevance', *Social Science Quarterly*, 2, pp. 97-115.

Fields, G. (1991), 'Growth and Income Distribution' , UK: *Oxford University Press.*

Findlay, R. and S. Wellisz (1994), 'The Political Economy of Poverty, Equity and Growth': Five Small Open economies, New York: *Oxford University Press.*

Hirway, I. (1985), 'Garibi Hatao: Can IRDP do it?' *Economic and Political Weekly,* Bombay, 6, March, 30.

IFAD (2001), 'Rural Poverty Report 2001': The Challenge of Ending Rural Poverty, USA: *Oxford University Press.*

Jaffer, P. C. (2008), 'India's National Rural Employment Guarantee Scheme' (NREGA): Localised Implementation in Gulbarga District of Karnataka. (http://www.solution exchange-un.net.in/NREGA/documents/NREGA-Gulbarg.pdf (cited on 9-9-09).

Khanna, R. S. (1996), 'Liberalisation and Unemployment in India', *The Indian Journal of Public Administration,* XLII, July-September issue, 1996.

Lal, D. (1999), 'Unfinished Business: India in the World Economy', New Delhi: *Oxford University Press.*

Mahatma Gandhi National Rural Employment Guarantee Act (2009), MGNREGA, Status Report (2009-2010), Ministry of Rural Development, Government of India, http://www.nrega.nic.in (cited on 29-9-09).

Mahatma Gandhi National Rural Employment Guarantee Act (2010), MGNREGA, Status Report (2009-2010), Ministry of Rural Development, Government of India, http://www.nrega.nic.in (cited on 1-7-2010).

Medhekar, A. (2005), 'Public Private Partnership for Infrastructure Development in India', *Proceedings of the 11th International Conference on Public Private Sector Partnerships: Enhancing Sustainable Development,* Lasi, Romania, May 25th – 28th: Facultatea de

Economie, i Admnistrarea Afacerilor Universitatea "Al. I. Cuza". UK: Sheffield Hallam University Press.

Mehta, H. R. (1997), 'Poverty Population and Sustainable Development', Jaipur, India: *Rawat Publications.*

MHDC (2000), 'Human Development in South Asia 2000': The Gender Question, Mehboob-Ul-Haq Development Centre (MHDC), Pakistan: *Oxford University Press.*

Nussbaum, M. C. (2000), 'Women and Human Development': The Capabilities Approach, Cambridge: *Cambridge University Press.*

Nussbaum, M. C. and A. Sen (1993), 'The Quality of Life', (Eds), Oxford, UK: *Clarendon Press.*

Press Trust of India. (2009), 'World Bank sees NREGS as a barrier to economic development in Business Standard, October 22-2009, http://www.business-standard.com/india /storypage.php?autono=351922 (cited on 8-10-09).

Planning Commission (PC) (2008), 'National Rural Employment Generation Scheme-(NREGS)', Ministry of Rural Development, Government of India, http://planning commission.gov.in/plans/planrel/11thf.htm (cited on 21-10-09).

Planning Commission (PC) (2009), Eleventh Five Year Plan (2007-12) Government of India, http://planningcommission.gov.in/plans/planrel/11thf.htm, (cited on 21-10-09).

Ravallion, M. (1991), 'Reaching the Poor through Public Employment: Arguments, Evidence and Lessons from South Asia', *World Bank Research Observer,* 6, (2), pp. 153-176.

Ravallion, M. (1992), Poverty Comparisons: A Guide to Concepts and Methods, Living Standards Measurement Study, Working Paper, no 38, Washington, DC.

Ravallion, M. and K. Subbarow (1992), "Adjustment and Human Development in India", *Journal of Indian School of Political Economy,* 4 (1), pp. 55-79.

Richards, M. (2003), Poverty reduction, equity and climate change: Global Governance Synergies or Contradictions? *Globalisation and Poverty Programme; Overseas Development Institute,* London.

Roy, K.C. and H.C. Blomqvist (2004), Government's Poverty Alleviation Programs for Women's Empowerment: Some Comments on the Indian Situation, Twentieth Century Development: Some Relevant Issues, New York: *Nova Science Publishers.*

Roy, K., H. Blomqvist and C. Clark (forthcoming 2012), Economic Development in China, India and East Asia: Managing Change in the Twenty First Century, Cheltenham, U.K.: *Edward Elgar publication.*

Roy, R. and N. Dey (2009), NREGA: Breaking new grounds, The Hindu June 21-09, Online Edition, http://www.hinduonnet.com/mag/2009/06/21/stories/2009062150010100.htm (cited on 8-10-09)

Sagar, D. (1990), 'Rural Development Policies of India: A Historical Analysis', *Indian Journal of Public Administration,* Delhi, 36, p. 2.

Squire, L. (1993), 'Fighting Poverty', *American Economic Review*, 83, May, pp. 377-382.

Solow, R. (1994), 'Perspectives on Growth Theory', *Journal of Economic Perspectives,* 8, pp. 45-54.

Tendulkar, S. D. and L. R. Jain (1995), 'Economic Growth and Equity: India 1970-71 to 1988-89', *Indian Economic Review,* XXX, (1), pp. 19-49.

Tendulkar, S. (1998), 'Indian Economic Policy Reform and Poverty': An Assessment, in I. J. Ahluwalia and I. N. D. Little (eds), India's Economic Reforms and Development, New Delhi: *Oxford University Press.*

The Indian Express (2006), 'India's Employment Guarantee Scheme', (TIE) (5-1-06), http://infochangeindia.org/20060306481 0/Poverty/News/India-s-employment-guarantee-scheme-to-be-launched-in-February.html, (cited on 9-9-09).

The Indian Express (2009), 'NREGS: UP Under Scanner, TIE', 9-October-2009, by Yadav, J.P., http://www.indianexpress.com/news/nregs-up-under-scanner/526942/#(cited on 10-9-09).

Todaro, M.P. and S. C. Smith (2008), 'Economic Development', Tenth Edition, Addison Wesley, *Pearson Education,* USA.

UNDP (2009), 'Millennium Development Goals Report 2009': End Poverty by 2015 (MDGs) http://www.undp.org/mdg/ (cited on 9-10-09).

Wall Street Journal (2009), 'NREGS and Rural Misery' (WSJ) July, 2009, http://www.livemint.com/2009/07/23233056/NREGS-and-rural-misery.html (cited on 9-10-09).

Wikipedia (2009), National Rural Employment Program, http://en.wikipedia.org/wiki/National_Rural_Employment_Guarantee_Act (cited on 20-10-09).

Wiebke, K. and A. Sen (2005), 'Amartya Sen's Capability Approach': Theoretical Insights and Empirical Applications, Berlin: *Springer.*

WTO (2004), 'Ministerial Conference on Cultural Tourism and Poverty Alleviation', Hue, Vietnam: 1-12.

World Bank (2004), 'World Development Report 2004': Making Services Work for Poor People, New York: *World Bank.*

World Bank (2009), 'World Development Report 2009': Reshaping Economic Geography, New York, www.worldbank.org/wdr2009, (cited on 20-10-09).

In: Development Management in the Twenty-First Century ISBN: 978-1-62100-699-2
Editors: Kartik Roy and Sandip Kar

Chapter 16

RECENT FINANCIAL CRISIS AND PUBLIC EXPENDITURE ON EDUCATION FOR POVERTY ERADICATION IN BOTSOWANA

Pelotshweu Moepeng*
Research Fellow, Botswana Institute for Development Policy Analysis (BIDPA)
Botswana

INTRODUCTION

The global financial economic recession of 2008/09 caught the world unaware and no amount of planning was found adequate to address the economic meltdown problems that were a result. In Botswana, diamond mining firms closed operations because there were no markets. Suddenly, there was a need to come up with coping strategies that would reduce the impact of the recession. The following year, in 2009/10, the government introduced fiscal measures that included cutting spending of new developments, the sale of some of its assets, increased borrowing and increasing the tax base and efficiency of tax collection. Public spending in education relative to GDP in Botswana is one of the highest in the world and for many years, this sector has attracted the largest share of GDP spending than any other sector. Fears of spending cuts that went across all sectors in the economy were thought to have serious impact in the education sector, especially its role in eradicating poverty. In Botswana, poverty is reported to be very high in rural areas than in urban areas (Central Statistics Office Botswana 2004). This article is organized by first outlining the objectives, then the methods used to collect data and analysis, and then a literature review is discussed, followed by a description of the Botswana economy and a display of the results of analysis. Finally the conclusions suggest that public education in Botswana had remained a government priority even in the midst of a global financial crisis and that prospects for eradicating poverty in rural areas are positive.

* pmoepeng@bidpa.bw.

OBJECTIVES

This Chapter aims to:

a) Explain whether the current budgetary options in public education spending encourage sustainable and desired outcomes that promote poverty eradication and the narrowing of income inequalities.
b) Determine how current budget cuts in response to the global financial economic recession have affected children from rural districts and children from urban districts.
c) Infer what is likely to be the trend of poverty in rural areas by the year 2016 in view of trends in budget allocation adjustments to shocks.

METHOD

The method used in collecting data and analysis is based on a desktop research. Secondary data sources were from the Central Statistics Office, the Ministry of Finance and Development Planning, the Ministry of Education and Skills Development; and the Ministry of Local Government. In addition, key stakeholders in departments working for the Ministry of Finance and Development Planning, Ministry of Local Government and the Ministry of Education were contacted and interviewed. The interviews did not follow any structured approach and requested informed views of stakeholders to establish the latest direction of government thinking in public education spending after the recent global economic recession.

Raw data was collected from Ministerial Reports and Budget allocations in terms of its appropriateness to the objectives of this article and analyzed using Microsoft Excel Software. Graphs showing trends and relative proportions were produced and are used in this study to demonstrate the results. The information about trends in education expenditure is used to inform development economics theory to derive the analysis in the discussion and also assist in arriving at the conclusions of this exercise. Data was also collected and reviewed from the international and domestic literature to inform the analysis. Information of public spending in rural and urban schooling, especially at primary levels and enrolment rates by location are also used to find out the relative public expenditure per child by location.

Peer review exercises were completed through presentation at Botswana Institute for Development Policy Analysis working paper seminar series in November 2010 and the International Institute for Development Studies Conference in Calcutta, India in December 2010.

LITERATURE REVIEW

If education is to be understood as a process of acquiring knowledge, then it is possible to consider it being a consumer good and a factor of production (McTaggart; et al. 1999). As a consumer good, knowledge is valuable because it can be used as a basis to increase one's income; and as a factor of production, education increases productivity. Knowledge such as basic education in reading, writing, and numbers learning equip people to be better able to communicate and interact with each other; which is a basis to develop better citizens. Investing in education has many positive external benefits which is included to enable citizens to communicate more effectively. Since, decisions made about the amount of education each individuals undertakes often undervalues the external benefits, the education market cannot be left to the unregulated market forces, lest there can be serious distortions in the allocation of limited resources. It is therefore critical that government intervention in terms of regulation, funding and quality assurance is an integral part of the education market.

An improvement in the education of people is a major requirement to the development process. This is demonstrated by the international and national commitments that place improving education of people high on the agenda. For instance, the UN's Millennium Development Goal (MDG) number two aims to achieve universal primary education by the year 2015. Further, Botswana's national Vision 2016 goal is about building an educated and informed nation. Thus the Vision 2016 of Botswana views investment in education and equality of educational opportunity as prerequisites that would enable the country to achieve a higher quality of human capacity and productivity in the future. Education attainment, and in particular literacy, has been observed as a major human resource input that, all things being equal, changes a poor economic environment into a more productive and sustainable environment (Todaro 1981). Hence, educated people are thought to bring more wealth than those without education. A healthier more educated person is capable of producing more than otherwise, and thus improved productivity is rewarded in the labour market (Bardhan and Udry 1999). Improvements in education have significant long term benefits of reducing poverty. For example, in India, empirical evidence suggests that states with a historical endowment of human resources, especially literate residents, performed better in reducing poverty than those with low levels of literacy (Datt and Ravallion 1998). Illustrations of the benefits of education include, but not limited to the following examples;

a) Literate farmers are more productive and more responsive to adoption of new technologies than illiterate farmers,
b) Trained mechanics are better able to keep up to date with changing car models.
c) More schooling years increase the chances of escaping poverty among the children of the poor.

There are socio-economic factors that are known to influence and determine the performance of a child's education attainment, which are beyond a child's control. These include among others, a child's family environment. If a child is from a poor family and the low levels of living in that family means that the housing and nutritional conditions are not conducive to learning, the educational process, even if it is free, might have little effect in changing the child's capacity for self-improvement and economic advancement. Empirical evidence has shown that more educated parents might provide the child with a more favorable learning environment at home, thereby lowering the cost of learning or increasing the market productivity of attending school for a given number of years (Schultz 1988). In some cases, it is thought that genetic transmission from an educated parent to a child might also explain the role of a family environment in the performance of a child's education.

In countries where public spending in education is constrained because such economies are very poor or education is not a major priority, government budget decisions in education can create a joint causation of human capital investment and income. In such cases, relatively wealthy individuals are able to invest in the education of their children and enable them to earn enough income at their adult age to remain wealthy. Whereas, the poor are unable to invest in the education of their children and thus earn low incomes and remain poor. Education spending that targets the poor and aims at reducing income inequalities is expected to allocate a larger share of the educational budget to the development of primary and secondary education as opposed to higher university and college education (Todaro 1981).

Schultz (1988) argued that many empirical studies in developed and developing countries had shown that basic primary and secondary schooling yield private returns between 10 and 40 per cent, and generally somewhat lower at university or college levels. Later, Bardhan and Udry (1999) have demonstrated that there is convincing evidence of a strong positive relationship between the schooling of a child and that child's future earnings. For women, the private benefits of their increased schooling years are observed in their ability to improve the health of their family members, produce a more nutritious diet for the same spending capacity and their ability to control more effectively their reproduction. The results of a positive association between increased schooling of mothers (women) and lower child mortality are well documented (Schultz 1988).

Externalities from education are more substantial at the basic primary level, and eventually fade out at the higher technical specialized levels of university training, where persons capture most of the social benefits from their education (Schultz 1988). Public spending to higher levels of education is better utilized when provided as loans than grants and subsidies. Once beneficiaries of education are required to bear a larger and rising proportion of their educational costs as loan repayments, and then the source of financing education would be sustainable. As a result, low income groups could benefit more from the system as a wider population would be covered by revolving funds in the system. In many instances in Africa, where returns to high levels of education are low, there have been experiences where high public education expenditures in high level professional training are known to promote brain drain and international migration of skilled professionals.

In circumstances where local university students transfer to Universities and other colleges abroad through generous government scholarships, there is a high likelihood that a country might experience a brain drain or some students failing to return home after completing their education. In the case of Botswana where merit determines eligibility for government sponsorship, students who are eligible for government grants who pursue science based subjects also stand a higher chance of finding employment abroad. These employment opportunities constitute significantly high private returns to the public sponsored students and their families.

Increased years of schooling enable the educated youth to access added private benefit of enhanced access to regular work opportunities in the market labor force and therefore lowers incidence of their long-term unemployment. In many developing countries, real wages in urban areas are higher than in rural areas. Migration from rural to urban areas tends to benefit the better educated more. It has been observed from empirical evidence in Colombia that nearly half of the gains to rural schooling is obtained through migration to urban areas (Schultz 1988). Hence, in many countries, including Botswana, the better educated are more likely to migrate and benefit more through employment in the modern sector.

In terms of public expenditures, education has taken the largest share or second largest share of public budget in many countries (Schultz 1988) and this is the case in Botswana for a long time to date. UNDP (2003) demonstrated that requiring poor households to pay for schooling was not conducive to achieving universal primary education and therefore unlikely to help achieve the MDGs. As indicated above, schooling is an important requirement in improving the prospects of future generations. Botswana has made significant progress in ensuring there is universal access to primary schooling and junior secondary education as a basic education entitlement to every child. The net enrolment rate (NER) in 2009 for the 7-13 year age group was 91.8 per cent, suggesting that 8.2 per cent of this group were not enrolled in schools (Central Statistics Office 2009). However, a major concern in Botswana is with high unemployment rates among the youth. For instance, the junior secondary school leavers constitute 36 per cent of all the unemployed (Central Statistics Office 2006). This could imply that the primary schooling and junior secondary education performance is very low in preparing the youth for work and life. In this article, the public expenditure in the education sector in Botswana, before and immediately after the global financial crisis of 2008-2009 are examined to determine their impact in objectives of poverty eradication and achievement of the Vision 2016 goals.

Botswana Economy and Observations of Public Spending in Education from 2003/04 to 2010/2011 Global Recession

Cash Flow Trend

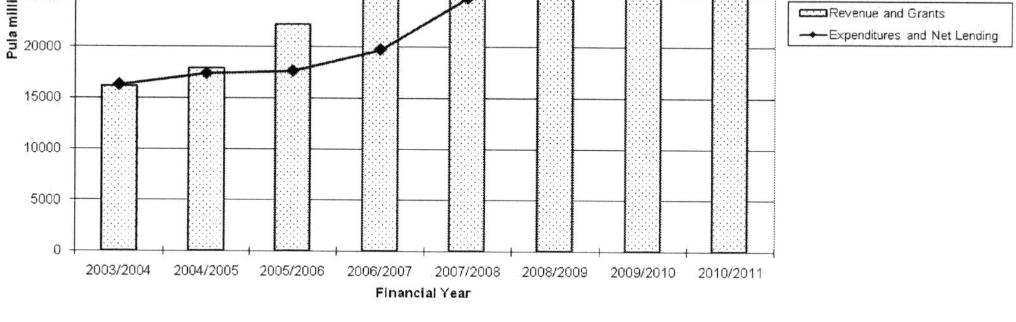

Figure 16.1. Botswana Cash Flow Trend 2003-2010. Source: Ministry of Finance and Development Planning (2010).

Figure 16.1 demonstrates the trends of Botswana's cash flow from the financial year 2003/04 to 2010/2011. Botswana has generally experienced surplus budgets until 2007/2008 financial year. The budget deficits began in the financial budget 2008/2009. The deficit was highest at the peak of the global financial crisis in 2009/2010. The situation has shown an improvement in the reduction of the budget deficit in 2010/2011 and during this time, the financial crisis was almost over. Diamonds, the main foreign exchange earner were now being exported.

Trends in Public Education Expenditure in Botswana

Despite the global financial crisis of 2008/2009, the Botswana government fiscal policy decided to ensure that public expenditure in education is not reduced. Figure 16.2, shows that the trend in public expenditure on education continued to rise through the financial years 2009/2010 and 2010/2011, despite the global financial crisis of 2009 that also affected the Botswana economy as demonstrated above.

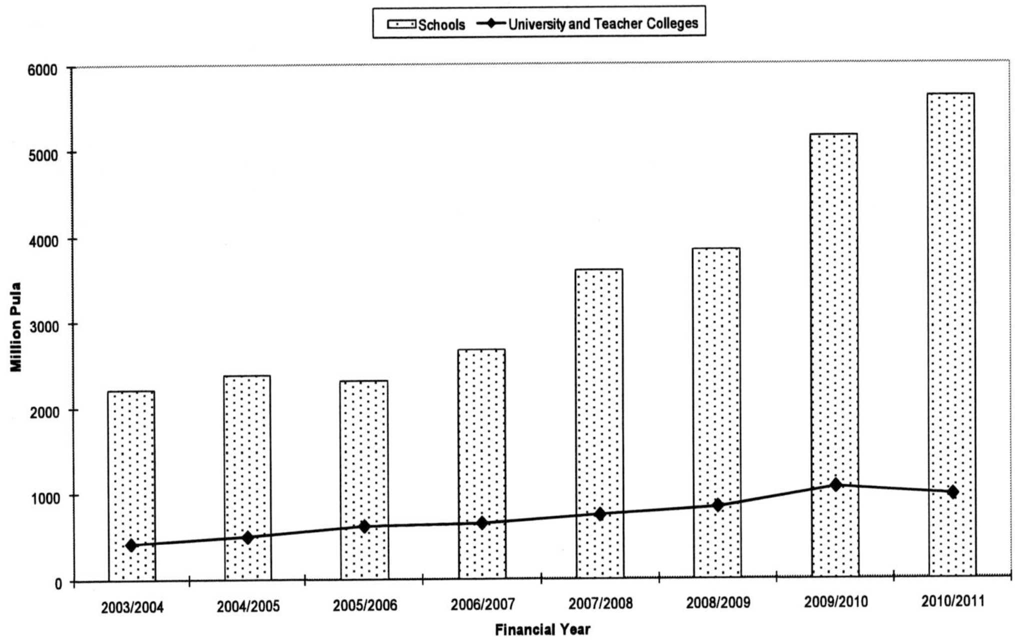

Figure 16.2. Trends in Public Expenditure on Education 2003/04 -2010/2011. Source: Ministry of Finance and Development Planning 2010.

Share of Education Expenditure in Overall Budget

During the period before the global financial crisis in 2007/2008, public expenditure in education constituted the largest share of total government expenditure at 38 per cent (Figure 16.3). After the Global Financial Crisis in the budget of 2010/2011, a year of the budget deficit recovery, public expenditure in education continued to receive the highest share of that year's budget at 43 per cent (Figure 16.4). Therefore, public spending in education remained a highest priority in government spending even during very difficult fiscal policy decisions.

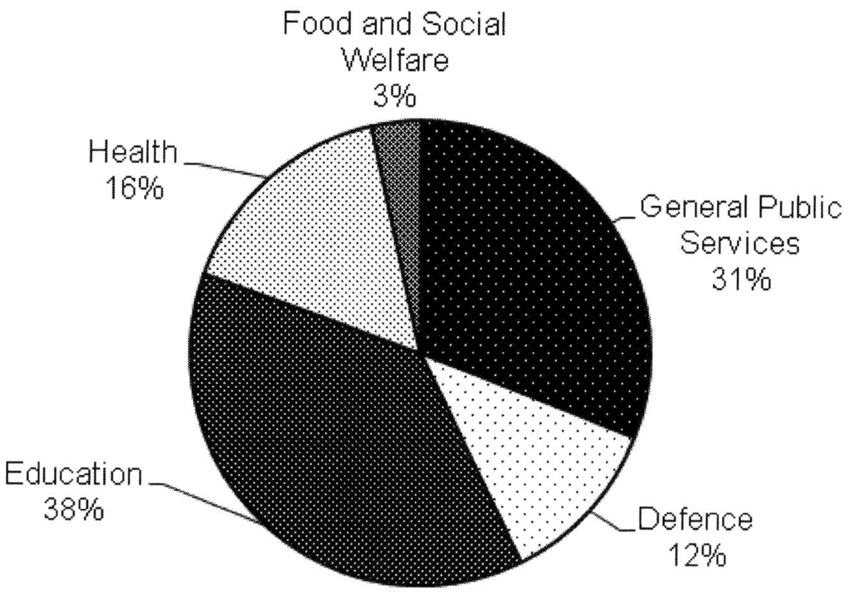

Figure 16.3. Share of Education Expenditure in 2007/08.

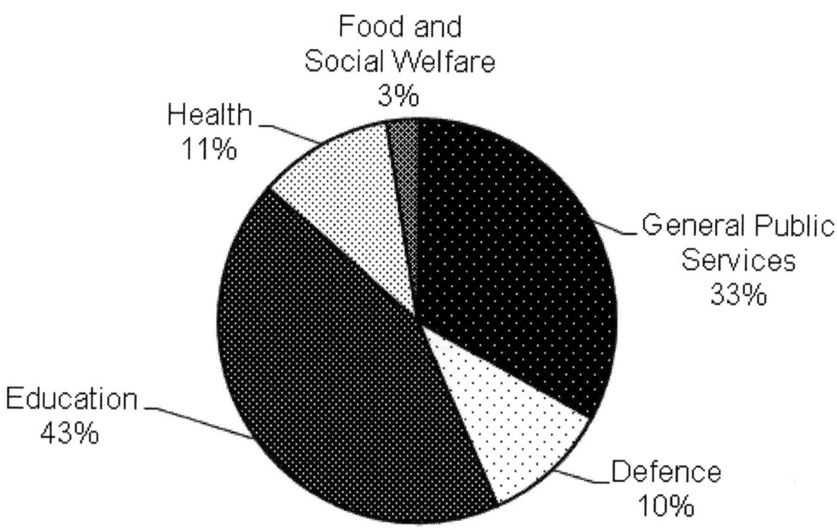

Figure 16.4. Share of Education Spending in 2010/11. Source: Ministry of Finance and Development Planning 2010

Trends in Public Education Spending by Education Sector

Figure 16.5 shows trends in public expenditure for "schools including student bursaries" compared to the public spending in "University and teacher Training Colleges". Public spending continued to increase during the period of global financial crisis until 2010/2011 for schools and student bursaries, whereas public spending for university education slightly declined in 2010/2011.

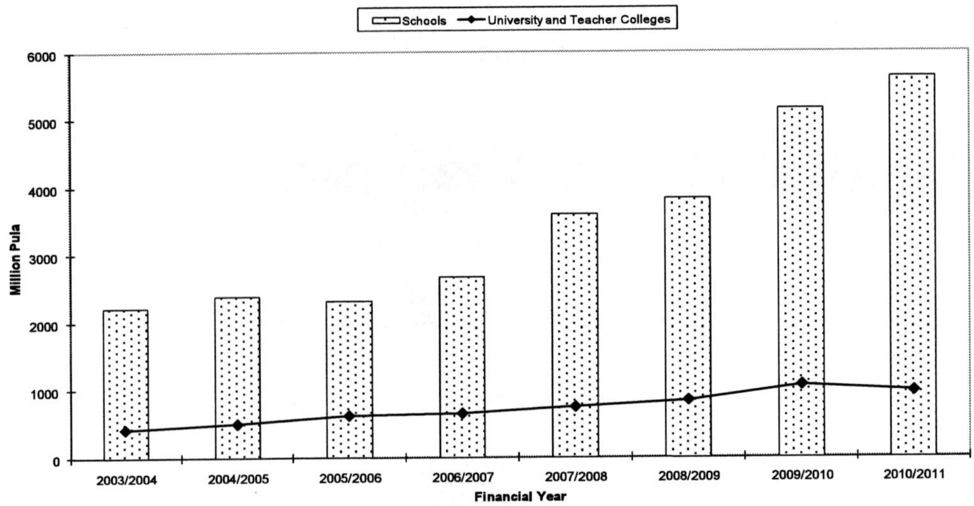

Figure 16.5. Trends in Public Spending between Schools and University and Teacher Colleges. Source: Ministry of Finance and Development Planning 2010.

Results of a Comparison of Expenditure for Primary Education between District Based and Urban Based Primary Schools

Public spending in district primary schools has relatively declined in 2010/2011 (Figure 16.6). The budget allocation for district schools in 2009/2010 was 40 per cent of the total three year budget for 2008/09 to 2010/2011 whereas the budget allocation for 2010/2011 is over 30 per cent of the total budget for that three year period, representing a relative decline in funds allocation to district primary schools.

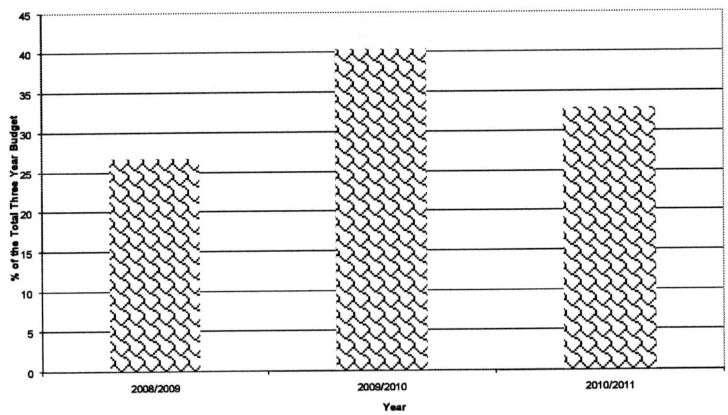

Figure 16.6. Public Spending in District Based Primary Schools. Source: Ministry of Local Government (2010).

The relative trend in budget allocation for a three year period from 2008/09 to 2010/2011 for urban schools shows an increasing trend (Figure 16.7). The share of urban schools budget in 2010/2011 was 40 per cent of the total budget for the three financial years period, higher than 36 per cent share for 2009/2010 and 24 per cent for the 2008/2009 financial year just before the peak of global financial crisis.

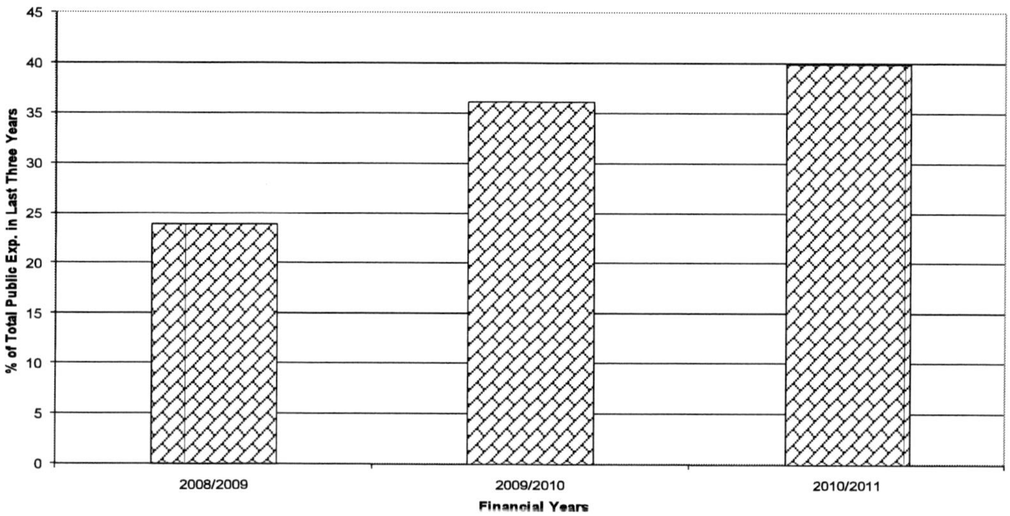

Figure 16.7. Public in Urban Primary Schools. Source: Ministry of Local Government 2010.

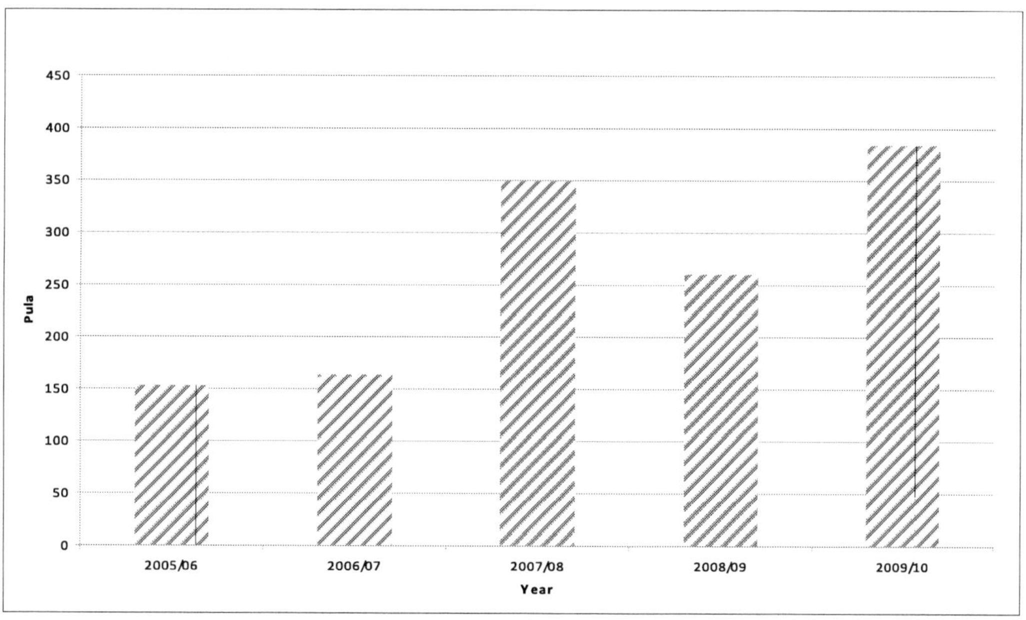

Figure 16.8. Cost in Pula per Pupil in District Schools. Source: Ministry of Local Government and Lands.

Figure 16.8, illustrates the yearly cost of schooling per pupil in district schools in Botswana. The trends in government payments towards schooling of each pupil in district schools shows an overall positive rise from P150.00 per pupil per year in 2005/06 to about P380.00 per pupil per year in 2009/10. However, in 2008/2009, the year of the global financial crises, district pupils experienced a reduction in government support from P350, in 2007/08 to P250.00 in 2008/09.

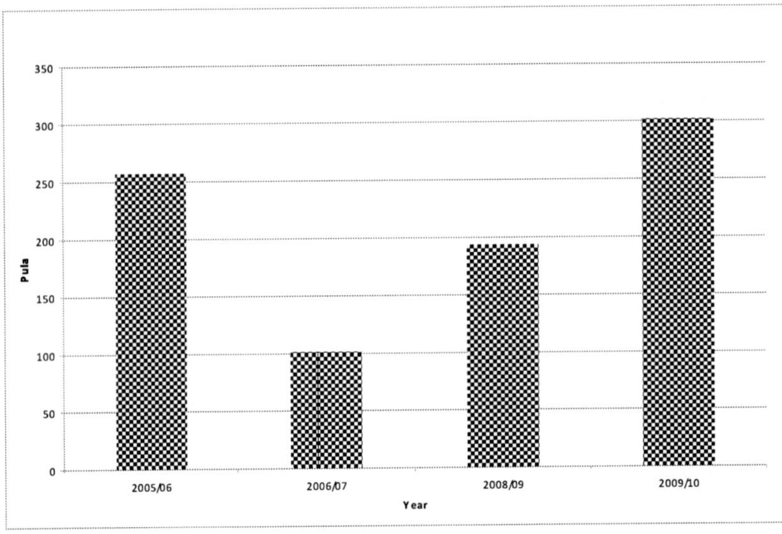

Figure 16.9. Cost in Pula per Pupil in Urban Schools. Source: Ministry of Local Government (2010).

The trend in yearly cost per pupil in urban areas is illustrated in Figure 16.9. In 2005/06, the government expenditure per pupil per year in urban primary schools was P250.00, which was higher than P150.00 primary schooling cost per pupil per year in district schools. However, in 2006/07, the cost of schooling a pupil per year in urban schools dropped to P100.00 and thereafter the trend was positive up to 2009/10. Although the government expenditure per pupil per year in 2008/09 increased to about P200.00, even though this was a year of global economic recession, the cost of schooling a child in urban schools was lower than that of schooling a child in district schools, which was P250.00 in the same year. In 2009/10, government expenditure on educating a pupil a year in urban schools increased to P300.00. Despite this increment in government expenditure per child per year in urban schools, the value was still smaller than the expenditure of government on a pupil per year in district schools that rose to P380.00.

DISCUSSION OF THE RESULTS

Progress in Contribution to Poverty Eradication and Inequality

Botswana's fiscal policy response after the 2008/2009 global economic recession maintained a positive trend in public spending on the education sector. This was a bold endorsement of government's commitment to the Vision 2016 Pillar of an "Informed and Educated Nation" as one of the primary instruments of poverty eradication in the long run. Maintaining a positive trend in education expenditure, despite the difficult global financial crisis of 2009, is strong signal that Botswana government believes is a key factor of production that can increase productivity and wealth for redistribution and poverty eradication. Although, public expenditure at primary school level shows that government increased financial support for urban schools when that for district (rural) based schools declined during the period 2008/09 to 2009/2010, the actual expenditure of government for schooling per child per year remained considerably higher for rural children than for children in urban areas. If the level of expenditure per pupil per year of schooling is used to determine whether government is addressing problems of inequality through expenditure in education, the answer is positive.

Impact of the Budget Cuts in Botswana in 2009/10 on Schooling by Rural and Urban Districts

Although Botswana experienced increased deficit problems in 2009/10 financial year which led to immediate budget cuts that affected many sectors of the economy, the overall budget for the education sector increased. During that year, the budget for urban schools increased while that for rural schools was reduced. Despite the cuts in rural schools budget, the individual benefit in terms of government expenditure per child in rural schools remained higher than that for a child attending in an urban school. Therefore, the effect of budget cuts as a result of the 2008/09 global recession were observed by cuts to expenditure in rural schools budget, but the pupils in the rural schools retained a higher spending benefit per pupil than those in urban schools.

Budget Adjustments to Shocks and Overall Botswana Poverty Eradication Objectives

If expenditure on public education implies increased acquisition of knowledge which is known as a major contributor to productivity and increased personal income opportunities, then the trend in public spending on education in Botswana suggests that the country will continue to experience declining poverty trends. High expenditure per child per year in rural areas, even when there was a negative shock in the economy because of the global recession means that the children in rural area's opportunities were maintained. If the schools themselves improve productivity and rural schools pass rate improve, then these children have a better chance of escaping poverty. Moepeng (2010) has shown that in rural Botswana, despite lack of relevant job opportunities for educated residents, there are many opportunities for the educated as a result of no restrictions of migration within the country.

LIMITATIONS OF THE STUDY

Access to data that can reveal overall funding expenses in the primary education of Botswana was very difficult. Primary education funding in Botswana is managed through three different ministries. The Office of the President through the Department of Public Service Management manages teachers' salaries and has no disaggregated data that differentiates teachers spending by school type and location. Hence this data could not be used. The Ministry of Education is responsible for teaching curriculum and quality of education and also had no disaggregated data available to show amounts spent for rural education and those for urban areas. The Ministry of Local Government budget allocation and spending information on primary schools is for school books, stationary, teaching materials, food and accommodation; and office equipment and furniture. This study has therefore assumed that the criterion for allocating teachers for both rural and urban schools is uniform.

CONCLUSIONS

Botswana economy experienced budget cuts in 2009/10 in response to the effects of the global economic recession that began towards the end of 2008/09. However, the budget for the education sector was instead increased, while other sectors such as health, social welfare and defense were experiencing cuts in spending. Within the education sector, budget cuts were observed in budget allocations for district schools while the budget for urban schools was increased. Despite these budget cuts in rural schools spending, the amount of funds spent on each child in rural schools per year remained higher than for each child attending public school in urban areas. If we assume everything else is uniform, the information about government expenditure per child per year between rural and urban schools suggest that government gives education a high priority instrument that contribute to poverty eradication. Therefore, if expenditure on schooling also suggests that expected outcomes will be positive, then children in rural areas of Botswana who attend public schools have an equal opportunity to escape from poverty as are children attending public schools in urban areas. Therefore, we can infer that, if there are no exceptional negative circumstances between now and 2016, rural poverty will be much lower in the year 2016 than is the case today.

REFERENCES

Bardhan, P. and Udry, C. (1999), 'Development Microeconomics', *Oxford University Press,* Oxford.

Central Statistics Office (2006) 2005/06 Labour Force Survey Preliminary Results, viewed 01/08/ 2007, http://www.cso.gov.bw/.

Central Statistics Office, (2009), 'Education Statistics 2009', *Government Printer*, Gaborone.

Central Statistics Office Botswana (2004), 'Household Income and Expenditure Survey' 2002/03, *Government Printer,* Gaborone.

Datt, G. and Ravallion, M. (1998), 'Why have some Indian States Done Better than Others in Reducing Rural Poverty', *Economica,* 65, pp. 17-38.

McTaggart;, D., Findlay;, C. and Parkin, M. (1999), 'Economics' Third Edition, Pearson Education Australia Pty Limited, Sydney.

Ministry of Finance and Development Planning (2010), *Consolidated Budget Estimates,* MFDP, Gaborone.

Ministry of Local Government (2010), Summary of Estimated Income for Years 2005/06 to 2010/11, MLG, Gaborone.

Moepeng, P. (2010), 'Rural Poverty in Botswana', Lambert Academic Publishing, Germany.

Schultz, T. P. (1988), 'Education Investments and Returns', in H. Chenery and T. N. Srinivasan (eds), *Handbook of Development Economics,* Elsevier Science Publishers, New York, I.

Todaro, M. P. (1981), Economic Development in the Third World, Longman Inc., New York.

UNDP (2003), 'Human Development Report: Millenium Development Goals', *Human Development Report.*

In: Development Management in the Twenty-First Century
Editors: Kartik Roy and Sandip Kar
ISBN: 978-1-62100-699-2

Chapter 17

A REVIEW OF ETHICAL ISSUES IN HEALTHCARE SERVICE

Prasanta K. Padhy [*,1] ***and Suresh Patnaik*** [†,2]
[1] Professor and Chairman- Board of Studies,
Department of Business Administration, Berhampur University, Orissa, India
[2] Assistant Professor, National Institute of Science and Technology, Palur Hills,
Berhampur, Orissa, India

INTRODUCTION

Healthcare is one of India's largest sectors, in terms of revenue and employment, and the sector is expanding rapidly. During the 1990s, Indian healthcare grew at a compound annual rate of 16%. Today the total value of the sector is more than $34 billion. This translates to $34 per capita, or roughly 6% of GDP. By 2012, India's healthcare sector is projected to grow to nearly $40 billion. The Federal emphasis on preventing healthcare fraud and abuse has provided a strong incentive for healthcare organizations to get their own programs in place to ensure that nothing illegal is occurring.

Cost of care can also be contained if the service levels in public sector can be substantially improved, referral systems enforced and the unfinished agenda of controlling infectious diseases achieved. The existing financing and payment systems are not suitable for countering market failures typical of insurance. Insurance services without availability of reasonable quality healthcare service delivery will not serve the intended purpose. It is necessary to ensure availability of health services for any insurance scheme to succeed.

The ethical problems of "trivial" or of chronic illness that the physician sees in his or her everyday life are discussed much less these days than the more spectacular and flamboyant ones deal with mercy killing, abortion or genetic manipulation. These problems are the far more frequent and often more vexing ethical problems that practicing physicians face today. They range from truth telling on disability forms, to the unwillingness of a managed care

* profpadhy@hotmail.com.
† sureshpreeti@yahoo.com.

organization to allow a procedure considered necessary by the physician, to dealing with inquiries about patients by persons the physician does not know, or to being frank with a patient who has been grossly mistreated by another physician with something which should have been remedied long before.

INDIAN HEALTHCARE SYSTEM: AN OVERVIEW

According to a study on the burden of diseases in India (NCMH, 2005), the number of Cardiovascular diseases is expected to rise from the level of 38 million in 2005 to 64 million by 2015, Diabetes from 30 million in 2005 to 45 million cases by 2015, and Cancer from 2 million in 2005 to 2.5 million cases by 2015. Today, nearly 50 percent of the world population is urban. India's urban population of 300 million represents 30 percent of our population. An urban slum growth rate of 5 percent is causing serious concern for the civic and health authorities in municipalities and towns. Health of urban poor and its implications on the entire urban population should be analyzed and an appropriate urban health policy should be arrived at.

Contaminated water and poor sanitation is responsible for large proportion of diseases in India. Poor hygiene and sanitation account for 9 percent of all deaths and an estimated 27.4 million years of life are lost each year in India. The Government's contribution to the total healthcare expenditure is only 20 percent, and therefore out-of-pocket expenditure is as high as 80 percent. The cost of healthcare is increasing rapidly. A large majority of India's population cannot afford healthcare expenses. In India, there are 16,000 hospitals with about 1 million beds. The average size of a private hospital is 22 beds, much lower than developed economies. India has only about 100 beds per 100,000 populations against the WHO norms of 300 beds per 100,000. The number of doctors per 1,000 population is also well below the WHO norms.

The provision of healthcare in India varies by state, with private healthcare accounting for more than 50 percent of all inpatients and more than 80 percent of all outpatients. Healthcare funding is primarily sourced from private out-of-pocket funds and accounts for more than 75 percent of the total healthcare spending. The demand supply gap is therefore large. Investment required to bridge the gap in the next ten years could range from Rs. 100,000 crore to Rs. 140,000 crore.

The development of organized private sector healthcare is a relatively recent phenomenon in India and focuses primarily on large super-specialty hospitals in urban locations. According to a report by McKinsey, outpatient care constitutes nearly two-thirds of the total healthcare spend by patients .And the domiciliary healthcare market, even in large cities, is extremely fragmented and unorganized. At the same time, urban Indians are subject to an increasing number of lifestyle diseases, and India is often cited as the world's capital for diabetes and cardiac ailments. Less than 5 percent of the population in India is covered by health insurance, resulting in almost 65 percent of healthcare spending being out of pocket. One Doctor is available for 20,000 patients.

The National Rural Health Mission (NRHM) is an articulation of the commitment of the Government of India to raise public spending on Health. It seeks to provide effective health care to the entire rural population in the country with special focus on 18 States which have weak public health indicators. It aims to undertake architectural correction of the health system to enable it to effectively handle increased allocations. It has as its key components provision of a health activist in each village; a village health plan prepared through a local team headed by the panchayat representative, strengthening of the rural hospital for effective curative care and made measurable through Indian Public Health Standards (IPHS) and accountable to the community; and integration of vertical Health & Family Welfare Programs and Funds for optimal utilization of funds and infrastructure and strengthening delivery of primary healthcare. Above all, it seeks to improve access of rural people, especially poor women and children, to equitable, affordable, accountable and effective primary healthcare. Reduction in Infant Mortality Rate and Maternal Mortality Ratio by 50% from existing levels in next 7 years is also an important objective of NRHM. Those who believe health care is an individual right support a universal health care system with the argument that every citizen deserves to have access to the right care at the right time and that a government's responsibility is to protect its citizens, sometimes even from themselves. Examinations of the ethical issues in health care reform are therefore of paramount importance as: "How should we as a society be acting so that our actions are morally correct rather than individually gainful?" Here are some questions that could be used in ethical decision making for health care reform. What action will bring the most good to the most people? What action in and of itself is a good act and helps us to fulfill our duties, obligations, and responsibilities to each other? What action in and of itself shows caring and concern for all citizens?

QUEST FOR ETHICS IN HEALTHCARE SERVICE

Ethics and morals are the words derived from Greek 'ethos' and Latin 'mores' respectively. Both of them seek to explain the custom, manners, or the disposition peculiar to a given people. In answering the question "How should *we* live?" one engages in a consideration of ethics—thinking about what is right and wrong. Ethics requires that we engage and offers a check on our moral intuitions as well as an opportune action and thus find better ways to live. Intuitively it is known to the doctors that prescribing penicillin to a patient with pneumococcal pneumonia is largely (but not merely) a "technical" matter, whereas not supplying nourishment to a terminally ill patient is largely (but not solely) an "ethical" one. Ethics is concerned with two key concepts: the concept of "good" and the more broadly, in defining the good concept of "right." The quest for the summum bonum—the ultimate good, that which is good in itself—is sometimes seen as the greatest good in a hierarchy of goods (e.g., rationality, for Aristotle), sometimes as the common denominator of all other goods (e.g., pleasure, for the hedonist), and, at times, as an almost mystical, religious good (e.g., God, for the religious).

ETHICAL DILEMMA IN HEALTHCARE SERVICE

Ethical choices in healthcare are also confronted with the dilemma. All physicians are trained to watch scientific changes and to intervene in the biological process so as to support homeostatic mechanisms tending to promote life and health. However, such work is difficult, demands a great deal of skill, and is often perplexing. Problems among the physicians are too critical and too close to the weal and woe of real people to permit the evading of choices. When healthcare professionals only pose the "can" question ("can I do something?"—e.g., treat a condition or make a diagnosis), and evade the more troubling "ought" question ("ought I to do what I can do?"—e.g., treat a condition or make a diagnosis), technology ultimately will drive itself.

Let us examine our own experience of getting severely hurt when we witness "hit and run" accidents—whether made with the best intentions or not. But hitting the bumper of the car parked in front of us without any visible damage is rather different from denting the same car and is again quite a different matter than hitting a pedestrian and leaving the scene.

In healthcare we need clearer instructions than "all medical mistakes" which may range from the trivial (viz: the doctor administered i.v. on a patient 15 minutes late"), to the fatal. Physicians are frequently confronting these issues merely not because of such mistakes, but because they too often create the impression of liability to patient and their family. Hence, one of the obligations that physician and allied health-care professionals have is to work towards creating a system with sufficient "fail-safe" mechanisms in the healthcare setting.

For example, a neglected colonoscopy may result in the late detection of a cancer that the physician who knows the patient suspects on grounds that do not quite meet the accepted criteria. Inventing blood in the stool (when none has been present) may need desired test but puts the physician into the position of lying and undermines the habit of truthfulness. The habit of truthfulness is not peculiar to health-care ethics but rather is a general and generally accepted principle of ethical behavior—no matter what system of ethics to which one may appeal. Patients who are ill enough and who know that they will require such illness to be certified are arguably obliged to communicate with their physician and get his or her recommendation to stay at home. However, patients may afterwards beseech their physician to withhold certain information. Hence, the questions we must clearly address are: (1) what is error in the medical setting? (2) how and by whom should an error be discussed with the patient or his/her family? (3) are the physicians obliged to reveal an error made by a previous physician, especially when they have referred the patient to a super-speciality hospital? More difficult than revealing one's own error is revealing to the patient that a prior (or referring) physician has made a severe blunder. Misdiagnosis or mistreatment by another or—most unpleasant—referring physician, nevertheless, must also be addressed. From the above revelation of ethical dilemma, it is clear how chaotic and stressful such dilemmas are. But, with good decision making power and sound analytical ability, it is possible to resolve the ethical issues in the workplace effectively. President Barack Obama of US expressed his opinion about behaving in a scientific and responsible manner while handling issues related to medical ethics. "As our nation invests in science and innovation and pursues advances in biomedical research and health care, it's imperative that we do so in a responsible manner."

Emerging Ethical Principle

In human thinking perception, curiosity, imagination, reason and emotion interconnect in forming a judgment. Health-care ethics would be lost without curiosity and imagination. A differential diagnosis requires curiosity and enlists imagination as it brings what we have learned into sharper focus. In health-care ethics our curiosity (or sensitivity) recognizes that a problem exists and our imagination begins to present us with a variety of options as well as the pros and cons of each. Many—if not most—of the greatest advances in physiology, medicine and biochemistry were made because of a physician's curiosity. To suppress what is truly human about the profession in order to reduce costs (and increase profits for those outside the patient–physician relationship) seems ethically problematic and in the long run pragmatically counterproductive.

PATIENT'S RIGHTS TO REFUSE TREATMENT

The patient is the center of attention and, in this sense, is the key "customer." The patient is not always right about medical treatment, however, and should not always get what he or she wants. It is essential, for good-quality medical care and for the just management of healthcare organizations, to recognize that a patient does not have a legitimate claim to treatment that, on the basis of professional medical judgment, is recognized as futile or non-beneficial. When a patient or family wants "everything" done to extend life that should be understood to mean everything that is medically appropriate and indicated.

There is a need to understand clearly the ways in which respect for patient rights relates to a variety of ethical responsibilities. Medical ethicists have been engaged in ongoing reflections on the nature and limits of patient rights. Concern that patients are sometimes subjected to unwanted treatment, especially near the end of life, has led to an emphasis on the patient's right to refuse treatment. Concern that physicians are being forced to practice bad (futile) medicine has led to an effort to define the limits of the patient's right to demand specific treatment. Recognition of the importance of the non-dramatic ethical issues ("everyday ethics") has led to concern about the rights of patients in relationship to institutional practices and concerns. The growth of managed care has led to efforts to clarify the rights of patients as enrollees in health- care plans. The growing interest in complementary and alternative medicine may well lead to additional refinements of the meaning of patient rights.

This is not to say that patients should not inform their physicians about their own insights into their health and that they should not challenge what they consider to be questionable diagnoses and prescriptions. They should be encouraged to do both. Nevertheless, physicians have a responsibility to provide evidence-based treatment. It is not ethical medicine to provide patients with the treatment they want when the treatment is not indicated or there is no reasonable expectation that it will be beneficial. As healthcare professionals and the public continue to grapple with the purpose of medicine and the meaning of "medical benefit," greater agreement may gradually result. It is likely, though, to remain very difficult to implement a judgment of medical futility in some specific situations.

When patients are understood as individuals and as members of a larger community, healthcare organizations need policies in place that permit patient- requested or family-requested treatment to be withheld when it is judged to be medically non-beneficial. To protect from an expanding or an abusive use of the concept of futility, however, these policies should require procedural safeguards. In disputes over whether a particular treatment is futile, patient rights are best protected by ensuring that the decision is not implemented without due consideration and reconsideration, not by simply doing what the patient/family wants.

It is not satisfactory simply to try to please the "customer," to do whatever patients want in regard to the kind of persons that will care for them. Requests for care- givers of a particular race, or excluding a particular race, should rarely if ever be considered sufficiently relevant to the quality of care or to legitimate patient interests to be honored. Requests for caregivers of the same sex may sometimes be relevant in terms of quality of care or legitimate patient privacy interests.

The healthcare professionals may take the position that despite the fact that certain medical interventions or procedures are legal and some patients are seeking them. However, they might not provide them because such procedures are considered contrary to the ethical beliefs adhered to by the institution. Abortion is a commonly recognized example, but there are a variety of other procedures as well that are sometimes prohibited within an institution. These acts also include: assisted suicide (where legal), some forms of assisted reproduction, genetic testing for certain indications, research on human embryos, and sterilization.

Balancing the Cost, Care and Ethics

Many engaged in healthcare services find it quite uncomfortable while comparing financial implications of appropriate care. Their tendency is not to think that cost does not matter, but to think that cost has to do with the "business decisions," not with "ethics decisions." However, viewing cost and ethics as separate considerations has unfortunate consequences. Most importantly, it keeps us from doing the hard work of determining when and how counting the cost contributes to the understanding of what is most ethically appropriate. The question is whether these other considerations should take priority over cost savings. The question is what the proper balance between cost and other considerations is in patient care. Certain minimum standards of quality must be met for all patients. There is a minimum level of basic and essential healthcare service that must be provided to all for whom the community has responsibility. Patients are owed the services, if medically appropriate, included in the benefits package of their health plans.

Good-quality healthcare means delivery of healthcare services in the setting or location that is most appropriate both in regard to the patient's healthcare needs and in regard to costs. A commitment to serving patients without regard to the ability to pay or to the source of payment should not be interpreted to mean that cost concerns are inappropriate for such patients. Efforts to control costs always need to be evaluated in terms of their impact on patient care. A commitment to high-quality patient care may require strenuous efforts to get the payment system improved.

Conclusion

Healthcare professionals are first of all committed to their patient's good—that is generally understood as being committed to their good when it comes to matters directly associated with their sickness or health. They should aim at health care delivery to improve health, to alleviate disability, and to provide access to appropriate health services to all persons regardless of their ability to pay. Caring for sick people is a social obligation that extends beyond the commercial realm. Health care delivery institutions or other organizations that deliver medical care must therefore ascertain that their services are rendered and remunerated under the stewardship of those in the health care system rather than merely sold to individuals or communities. In order to develop a more inclusive understanding of healthcare ethics, many have been suggesting that there should be a strong and visible focus on "business ethics" in healthcare institutions and in the education of future healthcare executives.

Since the practice of medicine is a social task, both patient and healer must respect each other's personal morality and moral agency. While health-care providers cannot—and act ethically—impose their own personal morality on the patient neither can the patient ask physicians to violate their own personal morality. The health-care providers may not simply follow the dictates of rules promulgated by the government (and may, in fact, be faced with quite unpleasant choices) and blame "the system." They should also carry the heavy responsibility in trying to resist dictates deemed harmful to their patient. Above all, they have to carry not simply the responsibility of accommodating themselves or resisting a system someone else builds for them, but play their proper part in building a system which is equitable to all members of the community and flexible enough to change their overall healthcare scenario.

There are several rules of thumb: the first and perhaps most essential is that, according to society's understanding, physicians and other healthcare professionals are, above all (unless there are highly unusual circumstances to the contrary), committed to their patient's good. This is not only society's understanding but is also a claim repeatedly made by the profession itself. And that claim has, at least until recently, generally been justified and has formed one of the pillars of the patient-physician relationship. That health-care professionals bear primary loyalty to their patients is the case for a number of reasons: (1) the societal understanding of the role of physicians from ancient times to the present; (2) the words and actions of physicians who claim to be primarily interested in the patient's good; (3) an inevitable imbalance in power which, under almost all situations, places physicians as the more powerful partner and, therefore, as the partner obliged to use that power with due care. In this sense it is a fiduciary relationship in which the patient knowingly puts his or her trust in the physician.

REFERENCES

Bhanumathi, P. P. (1977), 'Nurses' Conception of the 'Sick-role' and 'Good-patient Behaviour': A Cross-cultural Comparison.' *International Nursing Review.* 24(1), pp. 20–24.

Dewey J, Logic: The Theory of Inquiry. New York, NY: *Henry Holt & Co.,* 1938.

Dewey, J. (1938), 'Logic- The Theory of Inquiry'. New York, NY: *Henry Holt.*

Gorovitz S, MacIntyre A. (1976), 'Towards a Theory of Medical Fallibility'. *Journal of Medical Philosophy.* 1(1), pp. 51–71.

K.V. Ramani and Dileep Mavalankar (2005), 'Health system in India: Opportunities and Challenges for Improvements', Indian Institute of Management, Ahmedabad, India.

Kottow, M. H. (1986), 'Medical Confidentiality: An Intransigent and Absolute Obligation.' *Journal of Medical Ethics.* 12, pp. 117–122.

Lifton R. (1986), 'The Nazi Doctors'. New York, NY: *Basic Books,* New York.

Loewy, E. H. (1987), 'Clergy and Physicians Encounter medical Ethics'. *Humane Medicine.* 3(1), pp. 48–51.

Loewy, E. H. (1994), 'Friendship and Medicine'. *Cambridge Q Health Care Ethics.* 3(1), pp. 52–59.

Loewy, Erich. H. (2002), 'Textbook of Healthcare Ethics'.Kluwer Academic Publishers, New York.

Parsons T. (1981), 'Definitions of Health and Illness in Light of American Values and Social Structure'. In: Caplan A, Engelhardt HT, McCartney JJ, eds. 'Concepts of Health and Disease'. *Reading, Mass: Addison-Wesley,* 57–82.

Pellegrino, E.D. (1979), 'Toward a Reconstruction of Medical Morality: the Primacy of the Act of Profession and the Fact of Illness'. *Journal of Medical Philosophy*, 4(1), pp. 32–55.

Siegler M. (1982), 'Confidentiality in Medicine: A Decrepit Concept'. *New England Journal of Medicine.* 307(24), pp.1518–1521.

Szasz, T. S., Hollender, M. H. (1956), 'The Basic Models of the Doctor–Patient Relationship'. *Archive of International Medicine,* 97, pp. 585–592.

In: Development Management in the Twenty-First Century ISBN: 978-1-62100-699-2
Editors: Kartik Roy and Sandip Kar

Chapter 18

MANAGEMENT OF BEGGING AS ECONOMIC ACTIVITY UNDER CURRENT LAW IN INDIA

Subas C. Kumar*
Reader and Head, Department of Economics,
P. N. (Autonomous) College, Khordha, Orissa, India

INTRODUCTION

Days are over, when giving alms to beggars was considered as a part of religious, ritual and cultural activities. Today, it is increasingly believed that begging is an act of choice, fraud and organized crime. It is also referred as an informal economic activity in the sense that it is a part of "those economic activities that circumvent the costs and are excluded from the benefits and rights ......of formal society" (Feige 1990). Abject poverty, lack of education, lack of employable skill and employment opportunities are some of the important factors put forward to justify the reasons (of begging), as to why people beg for ? Or why do they join this marginalized informal economic activity? Thus, it is debatable whether begging as an income generating activity, is a matter of choice or compulsion.

Even if for the time being, it is accepted that people do start begging due to pressing compulsions, but why they do not prefer to undertake other avenues of income generating activities in informal sector like any other poor people do? Or is it an easier means of earning income? Does begging fetch substantial income and confirms to the work values? Because work by human beings is regarded as a "value in its own right, a noble and ennobling activity" (Bauman 1998). It is the nature of work performed brings status and enhances a person's identity. Thus, begging as an informal economic activity poses several issues like those raised above.

Against such a backdrop, an attempt has been made in this paper to reassess the common understanding of begging as informal economic activity of rational choice on the basis of demand for and supply of beggars. The paper also highlights the determinants of demand for anti-begging policy in general and the current Indian law in particular. It explores the

* kumar_orissa@yahoo.com.

implications of anti-begging legislation from the perspective of beggar's liberty and right to plead for subsistence while making suggestions for effective management of begging problems.

DEMAND FOR AND SUPPLY OF BEGGARS

According to a recent survey by Delhi School of Social Work (DSSW), the number of beggars has increased by almost a lakh during the last decade. There are some 60,000 beggars in Delhi and over 3, 00,000 in Mumbai (Action Aid: 2004), nearly 75,000 in Kolkata as per the Beggar Research Institute. According to police records there are 56,000 beggars in Bangalore. In Hyderabad, one in every 354 people is engaged in begging according to Council of Human Welfare report, 2005. The presence of these beggars is found in all most all locations i.e. at traffic posts, railway stations, bus stops, places of worship, footpaths and even in front of houses. Their presence in large number makes us to believe that people are still willing to opt for the age-old traditional begging occupation. In a market economy, the supply of any thing envisages or point to the inevitability of demand for it.

Supply of Beggars

One of the fundamental assumptions that form the basis of several laws and theories in economics is the rational behaviour of individuals. A rational individual always tries to maximize his/her satisfaction as a consumer, output as a producer, earnings as a wage earner and so on. Thus, given the rationality in the earning behaviour of individuals, it is expected that they opt for a profession or any economic activity in which not only their earnings but also happiness are maximized. Amidst the various constraints such as skill, physical capability, education, family and social tradition etc. one has to make a choice among occupations where he/she could realize pre-set goals with the best of his/her ability and capability. People also consider some other equally important criteria while making a decision to join in a profession/job such as self esteem, scope for career advancement, work environment, leisure and flexibility in working hours etc.

Let us consider the case of begging as an economic activity/ profession and find out the extent to which it satisfies the characteristics of a good job. There is no gainsaying of the fact that begging is always considered as a degrading occupation and a shameful activity. As regards prestige and self-esteem begging is found at the lowest rung of the job ladder. Even socially most hated job like prostitution is preferred to begging (HR Focus 1991). Thus, an individual joins the supply group of beggars, not because of self-esteem attached to the profession; it is due to either some compulsions or other induced factors. It implies that given the constraints of beggary if alternative jobs can be made available for them, the supply of beggars will decline.

Similarly, given the skill and competency an individual will prefer to join a profession if he considers that the average earning is substantial and stable in nature. Ordinarily, it cannot be believed that earnings from begging are substantial and stable; although studies reveal that in some cases/places the average earning of a beggar is more than the earning of a manual wage earner if calculated at the rate of minimum wage for normal working hours. The study, conducted by Subrata De (2005) in nine cities of four States, suggested that 85 per cent of the destitutes were earning far below the poverty line before they got into this practice. Most of the beggars are into it, not out of choice but out of compulsions. Several research findings (Ross, Fisher et al. 1986, Goldstein 1993, Lankenau 1999) indicate that beggars generally earn the same or less than the average earning of a full time wage earner at minimum wage rate. All the hypotheses that the begging yields an income above the poverty line, brings in earnings comparable to prostitution, and leads to a higher income for the migrant beggars and for beggars accompanied by children were summarily rejected by Stefan Adriaenssens and Jef Hendrickx (2008) in their research findings. Thus, it is the low wage and increasing unemployment in other economic activities push many people to the beggary. Their supply increases with the rise of unemployment and decline of wage rate.

The study made by Kassah (2007) reveals that several beggars tried to earn income through other means of economic activity but forced to begging either due to natural or unnatural forces. Further, unlike other professions there is neither a scope for career advancement nor a pleasant working environment for beggars. They are often subjected to violence in the streets and silently listen to filthy language and tolerate abuses without any protest.

The above facts clearly invalidate the general understanding that begging is a rational choice of individuals. More and more numbers of people are becoming beggars (supply of beggars is rising) because they are the victims of abject poverty, low wage, higher unemployment, lack of education and training, disability, mental illness, trafficking etc. At the same time, it would be wrong to dispute with the fact that some lazy and educated people (who, however, constitute a minority) too form the part of supply of beggars. They prefer to enjoy leisure and maximum freedom at work at the expense of their self-prestige and earning.

Demand for Beggars

The theory of economics holds that if there is a demand there will be a supply. The trend of increasing beggary not only suggests but also provides sufficient evidence towards inevitability of beggars in a market economy. In this shameful trade, it would be wrong to blame organized mafias alone but as a matter of fact the major blame has to be laid at the door of economic system and the society at large that continues to feed the demand for beggars. This can be substantiated from the findings of the survey made by the National Opinion Center, 1989, which revealed that the occupational prestige score of begging was 11, not zero. Thus, their presence in large numbers demonstrates the compassion and generosity that informs a large part of our civil society.

The religious people indulge beggars on the ground that they provide them with the opportunities to earn merit and the blessings of GOD. There are instances to show that people engaged in religious services contribute a larger portion of their income to charity (Independent sector 1992).

Many of us particularly reformists, social activists, and liberal political outfits attribute the rising trend of beggars in India to the failure of planned economic development and its assumption of so called trickle-down-effect. They observe that the benefits of development by-passed the poorest of the poor and reached those who needed them the least. The beggar-the poorest of the poor, therefore, needs to be supported through alms to save them from social exclusion and as an act of protest against the pro-rich socio-economic system.

In addition, the Indians are very emotional, kind hearted and believe in mutual help. A large number of people enjoy and derive satisfaction by giving alms to the beggars.

A demand-driven begging is no more elusive in the regime of increasing urbanization, which co-exists with the vast backward rural areas. There is a great demand for 'helpless-looking' children, which the beggars outsource from rural areas (Basu 2008). Basu reported about one such agency in Kolkata named as Pathshishu, which takes the children to the beggars in the morning and returns them to their parents in the evening-all for a fee of course. The child beggars, out of other categories of beggars are more in demand because they can easily draw the attention of passersby. In this regard, it is highly relevant to quote the speech of Mr. K.M. Munshi-the former home minister of Government of Bombay delivered at the Tata Graduate School of Social Work.

"Beggary would not be a profitable trade, if there were no children to attract the customer's attention. The beggar child, therefore, is the most valuable asset in the trade; and as such is sold, bartered or mortgaged".

In sum, begging as a profession or a marginalized economic activity will continue to thrive till there is a change in our religious behaviour, liberal attitude and alternation of the development policy, which are skewed in favour of the rich and the famous.

THE NEED FOR ANTI-BEGGING LEGISLATION

In recent years, there is a rising demand for eliminating beggars through anti-begging legislation. Several arguments are put forward to justify that begging is no less than a crime and the beggars are the social parasites. The advocates for it strongly argue that begging causes more harm than good to the society and an anti-begging law can solve the problem. Arguments put forward and reasons provided in support of anti-begging legislation can be briefly summarized as follows.

a) Begging is often considered as one of the antisocial behaviours clubbed with teenage vandalism, rowdiness, eve teasing, defacing walls with graffiti, sleeping in public place benches, public urination etc. The believers of 'broken windows' hypothesis (Wilson and Kelling 1986) are of the opinion that by eliminating low-level street disorder, more serious crime can be avoided.
b) It is alleged that begging in the streets negatively affects the public safety. The aggressive beggars often harass the pedestrians. Their activities at the traffic posts, bus stops and busy business centers cause traffic jam and accidents.
c) The business people contend that presence of beggars in large numbers has an adverse effect on their business because they deter potential customers.
d) Middle class elites feel that begging signals social decay and invites crime. Kelling and Coles (1996) in their article, 'Fixing Broken Windows' strongly advocated that beggars are a primary source of the kind of 'urban chaos' in which crime is alleged to flourish.

e) Some people are of the view that they are lazy; they do not work but earn their living as a parasite. They are worthless in their very nature.
f) Increase of beggars in a particular place increases the density of population and their activities create fears among the residents of that locality. This hypothesis holds that the beggars threat to one's economic security and quality of life.
g) It is also argued that the beggars are the soft target of mafias. Mafias and gangs abduct children and maim them to maximize their earning. In the process, the beggars are pushed to participate in organized crime.
h) The rich and middle class people often consider them a threat to their idealized and sanitized image.
i) Begging is a public nuisance and a threat to tourism. This argument is better known as 'hygiene argument', which holds that communities need to regulate public spaces in order to prevent or minimize chronic street nuisances.
j) Educated mass speak in favour of organized charity and against alms giving to individual beggar because they believe that beggars can be better helped through organized charity.
k) It is also argued that beggars are the victims of abject poverty due to their personal failings and therefore, society cannot be blamed as a whole.

All these arguments and hypotheses, intend to prove that the beggars are essentially engaged in illicit commercial transaction and therefore, no special attention should be given to them by the Government. On the other hand, they contend that there is a need to have anti-begging legislation to deal with the begging problem putting it on par with other criminal activities. The arguments in favour of anti-begging legislation, (a) that begging causes serious social harm and (b) criminalisation of begging will reduce or eliminate all public nuisances, however, need to be examined and critiqued.

Current Begging Law in India

Anti-Begging Act in India is an extension of the antiquated Bombay Prevention of Begging Act, 1959, which makes begging in public places a crime and a punishable offence. The law provides for jailing beggars up to three years and the term can be extended up to 10 years in case of repeated offences. The Act defines beggars as people "---------having no visible means of subsistence and wandering about or remaining in any public place in such condition or manner (as) makes it likely that the person doing so exists by soliciting or receiving alms". The scope of the Act is not confined to those seeking alms but covers all traditional artists, as singing, dancing, and fortune telling, performing or offering any article for sale. All these activities are deemed as offences under this Act. It is therefore, morally perplexing that in 21st century India, destitute beggars are considered as criminals and they are punishable under the law. According to Neeta Lal, a noted journalist of Delhi, the Act suffers from serious lacunae. Firstly, it addresses any one who appears 'poor' and 'destitute'. She observed that both the definitions are nebulous and open to the vagaries of time and whims of an inspector. A rag picker or a migrant labourer- who may never have been begged in his/her life – can be picked up at random and incarcerated in a beggar's home. Secondly, the nature of the Act itself is punitive, which makes the poor criminally responsible for their position. Moreover, the criminalisation of begging, has given rise to many contentious issues leading to clash of competing values such as social hygiene vs. freedom of expression; middle class discomfort vs. under class economic need and commercial interests of downtown business owners vs. beggar's right to plead for subsistence (Schafer 2007).

All these issues directly or indirectly pose challenge to any form of anti-begging legislation, intend to treat begging at par with other criminal activities and go against the liberty and rights of the beggars-the poorest of the poor in the society.

There is hardly any doubt that beggars are a seriously marginalized group in our society. They are almost always poor, frequently homeless, often suffering from extremely poor health, mental illness, and substance abuse, with few social support and even fewer opportunities to make their plight known to the policy makers of the country. They are socially excluded and trapped in a vicious circle of poverty and deprivation.

There is a substantial body of literature (Fontain 1967, Rodger et al. 1994, Silver 1994, Kumar 1999) on various dimensions of social exclusion. The beggars are the victims of all forms of social exclusion such as (a) exclusion due to abject poverty; (b) exclusion from employment and means of livelihood; (c) exclusion from housing; (d) exclusion from property (land) ownership; (e) exclusion from education; (f) exclusion from health services; (g) exclusion of old and infirm; (h) exclusion of windows, handicaps and disease; (i) exclusion of orphan children and a few more.

The dimensions of social exclusion become more comprehensive from the viewpoint of disadvantaged and marginalized class when notion of 'right' is incorporated in it, because exclusion of these people not only snatch away their 'entitlement' but also violate individual 'liberty'. For example, it is tantamount to violation of human right if there is exclusion from right to speak freely or peacefully seeking alms, right to express difficulties or right to have secured childhood.

BEYOND ANTI-BEGGING LEGISLATION

Begging is a complex social problem. It is primarily a problem of social exclusion. While analyzing the supply of beggars, it was observed that baring a few, no rational individual will like to become a beggar at the cost his/her self-prestige. Begging is usually the last resort to supplement income and satisfy subsistence needs. It is therefore, essential to conceive begging as a social and economic issue rather than a criminal activity. The beggars may look alike but the extent of deprivation among them is highly skewed owing to differences in their types and sources. Therefore, an anti-begging Act cannot bring any solution to the begging problem unless beggars are classified and treated according to the needs of each individual beggar.

Katayun H. Cama (1945) in her seminal article classified beggars into 15 categories such as (1) The child beggar, (2) The physically defective, (3) The mentally defective and mentally ill, (4) The diseased, (5) The able-bodied, (6) The religious mendicant, (7) The bogus religious mendicant, (8) The tribal beggar, (9) The employed beggar, (10) The small-trade beggar, (11) The temporarily unemployed who are employable, (12) The temporarily unemployed who are unemployable, (13) The somewhat permanently unemployed who are employable, (14) The permanently unemployed and unemployable, (15) The permanently unemployed who are viciously or incorrigibly unwilling to work.

While recognizing that her classification of beggars may not be an exhaustive one, she provided a detailed analysis of the nature and background of all these beggars. Her analysis clearly envisages that the need and intensity of destitution among the beggar groups widely vary. Therefore, there is no gainsaying of the fact that an anti-begging law, if applied uniformly, would certainly have disproportionate and detrimental effects on beggars.

Government agencies claim that there are beggar homes and rehabilitation centers; there is support and treatment available for their health needs and so on. In spite of their laudable claims, thousands of beggars are found in the nook and corner of each urban area of India. It implies that there are significant gaps in service provisions for the vulnerable population.

WHAT THE PUBLIC THINK

In order to ascertain the attitude of public towards beggars, 74 people from different strata such as teachers, lawyers, government employees, students, educated youth, housewives, religious people and police were interviewed during the month of September 2010 with the help of a well-structured interview schedule. The students of the Department of Economics, P.N. (Autonomous) College, Khurda, Orissa conducted the interview.

All most all people interviewed said that by far begging is a non-threatening and a passive activity. More than 97 per cent said that they give alms to beggars. Less than 3 per cent held that begging should be treated at par with other criminal activities if we want a beggar free society. On the other hand, majority were of the view that beggars genuinely need help. When asked how best to deal with the situation, except two out of 74 said that anti-begging law does not provide any solution to the problem rather, access to housing, education, training, employment and income source would certainly minimize their number to a considerable level if not completely eliminates begging from the society. Further, they stated that a stringent law banning begging might not facilitate social inclusion, which should be primary aim of such legislation.

RECOMMENDATIONS

The factors responsible for rising number of beggars as discussed in this paper prove beyond doubt that begging is not a profession by choice but a compulsion for most of the types of beggars. Therefore, legal penalties cannot be assumed to provide the best alternative available to manage the problem of begging and the inclusion of beggars into the mainstream society. Abject poverty and homelessness are the two main reasons attributable for rising number of beggars in India. Poverty situation in India or elsewhere is never been uniform in terms of intensity and severity among different classes of people. Therefore, Das Gupta (1993) in his study included social and political dimensions of poverty, or rather well-being. The most notable distinction he made is 'freedom vs. rights'. Similarly, Jean Dreze and Sen tried to explain social exclusion on the basis of 'capabilities and entitlements'.

Managing the begging problems and overcoming the aspects of social exclusion attached to it, is a herculean task for every one serious about finding a solution for it. The complexity of the beggar problem necessitates planning and effective implementation of multiple development programmes. Any development programme or a measure initiated by the Government, which benefits the beggars by enlarging the scope for 'social unit' and provide 'economic security' and 'safety' must be appreciated. Against this backdrop it is recommended that:

- In the context of poverty driven begging, the 'bottom-up' solutions will be better alternatives to the 'top-down' coercive legislation. Increasing emphasis should be laid on management strategies and measures to counteract deprivation, leading to social problems like begging. The bottom-up solutions need to be designed and executed in such a way that the supply of beggars is checked at source.
- Special provisions should be made in the development planning for destitute beggars. This would include facilities, which are easily accessible and provide employment opportunities with an assured income.
- Access to accommodation with minimum facilities to conduct daily life.
- Special service centers for health care and detoxification.
- Educational and recreational facilities especially for child beggars.
- Special anti-poverty pragrammes for beggars.
- Public-private peoples' participation (PPPP) in planning and implementation of programmes should be encouraged.
- Welfare of beggars should form one of the important priorities of Corporate Social Responsibility (CSR) programme of corporate houses.
- Policy to affect both demand and supply side of the problem.

In short, the society must be prepared to invest to meet their needs. Some of the State Governments in India have initiated programmes along these lines with moderate success. It is due to lack of adequate funding and political mindset. All the above bottom-up measures are no doubt expensive but will contribute significantly to ease the beggar problems and facilitate in the restoration of their self-dignity, freedom of expression and liberty.

REFERENCES

Action Aid (2004), New Delhi.

Barnabas, J. (1945), 'Legislation relating to Beggary', in J.M. Kumarapa, Eds., *Our Beggar Problem: How to Tackle It?* Bombay: Padma Publications Ltd.

Basu, Sreya. (2008), 'In Kolkata, an agency that supplies child beggars', *Thaindian News.* July-23, 2008.

Bauman, Z. (1998), 'Work, consumerism and the new poor', Buckingham, UK: *Open University Press.*

Cama, Katayun.H. (1945), 'Types of Beggars' in J.M. Kumarapa Eds., Our Beggar Problem: How to Tackle It? Bombay: *Padma Publications Ltd.*

Das Gupta, P. (1993), 'An Enquiry into well being and destitution': *Oxford Clarendon Press.*
De, Subrata. (2005), ' Begging not by choice': *The Hindu*, July-18:2005.
Dreze, J., and A.K.Sen Eds. (1991), 'The Political Economy of Hunger': Oxford Clarendon Press.
Feige, Edgar L. (1990), 'Defining and estimating underground and informal economies: the new institutional Economics approach', *World development,* (18), pp. 989-1002.
Fontain, La., (1967), 'Tribalism among the Gusil', *Gulliver.* pp. 177-192.
Goldstein, B. (1993), 'Panhandlers at Yale: A Case study in the Limits of Law', *Indiana Law Review* 27(2), pp. 295-359.
Harsh, Madar, (2009), 'The war against begging', *The Hindu*, Jan-25, 2009.
HR Focus (1991), 'Every job is Important, but is Every Job Respected'? *HR Focus* 68 (12), p. 22
Independent Sector (1992), 'Giving and Volunteering in the United States: Findings from a National Survey':Washington. D.C., USA.
Kassah, A.K. (2006), 'Begging as Work: a study of people with mobility difficulties in Accra, Ghana'. *Disability and Society, Routledge,* 21 (02). p.168.
Kumar, S.C. (1999), 'Economic Development and Social Exclusion in India', *The Fouth World:* No.10. pp. 58-84.
Lal, Neeta. (2008), 'Criminalising Beggars Instead of rehabilitating them', New Delhi.
Lankenau, S. (1999), 'Panhandling Repertoires and Routines for Overcoming the Non-person Treatment'. Daviant Behaviour, *An Inter Disciplinary Journal* 20: 183-206.
Lelling, G., and Coles, M. Catherine (1996), 'Fixing Broken Windows: restoring order and reducing crime in our communities', New York: Martin Kessler Books.
National Opinion Center. (1989), 'General Social Survey', Washington. D.C.,USA.
Rodger, Gerry, Et al., (1994), 'Overcoming Exclusion: Livelihood and rights in Economic and social development', Discussion Paper Series No. DP/72/1994. International Institute for Labour Studies, Geneva.
Rossi, P., G. Fisher and G.Willis (1986), 'The Condition of the Homeless of Chicago'. Chicago: University of Chicago, Social and Demographic Research Institute.
Schafer, Arthur. (2007), 'The Expressive Liberty of Beggars: Why it matters to them, and to us'. Canada: CCPA.
Silver, H. (1989), 'Social Exclusion and Social Solidarity: Three Paradigms', Discussion Paper Series. No. DP/69/1994. Geneva : International Institute for Labour Studies.
Stefan Adriaenssens and Jef Hendrickx (2008), 'The income of informal economic activities: Estimating the yield of begging in Brussels', *Hub Research Paper* 2008/16. April. pp.18-19.
Wilson, J., and G. Kelling (1982), 'Broken Windows: The Police and Neighborhood Safety'. *Atlantic Monthly 249*(3), pp. 29-38.

In: Development Management in the Twenty-First Century ISBN: 978-1-62100-699-2
Editors: Kartik Roy and Sandip Kar

Chapter 19

MANAGING DEVELOPMENT IN THE CONTEMPORARY WORLD: LESSONS LEARNT

Kartik Roy *
Research Professor, Auckland Institute of Studies St Helens (AIS),
Auckland, New Zealand

INTRODUCTION

The management of individual project involves the management of the process of making the decision for the construction and post-construction management of operation of the project. At the macro level, managing development involves the management of preparation, implementation and operational management of thousands of projects in a way that enhances economic growth as well as economic and human development in a country at any particular time.

The implementation of projects with significant positive externalities will also bestow on many ancillary project relevant positive externalities through out a country (Pearce et al., 1990). But successful management of development projects and of processes requires the presence in the country of favourable economic social and political institutions in the form of stable price level, low interest rate, deregulated labour market, outward oriented trade and investment regimes, congruence of social institutions, informal such as customary laws with formal laws and a highly proactive developmental state (Grabowski, 1999; Clark and Roy, 1997; Grabowski and Woo Cumings, 1994).

Further more, in the preparation and implementation of development programmes other requirements such as minimization of environmental damage, compliance with the formal laws of the global states will have to be met (Aron, 2000).

In the following sections, we make comments on the implementation of development programmes directed to achieving different developmental goals in individual countries.

* kartikr@ais.ac.nz; kcroy20@gmail.com.

Experiences Gained in Development Management

The creation and successful management of a largely open trade and export oriented industrial development regime can help a country achieve its growth and developmental objectives. Of all great success stories of trade led development, that of China stands out to be greatest. In Chapter 2, Ershad Ali discusses the main features of China's trade pattern which helped China to attain the status of an economic and political super power. The basic institutional changes that China has made are those which induce foreign enterprises to invest in developing counties including China. First, China's has preference always been to encourage the inflow of Foreign direct investiment (FDI) rather than portfolio investment. However, portfolio investment will inevitably flow into a country where FDI flow is taking place in massive amounts. The massive amount of FDI that have gone into China was primarily directed to export oriented industries. Apart from providing significant tax exemption to foreign companies, china significantly deregulated the labour market; disbanded trade union activities which disrupt industrial production deregulated factory hours and labour wages and allowed foreign companies to hire and fire labour as and when necessary. Further more, the foreign companies were also granted adequate supply of power, transport network and port facilities to take export items to their destinations. However, China's management of tariff regime which followed the same pattern as that followed by Japan, Korea and Taiwan included the maintenance of some form of import restriction regime which includes non-tariff barriers, some tariff barriers and anti-damping measures as well measures to promote export. The repatriation of profit of foreign subsidiaries in China to their parent companies was guaranteed. Many drawbacks still persist in China's management of trade. Many of China's rules and regulations relating to trade are opaque. Nevertheless, it has managed the growth of its global trade more successfully than any other country in the world during the late twentieth and early twenty first century.

Kartarzyna Nawrot, in Chapter 3, discusses how successful management of cooperation, competition and integration among south east Asian countries have helped them achieve respectable economic growth rate and impressive social and economic development. The management of agrarian transformation particularly in countries such as Vietnam, Malaysia, Laos, Cambodia and Indonesia has improved the economic condition of rural population and facilitated the process of industrialisation. The ASEAN has also been integrating with the two regional economic super powers China and India in trade and technology upgradation.

The changing global order also necessitates the formation, in each country, of new formal and informal institutions or modification of existing institutions to cope with the transformation of existing countries in the ASEAN and also to cope with the absorption of China, India, USA, Japan, the EU and emerging economies in a broad framework of cooperation and development. The entire region can then become the growth centre and a large market for global producers. The countries in the periphery also will benefit from a giant Asian triangle consisting of China at the top and India and ASEAN sitting below in two angles.

Maureen Dayan and Narendra Reddy, in Chapter 4, have discussed human resource and other management issues in service sector industries with particular reference to the post and telecommunications industry which has been split up into Post Fiji Limited and Telecom Fiji Limited under a reform programme. Extensive field surveys undertaken by authors reveal that the government did not follow clear guide lines in trying to restructuring the telecommunications industry. There was a clear absence of transparency, accountability and significant political interference by Government Ministers and Board members for collecting rents. The move to privatization of Fiji Post and Telecommunications Limited has resulted in a decline in government's reserve as efficiency of private sector industries does not always increase after privatization. In case of Fiji PTL, the privatization move has diminished employee's morale, the company's profit level and contributed to the departure of the highly experienced and skill employees of the company. The authors however hope that since the telecommunications is one of the most dynamic sectors in Fiji's economy, by improving technologies, management process and adopting learning by doing process, it will be able to improve its performance in service delivery in cost effective way.

In Chapter 5, Sandip Kar discusses the major management problem that arises in the process of completion of microprojects in special trade construction sector in India. An entrepreneur's capacity to maximize profit from a particular level of out put depends on the level of employment and on the productivity of labour measured as out put value per dollar worth of labour or as labour cost per dollar of out put or as contribution of one dollar worth of labour to value added in one dollar worth of out put. Extensive field surveys covering 5000 microprojects were carried out to collect information on measures undertaken to improve productivity of per dollar worth of labour engaged in production process. But by engaging in the production of same quantity of out put per day the same number of trained and untrained labours in two groups, the author found that the labour per dollar of out put produced by trained labour was significantly lower than the labour cost per dollar worth of out put produced by untrained labour. On-site training and learning by experience were found by the author to be the most effective means of improving the productivity of labour employed in microprojects.

Many countries in the world have been able to achieve and maintain respectable economic growth rates and social development by relying primarily on tourism. As every dollar spent by tourists in host countries creates more than one dollar of income the size of the increase in income resulting from the increase in expenditure by tourists depends on the size of the multiplier. Generally, the size of the multiplier is greater than one. Also the tourism industry being a conglomerate industry produces and supplies diverse range of products with different features. The increase in the number of tourist arrivals and in the per-capita expenditure of tourist dollars in the host country will encourage tourist related industries to increase employment in the country. A country may have many man made creations and natural wonders to attract tourists but without appropriate policies and infrastructure development it may not be able to achieve success in enticing tourists to visit the country. A country's agriculture, natural forests, wild life, ocean, and mountains, or man made wonders such as the Taj Mahal may compete with each other to draw tourists towards each of them. As a result of this competition if a man made wonder wins the hearts and minds of tourists, it will create employment and accelerate the pace of development of that region where this icon is located. This may contribute to a kind of mal development in other regions. Katarzyna and Lukasz Nawrot in Chapter 6 on the management of tourism development and competitiveness of Agricultural areas discuss the possibilities of promoting tourism in agricultural areas in Poland. These two authors suggest that steps should be undertaken to develop tourism market in the agricultural areas from both the demand and supply sides. In selecting a particular place in the agricultural region as a place of interest for tourists, a complex evaluation of natural, environmental and anthropological merits of the region ought to be carries out first. It is also necessary to secure the co-operation of subjects in the region to create a complex tourist product. Also private sector needs to be encouraged to invest in the particular agricultural region to build up the foundation of the tourist economy.

In recent years, increasing number of people from England, The United States, Australia and New Zealand are travelling to Thailand and India and also to China to receive medical treatment for their diverse ailments and health conditions at a very low cost. Since the number of such medical tourists has been rising and the cost of providing appropriate hospitals and other medical facilities to medical tourists have also been rising in India, the need for more public and private sector partnerships in the management of the growth of medical tourism in India has been gaining in importance in recent years.

Anita Medhekar has discussed all important aspects of the management of the growth of medical tourism in India in Chapter 7. To facilitate the promotion of medical tourism in India, the government of India has taken measures to create a special category of visa for medical tourists to lower restrictions on foreign direct investment in medicare facilities, and to improve hospital related infrastructure in India.

The partnership between the government of India and Medical Tourism Council is crucial to the growth of medical tourism industry in India.

Prakash Misra and Nirmal Sahu in their Chapter 8 on Tourism as an engine of Orissa's sustainable development discuss major issues to be addressed to ensure the sustainability of tourism for sustainable development of Orissa. The issue of sustainability of tourism has to be addressed from the demand side and supply side. Substantial increase in visits to sites by tourists, if not controlled properly, may damage the quality of these sites. Also in supplying tourism sites to tourists, the state has to ensure that the quality of the product does not deteriorate.

These authors feel that sustainable tourism development in Orissa requires tourists and provisions of tourist facilities and services to seek co-operation from environmental protection lobby and community residents as well as from their leaders who want a better quality of life for the current and future generations.

In Chapter 9, Yogesh Vansiya and Subadra Ragothaman have advocated the promotion of eco-tourism in Gujarat province of India because it lessens adverse effects on nature and is resources of tourists use of nature based tourist products. While eco-tourism can create local employment in many tourism related service sector industries, and help develop tourism in fratructure in regions where eco-tourism takes place, it can also produce some negative impacts on indigenous culture. The Government of Gujarat has been taking measures to improve infrastructure in areas such as Dangs where eco-tourism in rich forests, water falls, mountain range can take plalce. Extensive field surveys undertaken by Ragothaman and Vanisiya indicate that the local tribal population also want the government to promote tourism in the Dangs region.

Since climate change is said to be an environmental out come of massive proportions that has been occurring in the world particularly since the 1950s, one may like to investigate as to whether individual countries suffering from effects of climate change had put in place adequate legislative frame work for environmental guidelines to be followed in implementing development programmes. Lawson Smith, in Chapter 10, comments on environmental oversights that have occurred in implementation of development programmes in India. The author finds that there has been a systemic noncompliance by industry of environmental regulations and unwillingness by law – enforcing agents to force all sectors involved in economic and social transction to amply with environmental regulations. Consequently, as a result of public interest law suits filed by good Samaritan citizens, the Judiciary has taken the leading role in preserving the environment in India.

In Chapter 11, Dhulasi Birundha has commented on the impact of climate change on poverty in developing countries. The author provides a detailed account of how climate change increased economic poverty of the poor and thereby widening the gap between the rich and the poor vulnerability of the poor to many risks such as sudden illness or death of a member of family and reduces the per-capita availability to poor of food and nutrition. Also it contributes to the deterioration in health condition of the poor. In urban areas also rising CO_2 emissions per head is positively related to rise in common respiratory disease and spread of many unknown diseases.

Naturally, the author suggests that although policies to manage climate change impacts effectively will adversely affect growth, these will have to be undertaken. Use of price mechanism to reduce carbon emissions may not be very effective in developing countries where free market price mechanism do not seem to exist. Hence other state directed measures such as carbon labeling of traded goods, promotion of production and use of bio-fuels as well as implementation of green growth strategy are necessary.

In Chapter 12, Robert Gassler discusses thae ways in which climate change effects can be sustainably managed.

The economic and environmental problems of climate change cannot be solved by economic solutions alone. There is need also the need for institutional solutions. Unfortunately developing countries are lacking in such institutions. However, in developed countries also unlimited rise in expenditure on consumer goods encouraged big businesses to pay lip service to the implementation of measures to minimize adverse effects on the economy and human beings of climate change. The author has suggested several policy measures for implementation in countries where the adverse impacts of climate change on societies and human beings have been felt. A proper climate change policy implies that there is no trade off between environmental constraints and employment. There needs to be a clarity on the allowable quantum of CO_2 of extraction and emission as such a restrictions can be more easily applied than imposition of new taxes on products of polluting industries. Then also measures are required to be taken to redistribute income to these who suffered more from climate change effects. While accepting that global economic activities have increased phenomenally during the last three decades and that the world's environment cannot cope with such an increase in activities, we will have to take appropriate climate change minimizing measures now.

The consistent perusal of the strategy of achieving high rate of economic growth by all countries in Asia has inevitably entailed a significant rise in the consumption of fossil fuel and other natural resources which has increased pollution level in the atmosphere and caused substantial damage to the environment thereby making the goal of sustainable development less and less achievable in most countries in Asia, Africa and Latin America. Manoranjan Mohanty in Chapter 13 has contended that countries in the Asia-Pacific can minimize adverse effects of climate change by adopting the green development strategy which aims to transform an economy's production structures from high carbon generation to low carbon generation and thereby to promote sustainable economic growth. In this strategy a substantial share of total private and public sectors' investment expenditure in a country's GDP has to be directed towards the development of green technologies to make greater use of country's renewable energies, water supply from natural sources, green transportation, agricultural land and forests. Major Asian countries such as South Korea, China and India have already taken initiative to promote adoptions of green development strategy. About four per cent of South Korean's GDP is expected to be utilized to create jobs in industries producing goods with low carbon emissions. China has spent substantial amount of money to promote the production of renewable energy in industries which now employ more than a million labours. In India, almost thirty per cent of total energy supply is available from renewable energy sources. Since countries in the Asia – Pacific region have low level of energy efficiency, it is difficult for them to adopt adequate climate change mitigation measures. Nevertheless, countries in Asia-Pacific have been creating institutions to implement measures to minimize as much as possible, adverse effects of climate change on their economies.

Jamil Serwanga, in Chapter 14 examines the impact of climate change on poverty in Uganda, He contends, that due to unseasonal and seasonal heavy rain in rain fed regions of Uganda, sharp rises occur in water levels in lakes, which cause widespread flooding and push swaps to drift downstream to cause widespread blockage at the outlet of Nile from the lake. This leads to flooding of home lands and farm lands, as well as to a rise of water borne diseases. Similarly, in non-rain fed regions characterized by long, dry summer, lack of green pastures forces traditional pastoralists to migrate with their herds to neighbouring districts and game reserves contributing more to the environmental problem of these regions which pastoralists migrate to. Consequently, large number of additional victims of climate change effects, continues to fall below Uganda's poverty line income or expenditure. Furthermore land and forests continue to experience more degeneration, desertification, loss of natural habitats, loss of bio-diversity, soil erosion and siltation of rivers.

In Chapter 15, Anita Medhekar and Kartik Roy comment how effectively India's anti-poverty programmes have been managed. The performance of National Rural Employment Guarantee Act of 2005 renamed on 2nd February, 2009 as Mahatma Gandhi Rural Employment Guarantee Act (MGNRGEA), in terms of making provision of 100 days of employment for the poor has been discussed by these authors. Mekhekar and Roy's research reveals that the MGNRGEA has played a very important role in providing temporary employment to millions of poor Indians and has promoted in transparent governance in delivering jobs to millions of India's most provinces except in Bengal where 100 days employment opportunities were provided primarily to supporters of the Marxist communist party which ruled the province, irrespective of their economic needs. Also allegations abound that a substantial proportion of money transferred to village Panchayats under MGNRGEA were pocketed by local leaders of the Marxist political party. This programme in general has provided the rural poor with the right to demand work and thereby has helped them to regain their dignity and self-respect.

In Chapter 16, Pelotshew Moepeng has examineed the effects of global financial crisis led reduction in budgetary expenditure and how such a cut in budgetary expenditure has adversely affected the maintenance of the provision education of children of poor families in rural and urban districts in Botswana. The data for this study were collected from the primary sources via field surveys and from these secondary sources such as libraries and Government Departments in Botswana. His research reveals that even during the period of the global financial crisis (2007 – 2010), the share of public expenditure on education in the total budgetary expenditure remained very high and reached 43 per cent in 2010 – 2011 budget.

However, it is interesting to find that although during the three year period from the 2008 to 2011 the share of urban schools in total allocation of funds on schools increased, the annual expenditure for schooling per child per year remained substantially higher for rural children than for urban children. Moepeng rightly observes that the allocation of a higher share of total budgetary expenditure to education even during GFC, by the government of Botswana, has helped children in both rural and urban areas to be educated, be employed in productive economic activities and thereby be able to move out of economic and social poverty in Botswana.

In Chapter 17, Prasanta Padhy and Suresh Patnaik comment on issues which are very relevant to patients and medical practitioners but are neglected by hospitals and the entire health care industry. The important neglected issue is ethics. For many activities the end result may be good and welfare enhancing for individuals also have completed these activities, but the means adopted to achieve that end result may not have been ethically correct. Therefore, those who completed certain activities with the intention of achieving results which would be beneficial to many people, perhaps would not have undertaken such activities if they knew that their actions were not ethically correct. The primary responsibility of health care professional is to save human lives. But sometimes in individual cases a conflict emerges in the mind of a medical practitioner whether he or she should administer a particular treatment for a patient. For example, suppose, to save the life of a patient, a surgeons feels that both heavily damaged legs of a patient will have to be amputated. There is the ethical consideration that if both legs are amputated the patient would remain alive but would become a totally helpless and devastated individual. So in this case as a surgeon, one has to forget the ethical consideration and to do what is necessary to save the life of the patient. Padhy also comments that it has to be ensured that appropriate ethical values are being forced in hospital administration and granting of accreditation to a hospital would also require the hospital authorities to provide proof that ethical considerations are duly observed in day to day running of hospital activities.

Subas Kumar, in Chapter 18, has made a novel attempt to provide justification to begging as a rational economic activity in the informal market. The author uses Mancur Olson's rational behavior theory to suggest that a human being in trying to maximise return from a number of possible economic activities will inevitably chose the one which is the easiest to undertake and which involves least amount of financial cost to that individual. The fact that the supply of beggars in India still remains quite large and has not substantially declined, suggests that there is a demand for this particular type of informal economic activity. While the organised mafia groups take children from poor families and train them to be beggars under their supervision, the country's social and economic system recognizes act of begging is an occupation. Surprisingly, the author found that the prestige score value of begging as an occupation is 11 and not zero. The anti-begging law makes provision of jail terms for beggars upto three years and the term can be as high as 10 years for repeat offenders. But law can only makes sure and can justifiably be applied, if alternative means of occupation are made available to beggars by the state and society. The fact that the state has failed to do so, makes mockery of such a law. Kumar also found through field surveys that the majority of respondents feel that beggars need help from the state and the society to find graceful and non-begging employment. The author recommends that for different types of beggars different measures are needed. For those who are destitute beggars sleeping on the street corner, provision of shelters for them has also to be made. These measures will have to be implemented at the grassroot level through a bottom to up approach.

Concluding Remarks

In this chapter we have summarised the lessons of case studies of management of selected development issues in different countries. The management of trade pattern, broader economic and social development; human resources development; several aspects of tourism; climate change; poverty, health care and management of begging as an economic activity. The lessons that have been learnt and the experiences that have been gained in the management of the above noted development issues will be extremely useful to planners and policy makers in developing countries for formulating the unique strategy of development management applicable to each country.

References

Aron, J. (2000), 'Growth and Institutions: A Review of the Evidence', *World Bank Researdh Observer,* 15(1), pp. 99-135.

Clark, C.M. and Roy, K.C. (1997), 'Comparing Development Patterns in Asia', Bonlder Co.: *Lynne Rienner.*

Grabowski, R. (1999), 'The Developmental State: where does it come form'? *World Development,* 22(3), pp. 413-422.

Grabowski, R. and WooCummings, M. (1994), 'The Developmental State', Ethaca, NY: *Cornell University Press.*

Pearce, D., Barbier, E. and Markandya, A. (1990), 'Sustainable Development': Economic and the Environment in the Third World, London: *Earthscan.*

INDEX

A

B

C

D

E

F

G

H

I

J

K

L

M

N

O

P

Q

R

S

T

U

V